Crossing the Aegean

STUDIES IN FORCED MIGRATION
General Editors: Stephen Castles, Dawn Chatty, and Chaloka Beyani

Crossing the Aegean

AN APPRAISAL OF THE 1923 COMPULSORY POPULATION
EXCHANGE BETWEEN GREECE AND TURKEY

Edited by

Renée Hirschon

Berghahn Books
New York • Oxford

First published in 2003 by
Berghahn Books
www.berghahnbooks.com

Paperback edition published in 2004
Reprinted in 2006, 2008

©2003, 2004, 2006, 2008 Renée Hirschon

Library of Congress Cataloging-in-Publication Data
Crossing the Aegean : an appraisal of the 1923 compulsory population exchange between Greece and Turkey / edited by Renée Hirschon
    p. cm. -- (Studies in forced migration : v. 12)
    Includes bibliographical references and index.
    ISBN 1-57181-767 0 (cloth: alk. paper)
    ISBN 1-57181-562-7 (pbk.: alk. paper)
    1. Greco-Turkish War, 1921–1922--Refugees. 2. Population transfers--Greeks--History--20th century. 3. Population transfers--Turks--History--20th century. I. Hirschon, Renée. II. Series.
DF845.52.C76 2003
949.507'2--dc21   2002034452

British Library Cataloguing in Publication Data
A catalogue record for this book is available
from the British Library.

Printed in the United States on acid-free paper

ISBN 978-1-57181-767–9 (hardback)
ISBN 978-1-57181-562-0 (paperback)

Contents

List of Figures

List of Tables

List of Contributors

Ayhan Aktar
Associate Professor of Sociology, Department of Political Science and International Relations, Marmara University, Istanbul.

Alexis Alexandris
Historian; Associate of ELIAMEP, Athens.

Michael Barutciski
Lecturer, Law School and Department of Political Science, University of Canterbury, New Zealand.

Vassilis Colonas
Associate Professor, School of Architecture, University of Thessaly, Greece.

Stathis Gauntlett
Foundation Professor, Dardakis Chair of Hellenic Studies, La Trobe University, Melbourne.

Renée Hirschon
Lecturer, St Peter's College, and Research Associate, Refugee Studies Centre, Queen Elizabeth House, University of Oxford.

Çağlar Keyder
Professor, Sociology Department, SUNY-Binghamton, USA, and Sociology Department, Boğaziçi University, Istanbul.

Tolga Köker
Department of Economics, Hamilton College, Clinton, NY 13323, USA.

Elisabeth Kontogiorgi
Researcher, Research Centre for the Study of Modern Greek History, Academy of Athens; Lecturer in Modern History, Department of Geography, Harokopeion University of Athens.

Sophia Koufopoulou
Lecturer in Sociology at Michigan State University, and Department of Sociology, Anthropology, and Social Work, Central Michigan University. (Doctoral candidate, Department of Anthropology, University of Crete, Greece).

Peter Mackridge
Professor of Modern Greek, University of Oxford.

Hercules Millas
Currently teaches Turkish language and lliterature at the University of the Aegean, Greece. (Ph.D., Department of Political Science, University of Ankara).

Baskın Oran
Professor of International Relations, School of Political Science, Ankara University.

Vasso Stelaku
Architect, Secondary school teacher; Researcher in the Centre of Education Studies, Athens. (Ph.D., School of Social Sciences, University of the Aegean, Greece).

Thanos Veremis
Constantine Karamanlis Professor of Greek and Balkan History, Fletcher School of Law and Diplomacy, Tufts University, USA. Board Member, ELIAMEP, Athens.

Eftihia Voutira
Associate Professor, Department of Balkan and South European Studies, University of Macedonia, Thessaloniki.

Alexandra Yerolympos
Professor of Town Planning, School of Architecture, University of Thessaloniki.

Notes on Terminology and Orthography

In this collective volume I have not imposed a typology of terms to distinguish between various modes of forced migration. Contributors use the terms 'population transfer', 'population exchange', 'population expulsion' interchangeably, while 'ethnic cleansing', a term coined in the 1990s for events in the former Yugoslavia for what in effect took place in 1923, constitutes an anachronism.

I have urged for clarity in distinguishing between the Convention signed on 30 January 1923 and the wider Treaty of Peace of 24 July 1923. The first, the focus of this study, was concerned only with the terms for the compulsory exchange of Greek and Turkish populations (for the text of the Convention see Appendix I). The exclusion of the Orthodox inhabitants of the islands of Imbros and Tenedos, however, was specified in the later Treaty, as were the conditions for the protection of the remaining minorities.

Some further clarification of terms is necessary since they have connotations or usages which differ significantly in the Turkish and Greek contexts.

Geographical terms

Anatolia or Asia Minor
These two geographical terms, referring to the land mass which comprises the major part of Asiatic Turkey today, are used differently in Turkish and Greek usage. The term *Anadolu*, Anatolia, is used in contemporary Turkey, and is actually a Greek loan word, but the term Asia Minor is not familiar to most Turkish speakers.

In contrast, the term Asia Minor (*Mikra Asia*, *Mikrasia*) is standard in Greek today, while *Anatolia* is not used. This is possibly because the term Anatolia has strong orientalist connotations (see Gauntlett this volume). The use of the term Asia Minor, derived from Latin, is probably traceable to the nineteenth century when a 'purist' *katharevousa* form of Greek was promoted over the spoken demotic.

Another geographical term without precise connotations (but a long and complex history) and which has different usages is 'Roumeli'. The Turkish word *Rumeli* is inclusive and has a wide referent including all of the Balkans and Greece. In the Greek usage, though, *Roumeli* is a limited area in the central mainland, excluding Epirus and Thessaly.

Identity terms

Prior to the establishment of the Turkish Republic, formal identity in the Ottoman Empire was based on religion. Ottoman subjects were administered in religious communities, the 'millets'. Consequently, Orthodox Christians were members of the 'Rum' millet and were called *Rum* (pl. *Rumlar*) or *Romios* (pl. *Romioi*). The term 'Greek', strictly speaking, should refer only to citizens of the Greek state established in 1830.

This is reflected in the Turkish point of view which designates two categories of Greeks. The Greek Orthodox citizens of the Turkish Republic, i.e., those exempted from the exchange under the terms of the Lausanne agreements, are known as the *Rum Ortodoks* or just *Rum* for short. Citizens of the Greek state, including the so-called *établis* citizens of Greece who were also allowed to stay in Istanbul under the 1923 Convention of Lausanne and the 1930 Ankara Convention, are known as *Yunanli* or *Yunan*.

In the application of the exchange, Muslims of Pomak and Roma extraction in Greece, together with the Muslims of Western Thrace were exempted. According to the official Greek view, these Muslims are a religious minority recognised and protected by the final terms of the Treaty of Lausanne. In the recent period, following the 1974 Cyprus troubles, their self-designation as well as references to them as Turks, has become problematic and controversial (see Alexandris, Oran, this volume).

The terminology used to define identity also involves distinctions between words for 'refugees', 'exchangees', and 'migrants'. Interestingly, the Orthodox Christian newcomers to Greece themselves adopted the neoclassical nomenclature, and their original self-designation as *Romios/oi* was supplanted by the local Greek term. Thus, in Greece those expelled from Asiatic Turkey are known as 'Asia Minor refugees' (*Mikrasiates prosphyges*). Most commonly, these people referred to themselves as 'refugees', but seldom, if ever, as 'exchangees' (*antallaksimoi*).

In Turkey, the terms are used differently even within the population that was exchanged. Cretan Muslims who settled in Ayvalik and Cunda call themselves '*mübadil*', exchangees (Koufopoulou this volume), the term being specific to the 1923 compulsory exchange. However, the Muslims expelled from Greek Macedonia who were settled in Muradiye call themselves *muhacir*, refugees, and distinguish themselves from more recent forced migrants from the Balkans whom they call *göcmen* (Köker this volume), a Turkish neologism (*öztürkçe*) meaning migrant or settler. It should be noted, however, that *muhacir* has been the main word in Turkish referring to the forcibly displaced entering the Ottoman Empire and Turkey from the Balkans and the Caucasus, and *mübadil* the main word referring specifically to the 1923 exchangees.

The term 'refugee' does not apply technically to these groups of displaced peoples as defined in international law, however. This is because the Convention stipulated that they were immediately to be granted full citizenship rights in their respective host countries (Article 7). Nonetheless in the Greek context, it proved to be an especially durable term of several generation's depth with rich and varied connotations (Hirschon 1998 [1989]).

These different usages highlight the significance of indigenous terminologies which might indicate important qualitative differences in the experience of forced displacement. The terms people use to describe themselves are sociologically significant, and could constitute an important topic for further study (cf. Marx 1990, Zetter 1991).

Treatment of Other Terms

Place names have not been standardised in the volume so that, depending on the contributor and the historical period, a place may be referred to either by its Turkish (Izmir, Istanbul, Gökçeada, Bozcaada, Ayvalık) or Greek name (Smyrni, Constantinople, Imvros, Tenedos, Aivali) or by other variants, either in their native or anglicised spellings (Smyrna, Imbros, Thessaloniki or Salonica/Salonika).

There is no standard way of transliterating Greek script. The approach taken here follows a compromise preserving the phonetic with the visual, and allows for exceptions. In some chapters, Turkish words are incorporated as terms integral to the text. Where the plural form is required in English, for readability an 's' has been added to the Turkish word (e.g., muhacirs, misafirs, Rums), even if it is a plural form.

Preface

The Lausanne Convention specifying the conditions for the compulsory exchange of minority populations between the countries of Greece and Turkey was signed on 30 January 1923. One of a number of legal instruments related to the Treaty of Lausanne (24 July 1923), it set a precedent in international politics and is frequently used as a reference point in discussions about subsequent mass population displacements in many parts of the world. In a political context it is generally referred to as an example of a successful solution to interstate problems regarding minorities. Surprisingly enough, however, the multiple and far-reaching effects of the Convention on the two countries have been only partially studied.

The inspiration for this project came out of my experience as a social anthropologist with the Asia Minor refugees settled in Piraeus in the 1920s following the population exchange between Greece and Turkey under the Lausanne Convention of 1923. Having carried out intensive fieldwork in an urban refugee settlement in the 1970s, I was familiar with the picture from one side. It was only later that I realised how much the story of what had happened to the exchanged peoples of both Greece and Turkey remained unknown to the other side. From 1995, I became aware of this when I first met Turkish scholars at international conferences. At that time I was Chair of the Department of Social Anthropology at the University of the Aegean (Mytilini, Greece), with the Turkish coast only a few miles away, and my position there, that of an outsider–insider, convinced me of the need to establish a dialogue across national boundaries in which an overall perspective on issues of common interest might be promoted.

One evening at a memorable dinner party on the banks of the Bosphorus in Istanbul, a number of us – some contributors to this book – agreed that the region's history can only begin to be represented adequately by bringing together views from both sides of the Aegean. An initial attempt was a jointly-organised workshop hosted by Boğaziçi University (Department of Sociology) in April 1997 which focused on 'Our Common Cultural Heritage' and brought together Turkish and Greek scholars who presented views of the past based on oral as well as on documented historical sources. In 1998, the 75th anniversary of the Lausanne Convention, I organised an international conference focusing specifically and narrowly on the consequences of the

Convention (i.e., on the exchange of populations and not on the Treaty with its wider territorial and other specifications). At this event, hosted by the Refugee Studies Centre, Queen Elizabeth House, University of Oxford, participants from various countries, particularly Greece and Turkey, revealed the complex and far-reaching ramifications of the population exchange in political, economic, demographic, social and cultural spheres.

Over the four day period an additional aim of the meeting, that of providing a forum for amicable contacts and for building up interpersonal relationships, was also achieved. It was an early 'multimedia' meeting (now a more common occurrence at academic conferences) in which the proceedings included a video (Bringa's [1993] documentary of a Bosnian village during the war), and a live performance of unrehearsed music played by Turks and Greeks together. This demonstrated powerfully the 'common language' of these two peoples and the possibility of immediate communication through a long-standing shared heritage, too often forgotten. The performance has resulted in a CD recording by the Turkish and Greek players who continued their collaboration long after the conference ended.

This book comprises most of the conference papers, all revised. (The original papers can be consulted on the website of the Refugee Studies Centre). The intention of the conference and of the book is primarily to offer a case study of the consequences of the large-scale population transfer of 1923 between Greece and Turkey, examining its far-reaching effects on the development of these two nations over the past eighty years. The intrinsic interest of this volume then is regional, specific and empirical, showing for the first time the long-term ramifications of a mass population expulsion – nowadays termed 'ethnic cleansing' in a distasteful euphemism – in the Aegean region.

This study also has a wider significance, situated as it is in the context of the rapidly-growing field of forced migration and refugee studies. As mass population displacements are on the increase involving millions of people in all parts of the world, it surely behoves us to incorporate the historical experience of those countries that have dealt with the effects of absorbing displaced populations over the long term. Other suggestive cases for analysis would include those that could be surveyed over more than fifty years – the India–Pakistan partition, the establishment of the state of Israel out of Palestine. Thus, this aspect of the project provokes us to engage with the difficult issue of what can be learned from history. The contemporary relevance of insights gained from this specific case is another aspiration of the book, although it does not address policy issues directly. Nonetheless many of the contributions provide material in which the implications for practical application are available. Thus, a contemporary and comparative perspective is the wider conceptual framework in which this volume is set, with the hope that it might contribute to a deeper understanding of large-scale forced migrations and the many dimensions of their far-reaching consequences.

The project, however, also provokes an epistemological challenge, specifically that of how to achieve a less biased historiography with fewer inaccuracies. The aspiration to present a more realistic or reliable perspective might be dismissed in the post-modern condition (dissolving the subjective/objective problematic), but it is still a question that underlies much social science and historical research. Attempting to gain a less partisan approach is not easy and requires that several points of view on the same issue be consulted. When the viewpoint has developed within a national frame of reference, however, it is not surprising that the nationalist discourse might inform the work of researchers who focus on geographical areas defined by nation-state boundaries.

The problem of nationalistic bias is deep and insidious, then, and no less problematic for an outsider, i.e., the foreign researcher. My early experience in Greece was undoubtedly influenced by prevailing attitudes, through official as well as informal discourse but, as an anthropologist, I am committed to an ongoing process of examining assumptions and preconceptions. In writing the Introduction to this volume I consulted several colleagues with earlier versions, and was struck by their varied critical responses to my effort to produce what I saw as a satisfactory account that included both sides of the historical record. It seems that even the attempt to present a 'less biased' view is doomed to appear 'unfair', and it is certainly difficult to produce an account that is acceptable to everyone! In a recent review by an anthropologist, a specialist on Turkey, on the republication of my book *Heirs of the Greek Catastrophe*, I was criticised for my use of the phrase 'Asia Minor Catastrophe' to denote the events of 1922–23. Though not the common view in Turkey, this is after all the standard Greek term. Indeed, this term could even be used to describe the overall effect of events in that region for both sides, as some chapters in this volume reveal.

This highlights the key role of language and terminology which must be recognised in the attempt to minimise prejudice and inaccuracy, a point stressed throughout the conference proceedings and continued throughout the editing of this volume. As far as possible in editing the papers, I have tried to maintain sensitivity to political and terminological issues, in particular, to the connotations of terms that might be bound up in anachronism (e.g., avoiding the use of national labels before the existence of the states to which they belong), and to nationalist agendas. Patently this cannot be totally achievable – after all, language is itself a social and cultural construct – but it is hoped that possibly by raising these issues to an explicit level of consciousness we might achieve a greater sensitivity and better communication.

As it is, this is a first step in attempting to present history 'from both sides' and can only constitute a work in progress. At the very least it should alert us to the profound ramifications of the forced displacement of peoples in the Aegean region: the poignant relevance of this early attempt at 'ethnic cleansing' to the situation in the former Yugoslavia, and its parallels with Cyprus are clear. My own position inclines towards ways of promoting coexistence and symbiosis rather than the enforced separation of diverse peoples. In this era of advanced technological communication, it is surely imperative that we learn to accommodate our differences. It is only through contact that we might achieve the exchange of knowledge, the recognition of our common humanity, and greater mutual respect. I hope that this volume will contribute to an awareness and a wider understanding of the long-term effects of population expulsions in other parts of the world, wherever they occur, in these troubled times.

Renée Hirschon
St Peter's College
University of Oxford   April 2002

Acknowledgements

This volume is the product of many peoples' interest and collaboration, particularly those who participated in the 1998 Conference which was its initial stimulus (see Preface).

The Refugee Studies Centre, Queen Elizabeth House, University of Oxford, provided the essential base for the organisation of the Conference. I am most grateful for the support of the former Director, David Turton, and to all members of staff, academic and administrative, for their help. I would like to express my appreciation to Belinda Allan, former Development Officer of the Refugee Studies Centre, for her effective role in helping to procure extensive funding. My thanks are also due to Philip Robins and Peter Mackridge for serving on the Steering Committee.

I am particularly grateful to the following donors for their generous financial support without which this enterprise would not have been possible: the EFG Private Bank, the Onassis Foundation, the Hellenic Foundation, the A.G. Leventis Foundation, the Roberts Centre, and the U.K. Foreign and Commonwealth Office. The Turkish Ministry of Foreign Affairs (Cultural Affairs Section) and TUSIAD contributed towards the funding of most of the Turkish speakers. A timely and most generous grant from the J.F.Costopoulos Foundation facilitated the publication of this volume. My acknowledgement for help at various stages of the editorial task go to Hannah James, James Milner, Kerem Öktem, Rhianedd Smith, Charles Stewart, Evie Zois, and particularly to Robert McCaw for the major role he played.

The Preface, Introduction, and Notes on Terminology passed through various stages of revision in reponse to constructive criticisms and many useful comments. I am deeply indebted to Ayhan Aktar, Alexis Alexandris, John Campbell, George Dedes, Ersin Kalaycioğlu, Çağlar Keyder, Dimitrios Livanios, Peter Loizos, Peter Mackridge, Hercules Millas, Stephanos Pesmazoglou, Christos Retoulas, Dimitrios Theodossopoulos. Although it has not been possible to address all their observations, the text has improved considerably from points they have raised. In particular, Michael Barutciski's incisive criticisms of various drafts of my text have tightened the argument, and have expanded my understanding of legal and other issues associated with mass population transfers.

I am very grateful to all who have been involved in various ways with this work, especially to the participants who presented papers or chaired sessions at the Conference and all whose presence enlivened the proceedings: to the musicians led by Cahit Baylav and Matthaios Tsakourides whose unrehearsed performance created an unforgettable moment, to George Tsavliris who most generously sponsored them to produce a CD; to the Warden of Rhodes House for the formal venue of the Conference banquet, and to Iznık restaurant for the sumptuous meal. I am most grateful to Firdevs Robinson of the BBC World Service, to Nilgün Acar and to Gül Berna Özcan, whose support greatly aided in the effort. I am deeply appreciative of the intellectual stimulus that many colleagues have provided, especially at the Refugee Studies Centre and at St Peter's College, University of Oxford.

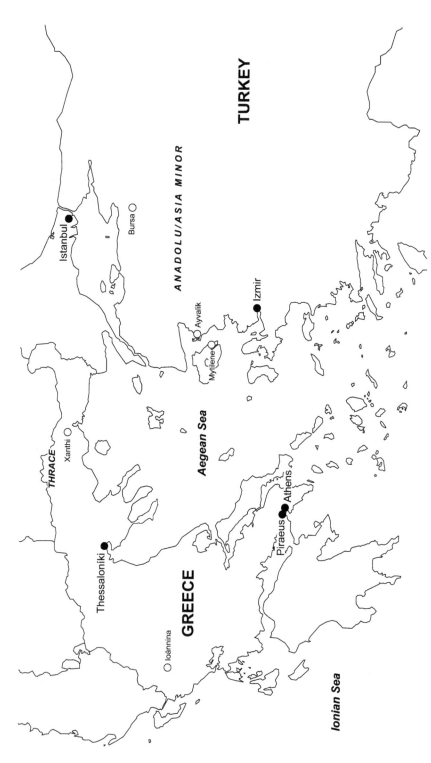

Map of Greece and Turkey showing contemporary place names

I

Introduction:
Background and Overview

1

'Unmixing Peoples' in the Aegean Region

Renée Hirschon

The background to Lausanne

The 1923 compulsory population exchange between Greece and Turkey involved the movement of about 1.5 million people. It had profound long-term consequences, radically changed all aspects of life in the Aegean region and, though historically distant from the ever-increasing patterns of forced migration, undoubtedly has poignant contemporary relevance. Our assessments of this event and its aftermath, discussed below, must be grounded in an understanding of the historical context and, for this, we need to look at the specific coordinates of the region (Ottoman) and the period (early twentieth century and post-First World War).

The period of the late nineteenth and early twentieth century was marked by the creation of modern nation-states. With the disintegration of the huge multiethnic Ottoman and Austro-Hungarian Empires, radical political and demographic changes occurred throughout the region of the Balkans and the Middle East. The Ottoman Empire had already begun to break up with the intensification of nationalist movements in Serbia, Bulgaria, and Greece all joining in the struggle to wrest territory from the empire. The Ottoman world was shrinking as bloody conflicts in the Balkans caused the mass displacement of its mixed populations. The ultimate exodus of much of its Muslim population and the unorganised influx of millions of destitute people into the Ottoman heartland resulted (McCarthy 1983a, 1995).

The Balkan Wars of 1912–13 were a critical turning point in a spreading climate of instability in the wider region, exacerbated by the upheavals of the

First World War when the non-Muslim residents in strategic areas were relocated to the interior of Anatolia, some later moving back, others migrating elsewhere. The recently published archives of the Bishopric of Smyrna illustrate particular cases, revealing, for example, complaints by Christian villagers that Bosnian Muslims had arrived in their villages and were expropriating land and houses by force (Alexandris 2001: 359–363). A view from the other side is given in the vivid account of the Ottoman regional governor in this area in 1914 dealing with the problems of settlement caused by the influx of Muslim refugees from the Balkans, and the issues raised are similar to those which occurred after the exchange (see Aktar this volume). Forced displacement in this region, then, had already affected millions of people, Muslims and Christians alike, years before the compulsory exchange of 1923 (McCarthy 1995, Zürcher 1998:170–2). In the wider setting, the Lausanne Convention was the legal framework for and the culmination of 'unmixing peoples', in Lord Curzon's much-quoted phrase, an ongoing process which was already underway a decade earlier. It had particularly affected the Balkans and Asia Minor littoral, and marked the experience of this final phase of Ottoman history.

Much historical writing that takes a political perspective focuses on the diplomatic negotiations following the end of the First World War. At that time, international power groupings were being rapidly realigned as negotiations defined the division of territories and spheres of interest – essentially what amounted to the spoils of war.[1] A number of important treaties were formulated and signed,[2] including those which effectively dismantled the Ottoman Empire and favoured Greece with major territorial gains. Amongst these, the Treaty of Sèvres (20 August 1920) proved to be of crucial significance to events in the Aegean region, for it was one of the contributory factors leading eventually to the compulsory population exchange between Greece and Turkey.

On the Greek side, despite the extreme political polarisation of the country known as the 'national schism' (see Veremis this volume) which developed early in the First World War between Germanophile royalist supporters and those of the pro-Allied Prime Minister Venizelos, Greece entered the War in 1917 on the side of the Allies. Among the promised rewards, its irredentist agenda of the *Megali Idea*, the Great Idea, was to be fulfilled. This expansionist dream of nineteenth-century Hellenism was to gain access to the Anatolian heartland of the Byzantine Empire and to recapture its capital city, Constantinople/Istanbul. Based on British support of these Greek ambitions, the Treaty of Sèvres promised the fulfilment of these dreams. However, rivalries between the Great Powers were intense at this time, alliances were shifting, and it is clear that Greece allowed itself to be used as a pawn in the larger game (Llewellyn Smith 1998 [1973]: 13ff). Italy had also made strong claims to territory in the Aegean region, but during the Paris Peace Conference these were blocked by connivance behind the scenes between the other Allies (particularly France and Britain) who encouraged Greece into an imprudent and precipitate venture (ibid.: 77–81). In the spring of 1919 Greek forces landed in Smyrna/Izmir and occupied the surrounding region (Vilayet of Aydin) amid scenes of triumphant nationalist celebration. Indeed, this premature move took place before the official Treaty was formulated. The Paris Peace negotiations were still underway, and during these protracted proceedings, competing claims to Ottoman territory were being settled with barely any consideration of the Ottoman delegation, and it appeared that '...they had been entirely forgotten' (ibid.: 74; cf. Zürcher 1998:149–153).

At this time, too, conditions in the Ottoman realm were changing rapidly: nationalist sentiments were in the ascendant and new political forces were formulating a different vision for the post-war situation. The Ottoman regime had supported Germany during the war; the end of the Sultanate was in prospect, and the organisation of the nationalist movement and army was taking place (Lewis 1968[1961]: 238ff; Ahmad 1993; Zürcher 1998: 153ff). Under the leadership of Mustafa Kemal (later Atatürk) these forces began regrouping, preparing to fight the Greek army and to establish a modern nation-state. The Treaty of Sèvres, finalised in August 1920, granted administrative powers to Greece over large areas of the Anatolian coastal region. Though it was signed by the Sultan's representatives, it was not implemented, however, not being recognised by the new political forces now organising Turkish affairs.

In a rapidly changing political scene, the foreign powers were reviewing their alliances and allegiances (Zürcher 1998:141,159–163). Despite this atmosphere of critical international instability and of the political flux prevailing in the two contesting countries, Greece imprudently continued its military campaign in Anatolia. To make matters worse for the Greeks, Venizelos lost the elections which he had called to renew his mandate, and his downfall provided the pretext and the opportunity for the withdrawal of Allied support, which in any case was essentially rhetorical and diplomatic. The Great Powers were shifting their positions in response to their competing interests in the wider region. Nevertheless, the Greek army proceeded with its campaign. The rising star of the Turkish political scene, Mustafa Kemal, had reorganised his forces in the Anatolian interior and was in a strong position to retaliate. Following an ill-conceived offensive in the interior, the Greek army was defeated and retreated in total disorder in the summer of 1922. This exposed the Christian population of Anatolia to reprisals by irregulars and the victorious Turkish army following the atrocities committed earlier by the advancing Greek army. The climax occurred in the destruction by fire of most of the thriving port of Smyrna/Izmir whose Christian inhabitants evacuated the city en masse (Pentzopoulos 1962: 45–7; Housepian 1972[1966]). Throughout the region, from villages and towns, the population fled with little more than their lives. Civilian casualties were high. Men aged between fifteen and forty-five were detained in the notorious labour battalions: many were sent on forced marches, or died of disease and malnutrition, and the active male population was decimated.[3]

The immense size of the exodus was remarkable, given that populations were much smaller at that time. Although accurate statistics do not exist, it is possible to arrive at a reliable estimate, and the consensus shows that in the last months of 1922 before the Lausanne Convention was agreed well over one million destitute refugees had arrived in Greece from the region (Hirschon 1998 [1989]: 36–9). An extreme humanitarian crisis resulted, its scale provoking widespread international concern and emergency assistance. Major agencies that dealt with the immediate needs of the refugees who had fled to the impoverished Greek state were the Near East Fund, the Red Cross, Save the Children Fund, and several U.S. philanthropic organisations (Bierstadt 1925; Morgenthau 1929; Psomiades 1968). In essence this was a continuation of what was occurring a decade earlier in the Ottoman realm, a major displacement of people under emergency conditions during and after the Balkan Wars. That earlier occurrence, however, received less publicity, and no international aid or intervention took place, the difference being that outflows from the Balkans involved a large number spread out over several years.

In view of the 1922 crisis, the League of Nations represented by Fridtjof Nansen, initiated peace talks in Lausanne on 30 November. The series of negotiations culminated in the first instance, in the Convention of 30 January 1923, 'Concerning the Exchange of Greek and Turkish Populations' (Appendix I). The ongoing negotiations (November 1922 to July 1923), which led to the Treaty of Peace signed on 24 July 1923, had as their aim to establish peace in the Near East, to revise the now defunct Treaty of Sèvres, and to redraw territorial boundaries, and with that the final dismemberment of the Ottoman Empire. This involved designating boundaries which carved up the Ottoman Empire into nation-states across the Middle East, each with its particular Great Power guarantor. These spheres of influence were already long-established as the major European forces had exercised influence and sought advantage through the nineteenth century, but they were also shifting in response to new geopolitical alignments (see Kent 1984).

Following the unprecedented scale of casualties and the radical disruptions of the First World War, the post-war negotiations and those at the time of Lausanne revealed contradictory concerns. On the one hand, an idealistic commitment to a just peace based on principles of 'self-determination and conciliation between victor and vanquished' was expressed but this contrasted with the victors' realpolitik drive behind the scenes to maximise gains through secret agreements in the spirit of the colonialist approach to the rest of the world. The rhetoric clothed 'in the idealistic language of national self-determination and justice' masked more pragmatic considerations (Jelavich 1983:120). In effect, concerns which guided the course of the discussions were those that promoted the establishment of independent nation-states, each with its ideally homogeneous population. The strong influence of American policy preferences was evident in the negotiations (Churchill 1929), particularly the ideal of self-determination encapsulated in U.S. President Wilson's Fourteen Principles. Following this direction, the nation-state won out over other possible types of polity.[4] Self-determination was the key word, for Point 5 specified the '...absolutely impartial adjustment of all colonial claims, based upon a strict observance of the principle that in determining all such questions of sovereignty the interests of the populations concerned must have equal weight with the equitable claims of the government whose title is to be determined' (Baker 1960: 43).[5]

In practice, though, the consequence for differentiated minorities within the new nation-states was to be disruptive. The delimitation of national territories by drawing boundaries through formerly mixed populations would involve population displacements (for example, the Greek–Bulgarian agreement for a voluntary exchange of populations in a protocol to the Treaty of Neuilly 1919), or the problematic task of providing security and rights for enclosed minority groups in states whose prototype was that of homogeneity of population. The presence of minorities became a difficult and complicating factor. One may surmise that the necessary imposition of guarantees for existing minorities was not welcomed by the leaders who were negotiating agreements to consolidate their new nation-states as entities independent of outside interference. This was indeed an important concern of the Turkish delegates at the Lausanne meetings who wished to break with outside interference in the Ottoman Empire such as had occurred under the Capitulations granted to foreign powers in the nineteenth century (Zürcher 1998:168–70; Göçek, 2002).

It can be said that the period after the First World War was that of a 'new world order' but it is important to be clear on the context of international law at the time of the Lausanne talks. International instruments were incipient and notably even the League of Nations did not receive support from the U.S. Congress. The notion of individual human rights, now a keystone in the current international regime, was not salient at that time; it became an articulated value only after the Second World War. International law was very different in that it dealt almost exclusively with relations between states. Although the protection of minorities was an explicit concern, it was conceived of as a collective issue (unlike contemporary human rights discourse which is founded in the notion of individual rights) and was contained only in specific chapters within treaties. Although the League of Nations Minorities' Regime included five minority clauses, 'no system of general application for the protection of minorities existed at the time of the League', a clause on minority rights being rejected from inclusion into the Covenant of the League (Meindersma 1997: 347).

Provisions and effects of the Lausanne Convention, January 1923

The Convention on the Exchange of Populations signed on 30 January 1923 comprises nineteen articles, separate from and the first of the legal instruments leading up to the comprehensive Treaty of Peace, signed on 24 July 1923. It defined those who were to be included in the exchange, those who were exempted from it, the conditions for transferring property and compensation, and the setting up of a Mixed Commission to supervise the emigration and to oversee the liquidation of property. The compulsory exchange involved 'Turkish nationals of the Greek Orthodox religion established in Turkish territory' and 'Greek nationals of the Moslem religion established in Greek territory...' and stated that 'These persons shall not return to live in Turkey or Greece without the authorisation of the Turkish Government or of the Greek Government respectively' (Article 1, see Appendix). It was absolute, precluding any choice: those who had fled with only their clothes were not allowed to return, and the expulsion was to include others defined by the criteria of religion and nationality laid down by the Convention. Significantly, this reveals a feature common to many examples of expulsions in conflict situations – the legal framework is placed upon and institutionalises an already existing de facto population displacement (cf. Schechtman 1962: 23; Barutciski this volume).

Exempted from the exchange was most of the Orthodox population of Constantinople/Istanbul who, following massive emigration between 1922 and 1924,[6] were left numbering about 100,000, and an equivalent number of Muslims in Western Thrace (see Appendix, Article 2; for the issue of proportionality, see Alexandris 1983: 85–7). At the later stage, in the Treaty of Peace of 24 July 1923, the Orthodox Christian inhabitants of Imvros and Tenedos, strategic islands overlooking the Dardanelles straits, were also exempted from the compulsory expulsion. Article 14 set specific stipulations regarding the protection of rights of the minority group in both countries.

Interestingly, the Turkish negotiators specified religion as the defining criterion of identity, reflecting an older administrative structure (the Ottoman *millet* system) which defined identity in terms of religious affiliation. A possible alternative criterion could have been language: this would have exempted the Turkish-speaking Christians of Anatolia, for example, and the Greek-speaking Muslims of Crete. In effect, Turkey was therefore largely emptied of its Christian population. Its citizens were to be treated with the reformation of their society modelled on various modern features (legal reform, parliamentary institutions, economic reorganisation) (Lewis 1968[1961]; Ahmad 1993; Zürcher 1998).

From the Greek side, a pragmatically grounded volte face was required. The acceptance of this reciprocal population exchange entailed renouncing the project of the Megali Idea. The territorial expanse of the (Greek-speaking) Orthodox settlements which had been the rationale behind irredentist claims of the previous century had now effectively ended.

It is important to stress that the population exchange which resulted was in no sense a repatriation for either the Muslims of Greece or the Ottoman Christians. The Anatolian landmass had been a location of Hellenic settlement and culture from antiquity, albeit with periods of decline and discontinuity (Vryonis 1971; McCarthy 1983a:1). During the nineteenth century there were established settlements scattered throughout Anatolia and the Black Sea region where people of the Orthodox Christian faith were a substantial minority or even predominant as in parts of western coastal Asia Minor (Kitromilides and Alexandris 1984–5: 9–44). For the Orthodox Christians the exchange was experienced as a harsh exile, and was expressed through decades of yearning for 'lost homelands' after their relocation to Greece (Mackridge this volume). Likewise, for the Muslims of the Greek state, their forced expulsion was a traumatic break (see Köker, Koufopoulou this volume), especially as most of their communities had been little, if at all, affected by the hostilities between the two states. On the Turkish side the Kemalist Republic was intent on consolidating the state within the boundaries set up at the 1918 Mudros armistice and on building the nation within it. In such a political climate, expressions of attachment to former homelands by Rumelian Muslims from the Balkans and Greece tended to be suppressed for they might have been seen as a kind of betrayal, and it is undoubtedly significant that Turkish literature for many decades was marked by 'silence' regarding this issue (Millas this volume).

For both sides, then, 1922 was a watershed in political, demographic and sociocultural terms. For the Greek state, the consolidation of the country's population within its national borders took place, while for the Turks 1923 marked the establishment of the modern nation-state. The ramifications of the Lausanne Convention, however, were far-reaching and differentiated, and more complex than is usually recognised, as the chapters in this volume reveal.

Assessments of Lausanne

Both positive and negative assessments of the Convention exist, and there is no doubt that the Convention is controversial – and indeed it was seen as such at that time.

Overall – and by way of summary – two opposed viewpoints can be distinguished. On the positive side are those writers who assert that the Convention and the wider Treaty ensured peace in the Aegean area and ended the conflict between Greece and Turkey. This reflects a political science, international relations and diplomatic perspective where security issues are given primary consideration, since most in the field of politics would tend to agree that the criterion for success is the absence of any major conflicts. In this view, the exchange of populations was a necessary step, even inevitable in the climate of the time. In the assessments of many in these disciplines, the larger Treaty of Lausanne constitutes a successful legal framework in which the relations between Turkey and Greece were stabilised. Its two main signatory states took a non-revisionist stance and have largely remained satisfied with their boundaries for most of the period. Indeed, the Treaty of Lausanne is held by many in these disciplines as one of the most durable of the twentieth century since it ended the political and territorial fragmentation in that part of the region (in contrast with the situation in the former Yugoslavia in the 1990s and ongoing instability in 2001).[7]

On the other hand, critical assessments of the Convention tend to be found in disciplines such as international law, economics, sociology and anthropology. These reflect humanitarian concerns giving priority to ethical considerations over the more pragmatic approach underlying diplomatic and politically-oriented views. An articulate exponent of this perspective is de Zayas who argues against the pragmatism of politicians' solutions, asserting that there is an inescapable ethical and moral component to population expulsions, a question which 'politicians prefer not to pose' (1988: 15).[8]

The ethical arguments mainly focus on the compulsory nature of the exchange. Indeed, the Convention's most notable and unique feature was its irreversible character, especially the stipulation forbidding return. Critics of the exchange at the time, mainly lawyers, expressed their disquiet that 'state interests were given priority over the legitimate human rights of the populations' with only some guarantees for the minority populations, and that the forcible population transfer had set a dangerous precedent in providing international recognition for a legitimate solution to minority problems. They further expressed their reservations in terms of the violation of the principle of free consent (Meindersma 1997: 347–351).[9]

There is also another perspective – viewing the hidden consequences of the expulsion. Though somewhat harder to demonstrate, it reveals another negative aspect, evident only because of the period of several decades over which they can be viewed. This is the subtle yet powerful separationist effect of the Lausanne Convention over the longer term. It is important here to distinguish analytically between short-, medium-, and long-term solutions. Separation of peoples who are caught up in deadly conflict is probably the only way of preventing further massacres and the only effective measure in the short term. However, short-term solutions are not necessarily the most suitable over a longer period, and the best policies should surely take into account different time scales, medium- as well as long-term.

From this perspective, the separation of peoples can be seen to produce serious problems in the longer term, and here the case of Greece and Turkey is illustrative. Through time, the process of separation rather than symbiosis inevitably entails diminished contact. The loss of shared experience is accompanied by growing ignorance of the ways of others; thus, separation entails the loss of ground for communication. What is lost is familiarity which carries with it the possibility for understanding and respect, and this is all too often replaced by suspicion, hostility and the inability to cooperate. At the sociopsychological level a process of projecting negative stereotypes onto the 'other' exacerbates the collective alienation (Papadopoulos 1997, 2000). This process is particularly acute in the case of the violent 'unmixing' of populations which have had closely interwoven relations over long periods of time. This is because nation-state building involves a process of constructing a distinct identity – in opposition to the 'other' – defining social, cultural, and psychological boundaries besides the more obvious political and geographical ones.

In order to foster a national identity after military conflict in states created out of mixed populations, particular mechanisms are often employed which intensify this alienation. These negative sentiments can be mobilised for political ends by the state, by particular interest groups, and/or by power-seeking individuals. The shared common past can be recast, with an emphasis on narratives of conflict, friction and violence, exacerbating hostility between peoples who, at the interpersonal level, might formerly have accommodated one another's differences in an atmosphere of mutual respect and symbiosis (Hirschon, 2003). From this long-term perspective, it is possible to see that the end result might be to raise the level of conflict from one of inter-communal violence to that of inter-state hostility, which ultimately poses a threat to international stability. In the contemporary context, India–Pakistan, Israel–Palestine, and Cyprus are some indicative cases which merit further consideration.

One critical factor in the sphere of international relations is the manner in which history is presented in order to serve the national interest, and here the study of national historiography is a fruitful field. For some time academics in this region have been aware of the effects of nationalism on the teaching of history (Millas 1991; Frangoudaki and Dragonas 1997; Berktay and Tuncer 1998; Avdela 2000; Pavlowitch 1999; Koulouri 2002), and how the national-ist policies and agendas of both countries affected people at all levels of society producing mutual suspicion, fear, and lack of trust as direct concomi-tants. Turkish and Greek historiography alike have been plagued with the 'victim complex', the assumption that its own side's suffering was greater than that of the other. The division of this region in 1923 into two hostile con-testing states led to an ever-increasing loss of understanding and knowledge about the situation on the other side of the national boundaries, even though there were periods of improved relations. Significantly, whenever relations between the two countries improve, one of the main items on the agenda is the revision of history text books. This has occurred at several periods in the past (Millas 1991) and also, notably, in the recent rapprochement meetings – the period of so-called 'post-seismic diplomacy' – between the Ministers of Foreign Affairs of Turkey and Greece following the earthquakes of 1999.

Any assessment of population transfers needs to be contextualised. The compulsory exchange of populations between Greece and Turkey is situated historically and in a macro-sociological framework. It provides one example of many cases of forced migration resulting from war and from peace nego-tiations where the doctrine of self-determination of peoples was a guiding principle. The Lausanne Convention ratifying this unique compulsory exchange was one of many international treaties signed in the aftermath of the First World War. It took place in and was an expression of the nation-state formation phase after the break-up of the great empires. At the time it was seen as the best solution to that particular situation. After some eighty years, we have the opportunity to survey the benefits and the costs of this radical displacement of populations in the process of creating nation-states.

The interesting issue is that this process of 'unmixing peoples' continues to occur as a de facto as well as an intended solution following violent inter-eth-nic and religious conflict, most obviously in the Balkans, but also in Africa and South East Asia at present. But to promote actively the establishment of ethnically homogeneous states is quite different in the contemporary world with advanced technology, communications, and mobility in the global economic system. We should therefore consider the feasibility, viability and indeed, the desirability of the long-term separation or 'unmixing' of peoples, as a way to go forward in the modern world.

Notes

1. Discussed with varying degrees of detail and explicitness in Toynbee 1922; Churchill 1929; Psomiades 1968; Llewellyn Smith 1998 [1973]; Kent 1984; Koufa and Svolopoulos 1991; Stevenson 1991; Göçek, 2002. General histories include Jelavich 1983; Mazower 1998; Pavlowitch 1999.
2. The Treaties of Peace 1919–1923, New York, Carnegie Endowment for International Peace, 1924.
3. Many English-language sources provide detailed information on events of the period and the war in Asia Minor, e.g.; Churchill 1929; Morgenthau 1929; Ladas 1932; Pallis 1937; Pentzopoulos 1962; Psomiades 1968; Llewellyn Smith 1998 [1973]. Abundant references exist on the Greek side, as well as archival sources (KMS 1980, 1982) and first-person accounts in literature (e.g. Doukas 1929; Venezis 1931; Sotiriou 1983 [1962]); fewer sources exist for the Turkish side, see Şimşir 1989, Arı 1995.
4. For discussion and speculation on possible alternative developments in the Austro-Hungarian, Ottoman and Russian Empires, see Barkey and von Hagen 1997; also Mazower 1998: 43ff.
5. Wilson's statements explicitly set out what was seen as a new direction in diplomacy (see Baker 1960).
6. It is estimated that about 150,000 emigrated out of a total of over 250,000 (Alexandris 1983: 50ff, 104).
7. For assessments of this kind, see Schechtman 1962: 22, 28f., and Henckaerts 1995.
8. de Zayas comments that politicians appear to prefer 'the apparent expediency of population transfers to the challenge of living together' (1998: 15). His position asserts the 'fundamental right of people to live on their native soil' and extends even beyond the range of human rights currently accepted in the international regime
9. See Meindersma (1997) for the articles of the Convention with an analysis of its implications for three case studies from the region, including Cyprus and Yugoslavia. Early commentators on the Lausanne Treaty include Tenekides 1924, Streit 1929, Seferiades 1928, Leontiades 1935 (ibid.: 347–51).

2

The Consequences of the Lausanne Convention

AN OVERVIEW

Renée Hirschon

My intention in this chapter is to present a synoptic picture of the effects of the population exchange for both Greece and Turkey, taking, as it were, an eagle's eye view over the Aegean. With limitations of space, I can only draw attention to the most outstanding features. The overall picture, based on chapters in this volume, is inevitably simplified and generalised. This summary indicates only the main outlines; each chapter with its special focus provides the detail to fill out the image.

Asymmetries

Overall, in assessing the consequences for the two countries, the most significant feature is the asymmetry of the experience. This arose as the result of two critical factors: the different historical and political significance of the events of 1922–23 for the two countries, and the difference in scale and the character of the populations involved.

Firstly, the asymmetry is most evident in the immediate political significance of the war which was entirely different for each side. For the Turks, the military conflict culminated in a major triumph. The year 1923 was celebrated as a liberation, the War of Independence which established a modern nation-state out of the Ottoman Empire. The establishment of the Turkish Republic as a nation-state constituted a regaining of recognition and power which had been eroded in the last period of Ottoman decline.

For the Greeks, however, this event constituted a major defeat, known as the Asia Minor Catastrophe, a greater disaster even than the Fall of Constantinople to the Ottomans in 1453, for it ended with finality the millennia-long Hellenic presence in Anatolia. At the time it constituted a major humanitarian emergency, with intervention by international agencies, both for short-term relief and for the long-term settlement of the displaced peoples. For Greece, the exchange of populations resulted in an ongoing process of long-term economic, political, cultural, and social adjustment and assimilation; through sheer weight of numbers it profoundly altered the Greek state and indeed all aspects of the society.

But what was a victorious event for Turkey also had its costs: the exchange which actually entailed the substantive loss of a major portion of the mercantile class, the bourgeoisie, and elite of Ottoman society was also the culmination of a process that had started years before with the loss of the Balkan provinces and of the majority of the Armenians in Anatolia. The population exchange, involving huge numbers in absolute and relative terms, destroyed existing social, economic and political structures and these could not easily be reconstructed. This had formative, even determining effects, on the way civil society developed in the new Republic (see below, Political patterns).

Demographic effects

It is important to note that the exchange comprised two phases: immediately following the Greek army's rout, the initial flight of the mass of refugees under emergency conditions in 1922, and later between 1923 and 1926 the more or less organised exodus of the Muslims from Greece, and the remaining Orthodox particularly from the Anatolian interior, excluding on both sides only those defined by the final signing of the Treaty (see Alexandris, Oran this volume). According to official records of the Mixed Commission, the 'Greeks' who were transferred after 1923 numbered 189,916 and the number of Muslims expelled to Turkey was 355,635 (Ladas 1932:438–9; using the same source, however, Eddy 1931:201 states that the exchange involved '192,356 Greeks from Turkey and 354,647 Muslims from Greece'). While accurate figures are impossible to ascertain, it is probable that the total number of Christians who entered Greece at this time was in the region of 1.2 million, the main wave being in 1922 during the period of hostilities (Bierstadt 1925: 248–250; Eddy 1931: 251; Ladas 1932: 438–442; Pentzopoulos 1962: 96–99; Kitromilides and Alexandris 1984–5; Hirschon 1998 [1989]: 36–9). Hence, the second aspect of the asymmetry was the scale and the character of the populations involved. The Lausanne Convention specified an exchange of populations which entailed a great disparity in numbers, in both absolute and relative terms.

An important differentiating factor is that the ratios in the host populations were incommensurate. For the tiny Greek state, a nation totalling around 4.5 million, the influx represented a massive increase by one-quarter of its population in just two years (equivalent to the U.K. currently receiving about 15 million refugees in two years), and created immense problems of settlement and absorption (Kitromilides 1992). But on the other side of the Aegean, as a result of previous displacements, the military campaign and the population exodus, parts of Anatolia were left with vast tracts of abandoned countryside and empty settlements. Estimates indicate that Turkey suffered an overall loss of population (1906 census returns registered 15 million, while the first Republican census in 1927 recorded 13.5 million) (see McCarthy 1993, 1995). Contrasting with the proportionately huge influx into Greece, the number of Muslims expelled from the Greek state and received by Turkey after 1923 was relatively small (350,000 in an estimated total of 13.5 million, or under 4 percent). Their impact on society as a whole was not very great – larger influxes had occurred over previous decades, especially since the Balkan Wars. It should be noted that over the longer period this region of the Ottoman Empire suffered immense demographic change (McCarthy 1993a), a fact which has largely been neglected in Turkish historiography until recently (ibid.; see also Toprak, 1998).

Significantly, this population decrease accompanied a dramatic alteration in ethnic and religious composition. The radical change in composition was striking on both sides since Turkey and Greece could subsequently claim to be homogeneous states (but see below, Social problems). Turkey lost an estimated two million people from its non-Muslim minorities through mortality as well as from forced displacement. This drastic loss meant that while 20 percent of the population – or one in five persons – was non-Muslim before 1923, after the war this proportion had gone down to 2.5 percent, or one in forty (see Keyder 1987, also Aktar, Keyder this volume). On the other side of the Aegean, an equivalent result occurred in Greece. Although the total number of Muslims expelled was smaller in overall numbers, mainly from Greek Macedonia and from the island of Crete, the effect was parallel, since Greece's Muslim population decreased from about 20 percent to 6 percent of the total (1928 national census). Again, the asymmetrical impact should be noted: it was the departures that were more significant for Turkey, while for Greece it was the influx that had the greatest impact.

Settlement Patterns

Effects on the social geography and settlement patterns were also radical. Again the asymmetry is striking for the problems were of a totally different order, almost as in a concave-convex mirror. In Anatolia, a population deficit occurred in some regions where settlements were emptied of the Christian inhabitants following the exchange, so that even today many houses, indeed whole villages, stand empty. The picture of a ravaged landscape emerges, of widespread post-war devastation in the wake of the passage of two armies. Following the exodus of the Christians from all over Anatolia (Orthodox and others, particularly the Armenians, who had previously been subjected to forced deportation and massacres), numerous villages were depopulated (Zürcher 1998: 170–2). The exchanged Muslims, far fewer in number, were allocated abundant Greek properties, but often homeless locals had already taken over, or plundered and looted these because they themselves were in need (see Köker, Aktar this volume).

The opposite occurred in Greece for the country suddenly experienced tremendous population pressure. The newly-vacated properties of the Muslims were insufficient to house the newcomers and an emergency settlement programme resulted (Yerolymbos this volume). The programme of land reform and redistribution was accelerated and over one thousand new villages were created in northern Greece alone (Pentzopoulos 1962; Kontogiorgi this volume). New urban quarters were established and towns expanded in all parts of the country, but even from the start these new housing schemes were overcrowded. Over the long term, the housing problem proved intractable, persisting even into the 1970s in some urban areas as a focus for grievance and of political disaffection (Pentzopoulos 1962: 114, 227; Hirschon 1998[1989]: 45–53). In fact, the chaotic experience of providing accommodation under emergency conditions formatively marked town planning practices in Greece, and effectively institutionalised ad hoc approaches which have blighted the urban landscapes to the present day (Yerolymbos this volume).

Economic effects

The economic effects were profound for both countries but of a different order, again because of the character of the populations involved in the exchange. In effect, Turkey lost its entrepreneurial class since finance, industry and commerce had largely been in the hands of the Christian populations – Greeks and Armenians. The exodus of traders and businessmen from trading towns and ports, excepting only Istanbul, radically disrupted the economic life of the region (Aktar, Keyder this volume). Izmir/Smyrna, a major commercial centre of the eastern Mediterranean, was almost totally destroyed by fire. Agricultural exports, the mainstay of the Ottoman economy, were badly hit as international trading links had been disrupted and as farming expertise lost in the exchange could not easily be reacquired (Aktar this volume), nor could artisan skills (Zürcher 1998:172). On the other hand, the void provided opportunities for some Turkish entrepreneurs who took control of abandoned businesses, for instance, olive oil production along the Aegean coast (Terzibaşoğlu 2001).

The Muslim incomers to Turkey from Greece were overwhelmingly small-scale farmers and rural dwellers. The advantage was that they could become self-sufficient in a short time and did not pose a major problem to the state. Unfortunately, however, their expertise was not properly deployed because, in many cases, they were settled in areas with unfamiliar crops and climatic regimes (Köker, Koufopoulou, Aktar this volume). Since they were almost entirely agriculturalists – and those who were townsfolk did not apparently have a noticeable impact on economic life – they brought no new skills, and simply swelled the already predominantly rural base of the economy (Keyder 1981).

In contrast, it is well known that Greece gained new skills and industries; textile and carpet manufacturing, ceramics, metal work and silk production were among these. Established industries benefited for, in addition to the newcomers' commercial expertise and skills, the refugee population provided a hugely increased market and labour force (League of Nations 1926; Mears 1929). But on the negative side, Greece had to meet the immense cost of settlement of the refugees in both rural and urban areas. Impoverished and politically in disarray, the country was backed by the League of Nations to establish the Refugee Settlement Commission which raised international loans to deal with the settlement programme (under high rates of interest given the humanitarian crisis) (Ladas 1932; Pentzopoulos 1962: 89ff). This recourse to outside help resulted in ongoing outside interference in Greece's affairs, a factor which was purposefully minimised in the Turkish Republic. In the 1930s, the financial burden of refugee settlement contributed to the country's bankruptcy and, over the following decades, continuing economic crises (Mazower 1991) had knock-on effects for political relations (Mavrogordatos 1983; Veremis this volume).

Political patterns

The refugee influx had a major impact on Greek politics, not surprisingly given the vast numbers of displaced people. Hailed early on as a success story, the policy of creating new settlements in northern Greece ensured the country's claims to territory, as the perceived ethnic homogeneity of the area increased (but a more complicated picture is presented in Danforth 1995; Karakasidou 1997; Cowan 2000). It was paraded as a prototype of a successful settlement programme for the displaced, and was visited by international agencies (Pentzopoulos 1962: 111; Voutira this volume). But in the longer term, the tensions between sections of the population, both urban and rural, exacerbated already existing rifts, continuing the 'national schism' of the First World War (see Veremis this volume). The polarity between liberals and right-wing royalists continued, with several military interventions in the 1920s. Following the rapprochement between Greece and Turkey in the 1930s when Prime Minister Venizelos cancelled out the issue of unsettled compensation, widespread disaffection from the Venizelist (liberal) party took place. Consequently, the Communist Party made marked gains in the elections of the early 1930s with extensive refugee support. In urban refugee quarters, support for the left was high from this time onwards, and the refugees played a critical role in changing political alignments in the country (Mavrogordatos 1983). The military dictatorship of 1936 was followed by the Axis Occupation and then the bitter civil war of 1944 to 1949 – the culminating expression of cleavages which revealed how accommodation of the refugees had only been partly successful (Veremis this volume).

An uninformed view that the exchange had no definable impact on Turkish politics is countered by analyses regarding the development of state–society relations in the new republic (Aktar, Keyder this volume). The departure of most of the Christian population constituting a major part of the empire's elite in the bureaucracy, as well as in business, had a deeply disruptive effect. Besides affecting commerce and banking, it entailed an upheaval in the functioning of state institutions and required the establishment of a new bureaucracy. Kemal Atatürk's modernising reforms were far-reaching but not easily applicable in the new context. With the hiatus in social structures, pre-existing patterns of the patrimonial state reappeared. As some commentators have noted, the republic soon began to operate more like the Ottoman state of a past period, and it seemed that the state had replicated the empire (cf. Keyder this volume).

Consideration of the political effects of the exchange must include difficult issues related to the recognised minorities of Turkey and Greece. The fate of those who were allowed to stay under provisions of the Treaty reveals how, in effect, they became hostages to the vicissitudes in Greco-Turkish state relations. For both populations – the Muslims of Greece, and the Rum Orthodox of Istanbul and the islands of Imbros and Tenedos – treatment by the host states over the decades depended on larger geopolitical issues, on international relations, as well as on internal political interests (the complexity and contentious nature of this topic is evident in contributions by Alexandris, and Oran this volume; see also Erginsoy 1998).

Cultural Influences

The exchange had a major impact on Greece in all areas of cultural life. With the influx of the Asia Minor peoples, a revival of Byzantine traditions in iconography took place and Orthodox Christian theology was revitalised, both of which had become ever more influenced by western patterns in the nation-state. Regional cultures in Anatolia were distinctive and the diversity of this incoming population was marked. Different culinary traditions were introduced by the newcomers and became signifiers of identity (Stelaku, also Koufopoulou this volume). Much attention has been directed to the influence of the Asia Minor refugees on urban popular music, particularly the 'rebetika' (see Gauntlett this volume); while local traditions in music and dance were further enriched by the introduction of Pontic and other regional forms from Asia Minor with the establishment of rural refugee settlements all over Greece (see Lemos n.d.; also, Williams 2003 for the effects of the expulsion on Cretan and Giritli music).

The effects on Greek literary pursuits were profound. A distinctive genre of literature flourished in Greece (Mackridge this volume) inspired by the vision of the 'lost homelands', and poetry and the theatre have also found deep veins of inspiration in this experience of displacement (see, for example, Fann 1996). Notably and in contrast, the exchange apparently had very little impact on literature in Turkey right up to the 1990s (Millas this volume). The existence of such an enduring silence is in itself remarkable, and suggestive of the different political processes each country has been involved in over the past eighty years. Overall for Turkey, however, the cultural effects of the 1923 population exchange appear to have been insignificant, probably because the demographic scale was so small, yet another aspect of the asymmetry of the experience.

Social Problems

The initial response to the enormous exodus of refugees from Turkey evoked international concern, and immediate widespread sympathy from the local Greek population. It was not long before this changed, however, and the acute problems, costs, and threats posed by accommodating their numbers lead to hostility and rejection, a common reaction noted in many such situations. In response, identity issues arose among the incoming displaced. In particular, those who had been supporters of the Greek cause in Anatolia were shocked by their exclusion and the prejudice they encountered, expressed in pejorative names: 'Turkish seeds' (*tourkosporoi*), 'baptised in yogurt' (*yiaourtovaptismenoi*) or 'orientals' (*anatolites*).

The common view that the exchange altered Greece's ethnic composition by producing a more homogeneous society has been powerful and persistent, and has had direct effects on current policies for refugee settlement (Voutira this volume). It is, however, oversimplified and masks a more complex reality. The incoming population, though all Orthodox Christians, was in fact highly diversified. From dispersed regions of the Ottoman heartland, these people were differentiated by wealth, by language, by dialect, and by regional cultural patterns, so they did not comprise a homogeneous group (e.g., Stelaku this volume; Hirschon 1998 [1989]: 22–28). Adjustment to the new conditions involved ways of maintaining continuity with the past; thus, in the longer term, existing social and cultural divisions persisted and were even reinforced at certain times (e.g., during the civil war).

Furthermore, the settlement of large numbers of Asia Minor and Pontic refugees in the city of Salonika had profound ramifications for its substantial Jewish community, which had essentially been the predominant group until the first decades of the twentieth century. The influx of the Orthodox Christian refugees in the 1920s affected not only the city's demographic profile but also civic policy and local attitudes. The community's dominant position was eroded, conditions became less favourable and at times they were subjected to outbursts of hostility. Finally, the end of the Ottoman diversity of the city ended in 1943 when its Jewish population, numbering around 50,000, was deported en masse by the Nazis, with only a few thousand surviving (*Sychrona Themata* 1994; Loizos 1999).

Until now little has been known of the experience of the Muslims exchanged and settled in Turkey, but a younger generation is showing an increasing interest in origins and identity, revealed in literature, and in current research (Yorulmaz 1997; Yalçın 1998; Yildirim 2002; Köker, Koufopoulou this volume). Interestingly, the experience of rejection was shared by the Muslim incomers who were stigmatised as 'half infidels' (*yarı gavur*) by local Turks, but here any assertion of a distinctive identity would not have been welcome in the prevailing Kemalist ideology of nation-state building.

On both sides of the Aegean, then, masses of people have experienced the sense of a 'lost homeland' through three and even four generations (Tsimouris 1997). This is the common factor then – in terms of human lives, there is no asymmetry. Forcibly displaced people everywhere share the experience of dislocation, of loss of home and place. This response can be documented from many parts of the globe: there is a continual process of definition and redefinition of identity, an emphasis on continuity with a compass point of reference to the place of origin. Lost homelands are not easily forgotten. People have enduring attachments to place, the sense of loss and disruption does not disappear easily and, interestingly, these bonds are often passed on to successive generations (Colson 1999). Elsewhere I have argued that this is explicable as a widespread response, not simply attributable to romanticism and nostalgia but something more fundamental, involved in the development of the human person in particular sociocultural contexts (Hirschon 2001a).

This explains why observable or objective similarities between incomers and hosts, the 'proximate host' assumption, does not always result in smooth assimilation. Even when common factors exist between the host society and the incomers which might lead to the expectation of accommodation, such as in the case of Greece and Turkey and their exchanged peoples (and indeed of Cyprus, see Loizos 1981, Zetter 1999), this expectation is not substantiated (nor is it in the case of internally displaced persons and those forcibly displaced through development projects). Empirical data show how enduring are these attachments to place of origin and how they can be revitalised after many years. The human costs of population exchanges are high indeed and constitute a factor in the equation which should be given considerable attention. Policy makers would do well to consider the longer term ramifications of population transfers whose far-reaching effects are illustrated in research conducted in this region.

The contemporary relevance of the Greek–Turkish exchange of population should be evident for situations which have arisen in India-Pakistan, in Israel-Palestine, in Cyprus, as well as for Albanians, Afghans, Eritreans, Iraqis, Kurds, Sri Lankans, Somalians, Sudanese, Tibetans, and other groups who have been forced to leave their homelands. This volume seeks to establish a deeper and more detailed understanding of the various ramifications of forced population displacement over the long time-span by focusing on the experience offered by a particular case. Overall, the asymmetries in the experience of the two countries are striking. This reveals how important it is to achieve an overview, as well as to assess these consequences from diverse points of view. By taking a stance which is inclusive and holistic, incorporating as many sides of the story as possible, we may achieve a deeper understanding of the consequences of mass population exchanges. The case of Greece and Turkey with its time depth of eighty years is a benchmark and will, it is hoped, inspire other studies of this kind.

II

Political, Economic and Policy Aspects

3

Lausanne Revisited

POPULATION EXCHANGES IN INTERNATIONAL LAW AND POLICY

Michael Barutciski

> To do a great right, do a little wrong.
> William Shakespeare, *The Merchant of Venice*

Introduction

From Biblical times to the end of the second millennium, the expulsion of populations has often been a strategy employed by belligerents to rid their territories of groups perceived to be a threat to effective political control. While the form of this practice has varied throughout history, the twentieth century is full of examples of premeditated mass displacement with the objective of consolidating political power. The unmixing of populations in Europe, the Indian subcontinent and the Middle East are among the more prominent examples of this form of violence in the twentieth century. This practice is not a feature of warfare confined to undemocratic or non-Western parts of the world: for example, mass deportations of German nationals were openly discussed in the American and British parliaments at the end of the Second World War. As Prime Minister Churchill declared in the House of Commons on 15 December 1944: 'The transference of several millions of people would have to be effected from the East to the West or North, as well as the expulsion of the Germans – because that is what is proposed: the total expulsion of the Germans from the area to be acquired by Poland in the West and the North.'[1]

Mass expulsions do not represent a modern phenomenon; the new factor is that developments in military and communications technology during the twentieth century have resulted in a destructive capacity that greatly increases the scale and effectiveness of coercive operations against civilian populations. Since the targeted minorities are often identified on the basis of membership in a national or ethnic group, these expulsions can be seen as examples of ethnic cleansing. The term 'ethnic cleansing' is used in this context to designate 'policies whereby the actual aim of the combatants is to drive out entire populations or ethnic groups in an attempt to establish homogeneous areas' (de Mello 1997: vi).[2]

This chapter addresses the dilemmas that arise when targeted populations in multiethnic territories are expelled or evacuated in order to prevent further violence. It suggests that if ethnic cleansing cannot be prevented, attempts at regulating by treaty certain issues related to population transfers can be appropriate to the extent that this approach contributes to promote peace and avoid massacres. This argument stems from the observation that ethnic cleansing and de facto population transfers continue to take place in contemporary conflicts despite the new human rights norms that have characterised the development of international law towards the end of the twentieth century.

One of the earliest and most controversial international treaties on this subject is the Convention concerning the Exchange of Greek and Turkish Populations signed in Lausanne on 30 January 1923.[3] Following the defeat of the Greek army in Asia Minor in 1922, the victorious Turks imposed this treaty which effectively legalised the ethnic cleansing of 'enemy' populations in both Greece and the emerging Turkish state. Centuries-old multiethnic coexistence was suddenly terminated and forced to cede to the harsh realities of exclusion that result from the creation of mono-national states. The crux of the issues debated at the Lausanne Peace Conference of 1922–23 can be found in the following commentary:

> Somehow in the course of the negotiations on a comprehensive peace settlement, peace and human rights have come to be conceived as opposite notions. In the interest of achieving peace, and of avoiding further violence and ending the war, any compromise that the warring parties agreed to sign, seemed acceptable. *Realpolitik* arguments were used against the reaffirmation of fundamental principles and too strong an insistence on human rights was perceived as an obstacle to consensus among the parties (Meindersma 1997: 636).

The preceding citation relates to the conflict in Bosnia–Herzegovina during the period from 1992 to 1995, yet the same themes were debated by participants at the Lausanne Conference. The international community's inability to prevent the violence that leads to ethnic cleansing obliges politicians to explore a variety of unpleasant options in order to achieve peace. In the difficult context of war, the exchange of populations continues to be a policy option that must be weighed in terms of its consequences for international peace and security, as well as for individual human rights.

The delicate issues raised by population exchanges make it a particularly contentious subject. Many commentators are morally outraged by the suggestion that national or ethnic identity can be used to settle civilian populations forcibly outside their country of origin in order to achieve peace (see Tenekides 1924: 72–88; Séfériadès 1928: 372; Meindersma 1997: 338–351). The declaration of Lord Curzon, the British Foreign Minister who presided over the Military and Territorial Commission established during the Lausanne Conference exemplifies this outrage: he described the proposal for exchanging Greek and Turkish populations as 'a thoroughly bad and vicious solution for which the world will pay a heavy penalty for a hundred years to come'.[4] Yet Lord Curzon ultimately accepted this solution and even provided justifications for why it should be compulsory. Likewise, both Venizelos of Greece (Séfériadès 1928: 373) and President Izetbegovic of Bosnia–Herzegovina (Barutciski 1996) at different times accepted the solution of population exchanges or territorial partition prior to the public reactions that made them adjust their positions. The fact that they also ultimately signed documents that effectively accepted ethnic cleansing suggests there may be a significant divergence between acceptable political statements for public consumption and confidential positions in diplomatic negotiations. Realistic approaches to the difficulties of ethnic cleansing clearly have to be examined to understand the solutions available to the international community.

This article adopts a pragmatic approach to the issue of population exchanges in recognition of the fact that these political options are available at moments of crisis in which quick decisions may have considerable consequences for the survival of targeted minorities. Moral arguments are also considered because sustainable policy responses to the problem of ethnic cleansing must be based on principles.

Mass displacement and international peace efforts

The Lausanne Convention was not the first attempt at formalising the unmixing of populations in order to attenuate tensions between states: the 1913 Peace Treaty between Bulgaria and the Ottoman Empire included a protocol on the reciprocal and voluntary exchange of Bulgarian and Turkish populations, and the 1919 Peace Treaty of Neuilly-sur-Seine included a convention providing for a 'reciprocal voluntary emigration of the racial, religious and linguistic minorities in Greece and Bulgaria'.[5] It may not be surprising that legal arrangements of this type were particularly encouraged by fascist and totalitarian governments during the Second World War. Indeed, Hitler announced in the Reichstag on 6 October 1939 that there would be 'a new order of ethnographical conditions ... a resettlement of nationalities in such a manner that the process ultimately results in the obtaining of better dividing lines' (cited in de Zayas 1975: 247). Along with the aggression and terror generated by the Nazi regime, a series of 'Option Agreements' involving numerous voluntary transfers[6] was concluded from 1939 to 1941 between Germany and Estonia, Latvia, the Soviet Union, Rumania, Italy and Croatia.

Perhaps the greatest example of this type of displacement in the European context is the expulsion of an estimated sixteen million German nationals that took place in the period from 1944 to 1949. While sanctioned by the Potsdam Protocol, the expulsions were conducted in violent conditions that led to the deaths of approximately two million Germans.[7] Even Albert Schweitzer condemned the victorious Allies for this practice when he received the Noble Peace Prize in 1954.[8] Whether they are intended to rid territories of troublesome minority groups or save threatened minorities abroad by allowing them to resettle, recent history unfortunately provides many examples of attempts to improve regional security by population expulsions.

Although the High Commissioner for Refugees, Fridtjof Nansen, was entrusted in 1922 by the League of Nations to deal with the Asia Minor crisis, it is interesting to note that the displaced Greeks and Turks were not 'refugees' according to the emerging body of international refugee law. Before the Lausanne Peace Conference had started, Nansen reported to the League Council that the Greek delegation had asked him to arrange an exchange of populations.[9] He was eventually asked to assist a Sub-Commission of the Conference in the drafting of an exchange convention. When the drafting was completed, Article 7 of the Lausanne Convention provided that:

> [E]migrants will lose the nationality of the country which they are leaving, and will acquire the nationality of the country of their destination, upon their arrival in the territory of the latter country. Such emigrants as have already left one or other of the two countries and have not yet acquired their new nationality shall acquire that nationality on the date of the signature of the present Convention.

The specific regime for the Greeks and Turks gave the transferees new nationalities, and it was consequently not necessary to introduce international protection under refugee law as a replacement for state protection.[10]

When considering responses to ethnic cleansing it is necessary to take into account the fact that humanitarian interventions have proven for centuries to be an unreliable response. Given that France, Great Britain and Italy were not going to intervene against the Turkish army to save the threatened Greek population of Izmir in September 1922, an alternative solution was obviously needed. If outside powers are unwilling to send their soldiers to prevent ethnic cleansing and there is a refusal to explore alternative solutions, then victimised populations will probably suffer even greater hardships. As Lord Curzon stated in 1923:

> I believe that an exchange of populations, however well it were carried out, must impose very considerable hardships, perhaps very considerable impoverishment, upon great numbers of individual citizens of the two countries who are exchanged. But I also believe that these hardships, great though they may be, will be less than the hardships which will result for these same populations if nothing is done.[11]

Insisting on certain principles in times when urgent action is needed can be unprincipled if the result is inaction. In this context, it should be remembered that the loss of life in Asia Minor was kept at a minimum following the signing of the Lausanne Convention (de Zayas 1975: 223) unlike the situation of the expelled Germans of 1944 to 1949, or even the Cherokees who were forcibly transferred across America in the nineteenth century (ibid.: 251). When considering the fate of the displaced Greeks and Turks following the defeat of the Greek army in Asia Minor, it should be kept in mind that several years earlier another victimised minority, the Armenians, was not able to escape violence and successfully integrate into a new state that would accept them. The Armenians found themselves in a territory where they were victims of extreme exclusion to the point that the authorities were determined to rid the territory of their presence altogether (Zolberg et al. 1989: 15). Their emigration proved impossible or unfeasible due to external conditions and this eventually resulted in large-scale massacres. From a humanitarian standpoint, it is better to have a population expelled than murdered en masse. The fate of the Jews in Nazi Germany two decades later emphasises this point.

Despite the great human hardship engendered by population exchanges, the improvement in regional stability cannot be ignored. The unmixing of populations in Asia Minor helped put an end to hostilities and secure pacification of the warring parties. It made possible the signing several months later of the Treaty of Lausanne, which constituted a comprehensive peace plan for the region.[12] Yet the negative consequences of this realist approach to ethnic cleansing and population exchanges should be underlined. The Lausanne Convention remains an example of perhaps the crudest expression of state power over the individual (Thornberry 1991: 51). It clearly involved the domination of state interests over individual human rights (Meindersma 1997: 350). To the extent that the state interests concerned relate to protecting populations and avoiding war, it is difficult not to consider them as legitimate. Nevertheless, population exchanges ultimately reward the use of force, and in doing so dangerous precedents are set for future belligerents who wish to have the international community acknowledge wartime *faits accomplis.*

Controversial legal issues of population exchanges

Compulsory or voluntary nature of agreements

Once political leaders and diplomats decide that a population exchange agreement would help to promote peace and avoid massacres, then one issue that has to be addressed is whether the exchange is going to be compulsory or voluntary in nature. The Lausanne Convention is a striking and unique example in that it explicitly involved a compulsory exchange. For many observers, this feature makes it an unacceptable model for the international community's attempts to deal with threatened minorities (Tenekides 1924: 85). They prefer the approach endorsed by the 1919 Treaty of Neuilly which provided for a voluntary exchange between populations in Greece and Bulgaria (ibid.). The absolute compulsory nature of the exchange in the Lausanne Convention has been contrasted with other voluntary exchange treaties and the general trend under the League of Nations for minority protection to be guaranteed within the home country (Meindersma 1997: 348).

The notion of compulsory exchanges has generally become so unpopular that even the origin of the suggestion in the context of the Lausanne Conference is contested. While High Commissioner Nansen promoted such an approach prior to the beginning of the Conference (ibid.: 338; Tenekides 1924:83), it is unclear whether Venizelos initially intended his proposed exchange to be compulsory. As soon as Greek refugees protested against the idea of a compulsory exchange and Muslims opposed the idea of being forced to leave their homes, international public opinion became outraged (ibid.: 86; Meindersma 1997: 341). Politicians thereafter began shifting the blame for the suggestion of a compulsory exchange (Séfériadès 1928 : 373). The following section argues that the issue of the compulsory or voluntary nature of an exchange is pertinent primarily to the extent that it affects the crucial issue of refugee return.

In assessing the implications of a compulsory exchange agreement, it should be noted that international instruments on this issue tend to be signed after substantial ethnic cleansing has already taken place. While official authorisation for the transfer of German populations followed the Potsdam Conference of 17 July–2 August 1945,[13] the reality is that German populations had already been systematically expelled from East Prussia, Pomerania, East Brandenburg, Silesia, Upper Silesia and the Sudetenland under conditions that even the International Committee for the Red Cross acknowledged were neither humane nor orderly.[14] Shortly afterwards, India and Pakistan signed the New Delhi Accord[15] on 8 April 1950 which sought to regulate the de facto exchange of millions of Hindus, Muslims and Sikhs that had taken place since the partition of the Indian subcontinent in 1947 (see Khosla 1949).

Even in the compulsory exchange provided for in the Lausanne Convention, Lord Curzon's statistics indicated that the pre-First World War Greek population of 1.6 million in Asia Minor had already been reduced to approximately 500,000 by the end of 1922.[16] Similarly, the estimated 800,000 Muslims in Greece had been reduced by half due to episodes of 'unmixing' prior to 1922.[17] The international Mixed Commission established by Article 11 of the Lausanne Convention transferred under its auspices 189,916 Greeks to Greece and 355,635 Muslims to Turkey during the period from1923 to 1926.[18] Although the Lausanne Convention was signed on 30 January 1923 and the exchange was to start officially on 1 May 1923,[19] the actual transfer of exchangeable persons began earlier than planned (Meindersma 1997: 344). Both governments accelerated departures, which resulted in disorderly transfers. Under these conditions, the voluntary or compulsory nature of agreements is largely irrelevant in terms of the departure of the affected populations.

The fact that no exchange agreement was signed by the Greek and Turkish sides in Cyprus did not prevent a de facto partition and exchange involving

200,000 Greeks and 65,000 Turks according to the United Nations High Commissioner for Refugees.[20] This was also the case in Bosnia–Herzegovina, although two important factors made the signing of a peace agreement possible (as in Lausanne seventy-two years earlier): all warring parties in Bosnia–Herzegovina had accepted in principle the solution of territorial partition (even prior to the outbreak of hostilities) and the war has led to almost complete ethnic cleansing on all sides.[21] The signing of the Dayton Accord in Paris on 14 December 1995[22] attempted to reconcile this reality with the international community's unwillingness to reward the use of force in this particular case.

These examples demonstrate that the controversial issue in population exchange agreements is not necessarily the imposition of an obligation for people to leave their homes, because this has usually already occurred by the time international instruments are signed. Rather, the issue of a compulsory or voluntary exchange affects the crucial question of whether the expellees are permitted or encouraged to return to the areas they have escaped.

The adoption of a population exchange agreement that is compulsory in nature can be explained by several factors. Victorious states in international armed conflicts can be expected to negotiate peace conditions largely on their own terms. Such was the case in October 1922 when the Turkish delegation presented itself for the Lausanne Conference[23] and insisted that the Greeks accept a mandatory population exchange.[24] The argument that a compulsory exchange would ensure that the transfer be implemented quickly was also presented at the Lausanne Conference: the goal was to avoid the lengthy process that would result from a voluntary exchange.[25] Once the principle of population exchanges was accepted at the Lausanne Conference, it soon became clear that it was in the interest of both the Greek and Turkish governments for the exchange to be completed as quickly as possible.

Despite the awkwardness of defending the exchange to domestic constituencies, the decision to make it compulsory is understandable if priority is to be placed on a rapid completion of the process of ethnic cleansing, thereby attenuating the suffering of the displaced. It can be argued that the refusal to exchange populations formally in the Bosnian example seven decades later simply prolonged the suffering while not changing the end result: the creation of ethnically homogeneous territories. Contrary to the declarations of many diplomats involved in the Bosnian crisis, the negotiators at the Lausanne Conference openly spoke of the balance they were trying to achieve in terms of realpolitik:

> The conference had only ceded to the demand that the exchange should be compulsory because all those who had studied the matter most closely seemed to agree that the suffering entailed, great as it must be, would be repaid by the advantages which would ultimately accrue to both countries from a greater homogeneity of population and from the removal of old and deep rooted causes of quarrel.[26]

Another related problem negotiators have to consider is that history shows that voluntary exchange agreements tend to turn into de facto compulsory transfers. The adoption of legal instruments that cannot realistically be expected to be upheld by the signatories can undermine the credibility of international law. In situations of war it may be more appropriate to acknow-ledge harsh realities and adopt a practical approach that relies on workable principles, rather than to experiment with untested positions based on ideal-istic visions of humanity. Even jurists opposed to the compulsory aspect of population exchanges acknowledge that 'quasi-voluntary' agreements have a role to play in some humanitarian crises if they can encourage orderly and humane transfers (de Zayas 1975: 250).

When population exchanges are compulsory, the actual application of the Lausanne Convention indicates that identifying the exchangeable individuals can be problematic, and carries long-term consequences for both the dis-placed and the remaining populations. Article 1 of the Lausanne Convention provided that 'there shall take place a compulsory exchange of Turkish nationals of the Greek Orthodox religion established in Turkish territory, and of Greek nationals of the Moslem religion established in Greek territory'. This is followed by an exception in Article 2: 'The following persons shall not be included in the exchange provided for in Article 1: (a) The Greek inhabi-tants of Constantinople. (b) The Moslem inhabitants of Western Thrace.'[27] In addressing the precarious situation of the populations that had fled prior to the signing of the Lausanne Convention, Article 3 stipulates that the 'Greeks and Moslems who have already, and since October 18, 1912, left the terri-tories the Greek and Turkish inhabitants of which are to be respectively exchanged, shall be considered as included in the exchange'.

The *rationae personae* application of the Lausanne Convention is unclear in that it possibly allows for all co-religionists to be transferred. It was therefore necessary to establish that the signatory states intended it to apply only to co-religionists who were presumed to share the national sentiments of the receiving country (see Eddy 1931: 203; Ladas 1932: 380). For example, Alba-nians in Greece who followed the Islamic faith were not to be included in the exchange. However, the national sentiments of certain populations were not as easily identifiable. Consequently, groups with questionable affiliation to the receiving country were included in the exchange. The transfer of Muslim Cretans to Turkey is a case in point.

The populations not included in the exchange were allowed to remain and were supposed to benefit from the League of Nations minority system. In effect, the Treaty of Peace with Turkey that was signed six months after the Lausanne Convention included a minority protection regime that applied to the remain-ing non-Muslim minorities in Turkey and Muslim minorities in Greece.

Option of return or compensation

Given that Venizelos admitted that his interest in signing the Lausanne Con-vention was to secure the departure of Muslims in Greece because Turkey had already driven out most of its Greeks (Ladas 1932: 465), the motivation for the Turkish delegation's endorsement may appear unclear. The answer lies in the second paragraph of Article 1: 'These [exchangeable] persons shall not return to live in Turkey or Greece respectively without the authorisation of the Turkish Government or of the Greek Government respectively.' Many of the Greeks who fled hostilities in Asia Minor may have wanted to return to their homes after a peace agreement, but the Lausanne Convention effectively denied them this right. While preventing refugee returns is a fundamental aspect of the unofficial policy for various factions in Bosnia–Herzegovina and in Israel, the Turkish delegation at the Lausanne Conference managed to obtain a provision that could justify a *de jure* prohibition on returns.

This strategic issue points to another important consideration in the drafting of population exchange agreements: the reparation offered to the victims of displacement. International documents that address the plight of displacees tend to offer them the option of return or compensation. For example, in resolution 194 (III) concerning Palestinian refugees, the UN General Assembly:

> Resolves that the refugees wishing to return to their homes and live at peace with their neighbours should be permitted to do so at the earliest practicable date, and that compensation should be paid for the property of those choosing not to return and for the loss of or damage to property which, under principles of international law or in equity, should be made good by the Government or authorities responsible.[28]

The Dayton Accord that brought peace to Bosnia–Herzegovina provides that:

> All refugees and displaced persons have the right freely to return to their homes of origin. They shall have the right to have restored to them property of which they were deprived in the course of hostilities since 1991 and to be compensated for any property that cannot be restored to them ... The Parties shall not interfere with the returnees' choice of destination, nor shall they compel them to remain in or move to situations of serious danger or insecurity, or to areas lacking in the basic infrastructure necessary to resume a normal life.[29]

These instruments formally attempt to mitigate some of the consequences of ethnic cleansing and provide some justice for the displaced, while acknowledging the complexities involved in achieving regional peace and security when mass displacement has occurred.

Responses to ethnic cleansing that emphasise the right to return generally ensue from the position that ethnic cleansing must be reversed.[30] While this is certainly a commendable position, it must be weighed against the practical problems encountered in refugee returns. Furthermore, these problems are considerable when peace results from the successful creation of homogeneous territories. In these situations, returning displacees represent a direct threat to the political entity that has consolidated power through extreme exclusion of minorities.[31] In terms of human rights considerations, even under peaceful conditions it is barely possible to resolve the conflicting and competing rights that result from the return of persons whose prolonged absence has led to property rights being assumed by new settlers (who may be refugees themselves).[32] The case of Bosnia–Herzegovina demonstrates that attempts at vigorously dealing with the concrete problems of voter eligibility and registration, acquisition of citizenship rights and property claims to be determined by the Commission for Displaced Persons and Refugees[33] become sources of further tension that do not necessarily promote the delicately achieved peace settlement.

If return is not always a realistic option in cases of ethnic cleansing, the appropriate international response is further complicated by twentieth-century examples which suggest that compensation mechanisms are perhaps impossible to implement in practice. The possibility of compensating exchanged populations has appealed to even the harshest critics of the Lausanne Convention (Tenekides 1924: 87). Yet the actual experience of the Mixed Commission established under the Lausanne Convention is revealing. Even though it was explicitly responsible for evaluating and liquidating the moveable and immovable property of the displaced victims[34] in order to provide individual owners with a debt that could be exercised against the country of immigration,[35] it was not able effectively to carry out individual appraisals and liquidations of the transferees' property.[36] Public declarations by Greek leaders suggesting that a general balance of claims between Turkey and Greece was being considered led to protests by Greek refugees, but this did not prevent the governments concerned from signing a treaty in 1930 that replaced the Lausanne Convention's elaborate compensation mechanism.[37] The new arrangement simply transferred ownership of the remaining property to the government of the country in which it was located.[38]

The experience of the UN Conciliation Commission for Palestine established under UN General Assembly resolution 194(III) also does not provide reasons for optimism concerning the effectiveness of international compensation schemes. Although it focused on the payment of compensation as soon as it realised significant repatriation was not going to occur,[39] it was confronted with the realisation that 'the compensation issue is extremely complex and it is, therefore, unlikely that it will be possible to pay individual compensation to the refugees concerned' (Takkenburg 1998: 339). The magnitude of the compensation issue is highlighted by the following account:

> Few are aware of the extent of abandoned property that Israel has acquired as a result of the 1948 war or of the value of that property. According to the Conciliation Commission, basing its estimates on Village Statistics of the former mandatory government, over 80 percent of Israel's total area of some 20,000 square kilometres represented abandoned Arab lands, although there was a great deal of ambiguity about the status of that land … Of the three hundred and seventy new Jewish settlements established between 1948 and 1953, three hundred and fifty were on former Arab property … The Palestinian Arabs left whole cities like Jaffa, Acre, Lydda, Ramleh, Baysan, Majdal; 388 towns and villages and large parts of 94 other cities and towns, containing nearly a quarter of all the buildings in Israel at that time (cited in ibid.).

If individual compensation is difficult to implement in a fair manner immediately following ethnic conflict as demonstrated by the unsuccessful attempts of the Lausanne Mixed Commission and the Dayton Commission for Displaced Persons and Refugees, then the Palestinian case indicates that it is almost impossible when considerable time has elapsed. Given the specificity of ethnic conflict, attempts to compensate victims individually appear particularly elusive as explained in the following comment that highlights the paradox of the situation:

> Theoretically, the Convention of Lausanne was drawn up with scrupulous regard to the rights of exchangeables, but practically the rights so granted were of no real value. No Convention of the sort could be put in practice in a satisfactory manner unless, coincident with the departure of an emigrant, he received the value of the property abandoned by him. In order that this should be possible, the two contracting countries must be at peace, and no pressure to bring about an exchange must exist. In other words, the scheme would only work at a time when it is improbable that anyone would think of putting it into practice (Eddy 1931: 228).

The dilemma resulting from the ineffectiveness of individual compensation schemes profoundly affects the question of compulsory or voluntary population exchanges raised in the preceding section. For involuntary exchanges to be politically acceptable, the displaced victims should be provided at the very least with compensation. Both the experiences of the Lausanne Mixed Commission and the UN Conciliation Commission for Palestine suggest that lump sums may be the only form of compensation that transferees can realistically expect.[40] Although even this would certainly be a considerable accomplishment in the difficult context of ethnic cleansing,[41] it may mean that populations will never voluntarily participate in an exchange agreement due to the likelihood of their never being compensated individually.

Conclusion: towards a pragmatic and principled approach to the dilemmas posed by ethnic cleansing

There are two distinct issues that should not be confused when considering responses to ethnic cleansing. The first issue relates to the political response regarding the perpetrators of the gross human rights violations that generally accompany ethnic cleansing. This involves, for example, possible punitive actions by the UN Security Council or other bodies that can confront the parties which are behaving contrary to agreed international principles. Once the violations have already occurred, however, the actual assistance offered to alleviate the plight of the victims constitutes a distinct problem. This second issue concerns the humanitarian response regarding the people who have fled or are being detained by belligerents. Both these issues are certainly interrelated and the approach taken with the former can help resolve the latter. Yet confusing these two distinct problems or invoking failures to punish the violators while refusing concrete action that resolves the humanitarian predicament of the victims cannot be considered a principled approach.

Regardless of the actions eventually taken against those responsible for ethnic cleansing, it is imperative to address the situation of the displaced populations realistically (and quickly). An absolutist position that refuses a solution to the second issue on the grounds that it leaves the initial violation of international law intact is inappropriate in the context of war.

While most observers would agree that condemnation of violations is not sufficient, it may be useful to acknowledge the unfortunate fact that many instances of ethnic cleansing proceed unpunished. With that perspective, it is dangerous to suggest that the only principled solution to ethnic cleansing is its reversal, because this almost inevitably entails the use of military force. By leaving states with little flexibility with regard to possible solutions, the risk of inaction is increased and the victims' plight can be prolonged. For example, if the international community insists that ethnic cleansing must be reversed in the Middle East and openly rejects any possible peace plan that involves compensating Palestinian refugees who cannot exercise a right to return, then it is unlikely that the Palestinian issue will ever be resolved.

These are among the difficult questions that the participants at the Lausanne Conference tried to address eighty years ago. International military intervention to prevent the displacement was not being contemplated by key members of the League of Nations and pragmatism suggested that a population exchange was the only way to mitigate the suffering. Consequently, High Commissioner Nansen proceeded to assist in the evacuation and settlement of Greeks and Turks. He refused to condemn the belligerents in order to maintain his humanitarian and 'non-political' role. While the above analysis suggests that such population exchanges are problematic in many regards, they were considered at the time to be the only realistic option that it was possible to negotiate between the belligerents.

Seven decades later, the United Nations and its commitment to universal human rights led to a somewhat different approach regarding the armed conflict in Bosnia–Herzegovina. Although lacking agreement on a forceful international intervention, the High Commissioner for Refugees initially challenged the displacement that was occurring. When the orchestrated violence reached critical levels, her representatives were left with the unenviable decision of whether to organise evacuations. Understandably, they chose to facilitate the movement of those persons who did not feel safe enough to remain.[42] If they did otherwise, the death toll would have been undoubtedly higher, as pointed out by the High Commissioner's special envoy: 'We decided to help people to survive. We chose to have more displaced persons or refugees than more bodies' (Mendiluce 1994: 14).

In order to save lives, the UN has therefore participated in recent de facto population exchanges in both Bosnia–Herzegovina and Cyprus.[43] It is difficult to imagine genuine principles that could justify a refusal to participate in exchanges under circumstances involving such examples of communal violence. Like Nansen at the time of the Lausanne Conference, Sadako Ogata, the High Commissioner for Refugees throughout the 1990s, was obliged to adopt a pragmatic approach in difficult war situations. Any other approach would have jeopardised the survival of civilian populations. Although it may seem contrary to progressive notions of pluralism, territorial partition accompanied by population shifts under international supervision is preferable to chaotic expulsion under gunfire. This is the palliative response to mass displacement that has traditionally been a fundamental part of the international refugee regime. It does not provide a remedy or fix the problems at their source, for that is dependent on the political will of other actors.

Notes

1. 406 Parliamentary Debates, House of Commons (5th ser.) 1713 (1944).
2. In the context of former Yugoslavia, the term has been used to designate actions 'rendering an area ethnically homogeneous by using force or intimidation to remove persons of given groups from the area'. See *Interim Report of the Commission of Experts Established Pursuant to Security Council Resolution 780*, UN. Doc. S/25274 (1993).
3. 32 *League of Nations Treaty Series* 807 (1925) [hereinafter Lausanne Convention].
4. Livre jaune, Conférence de Lausanne, tome I, p. 176.
5. Greco-Bulgarian Reciprocal Emigration Convention, 1 *League of Nations Treaty Series* 67. Signed at Neuilly-sur-Seine on 27 November 1919.
6. 'On the whole, it may be asserted that the transfer of some 600,000 *Volksdeutsche* from Eastern Europe to the Reich pursuant to the option treaties was legally unobjectionable, insofar as each transfer was on a voluntary basis and no physical abuse was connected with the resettlement. It was not an expulsion' (de Zayas 1975: 249).
7. For statistics, see ibid.: 238.
8. Speech cited in ibid.: 241.
9. Letter from Nansen to the Council of the League of Nations, Doc. A/48/24318/24318 (16 October 1922); Tenekides 1924: 83.
10. Only the displaced who found refuge in third countries were left stateless (such as the Greeks who fled to Egypt) (ibid.: 85).
11. Discussions on the Exchange Convention, *Lausanne Conference on Near Eastern Affairs*, p. 114.
12. Treaty of Peace with Turkey, 24 July 1923. The Treaties of Peace 1919–1923, vol. II, New York: Carnegie Endowment for International Peace, 1924.
13. Article 13 of the Potsdam Protocol reads: 'The three Governments having considered the question in all its aspects, recognise that the transfer to Germany of German populations, or elements thereof, remaining in Poland, Czechoslovakia and Hungary, will have to be undertaken. They agree that any transfers that take place should be effected in an orderly and humane manner.'
14. 'Close on fourteen million people affected by these measures were thus forced to abandon their homes at short notice, and those who had to leave them for a time because of the fighting, were prevented from returning. The ICRC at once received a great number of appeals, drawing its attention to the alarming conditions of food and health in which a great number of these people were living, after hasty expulsion from their homes and assembly in provisional camps, and also to the often deplorable conditions of their transfer to Germany. Had it been borne in mind that the repatriation of some 1,500,000 Greeks from Asia Minor, after the First World War, had taken several years and required large-scale relief schemes, it would have been easy to foresee that the hurried transplanting of fourteen million human beings would raise a large number of problems from the humanitarian standpoint, especially in a Europe strewn with ruins and where starvation was rife' (*Report of the International Committee of the Red Cross on its Activities during the Second World War, 1 September 1939–30 June 1947*, 1948, p. 675, cited in de Zayas 1975: 235).
15. 131 *United Nations Treaty Series* 3 (1950).

16. Discussions on the Exchange Convention, *Lausanne Conference on Near Eastern Affairs*, p. 114, cited in Meindersma 1997: 341.
17. Statistics cited in Zolberg et al. 1989: 14.
18. Statistics cited in Meindersma 1997: 346.
19. According to Article 1 of the Lausanne Convention. In terms of international legal obligations, the Convention is considered to have entered into force on 25 August 1923 after ratification by Greece (ratified by Turkey on 23 August 1923).
20. Statistics cited in Meindersma 1997: 341.
21. For statistics, see, for example, UNHCR, *Information Notes on Former Yugoslavia*, November 1994, p. 8.
22. General Framework Agreement for Peace in Bosnia and Herzegovina, 25 *International Legal Materials* 75 (1996).
23. 'Unlike previous conferences such as the Congress of Berlin [in 1878], the Conference of Lausanne found itself confronted, not by an abject conquered Sick Man, but by an invigorated re-awakened nation determined at all costs to maintain what it believes to be the sovereign rights of the Turkish people. The result has been that it was found necessary at Lausanne to seek a conciliatory adjustment of the Western and Eastern questions. The pretensions of the European Powers both among themselves and as against Turkey have naturally assumed a less important place than the claims of the Turks who felt that they had everything to gain and little to lose by an unyielding belligerent attitude' (Marshall Brown 1923: 290).
24. By the end of the month, the delegation insisted on a 'total and enforced exchange of populations' (Report by Nansen to the Council, League of Nations, Doc. C.736/M447, 5). See also Tenekides 1924: 83.
25. As stated by Lord Curzon: 'If the exchange were left on a voluntary basis, months might pass before it was carried out, whereas what was wanted was firstly to get the Turkish population back into Eastern Thrace so that they might till the soil early next year; and, secondly, to provide for accommodation in Greece of the refugees pouring in from other parts' (Discussions on the Exchange Convention, *Lausanne Conference on Near Eastern Affairs*, p. 114).
26. Lord Curzon, ibid.: 412.
27. Article 2 further states that: 'All Greeks who were already established before October 30, 1918, within the areas under the Prefecture of the City of Constantinople, as defined by the law of 1912, shall be considered as Greek inhabitants of Constantinople. All Moslems established in the region to the east of the frontier line laid down in 1913 by the Treaty of Bucharest shall be considered as Moslem inhabitants of Western Thrace.' See also the following legal opinion that deals with the interpretation of the word 'établis' in Article 2: 'The restriction was placed upon the application of the principle of exchange for several reasons. As regards the Greek inhabitants of Constantinople, one reason amongst others was to save that city from the loss which it would have suffered as a result of the exodus of a part of the population which constitutes one of the most important economic and commercial factors in the life of the city' (Permanent Court of International Justice, *Collection of Advisory Opinions*, Series B, no. 10, 21 February 1925, p. 18).
28. 11 December 1949, paragraph 11. Similar provisions have not been incorporated in UN Security Council resolutions on the Palestinian situation. Contrary to General Assembly resolutions, Security Council resolutions are binding in terms of international law. See Article 25 of the Charter of the United Nations (signed on 26 June 1945).
29. Article I(1)(4), Agreement on Refugees and Displaced Persons, Annex VII to the General Framework Agreement for Peace in Bosnia and Herzegovina (14 December 1995).
30. '[T]he obligation to cease and reverse the consequences of ethnic cleansing is not only incumbent on the violating State; a duty to ensure this outcome rests on the entire community of nations' (Meindersma 1997: 639).
31. 'Ethnic cleansing poses particular difficulties regarding the effective enjoyment of the right to return without causing further displacement or exposing returnees to renewed violence … Such return is, however, particularly difficult in conditions where peace may have been

brought about in part because the state was successful in its ethnic cleansing policies' (de Mello 1997: vi).

32. On the Palestinian example, see below. On the example of Rwanda, see Beyani 1997: 21.

33. Established by Article VII of the Agreement on Refugees and Displaced Persons, Annex VII to the General Framework Agreement for Peace in Bosnia and Herzegovina (14 December 1995).

34. Article 13 of the Lausanne Convention: 'The Mixed Commission shall have full power to cause the valuation to be made of the movable and immovable property which is to be liquidated under the present Convention, the interested parties being given a hearing or being duly summoned so that they may be heard. The basis for the valuation of the property to be liquidated shall be the value of the property in gold currency.'

35. Article 14: 'The Commission shall transmit to the owner concerned a declaration stating the sum due to him in respect of the property of which he has been dispossessed, and such property shall remain at the disposal of the Government on whose territory it is situated. The total sums due on the basis of these declarations shall constitute a Government debt from the country where the liquidation takes place to the Government of the country to which the emigrant belongs. The emigrant shall in principle be entitled to receive in the country to which he emigrates, as representing the sums due to him, property of a value equal to and of the same nature as that which he has left behind.'

36. 'La convention ne dit pas, ce qui pourtant est essentiel, à quel moment et sur quelle base aura lieu l'estimation' (Tenekides 1924: 85).

37. Greco-Turkish Convention signed in Ankara, 10 June 1930.

38. Until then the property left behind by Muslims in Greece had been assigned to the Refugee Settlement Commission created by the Protocol relating to the settlement of Refugees in Greece and the creation for this purpose of a Refugee Settlement Commission, 20 *League of Nations Treaty Series* 503 (1923). Signed at Geneva on 29 September 1923 and ratified by Greece on 2 November 1923. The Commission was disbanded in 1930.

39. Paragraph 11 of resolution 194(III) '[i]nstructs the Conciliation Commission to facilitate the repatriation, resettlement and economic and social rehabilitation of the refugees and the payment of compensation..'

40. An optimistic position in the Palestinian context could hold that it is 'to be expected that payment of compensation will benefit the rehabilitation and rehousing of the refugees at large' (Takkenberg 1998: 339).

41. For example, it is argued that this would greatly increase the 'absorptive capacity' of a new territorial entity for Palestinian refugees (ibid.: 336, 341).

42. 'ICRC and UNHCR remain committed to evacuate those who need protection, cannot get it and wish to leave. A change in this position will occur only if and when the situation is such that the victims themselves confirm they feel safe enough to stay' (UNHCR, *Information Notes on Former Yugoslavia*, 27 April 1994, p. iii).

43. On the participation of the UN peacekeeping force (established by UNSC res. 186 of 1964) in the transfer of Cypriot populations, see UN Doc. A/35/639.

4

The Consequences of the Exchange of Populations for Turkey

Çağlar Keyder

Introduction

The exchange of populations of 1923, together with the Armenian deaths and deportations during the First World War, can be argued to have constituted *the* most important factor in defining the new Turkish entity. In terms of the eventual effects on the Turkish nation-state, the two population expulsions were parallel in their impact, and together resulted in the formation of an ethnically 'cleansed' Turkish entity. As a result of these displacements, the Turkish Republic was founded on the basis of a relatively homogeneous population, or at least one in which such a claim of homogeneity did not risk much incredulity.

Before I discuss the specific case of the Turkish nation-state, it must be stated that the demographic and political turbulence of the period between 1914 and 1924 in Turkey was by no means unique. Indeed, it was a time during which many nation-states propounding some ideal of ethnic homogeneity were either brought into being or at least aspired to. They had, of course, been imagined during the previous century when the significant texts providing inspiration to nationalists everywhere were written. It was the war, however, that offered a unique opportunity finally to realise these goals, especially when both the American president and the leader of the Russian socialist revolution proclaimed that self-determination of nations would henceforth be the political principle underlying the formation of states.

Before the war, the nationalist path appeared as one of the various alternatives that might shape the future of the complex relationship between identities and political units, alternatives such as the continuation of empires or, perhaps, the formation of other non-nation-state entities under the aegis of global liberalism. Indeed, had there been a resurgence of liberalism, it is possible that empires and a global market for goods and capital could have survived into the twentieth century. The portrayal of pre-war empires as helpless and unwieldy mammoths, crumbling due to inertia and the inability to accommodate modernisation is inaccurate. They were in fact, if not vigorous, certainly workable entities adjusting to the times and evolving towards a modernised administration, the rule of law, and a measure of political representation.[1] Nation-states, of course, encapsulated a radically different kind of modernisation, with a new state–society relationship and the passionate ideology of nationalism that liberals so disliked.

Immediately after the war, as world opinion suggested that the formation of nation-states out of old empires represented the way world historical progress would move (Marrus 1985), several de facto or *de jure* population exchanges occurred in order to collect various peoples together in territories that were supposed to be areas of ethnic homogeneity. Vast numbers were displaced in the dissolving German, Austro-Hungarian, and Russian Empires. The exchange between Greece and Turkey, then, was seen as an inevitable consequence of the demise of the old order of empires. Although involving a huge and brutal displacement, it was thought of as a necessary measure correcting the incongruity of territory and nation, and it was accepted because it provided an accelerated route to nation-state formation. In this context, the aim of the Lausanne exchange may be seen as typical of the period, fulfilling as it did the negotiated and legally acceptable – hence civilised – version of ethnic cleansing.

The Ottoman inheritance

Among the empires, the Ottoman had been a latecomer to modernisation. It was only after the Tanzimat in 1839 that the political elite took reform seriously and started forming an administrative order based on the idea of a *Rechtsstaat.* By the end of the century, with citizenship and equality among the subjects and solidarity among the multiethnic elite, it appeared that the old empire had the chance of re-creating itself (Deringil 1998; see also Salzmann 1999). Law, not democracy, was considered to be the foundation of social and political order; this is what constitutionalism meant, and as long as capital flows and an expanding market guaranteed at least some economic improvement – with promises of more to come – social order could be maintained.

The elite shared loyalty to a belief in Ottomanism even if there were disputes as to its content. In this ideal, the state did not seek to homogenise the population in the name of a single ethnic, confessional or linguistic affiliation.[2] The subjects were free to construct and define their identities, usually within the bounds of their religious communities. Unlike the nation-state, the imperial state did not seek to provide its subjects with a single narrative of belonging; it was sufficient that they showed a 'patriotism' toward the empire. Otherwise they were free to declare themselves Arab, Kurd, Armenian, Greek, etc. This was the model under which the Ottoman government operated in the period leading up to the First World War. During the war itself, it was seen that patriotism along such lines was not an empty slogan: thousands of Greeks and Armenians volunteered to join the army and to defend the empire against their co-religionists.

However, it must be pointed out that in the closing period of the empire the hold of the original religious communities on individuals was no longer as effective as it was supposed to be according to the blueprint. There are no data to ascertain if certain types of boundary-transgressing behaviour such as intermarriage increased, but there certainly was an increasing willingness to consider old religious or *millet*-based categories as more flexible and open to change. Individuals converted with ease and positioned themselves within a newly forming empire-wide society (Deringil 1999). Large cities became cosmopolitan places where elites associated on the basis of politics and common interests. Municipal associations, masonic lodges and various clubs and associations provided examples of nineteenth-century urbanity where the ideal was the ability to juggle local and cosmopolitan identities successfully (Keyder et al 1993; Keyder 1999a). This is not to say that nationalist movements or the corporate identities of the millets were no longer in evidence. In fact, during the nineteenth century, and especially during the two short-lived parliamentary periods, corporate structures had taken on a new role, becoming almost representative in character. Compared with Ottomanism and imperial citizenship, this form of representation reflected a different conception of the empire, one that held it to be constituted of corporate groups. This conception was not that of the elite, but it did appear as one through which the elite recognised the different needs of their constituencies. This division might explain the local social bases of the eventual ascendancy of nationalist movements.[3]

The fact that there were nationalist movements did not necessarily imply the hegemony of separatist nationalism, for there were always competing currents within the same constituencies. Its eventual ascendancy, however, indicated that external circumstances, i.e., the war, were conducive to its victory (Keyder 1997). Under war conditions, nationalist sentiments, which had been nurtured by uneven modernisation and economic inequality, led to active strife; and with the disruption of commodity and capital flows during the war, the re-establishment of the liberal market could only be an impossible dream. The exchange and other similar accommodations of the nationalist ideal testify to the appreciation of this impossibility.

Aspects of the exchange

It was during the war and its immediate aftermath that the foundations for the formation of the Turkish nation-state were established. To attribute prior intention of forming an ethnically homogenous nation-state to the perpetrators of the Armenian massacres and the Greek exchange may not be justifiable. However, by the time the Turkish Republic was officially founded, the ruling elite could claim to have cleansed the territory of 'alien' ethnic elements. This understanding of 'alienness' was based on a religiously defined concept of ethnicity. In other words, 'the nation' was preconceived in the minds of its founders as one constituted of Muslims, and it was this principle that they applied during the exchange. In fact, several groups affected by it, such as the Turkish-speaking Karamanli Christian Orthodox and the Greek-speaking Cretan Muslims, wanted to remain out of the exchange. For politicians on both sides, however, conceptions of ethnic homogeneity counted for more than the principle of self-determination.

The events of the last quarter of the nineteenth century had already initiated the process of ethnic homogenisation within the territory that later became Turkey (McCarthy 1983; Karpat 1985). As the empire lost land to Russia, Austria and Greece, some two million Muslims emigrated from these territories to the heartland of the empire. The flow continued during the Balkan Wars, now including a reverse direction of Christian refugees as well. Between the Balkan Wars and the First World War, 130,000 Greeks from the empire were repatriated in Macedonia, the Greek islands and mainland Greece,[4] and a similar number of Muslim refugees, mostly from Greek-occupied Macedonia, arrived in Anatolia. Following this pattern, an exchange with Greece was first broached in April 1914 when the Ottoman government proposed an exchange of populations between Greeks in the Aegean littoral and Muslims in Macedonia, a plan that remained unrealised.

One of the ironic consequences of Ottoman modernisation, which sought to create equal subjects endowed with citizenship rights, was seen in the consequences of the 1908 law for universal conscription. Until then, Muslims served in the army, and Christians generally paid a tax to avoid military service. However, the new constitutional government made conscription universal. When the war began and the government called up the reserves for military service, it was still possible to buy one's way out. Poorer Greeks, however, could not pay the compensation and so had to face conscription (up to the age of forty eight), but many either did not present themselves for service or deserted at a later date. Some of their families were deported. Greek and Armenian conscripts were mostly stationed in labour camps in the interior to work on road projects. Many of them died either during the march to the camps or later in them. Then the events of the summer of 1915 occurred, during which between one-half and two-thirds of the Armenian population perished in massacres, or due to deprivation and disease, during forced marches. Most of those who escaped death ended up in other parts of the world.

During the war, a large number of houses abandoned by the Greeks as they fled or were deported from Anatolia were destroyed. In those that remained, the Turkish authorities had settled Muslim refugees from the Balkans and the Aegean islands. After the conclusion of the Mudros Armistice (31 October 1918), some of the Greeks who had left during the war started returning to Anatolia. These three factors taken together meant that one of the immediate problems the authorities of the Greek occupation faced was scarce housing. The situation worsened with the start of the Turkish War of Independence when Greeks from the interior of Anatolia began to take refuge in the Greek-occupied zone to the west. With the outbreak of active hostilities between Turkish nationalists and the Greek army, the pressure towards ethnic homogenisation acquired a new momentum. Some Muslims from the Greek-occupied area relocated in the interior, while a reverse flow of Orthodox Christians took refuge in western Anatolia. As it became clear that the Greek army would eventually be forced out, and that the British would not return to war, the outflow of the Orthodox population from Turkish-controlled areas accelerated. The final wave was, of course, in the late summer of 1922 when, under the most adverse conditions, more than half a million Greek Orthodox left Turkey and took refuge in Greece. Thus, the official exchange of populations applied only to the 150,000 to 200,000 Greeks who had been left behind – most concentrated in the Black Sea and interior regions – out of a population (excluding Istanbul, whose Greeks were exempt from the compulsory exchange) that had been around a million before the war; and to about 350,000 Muslims who were relocated from Greece and the Aegean islands to Anatolia.[5] In 1913, one out of five persons in the geographical area that is now Turkey was a Christian; by the end of 1923, the proportion had declined to one in forty.

The exchange and the Turkish Republic

The numerical and social impact of the newly arrived refugees on Greece was much greater than the impact of refugees in Turkey. Anatolian Greeks represented not only a huge addition to the existing population (some one-quarter) but also a generally more educated and wealthier group than the indigenous Greeks. However, the Muslims who arrived in Turkey represented less than four percent of the population, were dispersed in a much larger land, were mostly settled in the countryside, and generally did not have much impact on the political and social development of the country.[6] In other words, the impact of the exchange in the two societies was asymmetrical, not only because of the numbers involved but also because the type of refugee or exchangee differed greatly.

When the exchange was decided upon, Greece and Turkey were at different stages of nation-state formation. Greece had already existed as a nation-state for almost a century, and had fashioned an ideology commensurate with the nationalist ideal. So in Greece, the Asia Minor Greeks were faced with adapting themselves to the politics and ideology of an already-existing state. Although their absorption was difficult, their legacy was mostly visible only at the cultural, literary and musical level and in their support for left-wing politics. The Turkish nation, however, was itself formed through this process of ethnic unmixing. The exchange, as well as the Armenian deportations, constituted the foundation step in the formation of the nation-state ideal. For this reason, it is difficult to isolate the impact of the exchange on Turkish society from the wider process of nation-state formation. I propose to categorise the effects of the population movements on Turkish social development under two headings: impact on state–society relations, and impact on the formation of Turkish nationalism and national identity.

Changes in the state–society relationship

During the nineteenth century, the Ottoman state had undergone a process of modernisation towards the constitution of a liberal order. The state had started to embrace the idea of self-limitation so that a civil society based on citizenship and rule of law could develop. To a degree, the Porte's role had been transformed from running a state based on patrimonial principles to one with an increasingly rational bureaucracy respecting the legal order. The factors giving rise to this development derived from both the state and society. While state modernisation was in part a response by the political elite to international pressures, it was also carried out in an attempt to centralise and hence strengthen the empire. In this regard, the Ottoman case is a good example of the nineteenth-century dynamic in which imperialist imposition and modernisation from above reinforced each other in changing the character of the state–society relationship.

At the same time, too, developing within the empire was a social group whose demands paralleled the self-limiting reforms of the state. In other words, the liberal economy of the nineteenth century nurtured a rapidly growing peripheral bourgeoisie who expressed a clear preference for the liberal guarantees of property rights, and a predictable legal and policy environment. However, this trend was reversed during and after the war, perhaps the clearest illustration of which was the regressive impact of population movements on the evolution of the property regime.

The concept of property – the state's relation to, and the degree of respect for, property rights – is perhaps the principal index of achievement in the establishment of a successful liberal regime. Property rights are the basis of the civil rights that guarantee, through the rule of law, the integrity of the individual against the state. Without a well established conception of property, state rule remains arbitrary – perhaps committed to some sense of justice and equity but not formally rational. In the Ottoman case, land as property had always been a problematical concept, because essentially all land belonged to the sultan who in theory could confiscate it at will. Therefore, possession depended on political favour in Istanbul and the balance of power locally, not on legal enforceability. In addition, there was more land than the population could cultivate with the prevalent technology. Acquisition of land was not problematic since there was no scarcity or prohibitive purchase price. Even in the relatively densely populated Aegean coastal area, enough land existed for the immigrants of the nineteenth century to be comfortably accommodated.

The famous 1858 legislation, drafted in response to foreign pressure and as part of the state–led modernisation effort, specified the basic categories of individual property, although the wording of the legislation was ambiguous. But more importantly, as the Ottoman Empire became ever more open to the world market the value of agricultural land in the nineteenth century increased. With greater commercialisation, greater competition over land ensued. Especially after the 1890s when the pace of economic activity was accelerating on the back of increasing investments in agriculture-based industry, competition over land led to a more definite conception of landed property. This is one case where changing demographic and economic conditions created a demand for significant liberal legislation. As it so happened, legal change (in the form of adopting western concepts of property rights) was coming anyway, partly because state modernisation required it, and partly because of foreign pressure.

However, during the 1910s, political logic overtook economic concerns, and this liberalisation was reversed. As Armenians and Greeks left or were forced to leave, landed property was taken over by locally powerful or politically connected individuals. In fact, the provisions of the exchange stipulated that all abandoned property was to be considered 'nationalised', and reverted to the state. What this meant in practice was that land and houses that had not been seized by local power brokers were appropriated by the political elite and granted to their clients.

After 1923, the non-scarcity of land in Turkey and this system of distribution combined to reverse the liberal trend of the late Ottoman Empire, with the result that a capitalist conception of property was delayed for a long time. The republican state became a reincarnation of the classical patrimonial Ottoman state, dispensing land and benefits to its trusted clients, thereby able to perpetuate its patron status above the law. This situation had long-term and particularly adverse effects in urban areas where the post-1950 development of shantytowns was one of the direct consequences of the ambivalent legal framework regulating property and land.[7]

The material resources the republic had acquired during the wars preceding its establishment helped strengthen it afterwards. As the non-Muslim population was eliminated, their properties and positions became part of the dowry of the new state, which could now distribute them to the population. This distribution served both to expedite the creation of a native bourgeoisie and also to make it beholden to the state. At the same time, world economic conditions and the ideological *Zeitgeist* shifted to favour anti-liberalism and a state–directed economy. During the 1930s and the Second World War, these circumstances facilitated the process whereby the course of capital accumulation came under the full control of the state.

The land situation is symbolic and illustrative of the relationship between the state and society that was struck during the making of the republic and of the new social structure that emerged after the departure of the Christians. The peripheral bourgeoisie and the professional middle class of the late Ottoman era, which had also provided the social force behind the modernising efforts of the state, had been overwhelmingly non-Muslim. The world economy of the nineteenth century, based on free trade and the free movement of capital, had created a local bourgeoisie that initially engaged mostly as middle-men between foreign merchants and Ottoman producers of agricultural and mineral primary products. Gradually, however, these inter-mediaries became merchants who dealt directly with foreign markets, and subsequently became manufacturers themselves.

Initially living in and around the ports, their activities and life style came to be emulated by townsmen in smaller Anatolian cities as well. By the Young Turk era of the early twentieth century, Anatolian cities had become trading centers and were on their way to economic and social development, com-plete with nascent bourgeoisies and educated middle classes with their clubs, concert halls and imposing stone houses. In this emerging social structure, Muslims were left far behind. Thus, an inescapable consequence of the popu-lation movement and later exchange was the removal from Turkey of its economically and socially most modernised citizens. Furthermore, the Mus-lim businessmen who rapidly took over the business opportunities now available were far less independent of the state. They had acquired the material and political resources and networks left behind by the departing Christians through a political process under the jurisdiction of the political elite. Thus they felt indebted to the state, and were dependent on it in vari-ous ways. Besides, unlike their predecessors, they did not have the support and protection of the foreign powers, and so for a long time there was no possibility of their providing opposition to the state or forming an auton-omous base of political organisation (cf. Buğra 1994).

The state tradition that scholars identify in republican Turkey (cf. Heper 1985) is not, I argue, in direct continuity with the Ottoman past. The Ottoman state–society relationship had changed and Turkey was now revert-ing to an earlier version. The transition from empire to the republic constituted a reversal in a development that would have culminated in a strong and independent bourgeoisie capable of economic activity and capi-tal accumulation free from state involvement and interference. Compared with the late Ottoman state, the republican state was much less accountable, and therefore more autocratic and arbitrary. Concomitantly, society was in a much weaker position in terms both of the legal framework protecting it from the state, and of the civil societal institutions necessary for self-regulation. In short, one of the consequences of the exchange was the revitalisation of the pre-modern state tradition.

The nature of Turkish nationalism

Such a reversal in the trend of the state–society relationship could not occur without a change in the legitimating discourse of state authority. The imperial Ottomanist ideology of the top-level elite had to be abandoned. What took its place was a delayed reaction to, and appropriation of, what had led to the dissolution of the empire: nationalism. While they battled separatists and irredentists, the Ottoman-state elite had been slow in concocting their own brand of nationalism, which, of course, would have been self-defeating anyway since their attempt was to preserve the empire. Later, however, when the likelihood arose of a narrower territorial sovereignty after the First World War, the elite had no choice but to opt for Turkish nationalism.

Since the mid-nineteenth century, in countries as diverse as Germany and China, nationalism had provided the vocabulary for defensive modernisation. In the third world, the question of modernity had become inextricably bound up with the question of constructing the nation-state (Calhoun 1998). It was such nationalism from above that constituted the founding ideology of the new Turkish Republic. In this construct, the state demarcated the boundaries of the nation and could determine the margins outside of which the necessary unity of the collective body would be threatened. This was the perspective that had informed the implementation of the exchange; it also provided the justification for rejecting the possibility of fashioning a civic identity around which the population, as an aggregate of individuals, might find cohesion. Of course, it precluded the possibility of a citizenship constituted on a foundation of principles that would apply regardless of differences in religion, language or race. Instead, in this type of authoritarian nationalism, the emphasis was on unity and collective purpose (cf. Greenfeld 1992). The national body was supposed to express homogeneity deriving from ethnic unity, which would then be made concrete through speaking in a single voice. Hence, the collectivist vision necessitated an authoritarian implementation because it called for a cadre of interpreters and expressers to know and represent the unique voice of the nation. It was this cadre that was inducted as agents of the project of modernity.

In the process of reorganising as a republic, Turkish nationalism was transformed from being an elite discourse to a state ideology. Its content also had to be refashioned to accommodate the new centrality of the state and the specific way in which it had come into being. Throughout this process what is striking is the relegation of the masses to an entirely passive position. Turkish nationalism is an extreme example of a situation where the masses remained silent partners, while the modernising elite did not attempt to accommodate popular sentiment within the nationalist discourse. Another factor explaining the lack of any popular fervour is the continuity of personnel between Ottoman reformers and republican nationalists. However, notwithstanding such continuity, participation in the nationalist movement could have provided the unifying experience required for allegiance to the new regime, but here too there were problems. Military engagement with Greece had widely been perceived as a war against an outside aggressor rather than a struggle against a colonial presence; it was yet another military campaign to be endured by the already mobilised Anatolian youth. Indeed, for Anatolian peasants, as well as for most of the urban population, the new republic must have looked very much like a truncated version of the Empire, except for the unavoidable fact of the disappearance of the Christian population. Thus, the challenge for the new nationalist discourse was not only to legitimate the new state–society relationship, but also to make sense of a drastically changed population composition.

What had affected the masses directly during the transition to the Turkish Republic was the process of ethnic homogenisation: the expulsion, deportation, massacre and exchange of the Armenian and Greek subjects of the empire. Rather than being popularly acclaimed, however, the events culminating in the expulsion and disappearance of some nine-tenths of the Christian population were covered up both in official discourse and in the national psyche. Admittedly there had been Muslim resentment of the Christian subjects' rapid social and economic rise during the nineteenth century. In addition, the war years may have inflamed the sentiments against Greeks, especially in western Anatolia. Nevertheless, what transpired was way out of proportion with the degree of hostility that must have existed between the populations. Significantly, the newly emerging nationalist discourse made no mention of any indigenous strife. Instead it defined an external enemy – imperialist powers – against which national liberation had succeeded. There has never been any discussion of the ethnic composition of Anatolia in republican-era textbooks. Greeks and Armenians are hardly mentioned, and, until the last decade when scholars became interested in the multi-cultural heritage of the empire, there was no discussion of the demographic composition of Anatolia prior to the republic either. It is noteworthy that the principal event of the nationalist struggle was repressed in the collective memory of the nation. This silence may have been all the more necessary because of the material benefits that had accrued to the state following the physical removal of these ethnic minorities.

The aim of nationalist mobilisation is formulated as appropriation of the transcendent logic of the West. At the same time, a successful nationalist movement requires that its narrative resonate with popular experience and sentiments (Chatterjee 1986). The major problem with nationalist history writing in Turkey was that it did not take into account popular experience or sentiments. It did not result from a negotiation of the terms between what the nationalist elite were trying to achieve, i.e., modernisation, and what had motivated the masses to participate in the nationalist struggle, and it did not attempt to come to terms with the events that loomed largest in the experience of the participants. The story propagated through official discourse suffered from an all-too-obvious concealment of a crucial episode in the process of national construction, so that instead it became an exercise in pure artifice. Because of this artificial quality it was possible for the nationalist elite to treat the construction of history and national identity in an entirely instrumental fashion. The version they constructed was heavily biased toward the modernisation project, was woefully deficient in its accommodation of popular elements and treated the masses as passive recipients of the message, to be moulded according to the blueprint.

There are silences in every nation's history that underlie an active effort to forget.[8] Turkish nationalist historiography is distinguished by the enormity of the effort to negate the previous existence of non-Turkish populations in the land that eventually became Turkey. In fact, as the legitimising ideology of the new republic, however, Turkish nationalism was invented against the backdrop of major shifts in population composition. It is easy to see why this nationalism opted for an ethnic version of the national narrative: a concept of Turkishness was constructed in an attempt to present the remaining population as homogeneous, and it glossed over any real diversity. As in the case of all the rival nationalisms that emerged in the empire, this was done through employing the construct of an unbroken ethnic history reaching back to a mythical past. In the case of Turkish nationalism, an additional feature is that this ethnic history was said to originate not in the new heartland of Anatolia, but in a mythical geography as well.

What came to be known as the 'Turkish-history thesis' was a direct product of, and instrument to serve, this claim. Even today, school children learn that Turks populated all of Eurasia after their migrations from Central Asia. According to this teaching, the original inhabitants of Anatolia as well as those of most proximate lands were of Turkish extraction. Having accepted this proposition, it becomes easy to subsume the ancient populations of Anatolia into Turkishness – hence the discussions in primary-school textbooks about Hittite and Sumerian Turks. In the 1930s, extreme versions of this thesis also included a corollary claiming that the first human language was Turkish, and that all other languages derive from it.

The 'Turkish-history thesis' was a logical necessity as a basis for an ethnic nationalism. As stated in Ottoman historiography, Turks had gradually conquered Anatolia after the defeat of the Byzantine army in 1071. Given that just before the First World War – after centuries of empire and religious conversion and intermarriage – Christians still constituted one-fifth of the population of the inherited lands, it was very difficult to argue that Anatolia was the homeland and its population ethnically pure. If, on the other hand, the ancient populations were proto-Turks, the new awakening would constitute the reclaiming of a lost essence. Without specifically addressing this conundrum, official history managed to imply that the formation of the nation-state (after the deportation of the Armenians and the Greek exchange) had returned Anatolia to its rightful heirs.

The foundation myth chosen for nationalist discourse posited a territorial origin in a distant land, 'Orta Asya' or Central Asia, which furthermore was supposed to have undergone major environmental transformation causing the Turks to migrate. Consequently, the land of origin could only be imagined: it was unreclaimable not only because it was distant but also because it was irreversibly altered. Significantly, this imagined land held greater reality than the conquered and currently occupied Anatolia. National history in the republic was devoid of spatial reference. There was no glorification of geography, of holy sites, of character that sets space apart. Anatolia itself was not considered magical and mystical as England is with its landscape, Germany with its plains and rivers, France with its various sites and hexagonal space, or Russia with its holy *mir* (soil, land, community). Even more significant, particular locations and features of the geography were regarded with active suspicion. Izmir was considered infidel, Istanbul was Byzance, while the coastal stretches and islands were inhabited by 'others', those who were not really of us. Indeed, the transfer of the capital city from Istanbul to Ankara, a place without significations, testifies to the desire to locate the new project in a neutral space devoid of history and symbolic weight.[9] In a sense, then, a geography of nowhere was constructed to correspond to the claim in the official discourse that our real geography was elsewhere.

It is not difficult to argue that this geographical estrangement was prompted by an intense effort to forget and erase from memory the associations of places that had been populated preponderantly by Greeks; they were now approached as frontier land to be reconquered. This endeavour is evident in the frequent toponymic reconfiguring of Anatolia. Attempting to find Turkic origins for place names, the government often decreed a similar sounding name to replace the previous Greek or Armenian name. Where a Turkish name had also existed, it was usually allowed to remain unless it too contained an unacceptable reference, for instance, to a heterodox tradition. In other cases, the old name was domesticated through the device of a bogus story.

As the republicans opted for an inland nationalism focused on Ankara, the geography embodying this nationalist sentiment came to reflect a selective appropriation of the 'motherland'. Nationalist authors wrote about villages, about small towns, about the social transformation taking place in the 'heartland'. The selective emphasis on some aspects of national geography and the deliberate ignoring of others becomes apparent in the nationalist attitude towards the sea. In a country that is essentially a peninsula with a very long coastline, it is remarkable how minimal the population's relationship with the sea has been. The major reason is that the coast was regarded as the domain of the Greeks. Indeed, most of the coastal population of the empire – its sailors, fishermen and sea merchants – did not, by definition, derive from the Muslim Turkish element, for in Ottoman usage the word 'Turk' referred to Anatolian peasants and nomads.

In keeping with the selective appropriation of the motherland, the seaboard towns of Anatolia that had been predominantly Greek were left relatively empty until the 1960s. A small group of classicist intellectuals had initiated an ideological challenge to Ankara republicans by urging a recognition of Turkey's heritage in Anatolian civilisations, rather than in so-called Central Asia.[10] Slowly detaching itself from the hegemony of nationalist ideology, this same group introduced the Turkish intelligentsia to the practice of 'blue trips', i.e., coastal cruising in very basic conditions visiting ancient sites that ordinarily could not be reached by road. This is how the republican intelligentsia, reared on nationalist mythology and inland populism, came to know of a different, Mediterranean heritage associated with the land they called their own. After the 1960s, the village and the rural idyll were no longer idealised; instead the middle classes rushed to acquire flats and timeshares in coastal towns.

Conclusion

The exchange was a defining moment in the constitution both of the state–society balance and of the dominant ideology of nationalism in the Turkish Republic. It was, however, overdetermined, in the sense that the prevailing tendency of the time was towards the creation of ethnically homogeneous entities, and this goal was achieved in different contexts through the exercise of massacres, population exchange, and ideological coercion. Indeed, in the post-First World War era, the odds were not in favour of the survival of a multiethnic state with liberal accommodation of all its constituent groups.

Within this world context, the impact of the exchange on Turkey's future development was significant, both in the composition of social classes and in the formation of official ideology. As for social classes and their relationship with the state, the principal consequence of the departure of Ottoman Christians was the subsequent decimation of what could best be described as the nascent bourgeoisie of the Ottoman Empire, i.e., those who had achieved a degree of independence from the state in exploiting a market potential and in creating the foundations of a civil society in the form of a network of autonomous organisations. The Turkish Republic was thus left with a greatly diminished potential for independent bourgeois accumulation and for an autonomous society that could emancipate itself from the state.

The exchange's implications for the nationalist ideology that became the official historiography of the nation-state were no less consequential. In an important sense, the exchange, along with the Armenian massacres, was excised from national history. This national history in its official version became, and until recently continued to be, the unchallengeable foundation of Turkish identity. The republican founders of the state opted for a blatantly constructed artefact with no reference to lived history, which later emerged as the 'true story' of the land and its population. In this story, the prior existence of non-Muslims in the geographical territory that became Turkey was glossed over, and no reference was made to the tensions, hostilities, and the consequent expulsion and exchange of these populations. The very real experience of the coexistence of Muslim and non-Muslim populations, at most times peaceful, but terminating in hostility, was actively suppressed. Anatolia was presented as having been a land of the Turks from earlier times, and its reconquest after the eleventh century, only a reclamation. The heritage of modern Turkey was said to lie in the true heartland of ethnic Turkishness, that is, inner Asia. The rich cultural history of Anatolia was glossed over. This suppression, which was necessary for the coherence of the energetically propagated official version of national history and identity, could not accommodate the lived experience of the existing population or the abundant physical evidence of a prior 'non-homogeneous' population. The result has been a particularly schizophrenic existence for modern Turkey and especially for the identity of its inhabitants; the analysis is only now slowly getting under way.

Notes

1. See the collection of articles on the causes and consequences of the collapse of empires, Barkey and Von Hagen 1997.
2. For an argument about the different implications of empires and nation-states on identity formation, see Calhoun 1998.
3. A well known theory of nationalism, originally advanced as an explanation for the Arab case, may be informative for the separatism of the other millets, especially the Greek and Armenian (Dawn 1973). According to this hypothesis, nationalist ideas were fuelled by elite rivalry. While the old established elites participated in the Ottomanist ideal of a modernised empire based on true citizenship and *Rechtsstaat*, newly emerging elites, probably of a commercial inclination and in a position to exploit opportunities presented by the rapid growth of the world economy, were willing to strike out on their own. Thus, nationalism became attractive as an ideology of struggle, not only against the moribund imperial tradition, as is conventionally interpreted, but also against the old elite established within the same millet.
4. The following account of population movements prior to the exchange is based on Solomonides 1984.
5. Ladas 1932 and Pentzopoulos 1962 remain authoritative accounts of the exchange. See also Arı 1995.
6. The exception is the Dönmes from Salonica who moved in 1912 when Salonica fell to Greece, and also during the exchange. Dönmes constituted one of the stronger bourgeois groups in the new Republic (see Keyder 1993).
7. I have traced the impact of this ambivalence on the urban form in Istanbul's growth. See Keyder 1999b.
8. This is another way of expressing Renan's idea of getting history wrong. See Renan 1990 [1882].
9. As memorably documented in Yakup Kadri Karaosmanoğlu's 1991 (originally 1934) novel *Ankara*.
10. Cevat Şakir (who wrote under the pseudonym Halikarnas Balıkçısı – the fisherman of Halikarnassus, modern Bodrum) was one of the earlier propagators of this view. He wrote books and essays on Anatolian gods, Anatolian civilisations and Anatolian legends, as well as fiction, taking place in coastal towns. See also Bozkurt Güvenç's (1993) book *Türk Kimliği* (Turkish identity) which attempts to assert this vision of a territorial heritage as the basis of national identity.

5

1922: Political Continuations and Realignments in the Greek State

Thanos Veremis

The Greek state achieved its independence in 1830. The main themes of its development until 1922 included the consolidation of the new state's authority, the modernisation of state and public institutions, and the unification of territories inhabited by substantial Greek populations. It should be noted that the Greek state developed with remarkable speed and consistency, so that the two decades spanning 1860 to 1880 appear as something of a golden era of liberal democracy. In particular, Greek irredentism, encapsulated in the *Megali Idea*, the Great Idea, was a grand theme running through and beyond this period. It found its champion in the reformist politician, Eleftherios Venizelos, leader of the Liberal Party and Prime Minister over many years, who played a primary role in the events around the Lausanne negotiations.

With the outbreak of the First World War, Venizelos, an ardent Anglophile intent on territorial gains, was determined to enter the war on the side of the Allies. King Constantine, however, was convinced of Germany's military superiority, and opted for neutrality. The determination of the Prime Minister to prevail, and the King's intervention in coordinating a coalition against him in 1915 exacerbated a political and social polarisation that became known as the National Schism (*o ethnikos dichasmos*). The clash between Prime Minister and King was bitter and protracted, and created a major political cleavage that had long-lasting consequences for the country. With the triumph of Venizelos in 1916, however, Greece entered the war on the side of the Allies. Greece's presence among the victors of the War promised to confer substantial territorial rewards in the Paris Peace Conference of 1919, but a heavy cost was to follow (Llewellyn Smith 1998[1973]). An ill-conceived military campaign (1919–22) resulted in the defeat of the Greek army by Turkish nationalist forces under Kemal Atatürk, and culminated in the mass exodus and expulsion of the Greek populations of Asia Minor, Eastern Thrace and the Pontos regions (see Hirschon, this volume for background).

I suggest, therefore, that 1922 is actually the true divide between the old and the new century in Greece. Before 1922, the Greek state was preoccupied with national unification, the construction of a bourgeois state according to the designs of a visionary middle-class elite, the consolidation of parliamentary power, and irredentist claims. By 1922, Greece's expansion had reached its limit, Venizelos had already put the finishing touches to the liberal state, and the large estates of Thessaly – anomalous and anachronistic remnants of the Ottoman period – were being expropriated and parcelled out to landless peasants (Costis 1990: 40).

No one realised of course that most of the era's themes were to reach a grand finale in this 1922 *fin de siècle.* I say 'most' because one of the more pernicious – the continuing political cleavage between the Venizelists and the royalists – persisted as a sinister leit motif connecting the two eras. In a country without an *ancien regime* and no landed aristocracy, the existence of a national schism with the appearance of a clash between conservatives and liberals might appear strange. King Constantine's popularity after the Balkan Wars of 1912–13 was entirely due to his role as the commander-in-chief of the successful military campaigns which were the natural outcome of Venizelos's irredentist agenda. But by the end of the decade, Constantine had become the rallying point of the traditional parties which had joined forces against the innovating Venizelos in the elections of 1912, as well as of the war-weary population of 'old Greece', but scarcely of the inhabitants of the newly acquired territories.

The royalist parties opposed the presence of the Greek army in Turkey in 1919, but Venizelos's power and his conviction that Britain supported his decision prevailed. However, the anti-Venizelist, royalist coalition that defeated the Liberal Party in the 1920 elections lacked the courage to reverse the accelerating military campaign in Asia Minor. Despite the admonitions of one of their own, General Ioannis Metaxas (see below), they pursued a disastrous course that led to defeat, and then paid for the decision, one that they had not themselves made. The national schism climaxed in 1922 with the execution of five anti-Venizelist politicians and the commander of the Asia Minor forces, all accused of high treason. They were in fact executed for their responsibility for the Asia Minor Catastrophe, although they were not solely responsible for the disaster. It took the anti-Venizelists a decade to regroup and to manage again to win elections. For ten years, a period punctuated by numerous military coups and interventions (see Veremis 1997), factions in the Venizelist camp competed for power unopposed by their political adversaries.

The watershed of 1922 was marked by the influx of the refugees, whose presence was catalytic to all subsequent developments in Greece. The vast numbers of newcomers, both in absolute and proportional terms, had profound effects on the social, cultural, political and economic life of the country. They posed a social challenge that strained the tolerance of the natives; they introduced new perceptions in the insular society of the urban and rural centres; they changed the face of party politics beyond recognition; they gave the economy a vital transfusion by introducing their skills and labour; and they affected the views of the intelligentsia as no other single source of influence had done in the past.

Absorbing outsiders

The absorption of refugees was not a new phenomenon in the Greek state. From its very foundation in 1830, the inhabitants of Roumeli (central Greece) and the Morea (southern Greece), the first to be liberated from Ottoman domination, had acquainted themselves with the communities of their Cretan, Epirote and Macedonian brethren who sought support in their irredentist struggles. The latter trickled into the rebellious state, initially as volunteer warriors and subsequently as refugees after every failed uprising. The spectacle of makeshift camps was common in a state that was becoming familiar with the diversity of its future citizens. Although most were adherents of Orthodoxy, not all spoke Greek. Arvanites (Albanians), Vlachs and Slavs added variety to Greek-speaking representatives who met in Epidaurus in 1821 to draft a constitution that would unify the political fragments for a communal existence. In contrast with the Ottoman administration, which was based on a network of communities and used local notables for the collection of taxes, the Greek insurgents adopted the French blueprint, with its centralised administration and unitary state as a model.

The process of convergence of adversarial nationalist agendas was not without reversals and cleavages. In 1844 when a new constitution was being drafted, the parochial attitude of the autochthons, those born within the realm of the free state, prevailed (Kyriakidou 1892: 487–505). The Greeks born outside the realm, heterochthons, were not given the right to vote, and those in the civil service lost their jobs. However, before long the constitutional article which discriminated between native-born and outsider fell into disuse. A similar cleavage was generated following the Balkan Wars of 1912–13 as new territories and their populations were added to the kingdom. At this point Greece almost doubled its territory – from 25,014 to 41,993 square miles – and its population – from 2.7 to 4.8 million (Dakin 1972: 202). However, the established classes of 'old Greece' refused to share their privileges with the newly incorporated populations. They even resisted the continuation of the irredentist process itself when their control of the state began to hang in the balance. The political polarisation that developed during the First World War between a neutral stance and a pro-Entente commitment was another symptom of the growing pains of a small, culturally homogeneous state. The royalist slogan, 'a small but honourable Greece' expressed the old predilection of the autochthonous establishment for the status quo. However, the depth of the 1916 schism was unprecedented, as was the task of unifying under a single authority the newly acquired territory.

Inter-war politics and the refugees

The same was true with the 1922 influx of refugees. The threat, real or imaginary, that the dispossessed newcomers from Asia Minor posed to shop-keepers and small property owners all over Greece was linked in the public's mind with the ominous contagion of the Bolshevik revolution that haunted bourgeois Europe.

Despite clear evidence of previously existing internal tensions, Greek political parties were unprepared for inter-war radicalism, and displayed more alarm than its actual threat to the social order merited. Political manifestations of the period such as industrial action, general strikes, agitation and corporatism were perceived, in an exaggerated reaction, as signs of impending doom (Veremis 1982: 23–25). The national schism had resulted in a parliament dominated by the liberal camp, precluding a coalition of bourgeois political forces to face the crisis. By 1925 most liberal politicians were unwilling to take harsh economic measures since that would benefit the anti-Venizelist opposition and extra-parliamentary right-wing forces. Instead, they were prepared to abdicate their responsibilities by allowing a caretaker military figure like General Theodore Pangalos to step in and make the unpopular decisions. It was under such circumstances that military corporatism reached its brief heyday and became a melodramatic feature of the mid-1920s, in fact causing more sound and fury than real damage (Veremis 1997: 70–89). In a society where clientelism reigned supreme, the attempts by the military to introduce the element of professional corporatism into their interventions was ultimately doomed. The ponderous coup of 1935, masterminded by the only organisation established on corporatist principles (Elliniki Stratiotiki Organosis) failed miserably (Janowitz 1965: 68). Although patron-client relationships hindered attempts at horizontal organisation among the refugees, their overall social isolation and lack of connections other than their dependence on specific politicians encouraged the development of a corporatist as well as class identity which went on to affect Greek politics profoundly.

Through the population exchange, the influx of about 300,000 men of voting age, almost all in the liberal camp, determined the pattern of election results at least until 1932. Another new element with a special impact on the 1924 change of regime was the generalised anti-monarchist position of the refugees, as opposed to the specifically anti-Constantine sentiments of mainstream Venizelists. The native liberals opposed King Constantine as a person rather than the institution of the monarchy itself. His father, King George, although hardly a popular monarch, had steered the crown away from dangerous confrontations with parliament on several instances during his long reign, and had acquired his reputation for wisdom by striking compromises with parliamentary adversaries. If King Constantine had not challenged Venizelos's authority as the elected Prime Minister during the First World War, he would have been remembered for his presence in the frontline of the Balkan Wars. The refugees, however, did not share these recollections; instead, they harboured bitter memories of their eviction from their homeland, which they associated with the anti-Venizelist government then in power under its leader, King Constantine. Their loss of property and status had a revolutionary effect on their own social stratum that could not be compared to the more cautious radicalism of the natives.

The local congresses of refugees that convened through 1923 to determine a common position in Greek politics agreed that they owed their unqualified allegiance to Venizelos (Pentzopoulos 1962: 176). True to this commitment, the refugees supported the Liberals in the elections of 1923, 1926 and 1928. Without their support the Venizelist camp would probably not have been able to dominate the polls throughout this period (Dafnes 1961: 146). Yet in spite of their decisive electoral role, the refugees were under-represented as a group in parliament. While they comprised about 20 percent of the total population, on average they were represented by only 12–13 percent of all the deputies (Pentzopoulos 1962: 187), and the most seats they ever won was thirty-eight in the elections of 1932. The explanation for this under-representation lies in their geographical distribution and perhaps in the various representational electoral systems, which gave them a 'dominant voice in determining the victory or defeat of the old political parties of Greece but prevented them from forming an independent political force' (Pentzopoulos 1962: 188; cf. Legg 1969).

The Ankara Convention of 1930 between Greece and Turkey, with its provision cancelling the compensation due to the refugees for their abandoned properties in Turkey, instituted a watershed in refugee political behaviour. A significant shift to the left occurred in the 1930s that indicated the disillusionment of many with parliamentary politics. It also signalled the development of a class consciousness, a way of 'sublimating their alienation by struggling for an envisioned international order in which ethnic minorities would not constitute political problems' (Petropoulos 1976: 158–59). In the 1931 by-elections in Thessaloniki, where the refugees formed 48 percent of the total population, the Liberal candidate received only 38 percent of the votes compared with 69 percent three years earlier, and significantly the Communists doubled their gains (Pentzopoulos 1962: 192). The attraction of refugee votes at this time to the anti-Venizelist camp, represented by the Populist Party, was caused by false promises of compensation for their abandoned property, and it was only a temporary swing. Given its past history, the Populist Party could never achieve reconciliation with the refugees as a group. Thus, during the Venizelist coup of 1935 the refugees overwhelmingly backed the Venizelist rebels against the Populist Government of the time (Mavrogordatos 1983: 211–213).

In fact, the majority of refugee defectors from Venizelism turned to the communist camp, but the transition was by no means a smooth one. In 1924 the Comintern decided that Greek, Serbian and Bulgarian natives of the wider region of Macedonia should join up in a united autonomous entity under Bulgarian sovereignty in an autonomous Balkan federation. With their influence in the Comintern, the Bulgarian communists hoped to control this entity. The implications of such a decision for the Greek Communist Party (KKE) were grave, since it amounted to surrendering Greece's newly acquired territory to its vanquished Bulgarian rival. Party luminaries, such as Kordatos and Maximos, warned their comrades of the consequences this would have on the refugees and the masses in general. They were not heard and resigned in despair. The decision to fall in line with the Comintern caused a cleavage among Greek communists, and deterred many of the refugees who had been settled in Macedonia from joining the Party. The fear of becoming yet again an ethnic minority, this time in a united Macedonia with a hostile Slav majority, turned them away from the left and determined the political affiliations of the rural settlers for many years to come.

Refugees who did become members of the KKE soon realised that they would have to sacrifice their own special cause and accept the Party's priorities, which often clashed with their corporate interests. The predicament of the communist refugees is clear, given the Party's opposition to Venizelist 'imperialism' during the Asia Minor campaign, its subsequent support of native workers against the newcomers, and its condemnation of the massive refugee settlement of Macedonia and Thrace 'as part of a sinister plan of the Greek bourgeoisie for a forcible alteration of the ethnic composition of these regions' (Mavrogordatos 1983: 219).[1]

In 1934, the adoption of the 'Popular Front' strategy against fascism allowed the KKE to slacken its ideological rigour and to revise its position vis-à-vis the refugees. The policy for an independent Macedonia and Thrace was replaced by full national and political equality for all national minorities within Greece, and an extra effort was made to win over republicans who had become disillusioned with the Venizelist camp. The effect was notable. By 1935 about half of the Central Committee and most of the Politbureau members were refugees, including the Party Secretary, Nikos Zachariades (Mavrogordatos 1983: 222–23). As a distinct group, the refugees began to lose their cohesion, but offered their radical zeal to the communist movement.

Redefining Greek national identity

One of the most important new developments of the post-1922 era was the end of irredentist expansion and with it the fixing of Greece's boundaries. As the routes to the Balkans and the Near East closed one after another and the United States shut its gates on the immigrant incursion, the possibility of outward mobility for the Greek younger generation was halted. After 1930 the Asia Minor refugees abandoned hopes of returning to their homeland and chose to adjust to their new state of affairs or to rebel within the system.

The transition from the twentieth century's second decade of glorious expansion of the Greek state to the third decade of defeat and consolidation was not easy. Some Greeks felt trapped within the claustrophobic confines of a problematic state, others tried to rationalise Greece's predicament and exchange the dream kingdom of the Megali Idea for the ideal of westernisation and development. George Theotokas' novel *Eleftheero Pnevma* (Free Spirit), published in 1929, was a timely attempt to rid his generation of past illusions and to counter the pessimism expressed by writers such as Kariotakis or the mystical escapism of Sikelianos (Vitti 1978: 293–341). Theotokas praised the symbiosis of the worthy though contradictory elements that comprise Greek culture, the combined legacy of a folk tradition and of a scholarly achievement personified by Makryiannis on the one hand and by Cavafy on the other. However, his main preoccupation was to direct Greece back into the mainstream of European tradition of which it was part (Dimaras 1978: 487–89).

Ioannis Metaxas, general-turned-politician and then dictator, became a major player in the inter-war period, taking over Greek political life through his military coup of 1936. He also tried to establish a cultural continuum that would bring Greece into what he perceived to be the European mainstream. His idea of a third Greek civilisation was akin to Mussolini and Hitler's Eurocentric visions and was as much opposed to pessimism, escapism and communism as was Theotokas'. However, his scheme was exclusive, even insular, while Theotokas' vision was inclusive and cosmopolitan. Although some intellectuals sought to counter Greece's psychological contraction, parochialism was already setting in to define the revised content of what constituted the nation and national identity.

The autochthonous espousal of 'a small but honourable nation' proclaimed in 1844 was, however, countered by the expanding kingdom. As the nineteenth-century historian Papparigopoulos understood only too well, a concept of cultural unity could provide a bond in the new Greek state that would facilitate the acculturation of the many Albanians, Vlachs and Slavs who lived there. Isocrates's dictum, 'We consider Greeks all those who partake in our culture' became the basis of nineteenth-century Greek irredentism. The present cultural homogeneity of the Greeks owes much to the open and flexible notion of what constituted 'Greekness' in the era of the Megali Idea (Papparigopoulos 1976: 151–53; Dimaras 1978).

The content of Greek nationalism was being transformed during the inter-war period. Together with the Asia Minor Catastrophe and the consolidation of Greek borders, the Comintern posed a formidable challenge to Greece's territorial integrity, which was nonetheless adopted by a dutiful KKE. Thus the danger 'from within' posed by the communists constituted an entirely new threat to a state that up to this time had only known external adversaries. The new content of Greek national identity with its exclusivism and shifting emphasis on ethnic as opposed to cultural criteria can be seen as a negative reaction to the Communist Party's ideology. Historical materialism and the ideas of class analysis that cut across national distinctions directly influenced the state's ideological orientation. The internationalist assault on the notion of the social and cultural homogeneity of the nation-state by the Comintern provoked a strong counter-reaction. Whereas state ideology had reflected a generosity towards potential converts and a tolerance for ethnic varieties during the irredentist years, the inter-war state pursued its mission by recourse to a narrow and distant view of history. An exclusive relationship with classical antiquity became one of the two legitimising elements of Greekness. The other was ideological purity.

General Metaxas, like other theorists of the right such as Pericles Yannopoulos and Demosthenis Daniilides, relegated the role of religion in his state to a secondary position.[2] In his view, Ancient Greece and the classical heritage was the ideal and primary point of reference that differentiated the Greeks from their Slav neighbours and, by implication, the communists. In his anti-communism and anti-parliamentarianism he connected closely with contemporary fascists, but his racial discourse was limited. In his speech of 27 October 1936 in Serres, his first after seizing power, he spoke of the Greek race and its calling to be a 'chosen stock' (Sarandis 1993: 150). Although a rare occasion, the expression of this view constituted a significant departure from the culturally based nationalism of the past and set a precedent that would find its imitators in the post-Second World War period. His least successful innovatory idea was the cult of the state and its elevation to that of a living organism with a mission to unify the nation. For Greeks, unlike the concept of the nation, the state had always been an object of popular derision. Thus, in their time-honoured tradition they merely paid lip service to this grand design.

In Greece where the nation, *ethnos*, constituted the spiritual side of the system and the state, *kratos*, its secular and negative side, the latter could never mobilise the allegiance of its world-weary citizens to make up for its mischief (Just 1989). When on 28 October 1940 the Greeks closed ranks to resist the Italian invasion, it was because the fascist challenge was perceived as a threat to the nation, not the state. Nevertheless, the decline of liberal democracy after 1922, and its abolition between 1936 and 1945, would play a significant role in the future troubles that were to befall Greece.

Changing party political structures and alignments

Overall, the effect of widespread displacement and relocation of people in Greece in the early decades of the twentieth century undermined patron-client relationships and facilitated the advent of ideological party politics. The arrival of the newcomers disrupted the fabric of traditional political relations established in the nineteenth century both in the rural and urban centres and helped to redraw the grid of political camps and confrontations. This, however, was a gradual process and not accomplished overnight.

The attitude of political parties towards the 'other', whether refugees or ethnic groups, depended entirely on their point of entry into Greek politics. As long as the Venizelist-anti-Venizelist divide dominated politics, the refugees dedicated their allegiance to their political patrons, whereas the Jews and the Arvanites voted as a bloc for the anti-Venizelists. Venizelist liberals did not favour their refugee clients because of ideological inclination, nor did the conservative populists draw Jewish and Muslim support because of their party platform. It is different circumstances of political expedience that explains the support of these groups for each party.

Such a state of affairs continued even during the Metaxas regime when state relations with the 'others' were still based on their party allegiances.

Metaxas was better disposed towards the Jews, the Arvanites and the Muslims than the liberal Venizelists had ever been, and was certainly less so towards the refugees of the urban (as opposed to the rural) centres and to the Slav-speakers of Macedonia. Although Metaxas' anti-Venizelist 'Eleftherophrones Party' had benefited from the votes of Slav-speakers in the elections of November 1926, when he took control as dictator ten years later he was less concerned with winning potential friends and more preoccupied with warding off the enemies of the nation. Bulgarian propaganda among Slav-speakers in Macedonia was increasing and spurred the Metaxas regime of 1936 to promote the homogenisation of the non-Greek speakers under the licence of a dictatorship. The more Greek–Bulgarian relations deteriorated, the more pressure was put on Slav-speakers to disavow their linguistic loyalties (Carabott 1997: 267).

The Anatolian refugees who had been settled in rural Macedonia were mostly Turkish-speaking or Pontic Greek speakers (equally unintelligible to the locals) and for that reason they could not have exerted a strong Hellenising influence in the region. Their identity was based on the Orthodox Christian culture as the *Rum* community under the Ottoman regime. In the early period, however, they unwittingly became the cause of a significant cleavage with the natives of Macedonia. The competition of the Turkish-speaking refugees with the Slav- and Greek-speaking natives over the abandoned properties of the departed Muslims had far-reaching consequences for the society of northern Greece. Many disaffected Slav-speakers opted to support the Communist Party with its policy of a unified Macedonian state and later, during the 1946–49 civil war, many joined the Democratic Army, which had a secessionist agenda. A majority of the rural refugees, recognising their inevitable dependence on the Greek state as the most important source of support and security, were transformed into true patriots and became right-wing nationalists who supported the cause of the Greek state (Koliopoulos 1994). This contrasts with the situation in the poorer urban refugee settlements which became known as left-wing strongholds (see Pentzopoulos 1962; Hirschon 1998[1989]: 43–48, 51–53); Koliopoulos 1994).

The effect of the Second World War and of foreign occupation (Italian, German and Bulgarian) exerted the most radical influence on the reconstruction of the patterns of loyalties. The liberal–conservative divide was transformed into a right–left cleavage, and a shift of loyalties began to develop. Pre-existing differences among the refugees and native groups in Macedonia certainly played their part in deciding the subsequent position of each in the right–left spectrum as well as in the clash between loyalists and secessionists. However, it did not simply follow that right–left positions coincided with those of loyalists-secessionists. For example, the Cams of Epirus, certain Vlachs of Thessaly, and many Slav-speakers of Macedonia (extreme right-wingers) collaborated with the occupation forces hoping to establish their own states. On the other hand, certain Slavo-Macedonians (often the same who had fraternised with the Bulgarian quasi-fascist forces) sided with Tito's communist partisans and supported his post-war designs of Yugoslav domination. Nor should the pattern of behaviour of secessionists in the Democratic Army be equated with that of all members of the Greek Communist Party, as was often claimed by right-wing propaganda (Koliopoulos 1994).

The period of the occupation and civil war from 1941 to 1949 recast the entire question of refugees as a political force by practically eradicating their corporate position in Greek politics. However, those inhabiting the shanty-towns of Athens and the poorer urban quarters continued to remind the Greek state of their disaffected existence long after the left's defeat in the civil war by casting their vote for EDA (United Democratic Left) or the KKE (Communist Party of Greece) after it was legalised in 1974.

Conclusion

The watershed of 1922 is, as far as Greece is concerned, the true divide between the old and the new century. Before that time, Greece had completed its territorial expansion, political consolidation and political reforms. While the post-1922 period inherited the political cleavage between liberals and royalists, it added a new source of turmoil in politics – the Communist Party. Amongst Greek communists, however, the formidable predicament of being caught on the one hand between loyalty to the Party and, on the other, surrender of Greek Macedonia to a Balkan federation under Bulgarian influence created a rift, and the Anatolian refugees became a further catalyst for fragmentation in Greek inter-war politics. The subsequent political cleavage in Macedonia between slavophone natives and refugee newcomers can be explained by their local antagonisms regarding the reallocation of Ottoman property.

The entire transformation of the political discourse in Greece, from liberal–royalist, to left–right, was greatly influenced by the refugee factor. In the urban centres the refugees became associated with the communist 'enemy from within'; in rural Greece they were seen to have impeded the acculturation process of bringing the Slav-speakers into mainstream society and to have diverted their loyalties elsewhere. Civil strife bridged the political cleavages of the inter-war period. Venizelists and royalists slowly closed ranks against the left-wing threat. The grievances of some of the natives became a source of division that fed into the Greek civil war of 1949–51.[3] The new cleavage transformed the nationalism of the past into the 'national-mindedness' of the post-war state (Mavrogordatos 1995).

Notes

1. Mavrogordatos's point is well substantiated that, although the KKE sought to infiltrate the refugees, its own aims were often incompatible with their interests (1983: 218–21, particularly KKE sources in footnotes 109–19).
2. For the most systematic analysis of Metaxas's ideology, see Sarandis 1993: 159.
3. For a detailed discussion of this phenomenon, see Koliopoulos 1999.

6

Economic Consequences following Refugee Settlement in Greek Macedonia, 1923–1932

Elisabeth Kontogiorgi

Introduction

In the aftermath of the First World War and the failed Asia Minor campaign Greece received the largest influx of refugees in the Balkans: 1.2 million refugees – mostly women and children[1] – had to be integrated into an existing population of just five million. The arrival and settlement of so many refugees (equal to about one-quarter of the existing population) imposed heavy burdens on the national economy, both in the short term with the cost of initial relief,[2] but more importantly in the longer term when the debts incurred for the settlement of the refugees would prove crippling; indeed, it has been argued that these debts contributed to the bankruptcy of the Greek state in 1932 (Ladas 1932: 635ff.). The influx of numerous refugees also raised serious political and social concerns; the dangers of social unrest and the spread of epidemics and radical political ideologies were all feasible. Furthermore, there was the risk of hostility between the newcomers and the native population. The fact that the refugees enjoyed full citizenship rights as soon as they arrived in Greece (according to the Lausanne Convention) and were entitled to be established in the large Muslim estates (according to the Geneva Protocol of 29/9/1923), which local landless farmers expected to be distributed to them, increased antagonism over the resources available, and caused tension between the two groups during the implementation of land reform and settlement.

On the other hand, however, the refugees offered potential for economic growth. Not only were they an important labour source in a country needing to industrialise (Petropoulos 1976: 149; Pepelassi-Minoglou 1988: 148), but they also included many entrepreneurs and cultivators of cash crops, such as silk and tobacco (Mazower 1992: 120). Secondly, by their sheer numbers alone they promised the expansion of a small and limited domestic market, and in addition those refugees who were expelled from Turkey in relative order under the auspices of the League of Nations managed to bring considerable cash and valuables into the country.[3]

This chapter addresses some of the themes that emerge from the study of the refugee settlement process, mainly in rural Macedonia. The aim is to understand the consequences of the rural settlement policies adopted, to illustrate certain problems that affected the productivity and the socio-economic status of farmers in the 1920s, and to discuss the Venizelos government's policy for pursuing economic development based on agricultural growth.

Greece before Lausanne

At the time of the Lausanne negotiations, Greece was an underdeveloped country, plagued by ten years of war and internal division. After the disastrous war of 1897 with the Ottoman Empire the Great Powers made Greece subject to the International Financial Commission (IFC). Between 1897 and 1909 the policies of deflation and restricted government expenditure adopted under the supervision of the IFC led to the recovery of public finances and the stabilisation of the economy, so that by 1909 the value of the drachma was at a par with the French franc (Psalidopoulos 1989: 53–58). However, the strict economies adopted during this period also aggravated the long-standing social problems of the country, namely, the 'currant crisis' in the Peloponnese, the land reform question in Thessaly, the deplorable condition of the peasants and the increasing lawlessness throughout the countryside. Indeed, it is estimated that between 1899 and 1911 about 200,000 Greeks, mostly men in the productive age from rural areas, emigrated across the Atlantic (Fairchild 1911; Andreadis 1917; Evelpidis 1950: 1427).

After the considerable economic burdens of the Balkan wars, the country was then split by the 'national schism' (*ethnikos dichasmos*) with Prime Minister Venizelos being forced to resign over his stance that Greece should side in the Great War with the Entente, and not with the Central Powers. Henceforth the country was divided into two antagonistic camps: Venizelist – roughly speaking the republicans – and anti-Venizelist, who were royalists. Venizelos formed a provisional government in Thessaloniki in October 1916, which was eventually recognised by the Entente Powers who in June 1917 forced King Constantine to leave the country.

By 1922, still divided by the national schism and shattered by years of war, Greece was dependent on the outside world not only for capital but also for food supplies despite the fact that it was an agrarian society with almost two-thirds of its population involved in farming. This made Greece's domestic affairs particularly open to foreign-power interference.

Settlement objectives

The League of Nations and the Liberal governments of inter-war Greece had a common desire for peace, stability and security and, linked with that, for predominantly rural- as opposed to urban-based refugee settlement. Venizelos viewed the Asia Minor refugees as a human resource that could be used for the benefit of Greece's security in hellenising Macedonia and Western Thrace, thereby consolidating the northern and north-eastern borders of Greece. This would be achieved through the settlement of refugees in these regions and the concomitant departure of the Muslim and Slav minorities. Stressing the importance of this policy, in October 1922 he remarked:

> ... The very future of Greece is dependent on the success or failure of the solution of the refugee question. A failure would cause many calamities, while a success would allow Greece to recover in a span of a few years from the burdens bequeathed by the Asia Minor Catastrophe. After the collapse of Greater Greece, we can consolidate the borders of Great Greece only when Macedonia and Western Thrace have become not only politically but also ethnically Greek lands.[4]

In order to limit potential radicalism or communism, however, the other great concern was the creation of conditions conducive to the formation of a petty bourgeois class. Predominantly an agricultural economy, this would be pursued through government-backed redistribution of land. Inter-war liberal governments realised that a successful settlement of the refugees on lands allocated to them would give rise to a large class of peasant smallholders, which in turn might obviate peasant radicalism. Since there was no significant industrial working class in Greece, only a common peasant bloc could pose a threat to the democratic order. Consequently, in February 1923 the 'Revolutionary government' of Plastiras removed the constitutional requirement that land owners be compensated in advance for the expropriation of their lands, thus shifting the cost of expropriation from the government to the land owners themselves. In this way, large areas of cultivable land were freed and subsequently handed over to the Refugee Settlement Commission. During the process of settlement and land reform, plots were distributed to refugees and landless native peasants alike.

The Refugee Settlement Commission

The settlement project was carried out by the Refugee Settlement Commission (RSC), an international body established under the auspices of the League of Nations that operated from December 1923 to December 1930. The mandate of the RSC was to establish the refugees in productive work, agricultural or other, by using the land that the Greek government was obliged to transfer to it and the funds placed at its disposal. Charity and temporary relief were explicitly excluded from its functions. The Commission was concerned to ensure that all financial assistance channelled through its agencies to the refugees would be provided in the form of loans, and that the refugees would in due course repay their debt to the RSC. The RSC maintained close relations with the Greek government, and virtually all its staff was Greek.

As regards policy, the RSC also argued in favour of agricultural settlement in the northern regions of Greece. Such a policy would stimulate the production of foodstuffs, which in view of the large influx of people was very important. In addition, the RSC argued that the provision of a farm could provide the means of subsistence for refugee families, that the abandoned estates and houses of the exchanged Muslims, particularly in Macedonia, could accommodate immediately the needs of a considerable number of refugees, and that agriculturalists would be prevented from 'losing their desire for country life and becoming inefficient town dwellers'.[5] In short, this policy would fill the demographic vacuum left by the departure of Muslim cultivators, increase agricultural productivity and contribute to the recovery of the economy.[6] Finally, it was a necessary precondition for the provision of loans. Foreign lenders needed to be assured that they would be repaid, and it was considered easier to collect debts from farmers than from town dwellers.

Consequently, although the RSC recognised that among the refugees the proportion of town dwellers was larger than agriculturalists, its programme deliberately placed emphasis on agricultural settlement and it spent most of its funds on establishing refugee communities in Macedonia and Thrace. The settlement of 46 percent of the refugees in rural areas absorbed 86.35 percent of the total expenditure, whilst only 13.7 percent went to urban refugees, who formed the majority (Eddy 1931: 120). The RSC provided refugees settled in urban areas only with shelter, leaving urban projects and industrial planning and finance to the government.

In rural areas, however, the RSC's wide range of activities was striking. By 1929 the Greek government had assigned to the RSC 5,629,210 stremmata[7] in Macedonia, out of which 3,676,960 were cultivable (Afentakis 1927). Over half a million refugees (along with landless farmers) were settled on these lands in a total of 1,381 settlements, consisting of both new refugee settlements and existing villages, at a total expenditure of £8.75 million, an average of some £61 per family (Pallis 1927). Among its achievements the RSC organised a cadastral survey that extended to more than two million acres, built about 60,000 houses and provided livestock, seed and agricultural machinery and implements. It established model farms, experimental plots and stud farms. An early case of the way in which economic development can be linked to refugee settlement, the RSC constructed local roads, bridges, dispensaries and schools, and dealt with works for water supply, drainage and irrigation. Tractors and steel ploughs were introduced to cultivate the fallow lands of Macedonia and to increase the area of cultivated land. Rotation of crops was applied for the first time, and polyculture replaced monoculture.

These achievements impressed contemporary observers. For example, E. G. Mears remarked: 'The agriculture of Greece has benefited immensely from the influx of the refugees. Waste lands are being reclaimed, new methods and products are being tried out, and agricultural industries which have been in bare existence in Greece for many centuries are being pushed ahead with new vigour' (Mears 1929: 79). Jacques Ancel (1930)[8] also wrote enthusiastically about the progress achieved in rural Macedonia:

> Those miserable Turkish hamlets, nothing but hovels of mud and straw lying in the midst of an uncultivated plain or of unhealthy marshes, are now replaced by large cheerful villages... All around one sees sheaves of maize, fields of tobacco, kitchen-gardens, orchards and vines. What a miracle! (cited in Pentzopoulos 1962: 111).

The effects on farming

After 1922 the impact of land reform and refugee settlement was illustrated in a steady and rapid expansion of the area of land under cultivation, particularly in the regions of Macedonia and Thrace where it almost doubled, and in the increase of the number of people working in agriculture. In Macedonia, cultivated land increased from 275 million stremmata in 1922 to 550 million in 1931, and in Thrace during the same period from 72 million to 148 million stremmata (Mazower 1991: 79f.).

In its reports the Commission stated that the effect of refugee settlement on the agricultural production of the country was remarkable. It pointed to the fact that the total production of cereal crops in 1924 (the year the RSC commenced operations) was 544,729 tonnes. In 1926 it was 850,565 tonnes and in 1927 and 1928 over one million tonnes. The growth in production of wheat between those years was also remarkable: 210,226 tonnes in 1924 to 450,200 tonnes in 1928.[9] As a consequence, the importation of wheat was steadily decreasing: in 1924 wheat imports amounted to 407,161 tonnes, two years later to 313,605 tonnes. 'These figures would indicate,' reported the Commission's Vice-chairman, 'that the agricultural refugees are already producing more than sufficient for the consumption of the whole refugee population.'[10]

The figures for the tobacco industry were also impressive. Tobacco became the major export crop in the 1920s. In 1922 production totalled 25,300 tonnes. In 1927 it increased to 61,700 tonnes, in 1928 to 54,180 tonnes and in 1929 to 85,944 tonnes. Tobacco had long been grown in Macedonia and Thrace but the refugees found that its production brought the maximum value from their tiny plots and so expanded its cultivation. Refugee cultivators produced more than two-thirds of the total tobacco exported between 1924 and 1928, thus bringing foreign exchange to the value of £9 million into the country during those years. Over the same period the Treasury benefited from refugee tobacco cultivation to the value of £1.8 million. The Vice-Chairman of the RSC claimed:

> When the settlement is successfully concluded the League will be able to congratulate itself on one more instance of its beneficent work. And from the point of view of Greece it is already clear that what appeared to be a disaster of the first magnitude has been converted with the League's help into a source of prosperity and of strength for the nation.[11]

However, Greek economists and agriculturalists have contested this view and pointed out the shortcomings in the agrarian sector. During the 1920s, yields failed to reach 1914 levels. This was most striking in the case of cereals, which were grown throughout the country, mainly for subsistence, and which covered almost 75 percent of the total cultivated area (see Table 6.1). The country's need for cereals had in the meantime increased because of the massive influx of refugees. Despite the increase in production of cereals by one-third between 1922 and 1928 Greece still had to import over half of the wheat and flour she consumed and between one-sixth and one-third of other cereals; home production was not keeping up with the needs of the country.

As regards animal husbandry, the effect of settlement policies was without a doubt severely damaging. Two measures were responsible for this: the expropriation of chiftlik[12] properties and their distribution to refugees and landless farmers, and the abolition of the traditional system under which arable lands lying fallow on alternate years were made available to the semi-nomadic shepherds of the region (mainly Sarakatsans and Vlachs). The upshot of these measures during the inter-war period was spiralling pasture rents. In an effort to improve the situation, the government legislated against the eviction of those grazers who in the past had habitually used certain pastures for their flocks and who had paid their fees for grazing rights punctually. Nevertheless, Greece, which had kept livestock sufficient for its needs before

Table 6.1 Greece's Annual Cereal Production 1914–1930 (kg per stremma)

Year	Wheat	Barley	Maize	Oats	Rye
1914	81	98	122	87	185
1915	66	80	102	82	65
1916	61	72	78	68	61
1917	74	80	89	78	78
1918	85	94	97	90	90
1919	62	71	105	65	86
1920	70	86	106	94	89
1921	73	94	101	81	86
1922	57	86	85	98	78
1923	56	80	105	75	70
1924	45	56	78	43	65
1925	66	86	86	78	92
1926	64	81	89	65	86
1927	71	84	66	65	81
1928	66	78	70	68	80
1929	62	72	87	59	66
1930	47	79	78	63	73

Source: Annual Statistics, 1939: 440–41

the war, was obliged in the 1920s to import meat and dairy products from abroad (Kostis 1998: 151).

Land distribution

The activities of the RSC on the land and their impact cannot be viewed in isolation from its policy of distributing land itself, which to a great extent determined the efficacy of all its other initiatives.

The RSC's method of land distribution led to fragmentation of farmland. Allotments of land were based not on a calculation of overall productivity, but rather on current crop values, quality of the soil, and type of crop. The rationale behind this policy derived from a concern that all recipients of farmland should receive equal shares of the best quality land in each district. However, in most districts land of varying quality formed a patchwork pattern over wide areas so that in order to effect a fair division it was necessary to divide the estates into five or six categories before distribution could occur. Consequently, the fertile lands were divided into a complex pattern of small farms, and the plots given to each family were very rarely contiguous. Thus, the fragmented nature of the fields retarded economic development because profits, if any, were too meagre to allow for investment.

In addition, in many large estates on which both refugees and native cultivators were established, the latter often happened to possess small areas of the estate already and had the right to keep them. During distribution, arrangements to reduce fragmentation were hindered because the natives insisted on keeping the particular fields they possessed and tilled. For political reasons and in order to maintain social order there was no desire on the part of the colonisation departments to dispossess them and thereby create disturbances.[13]

This was the case in western Macedonia where most of the plots were made up of mountainous fields, unsuitable for cultivation of cereals and insufficient to provide for the needs of the families settled on them. In the fertile regions of Serres and Kavalla, on the other hand, the plots were very small, and the families settled on them had no other choice than to cultivate high value crops, mainly tobacco. Although the increase in tobacco production in the 1920s was hailed as a great success, it came at a price after the world economic crisis in 1929. Gross income per stremma of cereal crops was much lower than that of tobacco and, owing to the limited size of their holdings, production could not meet the family's needs, in most cases. Thus, in order to enhance their earnings, more and more farmers, particularly refugees, increased the amount of land given over to tobacco cultivation. The shift to cash crops limited the area for cereal cultivation, which not only had a negative effect on the production of cereals, but also had serious repercussions for the livelihood of many refugee families when tobacco prices fell due to the world economic crisis. Consequently, despite expansion in the fertile lands in the north and the vast increase in the number of farmers, harvests of cereals, in particular, were poor in the late 1920s and depressed the economy.

Other problems

Also of critical importance to refugees was *where* they were settled and allocated land. Due to the overall shortage of land some refugees were settled in areas where cultivation was in fact impracticable, such as on mountain slopes. In some areas the soil had to be broken up with dynamite.[14] At the same time many inappropriate allocations were made. For example, town dwellers and peasants from the mountainous Pontic regions were resettled in marshland plains where they made very inefficient agriculturists. With no experience of producing cereals they produced less than they needed for their own sustenance and, being unaccustomed to the climatic conditions, many succumbed to disease.

Productivity was further undermined by the fact that a considerable number of agriculturalist refugees either remained unsettled or lived in wretched conditions. At the same time, many failed to improve their standard of living despite being provided with land, equipment, and technical advice. Others, particularly in border areas, abandoned their settlements altogether and flocked to the cities to seek their fortune as wage-earners or small-traders.

It is noteworthy that in its nineteenth Quarterly Report (on the progress of the settlement project up to 30 June 1928) the Commission classified the agricultural refugees who had been settled in Macedonia into three categories. In the first category, representing one third of the total, were the contented families – those able to pay off their debts to the Commission and to enjoy 'successful village life'. In the second category, representing 40 percent of the settled refugees, were those who 'owing to a lack of a frugal spirit, or to want of agricultural skill' had not achieved the progress anticipated of them and needed further support. In the third class were the refugees, just over a quarter of the total, who had failed to make any progress at all, despite the provision of animals, agricultural implements, and seed. The Commission attributed this failure in part to personal qualities – as few were in fact true agriculturists – and in part to natural calamities. Sir John Hope Simpson remarked: 'Hunger is a frequent visitor to their homes; theirs is a hand-to-mouth existence, made up of loans from the moneylender or casual work with their neighbours, and the cultivation of their own fields is neglected.'[15] At the end of November 1929 the RSC estimated that there were still some 3,000 to 9,000 agriculturist refugee families whom the government was responsible to settle but as yet had failed to do so. In a general appraisal of the refugee problem the Council of the RSC reported to the Financial Committee of the League of Nations that 'the settlement of the agricultural refugees made by the RSC is not entirely complete and even after the expenditure of all the funds now available a good deal will remain to be done before their settlement can be regarded definitely as satisfactory.'[16]

Legal uncertainty

Another factor that adversely affected agricultural productivity was the legal uncertainty surrounding property rights. The cooperatives, which were supported by the National Bank of Greece and after 1929 by the Agricultural Bank, were only too keen to make credit available to cultivators who wanted to invest in equipment. However, most refugees were very reluctant to do so. For them the most discouraging factor against the investment of money and labour was the provisional allocation of plots and the resultant uncertainty over property rights. When settlement agencies began work in northern Greece there was an absence of cadastral surveys outlining the exact boundaries of properties, which made permanent assignment of plots impossible. The refugees received provisional titles, the so-called *parachoritiria*. Obtaining permanent titles was often related to further legal problems, e.g., inheritance rights and debt repayments. Numerous articles in the press, League of Nations reports, and statements of the refugees themselves stressed that the low yields and the resignation of many refugees to their poverty all derived from uncertainty as to their legal rights over plots of land. Considerable documentation exists in various sources on the actual implementation of land distribution. These reveal how technical, administrative and, in particular, ownership problems were encountered and how they impeded the finalisation of land allocations to refugees. In Macedonia, where there was great uncertainty over this issue, many disputed claims were often left unsettled for years with the result that allocations of plots remained temporary throughout the inter-war years.[17] Refugees who were settled in urban centres faced the same problem (Hirschon 1998[1989]: 70–73).

Rationalisation and investment were key to increasing output, but rationalisation threatened jobs – with the attendant fear of political unrest or destabilisation. Increased investment was inhibited by limited funds and, together with the uncertainty as to the precise boundaries of and rights over allotments, many individual farmers felt reluctant to borrow money for further investment in their fields.

The response of the state. Venizelos' government agrarian policy

In 1927, with progress on rationalisation and investment proving slow, the government introduced interventionist policies to support the production of wheat. The Minister of Agriculture in the Zaimis' coalition government, A. Papanastasiou, an important politician on the left of the Venizelist camp who had played a decisive role in the process for the implementation of land reform, introduced tariff protection and domestic price support aimed at equalising the prices of domestic and imported wheat in a bid to protect cereal growers. The following year the Central Committee for the Protection of Domestic Wheat (KEPES) was founded by the Ministry of Agriculture to protect wheat producers from dependence on merchants (Mazower 1991: 89–91).

When Venizelos returned to the political arena in the spring of 1928, he made explicit his preference for economic development based on the improvement of the agrarian sector. The tackling of the problems in agriculture received major priority in view of the balance of trade, demographic pressures, and the social problems that the country faced.

Low yields and tiny plots, insufficient to provide for the needs of an agricultural family, prompted politicians to seek the immediate exploitation of the natural resources of the plains in the North and the wider development of the agrarian sector. In order to finance large scale drainage and reclamation projects, for which plans had been promoted (but not yet realised owing to the lack of sufficient funds) ever since Macedonia and Thrace had been acquired by Greece, the Venizelos government floated large loans in 1928 and 1931. In 1928 he envisaged that the drainage and irrigation project in the the Axios and Strymon plains would be completed by 1932, including stamping out malaria, thereby freeing fertile lands for the settlement of refugee families, and allowing intensive cultivation of rich alluvial land by mechanised methods. However, when only 100,000 out of two million stremmata had been irrigated by 1932, it became apparent that even plans for the modernisation of agriculture in the marshland plains of Macedonia would have to be postponed (Pepelassi-Minoglou 1988: 160 n. 43).

In 1930 the Ministry of Agriculture, together with other measures introduced to improve cultivation techniques and increase wheat yields in order to make the country self-sufficient in cereals, made an effort for land consolidation in the northern provinces. The Director of Applied Agricultural Practice at the Ministry of Agriculture, E. Kypriades, attempted to have the principles that had previously governed distribution revised. He reasoned that it was necessary to consolidate the fragmented holdings in order to facilitate the use of modern machinery. Proposals were made to the RSC that the distribution policy should be based on the principle that shares had to be equal in value but not necessarily in acreage. However, these proposals were met with great reservation both by the RSC and by the Association of Greek Agriculturalists of Macedonia and Thrace. They argued that technical, economic and socio-political considerations lay behind the RSC's distribution policy. Firstly, it was pointed out that the existing policy was the only policy acceptable to the refugees and the native farmers themselves, who could not understand that it was fair for one family to receive sixty stremmata (even of inferior quality land) while another was limited to a holding of twenty stremmata. Sir John Hope Simpson, RSC Vice-Chairman, stated:

> It may be accepted as an axiom that no distribution is possible except with the consent of those among whom the land is to be distributed. The Survey Department has a wide experience of this question, and it is by force of circumstances that it has arrived at its present method of distribution, which is the only method acceptable to the refugees who get the land.[18]

The second argument put forward in favour of the existing policy was that it protected farmers against unfavourable topographical and weather conditions.

I. Karamanos, Director General of Agriculture at the time, pointed out that: 'Were plots to be distributed contiguously, the first adverse weather would destroy all farmers with holdings in that particular area, would create a social issue within the village and would give rise to civil strife which would be fanned by demagogues whilst the distribution system collapses like a house of cards'.[19]

Apart from the economic and socio-political objections put forward by the RSC, a more rational programme of land consolidation was further impeded because the government was bound to legalise all previous distribution made in the RSC's cadastral survey by the Convention on the Liquidation of the RSC (24 January 1930).[20] Furthermore, the Convention effectively prevented the government from applying a different policy in the areas still left to be distributed, for that would have been contrary to the Convention's spirit that all refugees must receive equal treatment. The legal framework devised under the supervision of the League of Nations aimed at protecting the interests of the refugees when the final distribution of plots would be effected. There was also still the fear that any change in policy would be strongly opposed by the refugees themselves. Thus, no government attempts to limit fragmentation were even put to the test, instead being deferred to the post-war era.[21]

Calls for further government action in order to restore economic vitality and keep the farmers in the country were put forward both by the Ministry of Agriculture and KEPES and also by the League of Nations.[22] The Venizelos government continued with intervention, most notably with its establishment of the Agricultural Bank (1929) with the RSC's urging, which provided necessary funds to farmers at reduced rates of interest, and with its further support of cereal farmers, its suspension of agricultural debts owed to private individuals for five years (1930). Combined with improved strains of wheat after 1930, the introduction of new systems of crop rotation and the expansion of cultivation in the irrigated lands of the north, wheat yields recovered as early as 1933. After the crisis of 1932, however, Greek technocrats, high level bankers, and supporters of the liberal neoclassical economic philosophy came increasingly to view state involvement in the economy as a practical solution to the socio-economic problems (Psalidopoulos 1989: 403–411). The Populists continued the strategy of intervention and allowed Venizelist institutions to expand their operations. By 1939 wheat production was three times that of 1925, which in turn had a positive impact on domestic manufacturing.[23] Economic recovery, particularly in the agrarian sector, came early in Greece compared with other European countries, as a result of continued state protection of cereal growers in the pursuit of the country's economic self-sufficiency.

The national debt

The only way the Greek government could provide sufficient funds for the RSC was to raise two loans on the international money markets. In 1924 the RSC concluded negotiations for a loan of £12.3 million at a real rate of interest of 8.71 percent. When the funds of the first loan proved to be insufficient the Greek government floated a 'stabilisation loan' in 1927 for £7.5 million at a real rate of interest of 7.05 percent; £5 million of this loan was given to the RSC. The high rate of interest on both these loans called into question their so-called humanitarian nature, for they added heavily to the country's already substantial external debt and impeded economic recovery after the world economic crisis in 1929.

Overall, the settlement project imposed a financial burden on Greece that the economy proved unable to sustain. In several of the years between 1922 and 1932 it is estimated that the programme of supporting and settling refugees absorbed more than 40 per cent of the country's ordinary budget and accounted for a similar proportion of external borrowing (Campbell and Sherrard 1968: 141; Pepelassi-Minoglou 1988: 164 n. 3).[24] As A. Papanastasiou remarked in 1932: 'From a financial point of view the refugee settlement has resulted in an excessive indebtedness of the state abroad as well as at home. Naturally, this indebtedness has aggravated the economic crisis in Greece' (cited in Pentzopoulos 1962: 149). Nevertheless, the commonly held view that refugee rehabilitation caused Greece's bankruptcy in 1932 has not been conclusively proved. As K. Kostis (1992: 31–46) argued, 'The data at our disposal are far too limited for any categorical affirmations.' The social and political priorities that determined the fiscal policy of Greece during the years of refugee settlement and the unwillingness of the Liberal governments to impose taxes on the produce of farmers (who still constituted the majority of the population) were equally responsible for the country's chronic budget deficit (ibid.; Dertilis 1993: 40–43). However, the fact that the settlement programme constituted an inordinate burden on Greece's finances cannot be disputed.

Conclusion

The rehabilitation of the refugees from Asia Minor and Thrace has been judged, and indeed in many ways was, a great and successful operation, unparalleled in Greek history, seeing Greece transformed into one of the most homogeneous states in Europe (Clogg 1979: 121). The significance of the refugees' contribution to the development of the economy during the inter-war years cannot be ignored. Greece's industrial sector was revitalised with the influx of cheap and skilled labour, while commerce benefited from a similar influx of entrepreneurs. Those refugees who managed to bring money and were settled in the urban centres established small factories and workshops and some introduced new skills and manufacturing to the country, such as carpet-making and silkworm breeding. The contribution of refugee women was particularly marked: for example, the capacity of the textile industry doubled between 1923 and 1930.[25]

The economic recovery of the depressed northern regions owed a great deal both to the re-population of existing villages and to the establishment of new agricultural communities. The refugees who were settled in the northern provinces outnumbered the Muslims and Slavs who departed. This not only determined the Greek character of the region but also met the need for a labour force.

The birth rate, too, was high in all the regions where the refugees were settled, and in the decade from 1925 to 1935 exceeded the death rate, thus contributing to the increase in Greece's population from 6,204,684 in 1928 to 6,933,000 in 1936 (Valaoras 1942: 24–61). This in turn contributed to the revival of local markets in the towns and commercial centres and helped to alleviate the economic damage resulting from the loss of the wider hinterland after the Balkan Wars.

However, the rehabilitation of refugees was not achieved immediately or without problems. The scarcity of arable land did not permit the allocation of viable plots to all refugees and native farmers, making the situation very complex in certain areas and leading to increased friction between the two groups. The conflicts between locals and refugees over the thorny issue of land distribution fuelled quarrels over disputed land throughout the inter-war period. In many mixed villages serious clashes occurred (Kontogiorgi 1996: 91–161). Uncertainty about their property did not encourage the refugees to exert themselves or to invest money in order to improve their plots. Refugees who settled in urban centres faced similar legal uncertainty.

After the 1930 Ankara Convention between Greece and Turkey, which all but annulled provisions in the Lausanne Convention regarding compensation, each government took on the obligations to its own exchanged people. Subsequently the label refugee served as grounds for compensation against the Greek government, a fact that continued for decades to be a source of friction between itself and the refugee communities.[26] This had the long–term effect of encouraging refugees to preserve a separate refugee identity, a mentality still observable today (Hirschon 1998 [1989]: 245–48; Karakasidou 1997: 159–61).

The predominance of national and political objectives over economic ones, i.e. homogeneity in multiethnic Macedonia and the prevention of civil unrest, partly accounts for the slow progress of development and modernisation, both in agriculture and in industrialisation and capitalist development.[27] Greek agriculture did improve in the 1920s but despite the high performance of tobacco, gross crop output failed to reach 1914 levels. The existing institutional framework left little scope for rational organisation and thoroughgoing modernisation and mechanisation of Greek agriculture. Increasing competition in world markets and the crisis in the international economy after 1929 imposed severe constraints on the expansion of agricultural exports, precipitating the tobacco crisis, and pushing down producers' incomes. This in turn aggravated Greece's balance of payments problem.

Confronted with all these constraints, it became clear that greater state intervention was necessary in order to consolidate and build upon the work of the Commission (League of Nations, 1931: 188f.). Furthermore, there were fears that farmers unable to make a living on their allotted plots would swell the numbers of the casual labourers and unemployed who were most liable to espouse radical and communist ideals.[28] Thus, the Venizelos government pursued an agenda of protecting the inefficient income of the large class of smallholders, of encouraging diversification of cultivation from tobacco to other crops, and of supporting wheat producers. As Mazower puts it, in 1931 the Liberals 'realised that the burden of relieving rural indebtedness would have to be borne by domestic rather than foreign creditors' (Mazower 1991: 133). One year later the state was bankrupt. However, after 1933 agricultural performance was so good, particularly in the northern provinces, that it stimulated short–term industrial growth and led to the economic recovery in Greece by that year, together with the effects of depreciation, and default on the external debt (Mazower 1991: 238–250, 301).

Notes

1. All Greek men between seventeen and fifty years old had been forbidden to leave Turkey, and instead were moved to the interior of Anatolia where many perished in the 'labour battalions'. Those who survived were allowed to depart for Greece only after 1924 (see Ladas 1932: 434ff).
2. From the budgets of 1922–23 state expenditure for the relief and early settlement of refugees amounted to approximately £1.7 million (Ladas 1932: 655).
3. According to Psalidopoulos, the movable property which the refugees brought into Greece amounted to about £25 million (1989: 80), while according to Campbell and Sherrard (1968: 40) it amounted to 56 million gold pounds.
4. *Istoriko Archeio tou Ypourgeiou Eksoterikon [Greek Foreign Ministry Archives]* (hereafter AYE), 1922/A/5(13), No. 3435, E. Venizelos to Greek Ministry for Foreign Affairs, London, 17/10/1922.
5. Archive of the League of Nations (LNA), C 124, 'The Greek Refugee Settlement Commission', J. Hope Simpson (autumn 1928).
6. British Foreign Office papers (hereafter F.O.) 371/9890, No 1281, 'Work on the Greek Refugee Settlement Commission', Extract from minutes of the 30th Session of the Council of the League of Nations, Fifth meeting , Geneva, 13/9/1924.
7. One stremma is equivalent to 0.1 hectare or 0.2471 acre.
8. Jacques Ancel, professor of the Ecole des Hautes Etudes Internationales is the author of the classic study *La Macédoine: Son Evolution Contemporaine,* Paris 1930.
9. League of Nations, *Official Journal,* October 1928: 1691–1692
10. LNA, C 124, 'The Greek Refugee Settlement Commission', by J. Hope Simpson (1928).
11. ibid.
12. Chiftliks were the large freehold estates owned mainly by Muslim landlords and cultivated by twenty to thirty families of tenant farmers. They were a combination of agriculture and pasture. By dividing their land into three sections – one for growing cereals, another for spring crops, and the third lying fallow (rented out to shepherds as pasture land) – the landowners avoided soil exhaustion and at the same time safeguarded their annual income against possible losses owing to bad weather conditions.
13. For such cases see *Genika Archeia tou Kratous* (GAK), *Topographiki Ypirisia tou Ypourgeiou Georgias* (TYYG), F.361
14. League of Nations, *Seventeenth Quarterly Report of the RSC,* C.51.M.25.1928.
15. League of Nations, *Nineteenth Quarterly Report of the RSC,* C.406.M.128.1928.II. 22/8/ 1928, p.4.; LNA, C 124.1, L2 (B), Sir John Hope Simpson to H. C. Finlayson, 6/11/1929.
16. LNA, C 124.1, L2 (B), Sir John Hope Simpson to H. C. Finlayson, 6/11/1929.
17. In the province of Serres, for example, only 46 out of 108 distributions were finalised between 1931 and 1933 for the period 1929–40 (Kavkoula 1999: 283). In the ten year period 1927–1937 a total number of 1,116 allocations had been made to refugees by the TYYG13

and a further 883 remained to be finalised (Kontogiorgi 1996:132–134).

18. LNA, C 124, Sir John Hope Simpson to A.Papadatos, 27 Feb., 1930.
19. Archive of K.D.Karavidas, File no.27: 'Note concerning the distribution of lands', by I.Karamanos, 1930. Karamanos, an agricultural expert educated in Italy, was previously a senior official in the RSC and had supervised the project of rural resettlement in Macedonia.
20. The Convention on the Liquidation of the RSC was signed at Geneva on the 24th January 1930 by A. Papadatos, for the Greek government, and the Chairman of the Commission C.B. Eddy. The text of the Convention on the Liquidation of the RSC was published in the League of Nations' *Official Journal*, March 1931:537–560. See also Eddy (1931:175).
21. Land consolidation measures were initiated after the Second World War but only in the 1960s did land consolidation take place, in selected districts, with the voluntary agreement of the owners of the majority of land (see Thompson 1963).
22. League of Nations, *Twenty Seventh Quarterly Report of the Refugee Settlement Commission*, C.444.M.202.1930, ii, Geneva 25/8/1930, p.18.
23. For a detailed and thoroughgoing analysis of these policies and their political and economic implications see Mazower 1991: 238–70.
24. There are different estimates of the cost of refugee resettlement, however, by the Ministère des affaires etrangères, *La Grèce et la Crise Mondiale*, Athens 1933, Rodocanachis 1934, and Pentzopoulos 1962; cf. Liakos 1993: 33f.
25. Among the most influential accounts of the beneficial effects on the Greek economy following the refugee rehabilitation are Mears 1929; Ancel 1930; Ladas 1932; Aigidis 1934; Lampsidis 1982; *Oikonomikos Tachydromos* [*Economic Journal*] 26 April 1973 (Special Issue 31: Refugees in Greece. Fifty Years' Contribution that Changed the Country). In the absence of sound economic studies evidencing the contrary, Kostis suggests that 'the refugees did not bring about the extraordinary transformations of Greece's economy that public opinion ascribes to them' (1992: 42–43). Instead he highlights other factors, such as changes in the international economy.
26. Cf. Pentzopoulos 1962: 201–5; on urban refugees, Hirschon 1998[1989]: 45–48, 70–73.
27. This policy was supported by the National Bank of Greece, as illustrated in the geographical distribution of its funds: Macedonia benefited more than any other province (see Dritsa 1998: 187).
28. I.Karamanos, a fervent supporter of interventionist governmental measures for protecting the farmers, warned: 'The agricultural workers who go to the towns and cannot find employment in industry would inevitably go to swell the ranks of those who depend for their livelihood on parasitic trades or casual labour. This class is already numerous and its existence precarious, and there is a risk that its members may one day join the extremist elements' (cited in Mazower 1991: 134).

7

Homogenising the Nation, Turkifying the Economy

THE TURKISH EXPERIENCE OF POPULATION EXCHANGE RECONSIDERED

Ayhan Aktar

There is no greater sorrow on earth than the loss of one's native land.
Euripides, 431 B.C.

No serious historian of the nations and nationalism can be a committed political nationalist ... Nationalism requires too much belief in what is patently not so.
Eric Hobsbawm (1990)

Introduction

Commenting in 1922 on the export of nationalism to Greek and Turkish societies, the British historian Arnold Toynbee noted that 'the inoculation of the East with nationalism has from the beginning brought in diminishing returns of happiness and prosperity' (1922: 18). The compulsory exchange of populations between Greece and Turkey demonstrates this point. The forced migration of well over one million Greeks and Turks not only increased chaos and despair among the migrants, but also profoundly changed the social and political texture of both countries. Concentrating mainly on Turkey, I argue that the exchange reduced the possibility of foreign intervention in her domestic affairs by homogenising the population along ethnic and religious lines, which in turn promoted the formation of a nation-state similar to western models. However, the exchange's effect on the economy of the new state was damaging, and necessitated many years of structural modification and readjustment.

A balance sheet: comparative advantages and disadvantages of the exchange of populations

The Ankara Convention of 10 June 1930, signed by Turkey and Greece, provided a solution to the problems still outstanding from the compulsory exchange of populations in 1923. A careful analysis of the U.S. archive documents of the period indicates that American diplomats had perceived the population exchange and its attendant problems as a great obstacle to restoring peace in the Balkans. Following the Ankara Convention, an extensive report on the population exchange prepared by Raymond Hare in October 1930 assessed the economic and political consequences of the exchange: 'By way of making a general summary of the situation, it might be said that Greece has gained economically and lost politically, and that Turkey has gained politically but lost economically (p.132).'[1]

For Greece, the political losses came in the form of outside interference. Between 1922 and 1930, Greece had spent more than £10 million on the settlement of Anatolian refugees. Mostly financed by foreign loans, the cost to Greece of this expenditure was a yearly debt-servicing burden of approxiamtely £2.9 million. Indeed, because of the cost of mobilisation and the Asia Minor adventure, Greece had been in desperate need of foreign assistance from the beginning of the 1920s, as a direct result of which Greek politicians adopted a development strategy whereby in return for financial aid they accepted a certain amount of political interference by outside powers (Petropoulos 1976: 160). Acceptance of foreign intervention thus became a *modus vivendi* for the Greek political establishment.

Conversely, Turkey's major political gain was to rid her domestic affairs of interference from the Great Powers, a problem that had plagued the Ottoman Empire throughout the nineteenth century, for with the emptying of Anatolia of its non-Muslim minorities there was no longer a basis for such interference.[2] In addition, unlike Greece, Turkey did not receive any foreign assistance to facilitate the integration of the Rumelian[3] refugees into the national economy. Although Turkey was economically shattered and the government could not even spend £1 million on settlement and other refugee-related programmes, the advantage for Turkey was that it incurred no financially and politically crippling debts to the Powers. Combined with strong economic protectionism and a clearly asserted neutrality in international relations, the consequent level of non-intervention that the Turkish political elite was able to enjoy is arguably the most important achievement of the Kemalist regime.

Transformation of the social fabric: a search for ethnic homogeneity in both countries

In the post-Lausanne period, Turkey and Greece were preoccupied with building nation-states, the distinctive feature of which was the emphasis on an ethnically homogenous population. In a long speech given to the Greek Parliament on 17 June 1930, Prime Minister Venizelos urged ratification of the Ankara Convention. In so doing, he analysed the dominant political tendencies of both countries as follows:

> Turkey herself – new Turkey – is the greatest enemy of the idea of the Ottoman Empire. New Turkey does not wish to hear anything about an Ottoman Empire. She proceeds with the development of a homogeneous Turkish national state. But we also, since the catastrophe of Asia Minor, and since almost all of our nationals from Turkey have come over to Greek territory, are occupied with a similar task.[4]

The fact that both political leaderships were busy completing 'a similar task' within their respective domains provided the objective basis of rapprochement between the two countries in the 1930s.

However, the process of forming ethnically homogeneous nation-states did not take place all at once, nor was it mainly the result of the compulsory exchange of populations between Greece and Turkey themselves. For Turkey, it was the result of the ten years of war between 1912 and 1922 (the Balkan Wars, the First World War and the War of Independence). The first examples of population exchanges between Turkey, Greece and Bulgaria took place just after the Balkan Wars of 1912/13. Then, during the First World War, the Armenians of Anatolia were forced into migration or worse, massacred.

The Ottoman population census of 1906 indicates that within the borders of present-day Turkey the population at that time was 15 million. However, the first Turkish population census to be conducted under the republican regime, in 1927, indicates that the population of the country had decreased to 13.6 million. McCarthy calculates that nearly 18 percent of the Muslims in Anatolia perished during the ten years of war (1983: 133). Changes in the ethnic and religious composition of the population were also dramatic: Keyder states that before the First World War, 'one out of every five persons [20 %] living in present-day Turkey was non-Muslim, after the war, only one out of forty persons [2.5 %] was non-Muslim' (1987: 79).

This drastic decline in the number of non-Muslims had severe economic consequences for Turkey. Observers of the period have noted the decisive role of Greeks and Armenians not only in petty trade and credit activities, but also in wholesale internal trade, in import and export, and in the overall financial structure of Turkey. As a careful observer of the pre-war period, Sussnitzki presents the fact that: 'The Greeks and Armenians are preponderant almost everywhere. Neither the Arabs and Persians, who are able traders, nor by and large the Jews can compete with them' (1966: 120–21). The departure of the Greeks and Armenians from Turkey meant that the most productive elements of the population, and a good deal of the entrepreneurial know-how, had left the country for good. Thus, when the republic was formed, the bureaucracy found itself largely unchallenged (Keyder 1987: 79), enabling the Kemalists to implement policies of turkification in the early years of the republic without much opposition.

For Greece, however, while the Muslims that left Rumelia were mostly peasants, the incoming Anatolian Greeks were mostly urban artisans or from the
commercial classes. Indeed, the influx of refugees from Turkey had positive
repercussions on the commercial and industrial life of Greece, and was in fact
responsible for a short-term economic boom in the post-Lausanne period. As
Yiannakopoulos clearly argues: 'The urban refugee population was a source of
cheap labour as well as skilled craftsmen. The country was enriched by men of
proven business competence and experience' (1992: 42). According to the survey conducted by the League of Nations in 1926: 'Of the 7,000 merchants and
industrialists enrolled in the Athens Chamber of Commerce, 1,000 were
refugees, while the proportion was even higher in Piraeus. In 1961, 20 percent
of Greek industrialists had been born in Asia Minor and Eastern Thrace' (cited
in Yiannakopoulos 1992: 42). Commenting on the economic prosperity that
Greece experienced in the 1920s, one foreign observer made the following
comparisons: 'Thus, we may expect the Asiatic Greeks to bring to Greece the
same kind of stimulus that England and America received from Huguenots
expelled from France in the seventeenth century, and that Turkey benefited by
when she welcomed the Jews exiled from Spain [in 1492]' (Mears 1929).

The influx of Anatolian Greeks and the departure of Muslim peasants
greatly contributed to the realisation of ethnic homogeneity in Greece. As the
Greek member of the Refugee Settlement Committee, A. A. Pallis, stated in
a report that was summarised in a U.S. diplomatic dispatch, '[Greece] has
been rendered racially more homogenous by the exchange, its minority
population now amounting to only six percent of the total population as compared to 20 percent in 1920' (Hare 1930: 94). This was no doubt a
considerable achievement, and very similar to the Turkish one.

Setting the stage for the final exchange: the Balkan Wars and their aftermath

A full dress-rehearsal of the population exchange of 1923 was staged in 1912
when the Ottoman army was defeated in the first Balkan War, and Turkish
territory overrun by troops from the Balkan states. The first group to suffer
was the Rumelian Muslims living in the war zone. When the advancing Bulgarian army was halted just sixty-five kilometres from Istanbul, nearly
250,000 Muslim refugees who were fleeing ahead of the army spilled into the
imperial capital (Toynbee 1922: 138). In Istanbul, all the mosques, including
the Hagia Sophia, had to be converted into shelters for the homeless refugees.
The tragic consequences of the Balkan Wars on the Rumelian refugees had
important repercussions on the collective consciousness of the Anatolian
Greeks too. As Toynbee rightly observed, 'The arrival of the Rumelian
refugees from the end of 1912 onwards produced an unexampled tension of
feeling in Anatolia and a desire for revenge; and so the Balkan War had two
harvests of victims: first, the Rumeli Turks on the one side, and then the Anatolian Greeks on the other' (1922: 139).

With the tension manifesting itself in hostile mob behaviour and a more nationalistic state bureaucracy, Greeks started to migrate from the western coast of Turkey towards the Aegean islands. At this point, Galip Kemali [Söylemezoğlu], the Turkish Minister in Athens, unofficially proposed 'an exchange of the rural Greek population of the Izmir province for the Muslims in Macedonia' (Söylemezoğlu 1946: 102–32). This proposal was subsequently approved by the Greek administration on the condition that the exchange not be compulsory. In the post-Lausanne period, this decision faced severe criticism. In particular, Prime Minister Venizelos was accused of being the first perpetrator of a population exchange that uprooted hundreds of thousands of Anatolian Greeks. Nearly sixteen years later, in June 1930, Venizelos felt the need to justify his position in his speech to the Greek Parliament:

> Finding myself, after the Balkan Wars, faced by the beginning of the expulsion of the Greek element in Turkey, I sought by every means to evade throwing the country into war. I sought, therefore, to come to an agreement with Turkey upon the following basis: let it recognise the cessation of the islands to Greece and I would agree, that is to say the Hellenic Government would consider itself morally bound, to advise a part of the Greeks in Turkey, whose presence in Turkey was considered as dangerous by the Turkish government, to consent, if possible, to exchange their homes in return for those of Turks in Greece.[5]

Although, due to the outbreak of war in October 1914, the exchange was not officially implemented, approximately 150,000 to 200,000 Greeks living within Ottoman borders had already left their homes and migrated to Greece (Hare 1930: 31).

Unfortunately, there are very few mentions in the memoirs of Turkish statesmen of how the exchange of populations took place during these years. However, Hilmi Uran is an exception. Uran was appointed the local governor of a small town, Çeşme, in May 1914, only a few months before the outbreak of the First World War.

The Greek community of Çeşme had been formed largely by late-eighteenth-century Greek migrants from Chios hoping to take advantage of changing trade patterns and the growing economic importance of Izmir at the expense of Salonica (Augustinos 1992: 92). In the nineteenth century, this community rented strips of land from local Turkish notables, which they then converted into vineyards. Subsequently, vines were supplemented by the production of cash crops, such as tobacco and aniseed. This agricultural commercialisation had generated a level of wealth and living standards that impressed the newly appointed local governor, but upon his arrival in Çeşme, Uran was confronted with innumerable legal disputes between Turkish landlords and Greek tenants (Uran 1959: 67). He goes on to describe how just a few days after his arrival, the Greek community in and around Çeşme started to panic and arranged the means of transport to the nearest island, Chios. Nearly forty thousand Greeks migrated in two weeks (ibid.: 69–71).

Çeşme's Greek community migrated to Chios in such haste that they left their homes and most of their personal belongings intact. One of Uran's most important responsibilities as governor thus became the protection and proper re-distribution of Greek moveable property. Soon, however, all his efforts became futile and the abandoned Greek property was plundered either by the local population or by Rumelian refugees arriving from Salonica.

These refugees were mostly wheat-growing peasants from the highlands of Macedonia. As Uran complained in his memoirs: 'These were people who could not adjust either to Çeşme's climate, or to its agricultural character; as a matter of fact, they did not. For instance, there were among them those who saw aniseed for the first time in their lives and, because of their ignorance, tried to use it as animal feed' (ibid.: 72). Some of the refugees even wore the clothing left by the Greeks. For instance, there is a humorous account in Uran's memoirs of a couple of refugees who, upon being assigned a house originally owned by a Greek priest, proudly took to the streets unwittingly promenading in their newly acquired robes, those of a Greek priest. Uran mentions that these 'men in black' must have created some suspicion among the local officers as to whether Greeks had returned to town. Some other refugees, not accustomed to the warm weather, used the black umbrellas they found to protect themselves from the sun. Uran was also very amused watching the refugees work their land holding fancy lacy umbrellas formerly belonging to urban Greek women (ibid.: 76).

Criticising the incompetence and lack of information in government circles with respect to refugee settlement, Uran also made embittered remarks about the transformation of the city:

> As a matter of fact the majority of the refugees who were sent to a place like Çeşme in that period did not even know the details of wheat production. They were Bosnian peasants who were very poor, very ignorant and quite primitive and did not even speak Turkish ... They were by no means suited to the advanced living standards which they had encountered in Çeşme. Finally, they did their best to reduce Çeşme to their own standards in a very short period of time (ibid.: 75)

This instance of settling Rumelian refugees in Çeşme provides the first example of the human tragedies that were to be experienced in abundance after 1923. Unfortunately, the Lausanne exchange was more complicated and painful due to the severe post-war conditions Turkey faced, making the settlement of refugees even more problematic.

Obstacles to refugee settlement in post-Lausanne Turkey

The prevailing view in most publications on the Lausanne population exchange is that the task of the Turkish Government was far easier than that of the Greek one. For instance, S. P. Ladas argues that the settlement problem in Turkey was easy enough to solve because of the abundance of land in that country (1932: 708). One can conjecture that this dominant theme emerges among Greek scholars working on the topic due to the fact that in the post-1922 period the number of exchanged Anatolian Greeks was substantially more than that of the Rumelian Muslims. However, the housing problem in Turkey was already serious before considering the needs of incoming Rumelian refugees. Since the western part of Turkey had been a theatre of war between 1919 and 1922, and was further ravaged by the retreating Greek army, there were actually thousands of homeless *local* Turks, who were trying to survive in properties that had been burned down during the military operations.

In order to administer the exchange, on 8 November 1923, the Turkish Parliament created the Ministry of Reconstruction, Exchange and Settlement (Arı 1995: 33). During the parliamentary discussions, some deputies proposed that the properties remaining after refugee land distribution should be given to homeless locals (Turkish Parliamentary Minutes 1975, Vol. 3: 303 – hereafter TBMM/ZC 1975).[6] Indeed, four months later, after one deputy's argument on 3 March 1924 that 'the true sons of this country whose homes were destroyed and razed to the ground and who are in real need of housing and shelter should be given homes after the refugees', the proposal was accepted and the law modified on 13 March 1924 (TBMM/ZC 1975, Vol. 7: 414).

The Anatolian Greeks, on the other hand, had started pouring into mainland Greece between the fall of Izmir on 9 September 1922 and the armistice signed in Mudanya on 11 October 1922. Hence, by the opening of the Lausanne peace talks on 1 December 1922, most of the exchangeable Greeks had already left Turkey. Ambassador Morgenthau, who travelled to Greece at that time, commented on the nature of their departure when he wrote, 'Within a few weeks 750,000 people were dumped like cattle at the ports of Salonica and Athens, and upon the larger Greek islands' (Morgenthau 1929: 48). This helps us to understand why the Greek delegation in Lausanne had to argue that the population exchange be compulsory. Only by the compulsory removal of the Muslim minority would their land be freed up for the thousands of Asia Minor refugees, and only by their compulsory removal could Greece itself achieve the level of homogeneity to which it aspired.[7]

The Muslim minority in Greece remained on their land for another year before being deported. However, Anatolian Greeks had already started to be settled in towns and villages throughout Greece with the result that during this transition period they often had to coexist in the same villages as the Rumelian Muslims. It is very significant that there are no records of serious inter-communal strife during this period, even though the Greek state confiscated some of the Rumelian Muslims' property and livestock and distributed it among the newcomers (Yalçın 1998; cf Köker, this volume).

At Lausanne, 1 May 1923 was set as the commencement date of the exchange, but according to the records of the Turkish Red Crescent, which was responsible for the transfer of Rumelian refugees to Turkey, the refugees started to leave Greece much later. The first ship sailed from Salonica to Turkey on 19 December 1923, while the major influx of Rumelian Muslims to Turkey actually took place later, during the first eight months of 1924 (Çanlı 1994). During the same period, the remaining Greeks in central Anatolia were transported to Greece, albeit in considerably lower numbers than the Rumelian Muslims. The official figures of the Mixed Commission for the exchange state that 354,647 Muslims were exchanged for 192,356 Greeks but, as noted, the bulk of Greek refugees (well over one million) had already left Turkey (Hare 1930: 64).

Between September 1922 and the middle of 1924, most of the abandoned property belonging to the Greeks in Turkey was either looted or occupied, or both. The following telegraph of Dr. Bahtiyar, the president of the Association of Settlement and Mutual Assistance in Izmir, was read in Parliament on 26 October 1924:

> In spite of the fact that the settlement regulations of Balkan War refugees were well-defined and obvious enough, some deputies, state officials from various ranks, army officers, local notables and homeless individuals – but not the ones who deserved assistance! – occupied the abandoned properties that originally belonged to the Greeks. Under the guise of being homeless due to fire, the unlawful occupation of abandoned Greek property has increased the feelings of despair and weakness, further exacerbating the disorder among the refugees (TBMM/ZC 1975, Vol. 9: 94).

The discrepancy between the early departure of Anatolian Greeks and the late arrival of Rumelian refugees had made this pillage easy. Building materials extracted from the so-called 'abandoned buildings' such as tiles, iron bars, window frames and doors were either sold on the market or used in the construction and repair of the houses belonging to locals. For instance, Cavit Paşa, in his criticism of government incompetence, mentioned how the plundered tiles were sold in the market-place in Samsun (TBMM/ZC 1975, Vol. 10: 36). As a result, the houses given to most of the arriving refugees had nothing but bare walls.[8]

In a dispatch to the Secretary of State for Foreign Affairs, R. W. Urquhart, the British Consul in Izmir, described how the Turkish Government's decision to pay salaries 'in kind' encouraged the army officers to participate in an unusual form of commercial activity: 'The officers have received during the past ten months a certain small percentage of their pay in cash, but part of it has been paid by drafts on the Commission de Liquidation des Biens abandonnés, which are accepted by that commission in payment of goods in its hands; so they have become dealers in old furniture.'[9]

In October 1924, the deputies from the opposition benches criticised the government's misconduct of the refugee settlement by recounting the stories they had heard or the cases they had observed in their election districts, and demanded a parliamentary investigation of the Ministers of Reconstruction, Exchange and Settlement. A two-week long parliamentary discussion of issues related to the exchange of populations and the settlement of Rumelian refugees in Turkey followed. In these sessions, all three consecutive Ministers of Exchange took the floor and faced fierce criticism.

Turkish parliamentary debates on the population exchange

Turkish parliamentary debates provide an extremely useful source for under-standing the structural limitations that prevented a more successful implementation of refugee settlement in the post-Lausanne period, as well as its immediate political repercussions. For instance, the speech of Hasan [Saka] Bey, one of the representatives in Lausanne, on 1 January 1923, provides a narrative of the population exchange discussions in Lausanne. He stated that the Greek delegation had proposed the exchange of populations and that the Turks willingly accepted it; he also noted that both sides agreed to keep the Greeks of Istanbul excluded from the exchange.[10] Another significant dis-cussion on the population exchange occurred two months later, on 3 March 1923, when Dr. Rıza Nur, the deputy-head of the Turkish delegation in Lau-sanne, specifically narrated the Turkish position on the issue of minorities.[11] During the Lausanne peace talks, Dr. Nur personally led the debates at the sub-committee level where the legal position of the non-Muslim minorities in the newly forming Turkish republic was negotiated. This was a critical issue since the Great Powers often used the position of non-Muslim minorities as a pretext to intervene in the domestic affairs of the Ottoman Empire. Dr. Nur quite bluntly stated that the compulsory exchange of populations had already resolved this question: as there would be no minorities left in Anatolia, there would be no foreign intervention. Furthermore, he argued convincingly that Greeks who had already migrated would never be allowed to return to Anato-lia. Dr. Nur articulated the reasoning behind this position later in his memoirs:

> The most important thing was the liberation of Turkey from the elements which through the centuries had weakened her either by organising rebellions or by being the domestic extensions of foreign states. Hence the making of the coun-try uniformly Turkish ... was a huge and unequalled responsibility. It would have been extremely difficult to make the Greeks agree to this or even to suggest this. Thank God, they were the ones to propose it (Nur 1967, vol. III: 1041).

Dr. Rıza Nur's position on the achievement of ethnic homogeneity in Turkey was endorsed by nearly all of the deputies, who were unanimous in their support of the exchange of minorities. The deputies considered the existence of minorities in Anatolia a potential threat to the national security of the young republic in terms, not only of inter-communal strife, but also in relation to the possibility they presented for foreign intervention. Their minds were influenced by bitter memories of the late nineteenth and early twentieth centuries when consistent and repeated Great Power interference occurred. For instance, Vehbi Bey, the deputy for Karesi, articulated these feelings when he stated on 5 November 1924, 'The arrival of every individual is a [source of] richness for us; and the departure of every individual who leaves is a blessing for us!' (TBMM/ZC 1975, Vol. 10: 25).

The parliamentary debates also illuminate the ideological concerns of the deputies in the execution of the exchange. The neglect of the linguistic criteria in the settlement process was one of the first criticisms the Ministers of Exchange had to face, especially from prominent nationalist deputies who criticised the settlement of the Albanian- or Greek-speaking Muslims on the western coast. For instance, the ardent nationalist Hamdullah Suphi [Tanrıöver] Bey brought the question to the attention of the Parliament in the following statement: 'They settled the Greek-speaking masses right across the sea from the islands. A grave mistake! Soon, when peace truly reigns and relations between the islands and our shores pick up and Greek islanders and the Greek-speaking masses reestablish contact, then it will be impossible ever to eradicate this foreign language' (TBMM/ZC 1975, Vol. 9: 92). Among other deputies who were more critical of the cultural consequences of the settlement, Ali Şuuri Bey, the deputy of Karesi, complained: 'Among the refugees settled on the coast, the dominant dance is the polka instead of our national dance; the dominant musical instruments are the mandolin and the bagpipe instead of our national instruments; the dominant language is Albanian and Bosnian instead of our national language!' (TBMM/ZC 1975, Vol. 10: 28).

The concentration of Greek- or Albanian-speaking refugees in certain regions created further suspicion among the nationalists, who desired complete homogeneity of the population. For them, this was a clash between the 'ideal' and the 'real'. Instead of an imagined community they hoped would be similar to their own, they encountered, in their view, a group of people from a rural background, speaking foreign languages and with very different life styles. Needless to say, the Turkish nationalists were disturbed by the cultural discord created by the influx of refugees. Here the process of turkification worked in the opposite direction: it created distrust and suspicion among the ruling nationalist elite towards the repatriated masses. Bernard Lewis demonstrates the absurdity of the nationalists' expectations on both sides of Aegean as follows: 'A Western observer, accustomed to a different system of social and national classification, might even conclude that this was no repatriation at all, but two deportations into exile – of Christian Turks to Greece, and of Muslim Greeks to Turkey' (1968[1961]: 355). The reactions of the Turkish nationalists were especially significant in that they came to constitute the backbone of the 1930s cultural xenophobia that eroded the cosmopolitanism of the late Ottoman period.

The structural impediments to a better settlement: determining the material basis of chaos and despair

A careful analysis of the scholarly works on the compulsory exchange reveals that there was a substantial amount of ill-considered and inappropriate settlement in both Turkey and Greece. For instance, tobacco producers from both countries were resettled in regions where tobacco production was virtually impossible. Even worse, wheat-producing peasants were forced to settle in regions with olive groves. Unaccustomed to growing olives, the refugees simply cut down the trees and used them as wood for their stoves, planting wheat or barley in their place. These unfortunate events were naturally blamed on the governments.

The answers given by the Ministers of Exchange to the deputies' criticisms in the Turkish Parliament reveal the nature of the social and economic problems the young republic faced in its settlement efforts. The most important problem in the exchange was the contrast between the departing Anatolian Greeks and the incoming Rumelian Muslims. While the Anatolian Greeks were predominantly urban, the Rumelian Muslims were largely rural. Even if the armies had not burned down the villages during the war, even if the homeless locals had not occupied most of the abandoned property, this dissimilarity in populations would have complicated matters in and of itself. The Minister of Exchange, Mahmut Celal [Bayar] Bey therefore had to admit in Parliament that:

> [T]he lifestyles and economic conditions of those arriving are not similar to those of the departing [Greeks]: those departing are mostly tradesmen or merchants. However, those arriving are generally farmers. Gentlemen, the overwhelming majority of those arriving are peasants; the overwhelming majority of those departing are urban dwellers! I leave it to your judgement to decide if it is at all possible to succeed in [the matter of] settlement under such irreconcilable conditions (TBMM/ZC 1975, Vol. 10: 52).

The second structural limitation preventing a successful settlement of refugees was the lack of information. In the immediate post-Lausanne period, the government in Ankara lacked even the most basic information about the society it was trying to rule. Social statistics about the various forms of livelihood within the Turkish population were either non-existent or had become obsolete. Furthermore, the republican elite proved inefficient in gathering information about the country and developing a sense of control over its economic and social issues. Under these conditions, the settlement of refugees was conducted at best in an ad hoc manner. When the Ministers of Exchange were accused in Parliament of forcing people from plains to settle in valleys and vice versa, one minister, Refet [Canıtez] Bey, had to acknowledge the following:

> Gentlemen, how much of the land in the villages is in the plains and how much of it is in the highlands? What is the sum of arable land in the villages? How many persons could be engaged in cultivation? What is the actual level of agriculture? It is necessary to conduct extensive research on these issues. Yet it is impossible to obtain this information now. Since this type of information does not exist, it is necessary to progress in general terms and that is what we are undertaking now! (TBMM/ZC 1975, Vol. 10: 43).

Lacking any kind of scientific information like a population census, industrial and agricultural surveys or cadastral maps of Turkey, the government relied on the information gathered informally at ports during the arrival of the refugees. Their final destinations were decided on this scant information.

The third structural problem arose from the poor quality of the staff employed. Immediately after the formation of the Ministry of Reconstruction, Exchange and Settlement on 8 November 1923, many of its positions were filled by retired army officers, and then by bureaucrats dismissed from their posts in other ministries. Indeed, references are frequently made in the parliamentary debates to the harsh, inflexible and irresponsible attitude of these state officials towards the refugees.

Collapsing system of communications: government support for the turkification of Anatolia

After the ten years of war between 1912 and 1922, not only was much of Turkey's agricultural land in a state of ruin, but homes and cities had been torched, leaving many people destitute. Moreover, at a time of such need, the country's reserves of entrepreneurial know-how and artisanry had been almost totally drained with the departure of Anatolia's minorities. The non-Muslim commercial bourgeoisie of relatively developed Anatolian cities such as Samsun, Trabzon, Erzurum, Adana and Gaziantep had been subjected either to forced migration and massacre – as in the case of the Armenians – or to exchange – as in the case of the Greeks – while artisans and craftsmen had found their way either to Europe or to neighbouring countries. The newly emerging Turkish bourgeoisie and urban artisans could not replace the minorities in all sectors of economic and social life.

The loss of entrepreneurial know-how was critical in trade, especially in western Anatolia. Traditionally, Izmir had been an important centre for the export of Turkish agricultural products. Basic agricultural goods exported from Izmir such as tobacco, sultanas, cotton, dried figs and hazelnuts had constituted nearly 60 percent of Turkish export revenues (Keyder 1982: 109). However, when the Greek, Armenian and Levantine merchants who had been acting as intermediaries between local producers and foreign buyers were removed, trade proved difficult. This is evidenced by the following correspondence received by the British Chamber of Commerce of Turkey from a dried-fruit importer in Bristol in October 1923:

> Owing to the recent troubles in Smyrna we have lost several of our old connections and shippers of sultanas, and this season and the last we have not been in a position to import, or to offer, on account of being unable to obtain offers of Smyrna fruits.
>
> We shall be very pleased if you will put [us] in touch with reputable houses and shippers, who will immediately forward us type samples ... We are [also] interested in dried plums and prunes, and [if] it is possible you may be able to put us in touch with a shipper.[12]

Soon the Turkish Government attempted to fill the vacuum with local Turkish merchants. Already, some local notables with good contacts in Ankara had profited from the distribution of abandoned Greek property, not only by occupying the most fertile agricultural holdings, but also by claiming the abandoned industrial establishments and workshops. Parliamentary debates reveal, for instance, that a deputy from Balıkesir had acquired for himself a house in the town centre, a summer residence, thousands of olive trees and a soap factory around Ayvalık (TBMM/ZC 1975, Vol. 10: 36). Even though this emerging group of Turkish businessmen had very limited experience in international trade and business transactions, they volunteered to replace the non-Muslim entrepreneurs. Although they lacked commercial expertise, they nevertheless had the advantage of government support from Ankara.This dependency on the state, however, ultimately limited their development as an independent bourgeoisie.

By the mid-1920s, the native commercial class was gradually beginning to fill the vacuum left by the departing minorities. For instance, in May 1925, a report written by Alaiyelizade Mahmut Bey, the president of the Izmir Chamber of Commerce, stated that many Turkish businessmen had settled in Izmir after the liberation, opening about fifty-four stores and selling mostly imported European textile products. Many companies specialising in the export of agricultural products were also formed in Izmir. Indeed, Mahmut Bey provided a detailed account of the levels of production reached for certain agricultural products such as sultanas, dried figs, tobacco, olive oil, cotton, and convincingly argued that thanks to the continuous support of the government in Ankara, pre-war production levels had already been reached (Koraltürk 1996–97: 197).

In contrast to these positive accounts of Mahmut Bey, however, the foreign diplomats stationed in Turkey presented an altogether different and dire picture of Turkish economic performance in their dispatches: all were highly critical of the turkification policies being implemented in the early years of the republic. For instance, in November 1929, British Ambassador Sir George Clerk evaluated the performance of the newly formed Turkish firms as 'incompetent', and continued with the following scathing assessment:

> This incompetence is repeated in the numerous Turkish firms of smaller import-
> ance which have endeavored to replace the Greek and Armenian middlemen
> who were always the backbone of Turkish commerce. Almost invariably these
> new Turkish firms start business as commission agents, but they have neither
> the patience, the experience nor the temperament to build up their fortunes
> slowly in the same way as their Christian predecessors. In most cases they drift
> to Ankara, to the neglect of their agency commitments, and endeavor to get
> rich quickly by dabbling into large contracts. Further, commercial morality
> here has declined of late years.[13]

Ambassador Clerk's remarks reveal that at least in some cases continuing support from government circles had not been sufficient to create the desired outcome. Perhaps if the group replacing the minorities had received less protection and tutelage from Ankara, it might have been forced to develop its entrepreneurial capacities much more effectively and successfully. Mostly due to the lack of business skills of this emerging bourgeoisie, as well as the destructive effects of the Great Depression in 1929, the founders of the new Turkish state were forced in the 1930s to move towards a more protected and autarchic model of economic development. Subsequent growth in the size of the public sector and the newly formed state economic enterprises to compensate and eventually replace private initiative not only dwarfed the Turkish business elite in size, but also consolidated their immaturity. I personally view this as the most significant and negative outcome of the population exchange in Turkey.

The turkification policies implemented in Istanbul

By mutual agreement at Lausanne, the Greek community of Istanbul was excluded from the compulsory exchange. Nevertheless, especially in the second half of the 1920s, the remaining minority merchants and foreign companies were forced to suffer continuous pressures, the most significant of which came as a result of the emerging trend of nationalist economics. Under the dominant slogan of the period 'Turkey for the Turks', Muslim Turkish merchants organised themselves in the Chambers of Commerce that had previously been dominated by non-Muslims. With government support, they then identified themselves as 'national merchants' (*milli tüccar*) thereby implying that the minority businessmen who remained in Istanbul were not national, and therefore of suspect loyalty to the regime. In other words, the aim of the turkification schemes was not merely to create a nationalist bourgeoisie, but to do so at the expense of existing minorities and foreign-owned companies. The turkification programme can thus be defined in practice as a set of policies aimed at establishing the unconditional supremacy of Turkish ethnic identity in nearly all aspects of social and economic life.

The policies implemented in the 1920s consisted of measures such as mandating that foreign companies must keep their books in Turkish, allocating certain professions and state employment exclusively to Muslim Turks, and ruling that foreign-owned companies should have Muslim Turks comprise at least three-quarters of their employees. In one dispatch to London, British Ambassador Sir R. Lindsay grumbled about the news that 'in the future only Turks would be allowed to act as chauffeurs'.[14] Similar pressures were also exerted on foreign concessionaire companies like the Izmir–Aydın railway company (The Ottoman Railway from Smyrna to Aidin). A representative of the company paid a visit to the British Ambassador on 18 March 1926 and mentioned that the Turks were demanding that the personnel of the railway should be entirely Turkish. The railway company was willing to employ Turks as far as possible, but could not find any suitable.[15] In this period firms, shopkeepers, companies and sometimes even professionals such as doctors and lawyers were told to dismiss their non-Muslim employees and hire Muslim Turks instead. Perfect examples of the discrimination against non-Muslim minorities, most of these demands had neither a legal basis nor any constitutional justification; they were simply de facto pressures exerted by the Turkish bureaucracy.

In another of his dispatches, also in 1926, the British Ambassador Sir R. Lindsay examined the psychological factors behind the turkification programmes:

Imbued with a profound distrust of all non-Turkish elements, a distrust due to the policy of the Powers towards Turkey for more than a hundred years, the republic is resolved to surround itself with a Chinese wall of exclusiveness and reconstruct a State in which there shall be no room for the exercise of foreign influence even by individuals and traders. This policy is being pursued with remorseless pertinacity ... and it receives the cordial support of the whole population.[16]

The construction of the 'Chinese wall' would be completed in the next decade, with *étatist* development models and autarchic trade regimes forming its cornerstone. Moreover, while the turkification policies implemented in the 1920s had been de facto administrative policies, later policies eventually acquired legal force so that the discriminatory practices against the non-Muslim minorities became *de jure* expressions of nationalist ideology. The notorious law (number 2007) passed in 1932 'Restricting certain Professions and Trades to Turkish Citizens only'[17] is an example of this transformation. As a result of its implementation, nearly nine thousand non-exchanged *établis* Greeks lost their jobs, and soon after migrated to Greece for good (Aktar 1996a). Indeed, there is no doubt that the policies of turkification were responsible for the haemorrhaging of non-Muslim communities from Istanbul during the early years of the republic, despite the clauses specifying minority rights in the Treaty of Lausanne.

A final note: the transformation of Turkish nationalism

It is widely accepted that Turkish nationalism was first formulated and codified by Ziya Gökalp (1876–1924) during the Balkan Wars. Unlike most formulations for national identity, which emphasise race and ethnicity, Gökalp's criteria for membership of the 'national community' were cultural and linguistic. Gökalp defined the nation as follows:

> ... [The] nation is not a racial, ethnic, geographical, political, or voluntary group or association. [The] nation is a group composed of men and women who have gone through the same education, who have received the same acquisitions in language, religion, morality and aesthetics ... Men want to live together, not with those who carry the same blood in their veins, but with those who share the same language and the same faith. (1959: 137)

It was the multiethnic and multi-religious nature of the Ottoman Empire that necessitated such criteria, an empire in which it was practically impossible to preach particularistic nationalism even during the Balkan Wars. In formulating the principles of Turkish nationalism, Gökalp inevitably had to recognise the significance of the *millet* system even if it had already disintegrated. Furthermore, for Gökalp, religion was significant only insofar as it was a factor of shared culture; he emphasised Islam only as a moral force that would help bring about social solidarity, and not as a necessary condition for being a Turkish nationalist. Gökalp's place for Islam might also help explain why Jewish intellectuals like Moise Cohen Tekinalp (1883–1961) and Abraham Galante (1873–1961) played an active part in the ideological kitchen of Turkish nationalism (Aktar 1996b: 272).

Gökalp's conceptions of nation and nationalism were accepted until the second half of the 1920s, at which point an ideological break set in and the model underwent a radical reconstruction. Gökalp's idea of an individual's ties to the national community being along cultural and therefore civic lines was superseded by an ethnic definition tailored by the republican elite. The formation of the rhetoric on nationalism can be traced through the Turkish parliamentary debates on the exchange and settlement. Earlier in this article, I noted that the Ministers of Exchange and Settlement were criticised because of their neglect of linguistic criteria. When Dr. Rıza Nur was especially harsh in criticising the settlement of Albanians in and around Izmir, some deputies pointed out that he had been politically very accommodating to the Albanian deputies when he served in the Ottoman Parliament. His reaction was quite revealing:

> At that time the Albanians were part of the ingredients of this land. From Basra all the way to Iskodra [in Albania] there were fifteen to twenty national groups; under such conditions I could not possibly pursue the line of argument of Turkism. You know as well as I do that the 'Union of all Ottomans' was in fashion then. It was truly impossible to pursue any other policy. Later, I began on the path of Turkism [when it became politically viable](TBMM/ZC 1975, Vol. 10: 152).

The majority of the republican political elite soon followed Dr. Nur in accepting this new understanding of nationalism, so much so that the republican version of ethnic nationalism soon became the mainstay of official Turkish ideology. In this context, the non-Muslim minorities – even though they were Turkish citizens – were clearly left out of the national community, and became technically impossible to incorporate. As a consequence, they started to be discriminated against and treated as outsiders in their own lands: ethnic nationalism thus became the archenemy of cosmopolitanism.

However, one has to concede that the new regime in Ankara, stripped of its imperial traditions and confined in its sovereignty to Anatolia alone, could not have responded otherwise. The already-turkified human geography of Anatolia made it impossible for the republican elite to provide an umbrella sheltering Greek tinker, Armenian tailor and Turkish soldier all at once (Aktar 1996b: 287). The sociologically defined Gökalpian culture that functioned as a collective conscience to homogenise peoples of varying status, class, religion, sect and in some cases ethnicity was no longer meaningful. Gökalpian cultural unity was designed to mould a conglomerate of ethnically diverse individuals into one nation, but it became outdated. The political formulations of an ethnically and religiously heterogeneous empire had become antiquated in a mere ten years.

Notes

1. Special report prepared by Raymond Hare on 'The Origin and Development of the Greco-Turkish Exchange of Populations Question' dated 15 October 1930. Document no.

767.68115/143 in *Records of the Department of State Relating to the Political Relations of Turkey, Greece and the Balkan States, 1930–1939.* Raymond Hare later served as the U.S. Ambassador in Ankara between 1961 and 1964.

2. However, issues surrounding the Greek minorities in Istanbul and the Aegean islands continued to pose problems for decades (see Oran and Alexandris, this volume).

3. 'Rumelia' denotes Ottoman or former Ottoman domains west of the Straits, including Aegean possessions.

4. Official translation of Venizelos's speech is attached to Robert Skinner's dispatch sent from Athens to the U.S. Secretary of State, Washington, dated 20 June 1930. Document no. 767.68115/136. *Records of the Department of State Relating to the Political Relations of Turkey, Greece and the Balkan States, 1930–1939.*

5. See Skinner's dispatch sent from Athens to the U.S. Secretary of State, Washington, dated 20 June 1930, 767/68115/136. *Records of the Department of State Relating to the Political Relations of Turkey, Greece and the Balkan States, 1930–1939.*

6. *Türkiye Büyük Millet Meclisi – Zabıt Ceridesi (1975) Devre 2,* Ankara, TBMM Matbaası. [Turkish Grand National Assembly – Record of Minutes (1975) 2nd Election Period, Ankara, TBMM Press.]

7. As Pentzopoulos rightly argues, the agreement reached in Lausanne indeed alleviated some of the problems of refugee settlement in Greece. As the Greek government had already confiscated and distributed the lands that formerly belonged to Rumelian Turks, Pentzopoulos suggests that: 'The remaining 350,000 hectares were to be land [sic] left behind by the exchanged Turks and Bulgarians. This figure shows the tremendous importance of the transfer of populations in the settlement of the Greek refugees. It is obvious that without the vacated Moslem properties the solution of the refugee program through an agricultural settlement would have been very difficult indeed' (1962: 104).

8. A recent Turkish book contains valuable interviews conducted with ageing Greek and Turkish refugees on both sides of the Aegean. They both tell of their frustrations during the population exchange and most still complain about the miserable condition of the property assigned to them (Yalçın 1962).

9. Dispatch sent from Acting Consul-General in Izmir to the Marquess Curzon in London: *FO 424: British Confidential Reports* / Document dated 21 July 1923 / E 8317/199/44.

10. *Türkiye Büyük Millet Meclisi – Gizli Celse Zabıtları (1985) Ankara, Türkiye İş Bankası Kültür Yayınları.* [Turkish Grand National Assembly – Closed Session Minutes (1985), Vol. 3: 1173, Ankara, *Türkiye İş Bankası Kültür* Publications.]

11. A detailed account of the Lausanne peace talks and the formation of different national narratives in relation to Lausanne can be found in Fatma Müge Göçek's recent study (2002).

12. Journal of the British Chamber of Commerce of Turkey, Vol. 11, No. 73, October 1923: p. 541.

13. Dispatch sent from Sir George Clerk in Istanbul to Mr. A. Henderson in London: FO 371: Foreign Office Correspondence / Document dated 13 November 1929 / E 5984/89/44.

14. Dispatch sent from Sir R. Lindsay in Istanbul to Sir Austin Chamberlain in London: FO 371: Foreign Office Correspondence / Document dated 3 March 1926 / E 1571/373/44.

15. Resume of the conversation between Sir R. Lindsay and Lord Howard of Glossop. FO 371: Foreign Office Correspondence / Document dated 18 March 1926 / E 1874/373/44.

16. Dispatch sent from Sir R. Lindsay in Istanbul to Sir Austin Chamberlain in London: FO 371: Foreign Office Correspondence / Document dated 15 February 1926 / E 1072/373/44.

17. Düstur, Üçünü Tertip, Vol. 13: 519.

8

The Story of Those Who Stayed

LESSONS FROM ARTICLES 1 AND 2 OF THE 1923 CONVENTION

Baskin Oran

Introduction

Historical context of the 1923 exchange of populations

The compulsory exchange of populations of 1923 between Greece and Turkey is a component part of the Lausanne Peace Conference, which took place at the end of the Turkish War of Independence (1919–22). That war concluded when the armies of the Greek occupation of Anatolia supported by the Allies at the end of the First World War were defeated in August 1922 by the Turks. The Convention and Protocol on the Exchange of Greek and Turkish Populations (hereinafter 'the Convention') is one of eighteen instruments created at the Lausanne Conference on Near Eastern Questions, 1922–23. Sixteen of these instruments, including the Lausanne Peace Treaty itself, were signed at the end of the Conference on 24 July 1923. The remaining two, the Convention and the Turkish–Greek Agreement on the Extradition of Civil Hostages and on the Exchange of War Prisoners, were signed on 30 January 1923, about two and a half months after the start of the Conference and about six months earlier than the other sixteen. The subject matter of these two instruments 'had nothing to do with the Peace Treaty' but had to be 'dealt with at the earliest possible time'.[1] The Convention was thus a prerequisite for the Peace Treaty, as shown by its early signature.

From the outset, I would like to make a note on the terminology I use for the respective minorities exempted from the exchange by Article 2 of the Convention. For those exempted in Istanbul, Article 2a used the term 'Greeks' (see Alexandris, this volume). Later, the inhabitants of the islands Gökçeada and Bozcaada were also included. In its place, I prefer to use the term *Rums*, which denotes the almost-exclusively Orthodox population of Byzantine descent of the Ottoman Empire and Turkey. The Rums were usually bilingual, but their mother tongue was Greek. Since the 1820s, 'Rum' has been used in Turkish for any Hellene living outside Greece and who is not a citizen of that country. Not only is this term more accurate, but, coming from *Romios* (pl. *Romioi*), meaning 'from [eastern] Rome', it also reflects the Rums' own view of themselves. Although the Rums see Greece as their kin-state, they believe that they can trace their lineage directly back to Romano-Byzantine Constantinople (Alexandris 1983: 17). Preference for Rum instead of Rum Orthodox is because, notwithstanding the small number of Catholic and Protestant Rums, Rum has always been synonymous with Rum Orthodox.

Article 2b of the Convention used the term 'Moslems', not 'Turks', for the minority in Western Thrace, probably for the following two reasons. Firstly, at the time of the exchange, religion and confession counted far more than ethnicity; and secondly, just as Turkey wanted all the Muslims of Western Thrace to remain – not just those of Turkish ethnicity – it is probable that the Allies and Greece wanted all the Muslims to be subject to the exchange (hence this expression in Article 1). However, I prefer to use the term 'Muslim-Turks'. Firstly, in the Balkans especially, Turk and Turkish have always been, and to a large extent still are, synonymous with Muslim, probably because Turks were the founders and the main element of the Ottoman Empire and *a fortiori* of its *millet* system, which considered all Muslims as one single community.[2] Secondly, and more importantly, this preference is made because this profoundly religious minority of 110,000 – composed of approximately 70,000 Muslims of Turkish ethnic origin, 35,000 Pomaks (slavophone Muslims) and 5,000 Muslims of Romany ethnic origin – now feels very strongly about denoting itself as Turkish and fully considers Turkey its kin-state (cf. note 24).

The exchange, and especially its compulsory nature, is of particular importance in the 1990s. However, in order to learn anything from this experience that might contribute to today's minority, exchange and refugees debates, the following question must first be resolved: who wanted the exchange, who wanted it to be compulsory, and why?

The exchange and its compulsory nature were proposed by the Allies, in particular Great Britain.[3] Lord Curzon thought the exchange should be compulsory for the following reasons: that it would otherwise take months to implement the Convention; that the exchanged Turks should be able to start tilling Thrace as soon as possible; that it would help Greece to make place for the influx of refugees; and that it would also make it easier to compensate the exchanged people for the property they would be leaving behind (1 December 1922, Meray, Lausanne: 123). His real reason, however, was that the Allies thought a radical solution to the question of minorities would ease their task of guaranteeing the stability of the new international order, for the very fact that the issue of minorities in Europe, as explained also by de Azcarate, was one of the two main causes of the First World War (1969: 9).

The second party that desired the exchange was Greece, above all because of the pressing need for space to settle the large number of Asia Minor refugees who fled Turkey along with the withdrawing Greek armies – approximately one million people, or a quarter of Greece's population at the time. As for the compulsory nature of the exchange, the Greek Prime Minister, Eleftherios Venizelos, declared that it should be voluntary, but added that he was prepared to discuss the issue. Of much greater importance to Venizelos, though, was the exclusion from the compulsory exchange of the Rum population of Istanbul (about 110,000 Rums in Istanbul were finally designated as non-exchangeable). The reason he gave was that the Rum population of Istanbul would so greatly augment the number of refugees coming to Greece that Greece would feel obliged to ask the U.S.A. to increase her emigration quota. Of course, Venizelos had another, probably more important, reason for this. He was the champion of Greek irredentism, known as the *Megali Idea,* 'the Great Idea', and had long been fuelling Greek public opinion with the idea that 'Ionia' (western Turkey) would become part of Greece. Thus it would be very difficult to have the public accept the exchange of Istanbul Rums because, Istanbul being 'the Second Rome' and the seat of the Holy Phanar Rum Orthodox Patriarchate, this would unequivocally mean the end of the Megali Idea.[4] In addition, the Patriarchate would most probably have had to move to Mount Athos in Greece, and this would inevitably have caused great friction between it and its rival institution, the autocephalous Church of Greece. The exclusion from the exchange of a substantial number of Muslim-Turks just within the Greek border was a price Venizelos had to pay to ensure that the Istanbul Rums and the Patriarchate crucially stayed where they were in Istanbul.

The third party that desired – and very much so – a compulsory exchange was Turkey.[5] Ismet Pasha, head of the Turkish delegation at Lausanne, said that in the event of such an exchange, all the Rums of Turkey should be included (1 December 1922, Meray, Lausanne: 121) even though he thought the Muslim-Turks of Western Thrace should be excluded. Ismet Pasha wanted all the Rums expelled from Turkey for numerous reasons. Firstly, Christian minorities had always been the main pretext on which the Great Powers interfered in the domestic affairs of the Ottoman Empire. Secondly, the Peace Treaty towards which the parties were working was to include a section titled Protection of Minorities. Ridding Turkey of as many Rums as possible (the most significant non-Muslim minority) would minimise the potential for recourse being sought to these rights. Thirdly, the way the Rum minority and the Patriarchate had collaborated with the occupying Greek armies was still in the forefront of the Kemalists' minds: they were eager to destroy Greek irredentism once and for all while they had the opportunity. Furthermore, there was also an unarticulated agenda behind the Turkish desire for a complete and compulsory exchange. Like many of the states of eastern Europe and the Balkans at the time, Turkey too was ready to embark on a full-scale nation-building process, and her non-Muslim minorities were considered a real stumbling block to this endeavour. The reason Ismet Pasha wanted Western Thrace to be excluded from the exchange was probably twofold. On the one hand, the Turkish delegation drew attention to the country's National Pact,[6] stressing that the pact's third point asked for a plebiscite in this region where the Turks were in a majority. On the other hand, with the exclusion of the Istanbul Rums from the exchange now inevitable, it seemed that Turkey, which deplored the idea of having to keep them, was seeking to create a symmetry in the region by counter-balancing them with the Muslim-Turks of Western Thrace.[7] This symmetry was to find its expression in the second article of the Exchange Convention in which provision was made for the two minorities to be excluded from the compulsory exchange.

Legal and socio-political aspects and consequences of the exchange

Article 1 of the Convention specified a compulsory exchange. It defined those who must leave: from Turkey, Turkish nationals of Greek Orthodox religion;[8] and from Greece, Greek nationals of Muslim religion. As a consequence, 355,635 Muslim-Turks were expelled from Greece for Turkey, and 189,916 Rum Orthodox were expelled from Turkey for Greece (Macartney 1934: 446). However, as mentioned above, Greece actually had to receive a total of 1.2 million expellees because she had already received some one million refugees who had fled Turkey on the defeat of the Greek armies in August 1922, what the Greeks refer to as the *Mikrasiatiki Katastrophi*, the 'Asia Minor Catastrophe'.[9]

Article 2 of the Convention set the exception. It defined those who would be excluded from the exchange, the so-called é*tablis.* These were, in Turkey, Rums (in the Convention 'Greeks') settled in the Istanbul[10] prefecture prior to 30 October 1918, and in Greece, the Muslim-Turkish (in the Convention 'Moslem') inhabitants of Western Thrace. As a consequence of Article 2, around 130,000 Muslim-Turks stayed in Western Thrace, and about the same number of Rums in Istanbul.

Under the terms of the Lausanne Peace Treaty (concluded six months later in July 1923) two islands at the mouth of the Dardanelles – Gökçeada (Imbros) and Bozcaada (Tenedos) – were ceded to Turkey for security reasons. Article 14, paragraph 2 of the Peace Treaty excluded from the exchange the populations of these two islands (substantially composed of Rums). In 1920, about nine thousand Rums were living on Gökçeada and Bozcaada (Alexandris 1980: 27).

Article 1 created emigrants. These people had to leave practically with what they could carry. In their respective kin-states they were to receive property equivalent to what they had left behind. These emigrants suffered greatly for a number of reasons. Firstly, during the implementation of the Convention, a large number of unforeseen problems emerged that were not solved until almost eight years later. At the root of most of these was the disagreement between Greece and Turkey regarding the immovable property left behind by expellees. These people had to leave everything behind – their homeland, their neighbours and, indeed, their way of life. Some of them did not even understand the language of their new country,[11] while for a considerable length of time both groups were considered strangers by their new compatriots.[12] The numerous problems inevitably raised by such a radical exchange (see below) continued to poison Turco-Greek relations right up until 1930. In that year the Ankara Convention conclusively settled problems concerning the property rights of the exchangeables. Owing to the statesmanship of the countries' two leaders, Venizelos and Atatürk, relations between the two states normalised (and even became friendly) after this date.

Article 2 created national minorities, who were allowed to stay. They were given minority rights in the Peace Treaty as formulated in the section titled Protection of Minorities. Articles 37–44 of this section (which were based on the Polish Minorities Treaty of 1919) concerned, *inter alia*, Turkey's non-Muslim minority, the Rums, while Article 45 set down a principle that would in turn govern Greece's behaviour towards its Muslim minority.[13] However, most of these rights existed only on paper. As a consequence, the experience of those who were allowed to stay proved to be even more difficult than that of those who had to leave. Although those who had to leave under Article 1 suffered a great deal, their problems were more or less limited to one generation. These problems diminished considerably, and even faded away altogether as the 1923 expellees adapted to their respective new countries (but see Köker, Koufopoulou, Stelaku, this volume, and Hirschon 1998 [1989]: ch.3).

It is for a number of reasons that ultimately the experience of those who were allowed to stay has proved to be more difficult. Firstly, for eighty years the minorities have never been considered by their host-states as their own people and they have always been forced to live a separate life, sometimes subjected to harassment. Secondly, the intensity of the negative attitude shared by both Turkey and Greece towards their minorities did not diminish with the passing of time. On the contrary, the respective lives of the two établis communities were made even more difficult after the 1960s, when another issue, the Cyprus question, came to poison Greco-Turkish relations further. Thirdly, and of particular relevance, the two établis communities were forced half a century later to share the fate of those who had to leave in 1923: they had to emigrate to their respective kin-states, some of them even becoming refugees and stateless persons.

The numbers speak for themselves. Typical of city-dwellers, the Rum minority of Istanbul has a very low rate of population growth and has practically withered away, diminishing from some 110,000 people in 1923 to around 2,500 today. The Rum population of Gökçeada and Bozcaada has fallen approximately from 9,000 to 500 over the same period (Whitman 1992a: 29). The size of the Muslim-Turkish minority in Western Thrace, the rural nature of which is reflected in a very high rate of population growth, is now smaller than the 120,000 it was in 1923. This is because an estimated 300,000 to 400,000 of them have left Greece since 1923.[14] In this respect, the story of those who were allowed to stay has a lot more to teach us than the story of those who had to leave. In examining this issue I shall analyse the predicament of the two respective minorities both in the context of Greco-Turkish relations and with respect to their rights as laid down in the 1923 Convention and Peace Treaty, in the 1930 Ankara Convention and in other instruments.

The two minorities and Greek–Turkish relations

For centuries the issue of respective minorities influenced relations between what are now present-day Turkey and Greece. However, that causal link was reversed in 1923: since then it has been the relations between the two countries that have been the determining influence on the lives of the two minorities, and with incomparably greater effect. This new period can be subdivided into three: 1923 to 1930, 1930 to 1954, and 1955 onwards.

1923–1930 Initial violations: emptying strategic territories of their établis

Violations started as soon as the Convention began to be implemented. Firstly, both Turkey and Greece made efforts to dislodge the établis who constituted a majority on certain strategic territories. Greece dislodged them from its Turkish border (Evros) immediately, and Turkey dislodged them from the islands of Gökçeada and Bozcaada a few years later.

In Greece, as the Evros province was emptied of Muslim-Turks and as the incoming Rums were settled in Western Thrace, the Muslim-Turks, who formed the majority there in 1922 (129,120 Muslims compared with 33,910 Greeks) and who held 84 percent of the land, became a numerical minority (23 November 1922, Minutes no.3, Meray, Lausanne: 41f., 54, 61). This situation only came about because the Rum refugees from Eastern Thrace, crossing the Maritza river in the autumn of 1922, were able freely to seize the property and livestock of the Western Thrace établis; the security forces did not stop them. In the end, Muslim-Turks had to abandon everything and take refuge in Turkey (Alexandris 1983: 120–21).[15] One year later (1924) the number of Greeks in the area had risen to 189,000 (Pallis 1925: 327). Also in Greece, Law No. 2345/1920 was never implemented. The law was promulgated in order to meet the requirement of the 1913 Athens Treaty (see note 13) with regard to the election of the Mufti and Head-Mufti by the Muslim-Turkish community. As a consequence of its non-implementation, the community was never able to elect its religious leaders. This situation has still not been resolved in 2002 (but see Alexandris, this volume).

In Turkey, the special self-administration privileges given to the inhabitants of Gökçeada and Bozcaada under Article 14 of the Peace Treaty were never honoured. Even the Rums' right to education in their mother tongue was denied in 1927 (Law No.1151).[16]

1930–1954 The rapprochement period

It can be argued that for two decades Greece and Turkey had friendly relations. The établis question and other bilateral problems were settled in 1930 through the Ankara Convention. Common fears concerning the Italian 'Mare Nostrum' policy of Mussolini in the 1930s and the Stalinist policy of the Soviets in the 1940s and early 1950s acted to promote friendly relations between Greece and Turkey. This atmosphere of rapprochement was also reflected in the treatment of the two établis communities, and it served in some measure to alleviate their problems. Under the Culture Agreement of 1951, an exchange of teachers for minority schools in both countries was foreseen and there was an undertaking to purify school textbooks of 'mutual defamation concerning both nations' moral values'. In Greece, the minority schools were officially called Turkish instead of Muslim for the first time in 1954 (the 'Papagos law', Law No. 3065/1954). In Turkey, the Rum minority's 'golden age' started with the arrival in 1930 of many Greek citizens (probably those who were born in Istanbul and left in 1922) coming to live and work in Turkey with work and residence permits.[17] The two countries became the closest partners in the Balkans. In the early 1950s, Greek started to be taught again on Gökçeada and Bozcaada. Under American influence bilateral relations prospered, which also allowed a revival of the Patriarchate.

On the other hand, the core of the problems for the respective établis communities remained untouched. In Greece, the 'forbidden zone' was declared in 1953 as a measure against communist infiltration from Bulgaria. Encompassing one-eighth of Western Thrace, it was in fact used, together with the military restricted zone running parallel with it in the south, to keep the Pomaks in the northern mountains separate from the Muslim-Turks in the south.[18] This practice, by which a special pass was required to enter the zone – issued only to the Pomaks domiciled there – was abandoned in November 1995. In addition, complaints about land problems began in May 1952, as recorded in various subsequent news items in *Trakya* (e.g., 14 July 1954, in Oran 1991: 237).

In Turkey, it was the heyday of Turkish secular nationalism. Religious institutions and their clerics were being intimidated with Turkist slogans and measures such as the obligation to sing the call to prayer – the *ezan* – in Turkish instead of Arabic. This mood also affected the Rum community, particularly in the form of the pressure exerted by the Turkish Orthodox movement of Papa Eftim, a Karamanli Rum Orthodox priest. This movement, which was never recognised by world churches, pressured the most important Rum institution in Turkey, the Patriarchate.[19]

1955 onwards. The point of no return: the Cyprus imbroglio begins

(a) The Cyprus question[20]

The Cyprus question was first taken to the United Nations by Greece in 1954. Since then this issue has proved disastrous for both minority communities. On 6–7 September 1955 street demonstrations in Turkey in reaction to the

Cyprus affair soon degenerated into widespread vandalism and violence, during which Rum property in Istanbul and Izmir was ransacked and lives were lost.[21]

The murder of Cypriot Turks at Christmas in 1963 by Cypriot Greeks caused in turn a Turkish reaction in 1964 that was to have serious ramifications for the Istanbul Rum community. With the aim of retaliation against Greece, the Turkish Government cancelled the work and residence permits of some 13,000 Greek citizens who were living and working in Istanbul under the 1930 Convention. These Greeks were not only those who had come from Greece as a result of the 1930 Ankara Convention but were also Istanbul Rum établis who had Greek, not Turkish, citizenship. They were all expelled. In due course, however, the core of the Istanbul Rum community also left, because many had intermarried with the now-evicted Greek community, and because they feared the consequences of the seemingly interminable Cyprus issue. As a result, Istanbul was almost emptied of its historical Rum community. Also in 1964, education in Greek was once again forbidden on the islands of Gökçeada and Bozcaada, and in 1965 many Rum properties were expropriated to build an open agricultural prison, as a result of which many more of the islands' Rum inhabitants took refuge in Greece (see Erginsoy, 1998, and Alexandris this volume).

(b) Grievances of the Turkish minority

The events of 1964 marked not only the beginning of a period of increased hardship for the Rums, but also for the Muslims of Western Thrace.[22] Now that so many Greeks and Rums had left Turkey, there was no longer the same incentive for Greece to treat its Muslim-Turkish minority equitably. Following the coup d'état of the colonels in 1967, conditions for the Muslim-Turkish minority deteriorated.

Article 40 of the Lausanne Peace Treaty gave the Muslim-Turkish minority the right to 'found, administer, and inspect' its schools. However, after the coup, school-board elections were no longer permitted. All school and association signs that had the word 'Turkish' on them were forbidden (see *Akın* and *Azınlık Postası* newspaper items in Oran 1991: 121–25; for pressures on minority education see Whitman 1990: 14–17, 39–42). The Papagos law was repealed by decree 1109/1972 and Turkish schools were again called Muslim schools. Law No. 695/1977 stipulated that graduates of the Salonica Special Academy of Pedagogy (SSAP), an official teacher-training school established in 1966 to train young Pomaks to turn Turkish schools into Greek-medium schools, were appointed by priority, causing interminable school boycotts,[23] especially by students of Pomak origin.[24] As of 1984, the lycée students had to sit their exams in Greek, even for Turkish-medium courses, as a result of which after 1985 students were no longer able to pass their exams successfully and graduate from the Komotini lycée, the only official Turkish-medium high school. Furthermore, teachers and books that should have been arriving from Turkey were not allowed into Greece. As a result, many youngsters (who, unlike their counterparts in Istanbul, do not have the opportunity of going to American or European lycées) try to go to Turkey for their secondary and higher education. The great majority of those who leave do not come back, largely because university diplomas obtained in Turkey are not recognised in Greece by the official body which accredits foreign higher education qualifications (DIKATSA). (This policy was abandoned at the end of 1994 except in two fields: Turkish language and theology.)

According to provisions of Law No. 2345/1920 the religious leaders (*muftis*) of the Muslim-Turkish community were to be elected by the Muslim community itself. This law was never applied, however, and when it was repealed in December 1990 the new decree (No. 182) provided for a mufti appointed by the Minister of National Education and Religious Affairs. The community sees this as a severe blow to religious freedoms and calls this mufti 'the Mufti of the Christians'. In the same vein, since presidential decree No. 1 of 3 January 1991, *wakfs* (the pious foundations that form the economic and social backbone of the Muslim-Turkish community) have come under the strict administration of provincial governors. In contrast, the Greek state has no involvement at all in the selection of Orthodox clergy and administration of Orthodox institutions (see Oran 1991: 155–71; also Whitman 1990: 26–9).

As for civil society, the three main associations of the Muslim-Turkish minority, namely the Xanthi Turkish Union (founded 1927), the Komotini Turkish Youth Union (1928), and the Western Thrace Turkish Teachers' Union (1936), were closed down in November 1987 on the grounds that the word 'Turkish' in their titles should only refer to citizens of Turkey, and that its use to describe Greek Muslims endangered public order. As a result, a large demonstration took place in Komotini, supported mainly by Pomaks coming from the forbidden zone in the north (Oran 1991: 172–81; also Whitman 1990: 16–17).

Whereas in the past the Muslim-Turkish minority was subjected to oppression only from the police, in reaction to the growing expression of Turkishness within the minority, the authorities recently connived in other forms of pressure. Mass attacks on life and property started to occur. On 29 January 1990 several mobs damaged Muslim-Turkish workplaces in Komotini following the broadcast of an erroneous news item on a local radio station. In addition, fifty people, including the acting mufti and a Muslim-Turkish MP, were injured. The police did not intervene. Similar mob attacks took place in August 1991 and again in December 1997 and July 1998 in Komotini with no effective police intervention.

Not only the right to petition, vote and be elected, but also the right to a fair trial had ceased to exist for the Muslim-Turkish community in Western Thrace. This can be illustrated in the case of Sadik Ahmet, an MP (who later died in a controversial car accident on 25 July 1995). After he prepared a petition titled 'Grievances and Requests of the Turkish-Muslim Minority Living in Western Thrace' supported by 13,000 signatures, he was sentenced on 24 June 1988 to thirty months in prison and fined 100,000 drachmas. In addition, under the charge of 'openly or indirectly inciting citizens to violence or creating division among the population at the cost of social peace' –

by using the adjective 'Turkish' in their campaign literature – he and Ibrahim Şerif, an MP, were each sentenced on 26 January 1990 to eighteen months in prison and were deprived of their political rights for three years. Some seven months after Dr. Ahmet became an independent MP in the national elections of April 1990, the electoral system was amended. The amendment set a 3 percent minimum vote requirement for independent candidates, making the election of an independent Muslim-Turk impossible.[25]

Under the terms of Article 19 of the Greek law on citizenship (3370/1955), the Muslim-Turks of Western Thrace risked losing their citizenship without a hearing or an effective right of appeal, in the process becoming stateless persons. This provision stated that a person of 'non-Greek ethnic origin' going abroad 'without the intention of returning' may be deprived of citizenship. Article 19 put Greece in an indefensible position. In 1990 it was referred to by the U.S. State Department in its Country Reports on Human Rights Practices in the following terms: '[In Greece] exile is unconstitutional and does not occur, except in the form of an administrative decree on the loss of citizenship by non-ethnic Greeks' (Section Greece, 1/D). Article 19 was used in conjunction with another method to inhibit the freedom of movement of the minority in Western Thrace: from 1985 the police began crossing out 'including return' in the passports of Muslim-Turks, mostly illiterates, visiting Turkey. These people were then denied re-entry upon return to the Greek border and were also deprived of citizenship under Article 19. Moreover, movement is not only restricted between Greece and Turkey: because of the forbidden zone it is restricted within Western Thrace as well. Article 19 was denounced in 1991 by Prime Minister Constantine Mitsotakis as 'the product of another era', but it was only repealed in July 1998 under pressure from the European Union, but without retrospective effect. The numbers of the stateless persons it created from 1955 to 1998 are not known exactly, but estimated at ten thousand by the Western Thrace minority.[26]

The Muslim-Turkish minority in Western Thrace is 70 percent peasant. In 1922 it owned 84 percent of the land in Western Thrace, but now the minority estimates this figure to be 20–40 percent. This stems from various practices of the Greek administration. Firstly, the Orthodox population is encouraged to buy Muslim-Turkish land with soft loans granted by the state for this purpose.[27] Secondly, laws are systematically applied in a discriminatory way. Fertile land under the ownership of the minority is expropriated for political motives such as for the building of prisons and universities (see Oran 1991: 240–44; also Whitman 1990: 35–36). At the same time, the policy of *anadasmos* (land consolidation) also works against the minority (see *Akın*, 6 May and 21 June 1977 in Oran 1991: 245). Thirdly, possession documents and title deeds are not recognised (see Oran 1991: 247–60). Lastly, between 1965 and the end of the 1990s, Law No. 1366/1938 was used to stop the minority purchasing new property. Under this law, purchase and sale of real estate and even the use of possession rights were subject to special licence. Law No. 1366/1938 applied in the coastal areas, frontiers, and on the islands – in all, nearly half the total area of Greece. Christians had no problems, but

Muslim-Turks did.[28] However, this problem too has eased in recent years, again following pressure from the European Union, this time after a British citizen encountered problems buying land in a coastal area (see European Court of Justice decision dated 30 May 1989).

The minority also faced particular difficulties in opening and running businesses. When a Turk applied to open a business the authorities were zealous in insisting on absolute compliance with even the most minor and unimportant rules and regulations, a standard not applied in practice to ethnic Greeks (see Whitman 1990: 57 and 36–37; also Oran 1991: 227–30). In addition, once a business started, its running was hindered through harassment by tax officers.[29] The minority has also been discriminated against when applying for various licences (tractor driving, hunting rifles, etc.) but these measures have also been alleviated in recent years (see *Ileri*, 1 October 1982 (a Xanthi newspaper) in Oran 1991: 227; also Whitman 1990: 37).

The Greek administration seems to have a dual aim in Western Thrace: to assimilate the Muslim minority of Pomak ethnic origin, and to encourage the emigration of the Muslim minority of Turkish ethnic origin. As a consequence of pressure, the Muslim minority of Turkish ethnic origin has been inclined to migrate to Turkey. Others have chosen to work in Germany, where they have set up active associations to inform European public opinion of the violations in Western Thrace. As stated above, some 400,000 people are estimated to have left Western Thrace since 1923. Some of this number are stateless persons as a result of Article 19. However, several factors keep the numerical size of this minority more or less stable. Firstly, Greece offers better economic opportunities than Turkey. Secondly, Turkey was shaken with anarchy after the end of 1960s and with terrorism after 1984. Thirdly, the minority is a community mainly of peasants; people do not readily leave their land. Lastly, and most importantly, the Western Thrace minority's population growth rate is as high as 2.8 percent, while the average for Greece is 0.7 percent.

(c) Grievances of the Rum minority[30]

The Rums of Turkey have experienced very similar problems to those of the Muslim-Turks of Western Thrace in the field of education: books and teachers in short supply, difficulty with school administration and repairs to buildings, etc. However, there is one difference with the situation in Western Thrace: there has been no denial of the Rums' identity.[31] School signs that read 'Rum Minority School' were kept in place, with only one exception that I know of: the sign at the entrance to the Istanbul Rum Phanar Lycée that reads in Greek letters, 'The Great School of Our Race'. It was removed in May 1970 in retaliation for the breaking of the marble sign in Arabic letters on the 114–year-old Xanthi Clock Tower.

In the religious and social spheres too, the Rums of Turkey have generally had the same kind of problems as their Muslim-Turkish counterparts in Western Thrace. Although the Patriarch is elected by his fellow clergymen, the Turkish administration, in accordance with the custom based on the *Rum*

Patrikliği Nizamatı (Rules Concerning the Rum Patriarchate) of 1862, has always interfered with all but the final of the election lists prepared by the clergymen by crossing out some of the names. Perhaps more importantly, the Halki School of Theology was closed by a decree of the Constitutional Court in 1971 nationalising private institutions of higher learning, making it impossible to educate the Orthodox clergy in Turkey. Partly as a result of this, but also because the numbers of Rum Orthodox have diminished to under three thousand, the Patriarchate itself is on the road to extinction. In addition, Rum pious foundations have come under pressure. The Turkish administration has declared that all donations made to the communal institutions of non-Muslim minorities are the property of the government. Other violations concerning fundamental or economic rights have also consistently occurred. Most notably there has been harassment from the police and interference in the election of school and religious-foundation board members by the Governor of Istanbul.

As a consequence of these pressures and violations, the Rums of Istanbul and of the islands Gökçeada and Bozcaada have migrated to Greece, leaving very few of their number behind. These migrants usually retain their Turkish citizenship, but their grandchildren have become Greek citizens and do not speak Turkish. Consequently, the Rum minority of Turkey is almost extinct, numbering no more than 2,500, most of whom are senior citizens. However, there are also other reasons why the Rum minority in Turkey has failed to maintain its numbers in the same way that the Muslim-Turkish minority in Western Thrace has. Firstly, the marriage opportunities for the Rum community in Turkey became increasingly limited because, after the expulsion of Greek citizens from Turkey in 1964, many young Rum men who did not want to serve in the Turkish army (where they were not made reserve officers) left for Greece. Secondly, there is the factor described by one Japanese researcher as the 'footloose Greek merchant' (Kamozawa 1982: 129). The Istanbul Rums had lived for several centuries as more or less wealthy city dwellers and so, unlike the peasants of Western Thrace, they were not dependent on land. Consequently, their horizons were not as limited. When the pressures on the Rum community intensified after the Second World War because of the events unfolding in Cyprus, they were better placed to migrate owing to their long-maintained commercial links with Europe. Migration to Greece was further encouraged by the relative strength of the Greek economy (per capita income four times that of Turkey) and by Greece's eventual membership of the EEC. The Rums transferred what capital they had to Athens and reorganised their businesses there. Thirdly, besides police harassment, the Rums, an upper middle- and middle-class community, were greatly disturbed by the anarchic atmosphere prevailing in Turkey from 1968 until the end of the 1990s. Lastly, as city people, they had a very low rate of population growth.

The Rum inhabitants of Gökçeada and Bozcaada were not, of course, city folk like the Istanbul minority. Nevertheless, they too left. It seems that the psychological atmosphere of foreboding created by the quasi-extinction of the Istanbul Rums, together with the background of ongoing pressures, including withdrawal of the right to education in their mother tongue, has been too much for them to bear.

Lessons to be drawn from the 1923 experience

The end of the Soviet Union heralded a new era in international politics in the 1990s. In the Balkans this could justifiably be called the opening of 'Pandora's box', for the suffering of minorities and the creation of refugees – considered things of the distant past in Europe – came on to the international agenda with renewed urgency. But can we draw any lessons from the most radical solution adopted so far for this kind of problem, the compulsory exchange of populations between Greece and Turkey in 1923? Bearing in mind the important parallels between the post-First World War situation and the post-Cold War era of today, a review of the relative successes and failures of the Convention and its implementation would, I believe, be particularly timely.

Both eras mark transitory periods of striking importance for the nation-state, i.e., the 'motherland'. In the first, the keynote was the transition from imperialism to nationalism; in the second and current era it is the transition from nationalism to globalisation.[32] The current era, like the post-First World War era, plays host to two main trends concurrently: nationalism and globalisation. The post-First World War era saw a continuation of the irredentist policy of Greece in the 1820s on the one hand, and on the other, in response to the Greek threat, a burgeoning Turkish nationalism. In the current era, on the one hand we see a continuation of the irredentist policy of Serbia, whose expansion was prohibited in the first era, and on the other, in response to the Serbian threat, the Bosnians attempting to construct their national identity, while Albanians and Macedonians try to build their nation-states. The post-First World War era marked the zenith of a second period of globalisation (1890s) in world history. (A previous wave occurred from the 1490s mercantilist period through colonialism.) The post-Cold War era marks the beginning of a third period of globalisation in which it seems inevitable that in the long run there will be a blurring of national identities under the homogenising influence of the global market. For different reasons, both eras have borne witness, to outbursts of nationalist excess.

Let us now proceed to the final observations on the eighty year experience of the exchange by re-evaluating the two main articles of the Convention in a contemporary context.

Article 1

The implementation of Article 1 was very successful insofar as it came to realise the purpose of cleansing the nation-state. It is true that the exchange and the resettlement of refugees took considerably more time and effort than anticipated, and in the process gave rise to a great deal of suffering. In the international arena, however, and strictly in terms of the Convention itself, the issue had come to a close by the end of 1930. The overriding reason for this success was the fact that Great Britain, Greece and Turkey all strongly desired a radical exchange of populations, even a compulsory one. It does not follow, however, that a similar exchange could be undertaken in today's world. In the post-First World War era it was the concept of minority rights, not human rights, that informed the prevailing opinion of the international community. Today the concept of universal human rights is in the ascendancy. This being the case, it is improbable that the international community would again sanction such a large-scale forced exchange of populations.

Article 2

The outcome of Article 2 has been a failure in that it was unable to bring about its declared purpose, i.e., accommodation by Greece and Turkey of culturally, ethnically and religiously diverse societies. The stipulations of Article 2 were met with such reluctance that those who were excluded from the exchange, the respective minorities, never felt themselves a component part of their host-state, and the host-states persisted in considering them as an alien element to be ejected. The reasons for this are numerous.

- With hindsight, the fate of the respective minorities was sealed the very day the Convention was signed. Greece and Turkey – and many other states of eastern Europe – were eager to build their own ethnically and religiously homogenous nation and nation-state. However, in their view, the provisions for the protection of minorities imposed on them by the Great Powers undermined the nation-building project. Greece and Turkey, questioning the true motives of the Allies, made attempts to resist these provisions and even to rid themselves of the minorities altogether by making life for them as difficult as possible. Therefore, the main reason for the failure is the fact that, from the outset, the respective minorities were unwelcome elements in both countries. Greece and Turkey accepted them as a necessary evil, or worse, considered them as a Trojan horse left behind by the other side.
- Greece and Turkey were not ideal partners for this very difficult undertaking. Their recent history was one of war and bloodshed, they were both in the process of nation-building, and their religions are different. To make matters even worse, other points of conflict have arisen since the exchange, most seriously over Cyprus and the rights to the Aegean.
- Permitting minorities to remain in two strategically important areas, i.e., in the Evros province of Greece contiguous to the Turkish border, and on the Turkish islands of Gökçeada and Bozcaada at the mouth of the Dardanelles, does not seem to have been conducive to their security and fair treatment.
- The guarantee that reciprocity was supposed to deliver was the last hope of both minorities, but this proved to be a cruel one. The moment one state acted unfairly towards its minority community, the minority community of the other has been subjected to retaliatory measures.

It does not follow, however, that a similar project could not be undertaken today. With the spread of globalisation, multi-culturalism is set to become one of the defining characteristics of the post-Cold War era. For example, Greece's record in the last few years seems to suggest that certain external dynamics (globalisation) can play a positive role in discouraging a state's mistreatment of its minorities. Greece's full membership of the European Union has, for the time being, brought meaningful amelioration to two of the Muslims' most significant grievances: the non-deliverance of building and repair licences and of the requisite permits to buy property, and the application of Article 19 of the citizenship code. On the other hand, the Balkans are still far from ideal as an area for such an initiative.

The nationalist excesses of the 1920s marked the beginning of the era of nationalism; those of the 1990s now mark its end. It is only natural that the forces of destruction unleashed at the close of the era should be even greater than those that attended its inauguration.

Notes

1. As expressed by Mr. Montagna, President of the Sub-Commission on Minorities (and on the Exchange) on 10 January 1923. (Professor Seha L. Meray, integral Turkish translation in eight volumes of the Lausanne Peace Conference, Minutes and Documents, Series 1, Volume 1, Book 1: 321. From here on, references will be made to this Turkish translation as 'Meray, Lausanne', but dates of sessions and numbers of minutes taken will also be given to enable the reader to follow in other language editions).

2. The Empire itself was usually marked 'Turkey' or 'Turquie' in the numerous maps drawn by the Europeans of the period. The French expression *se faire Turc*, literally 'to make oneself a Turk', means to become Muslim. In addition, the Arabs and Palestinians who migrated to Chile at the beginning of the century are still called *Turkos*.

3. After discussing the territorial questions and the Straits, the Conference convened on 1 December 1922 to discuss an exchange of war prisoners. But Lord Curzon, British Foreign Minister and President of the Conference, announced that Dr. Nansen, the renowned High Commissioner for Refugees of the League of Nations, would be reading a report on the exchange of Greek and Turkish populations, an item that did not figure on the agenda. According to Dr. Nansen, the question was of real importance for peace and economic stability in the Near East, as well as for peace in Europe. He had been invited by the representatives of four Great Powers in Istanbul to prepare a treaty for the exchange of minorities to be implemented immediately, before the concluding of the Peace Treaty. He had already obtained the official approval of the Greek Government, and talks were more or less on the way with the Ankara Government, which declared to him 'at least four times' that it took a positive stand on the exchange issue (1 December 1922, Minutes no. 8, Meray, Lausanne: 115f.).

4. In the later stages of the Conference, Venizelos seemed to withdraw from the idea of a compulsory exchange, but this was no longer realistic, and was probably only a diplomatic move. Dr. Riza Nur, the Turkish delegate on the Special Committee on Minorities, explains this in his memoirs (written in 1928) by pointing to the probability of the Greek Government of the time, of which Venizelos was not a member, being against the exchange (1967, vol. III: 1113).

5. The Allies' proposal for a compulsory exchange was a most pleasant surprise for Dr. Nur, who wrote: '...I was astonished. I had been wondering all along how in the world I could propose such a thing to them, something unheard of in history. It came all by itself. It was like a present from Heaven' (1967, vol. III: 1040).

6. The National Pact (*Misak-ı Milli*) was a declaration by the last Ottoman Parliament on 28 January 1920 regarding the minimum requirements for a just and durable peace. It laid claim to the lands still in the hands of the Ottoman armies as of 30 October 1918 – the date of the Mudros Armistice – which would give the country defensible boundaries, more or less corresponding to the present borders of the Turkish Republic, with the exception of Batumi in Georgia, the Sandjak of Alexandretta (joined to Turkey in 1939) and Mosul in Iraq. The Kemalists considered the *Misak-ı Milli* their holy aim.

7. Ismet Pasha profited from the fact that the exclusion of Western Thrace from the exchange was proposed by Lord Curzon at the very outset. See 1 December 1922, Meray, Lausanne: 124.

8. Thus the exchange did not include Catholic or Protestant Rums. However, the Turkish delegate would have preferred the group subject to the exchange to be defined as 'Rums of Turkish citizenship' so that 'Greek irredentism disappears from Turkey' (16 January 1923 afternoon session, Minutes no. 4, Meray, Lausanne, Series 1, Volume 1, Book 2: 312).

9. According to Article 3, those now subject to the exchange who, prior to 18 October 1912, had left the territories were to be considered in the scope of Article 1, i.e., exchangeables. The number of the Rums who fled Turkey in August 1922 is generally given in Western sources as some one million, bringing the total number hosted by Greece to around 1.2 million. However, Bilal Şimşir, a Turkish historian, notes that the number of those who fled around August 1922 before the exchange was less than half a million and that 150,000 of them were those who had come to settle in Turkey after 1919. According to this calculation, the number of those hosted by Greece is around 700,000 (see Şimşir 1989: 381).

10. Therefore, in contradistinction to Article 1, all the Rums of Istanbul (not only Orthodox Rums) were declared non-exchangeables. Some of these were citizens of the Greek state.

11. As in the case of the Karamanli Orthodox who spoke only Turkish and of some Muslims (Cretans in particular) who spoke only Greek (see Stelaku and Koufopoulou, this volume).

12. Many Rum Orthodox who left Turkey for Greece, especially those from the Izmir and Istanbul areas, belonged to a higher social class than the mainland Greeks. As a result, they were met with jealousy and despised as *tourkosporoi* (Turkish seeds). In addition, they also segregated themselves from indigenous Greeks. Izmir Rums founded Nea Smyrni and a sports club called Pan-Ionion, and many Istanbul Rums live in Faliron where they support the athletic club AEK (*Athletiki Enosis Konstantinoupoli*). On the other hand, the habits of many of the Muslims who left Greece for Turkey were much more liberal than their new, rather conservative compatriots. Indigenous Turks considered them *yarı gâvur* (half-infidel), despised them as *muhacir* (immigrants), and for a long time abstained from intermarriage with them (see Köker, this volume).

13. While the rights of the Rum minority consist solely of those laid down in the Lausanne Peace Treaty, the Exchange Convention and the Ankara Convention of 10 June 1930, the Muslim-Turks of Western Thrace also have minority rights as laid down in two other instruments: the Athens Treaty and its Protocol no.3 (14 November 1913) and the Treaty on the Protection of the Minorities in Greece (10 August 1920). The Athens Treaty is a bilateral treaty concluded between Greece and the Ottoman Empire at the end of the second Balkan War to protect the rights of Muslims in Greece (see Oran 1991: 62–64; for the text of the Treaty (in Turkish) see Erim 1953: 477–88. The Treaty on the Protection of Minorities in Greece is a multilateral treaty concluded between Greece and the Great Powers (see Oran 1991: 72–75; for the text of the Treaty see British Foreign and State Papers, Vol. 113, p. 471). For a legal appraisal of the validity of these treaties and an analysis of the probable political reasons for Greece declaring that it does not recognise these two, see Oran 1991: 101–12.

14. Whitman (1990: 2) estimated that, even with a population growth rate of 2 percent (which is an underestimate) the size of the Western Thrace minority today ought to be around 500,000.

15. This situation, which was implicitly acknowledged by Venizelos at the Conference (1 December 1922, Meray, Lausanne: 122), was allowed to come about when the Greek Minister of Agriculture, Anastas Bakkalbasi, revoked an eviction order demanding sixty thousand Rum refugees leave the homes of the Muslims in Western Thrace on page 2 of an election pamphlet he published in his bid to be re-elected in 1950. See *Trakya*, 24 May 1954 (a newspaper in Turkish published by O.N. Fettahoğlu from 1932 to 1964 in Xanthi/İskeçe).

16. In addition there was considerable pressure on the Rum Orthodox Patriarchate in 1926 to renounce the first paragraph of Article 42 of the Peace Treaty (concerning personal and family status). I do not mention this in the text because it did not concern the Rums only, rather all non-Muslim minorities. However, it should also be included among the Rums' grievances. At that date, the Swiss Civil Code was adopted, which made civil marriage compulsory. Non-Muslim minorities were urged to comply with the law and have civil marriage executed first, the religious ceremony later. The Jewish and Armenian communities complied, but the Rums were 'persuaded' only much later (see Alexandris 1983: 136–38).

17. At that time there was a labour shortage and a need for specialised skills in certain sectors in Turkey because of the vacuum left by the departed non-Muslims, while in Greece there was excess population and unemployment. A special dispatch from Robert Skinner in Athens to the U.S. Secretary of State in Washington D.C. (25 October 1930, no. 767.68/684) suggests that Venizelos badly needed 'new avenues of employment' when he visited Ankara in 1930 to make these agreements (see Records of the Department of State Relating to the Political Relations of Turkey, Greece and the Balkan States, 1930–1939, microfilm no. MT1245 – I thank Dr. Ayhan Aktar for this document). One of the three agreements signed on 30 October 1930 provided for free circulation between the two countries enabling unemployed Greeks to come and settle in Turkey, particularly in Istanbul. Their number is unknown. However, the large advantages conferred by the 30 October 1930 Ankara Convention were definitely more significant for the Greek-citizen Rums of Istanbul than for the few Greeks (numbers unknown) who came from Greece.

18. For the forbidden zone, see de Jong 1980: 98, Whitman 1990: 14.

19. For the story of this movement, which while not created or supported by it, was nevertheless shown much tolerance by the Turkish government, see Alexandris 1983: 149ff; O'Mahony 2003. The reason that I do not mention the 'Citizen, Speak Turkish' campaigns, the turkification of commerce of the 1930s, and the Wealth Tax (*Varlik Vergisi*) of 1942 is that these were 'nationalist' initiatives targeted at all the non-Muslim minorities, not against the Rum community in particular. For instance, the economic nationalism of the Kemalists used the notorious Wealth Tax to break the quasi-monopoly that the non-Muslim bourgeoisie exercised over the economy. What began as a badly needed extraordinary tax in the miserable war years developed in the pro-fascist atmosphere of the period into a shameful discriminatory practice against non-Muslim minorities. It goes without saying that the Wealth Tax in particular and the other nationalist initiatives of the period in general should be considered among the grievances of the Rum minority.

20. The independence and constitution of the island, the population of which at that time was one-fifth Turkish and four-fifths Rum Cypriot, was guaranteed by Turkey, Greece and Great Britain. However, Greece and the Cypriot Greek community were pressing for Enosis, union with Greece.

21. This shameful event (which also affected other non-Muslim minorities) was initially a display of anti-Rum feeling organised by the Cyprus Is Turkish Association, but it was obvious that it enjoyed the tacit approval of the Government, which hoped that the demonstrations would show that it enjoyed the support of public opinion during the ongoing London Conference on Cyprus. However, the mob ran free, the police stood by, and the demonstration turned into a frenzy of looting and plundering. When Prime Minister Adnan Menderes was tried after the coup d'état of 1960, the Turks learned that the bombing of Atatürk House in Salonica that triggered the violence was in fact instigated by the Turkish secret police.

22. The main problem with documenting discriminatory practices is that, except for some limited cases (as in the case of Article 19 of the citizenship law, repealed in 1998), the text of the laws is not discriminatory in itself: their official application is. For example, Law no. 1366/1938 does not state that the minority shall not be given permission to buy land in coastal areas etc.; the rules of *anadasmos* do not state that the minority shall be given less land or land in arid areas after the lands are unified; nor that tax inspection rules for Muslim-Turkish shops shall be much more strict; nor that Muslim-Turkish title deeds to property shall not be recognised. Nevertheless, such extensive discriminatory practice took place between the mid-1950s and the end of the 1990s, at which point European Union efforts

obliged the Greek state sensibly to ease these pressures and even to end some of them, as in the case of Article 19 in 1998. Probably the most detailed account and analysis of these human and minority rights violations (and on the question of Western Thrace in general) is my book, *Türk-Yunan İlişkilerinde Batı Trakya Sorunu* (Oran 1991). The non-Turkish speaking reader can follow (and see confirmed) the same violations through the less detailed report on the Turks of Greece by Whitman (1992) and also through the Country Reports on Human Rights Practices, Section Greece, published yearly by the U.S. Department of State.

23. For reports of boycotts by students of Pomak origin see *Trakya'nin Sesi*, 25 September 1982 (published in Xanthi); for a letter concerning Pomak students' complaint about SSAP teachers to the Minister for National Education and Religious Affairs, Apostolos Caclamanis, see Oran 1991: 133–34.

24. In Western Thrace the Pomaks are known for being 'more Turkish than the Turks' and the Romany for being 'more Turkish than the Pomaks'.

25. On cases against Dr. Sadik Ahmet see Oran 1991: 195–210; also Whitman 1990: 17–22.

26. On Article 19 and on violations concerning passports see Oran 1991: 213–19; also Whitman 1990: 11–13.

27. According to the agreement dated 22 November 1966 between the Greek Central Bank and the Agricultural Bank concerning credit facilities to be extended to 'Hellenic nationals of Christian religion willing to buy lands and agricultural constructions belonging to the Muslim-Turks of Thrace', such Hellenes receive a credit covering the price of the land and/or farmhouse with surrounding land, and also all expenses pertaining to such a purchase. The last two articles of the agreement signed between the bank and the individual are as follows: 'The above-mentioned sum will be paid back over twenty years in the form of equal instalments, to be started two years after the credit has been appropriated' and 'In case of misuse of this credit [i.e., if the credit is used for any other purpose] the Agricultural Bank is entitled to ask for the immediate restitution of the said credit.' Both left and extreme right-wing newspapers in Greece have severely criticised the application of this practice saying that, *inter alia*, it created 'many billionaires' as many borrowers exaggerated the price of the land and used the rest of the credit for other purposes. See *Embros*, 25 September, 30 October, 5 and 6 November 1985 (a left-wing newspaper printed in Xanthi) and *Hronos*, 30 October, 12 November 1985 (an extreme right-wing newspaper printed in Komotini); also Oran 1991: 237–40; Whitman 1990: 39.

28. On cases of official refusal to sell land to the minority see *Akın* 14 November 1969, 6 and 21 November 1972, 7 February 1975, 13 February 1978, in Oran 1991: 261. For the list of thirty-three non-answered demands of repair made between June 1973 and June 1981 see ibid.: 268 footnote 163. On official refusal to grant repair permits to houses and mosques see *Akın* 4 September 1976 in ibid.: 222; also *International Herald Tribune*, 28 December 1982; and Whitman 1990: 32–35

29. On this issue see the text of a collective and detailed complaint written in Komotini, dated 29 August 1984 and sent by nine minority leaders to the Undersecretary of Finance Dimitrios Tsovolas, in Oran 1991: 231–34.

30. My main source is Alexis Alexandris, the undisputed expert on this subject, with particular reference to his 1983 book *The Greek Minority of Istanbul and Greek–Turkish Relations, 1918–1974*, and to his 1980 article, 'Imbros and Tenedos: A Study in Turkish Attitudes Toward Two Ethnic Greek Island Communities Since 1923'. The plight of the Rums in Turkey can also be followed from the Helsinki Watch report on the Greeks of Turkey (Whitman 1992a), and from the U.S. Department of State's yearly Country Reports on Human Rights Practices, Section Turkey.

31. Whitman in 'The Greeks of Turkey' (Helsinki Watch 1992a) is wrong to look for a parallel in this respect. As already noted, the term 'Rum' has been the denotation given by the Istanbul minority to themselves since time immemorial. It comes from *Romios* (pl. *Romioi*), which means 'from [eastern] Rome'. They never called themselves '*Yunanlı*' meaning 'Greek, citizen of Greece', a term coined after Greece's independence following the 1821 revolution. In this respect, it is interesting to note that after the conquest of Constantinople in 1453 the Ottoman Sultans started to call themselves '*Sultan-i Iklim-i Rum*', meaning 'Sultan of the

Rum Lands'. In the same way, after 1639 (when Kurdistan came under Ottoman rule) Kurds called the Turkish soldiers *Rum Askeri (*Rum soldiers) for the same reason.

32. Globalisation is a much-discussed topic and can best be defined as the universal expansion of the Western system, carrying with it both an infrastructure (capitalism), and superstructure (rationalism, secularism, human and minority rights, democracy, etc.) (see Oran 2000).In the present context, it is very important to note that globalisation will bring a radical change to the concept of territory and therefore to the concept of 'motherland'. From 'clan territory' to 'manor' to 'kingdom' to 'national state' – every time the economic market was enlarged, the concept of 'motherland' kept pace with it. There is no reason why this all-important evolution should not alter our concept of motherland now that globalisation carries the economic market from the national state to a much larger and more ambiguous territory called the globe, radically transforming the focus of the supreme loyalty of men.

9

Religion or Ethnicity

THE IDENTITY ISSUE OF THE MINORITIES IN GREECE AND TURKEY

Alexis Alexandris

Introduction

At the Lausanne Conference, the international community allowed some relatively small minority groups in Greek Thrace, Istanbul and the islands of Imbros and Tenedos to escape the ensuing population exchange. These minorities were entitled to enjoy religious, educational and linguistic freedom, retained the right to administer their pious communal properties (*vakıfs*) and were allowed to settle questions of family law and personal status in accordance with their customs.[1] As worthy as these principles were, the Lausanne arrangements for minorities had serious practical flaws the consequences of which were to blight the minorities' lives for years to come.

Firstly, the Treaty of Lausanne defined the minorities in religious terms and evaded addressing the issue of their ethno-national identity. Secondly, although the reciprocal character of the rights that were to be enjoyed by the minorities in Greece and Turkey and the preservation of numerical balance between the two minority populations created a sense of bilateralism, no effective multilateral mechanism for assuring the respect of these protection clauses was installed. As a result, the minorities could genuinely prosper only as long as Greek–Turkish relations were good, as in the 1930s and early 1950s. This essay addresses the impact that these issues have had on the Lausanne minorities, and concludes with an appraisal of what the future could hold for them in the post-Cold War era.[2]

The Greek Orthodox of Istanbul

Of the110,000 Greek Orthodox in Istanbul who were exempted from the exchange the two-thirds that had been Ottoman nationals were given Turkish citizenship. The other one-third were nationals of Greece who had been established in Istanbul before October 1918. They were allowed to remain *in situ*.[3] Following the 1923 arrangement, the Greek Orthodox with Turkish citizenship (*Rums*) and the Greek Orthodox of Greek nationality (*Yunanlıs* or Istanbul Hellenes) continued to form a single minority group in Istanbul. In October 1930, the right of the Constantinople Hellenes to remain in their native city was reaffirmed with the signing of the Greek–Turkish Establishment, Commerce and Navigation Treaty.[4]

The Turkish delegation at Lausanne adamantly refused to accept national minorities within the frontiers of the new Turkish Republic and insisted on defining the exempted minorities in religious terms. Thus the Istanbul Greek Orthodox were always considered a religious minority by Turkey, and as such were not allowed to make their ethnicity a political concern. It is for this reason that so much stress is laid on the distinction in Turkey between Greek Orthodox (*Rum Ortodoks*) and Greek (*Yunanlı*), i.e., national of the Greek State. For instance, the Greek Orthodox Patriarchate is known as *Rum* but never as *Yunan Patrikhanesi*, for the latter would have national connotations and cast doubts on the loyalty of the institution to the Turkish state. However, the model of a secular and nationalist Christian identity (*Hıristiyan Türk kimliği*), advocated by a group of the Turkish Orthodox headed by a renegade Anatolian priest Papa Eftim, was encouraged by the Kemalist authorities. In 1936, one of the main exponents of this movement and a close collaborator of Papa Eftim, İstamat Zihni Özdamar (Stamatis Pouloglou), was appointed deputy in the Turkish Parliament representing the Christian Orthodox minority. In contrast, Ankara prevented Turkish citizens of Greek Orthodox background from forming or participating in associations emphasising their ethnic identity. Thus, in 1925 the historic Constantinople Greek Literary Society (*Ellinikos Philologikos Syllogos Konstantinoupoleos*) was banned and its contents confiscated (Moraux 1964: 3–24; Stavrou 1967: 309–13). Nevertheless, during the Greek–Turkish rapprochement of the 1930s, the establishment of a Greek ethno-cultural society in Istanbul was permitted in response to the Greek Prime Minister Eleftherios Venizelos allowing Turkish Kemalist associations to function in Thrace. Thus, in 1933, the Greek Union of Istanbul (*Elliniki Enosi Kostantinoupoleos*) was formed. However, membership of this association was restricted to the Istanbul Hellenes, for the ban on the Rums from forming ethnic associations continued even during the 1930s.

The Greek Union was tolerated by Ankara so long as Greek–Turkish relations remained friendly. However, with the emergence of the Cyprus crisis the Turks revised their position on the issue and in 1958, accused of 'activities detrimental to Turkish national interests', the Greek Union was shut down (Alexandris 1983: 272, 284). Currently, there are twenty-six Rum associations registered with the Turkish authorities, of which none deals with Greek ethnic or cultural matters. These are minority associations managing pious foundations (*vakıfs*) and other communal institutions, like 'the benevolent society for the sick and needy elderly of the Balıklı *Rum* hospital' (Anastasiadou-Dumont 2000: 94).

Semi-official nationalist organisations such as the Turkish Hearths (*Türk Ocakları*), the Citizen Speak Turkish movement and the Cyprus is Turkish Society systematically discouraged any ethnic Greek assertiveness on an individual level (Alexandris 1983: 183). Kemalist nationalists continued to regard the Greek Orthodox of Turkey as an unwelcome remnant of the Ottoman Empire and as agents of Pan-Hellenism (Şahin 1980: 124ff). During the interwar years, but also throughout the Second World War, the Rum Orthodox fell victim to the government's policies of turkification (*türkleştirme politikası*) targeted at all the non-Muslim minorities (Aktar 1996c: 324–38; Bali 1999: 102 ff). The enforcement of the infamous Wealth Tax (*Varlık Vergisi*), an extraordinary levy imposed almost exclusively on Christian and Jewish Turkish citizens during the period 1942 to1944, reflected the deep-seated perception in Kemalist circles that Muslim equals Turk, and non-Muslim equals non-Turk (Ökte 1951; Akar 1992: 97–149; Bali 1999: 424ff).

Suspicions of the Greek Orthodox minority were greatly reinforced during the 1950s when Archbishop Makarios became the symbol of the Greek unionist movement in Cyprus (Armaoğlu 1963: 155ff, 1959: 57–86; Bahcheli 1990: 171). As the Cyprus crisis deepened, the Greek Orthodox minority was used as a national scapegoat. Anti-Greek sentiment came to a head during the government-sponsored riots of 5–6 September 1955 (Alexandris 1983: 256ff; *Tarih ve Toplum* 1986: 11–26, 50–52; Hatzivassiliou 1990: 165–76; *Aktüel* 1992: 22–29; Dosdoğru 1993: 190–192). Inter-communal disturbances in Cyprus and the deterioration of Greek–Turkish relations during the 1960s had a direct impact on the Greek Orthodox in Turkey. The Istanbul Orthodox with Greek citizenship were the first group to be affected when on 16 March 1964 Turkey unilaterally denounced the Greek–Turkish Convention of Establishment of 1930, even though the right of these people to remain in their native city was guaranteed by the 1923 Lausanne agreement (Demir and Akar 1994: 63ff). By 1967, almost the entire Istanbul Hellene community had been expelled and their assets in Turkey frozen (Bitsios 1964–1965: 108–18, 127–29).[5] The exodus of the Istanbul Hellenes and the intense anti-Greek climate in Turkey affected those with Turkish citizenship too: some 40,000 members of the minority left Turkey of their own accord between 1964 and 1967. Thus the Greek Orthodox population of Turkey, whose numbers were just over 125,000 in the official Turkish census of 1935 (*İstatistik Yıllığı* 1936–37: 41–43), decreased to under 10,000 some forty years later. By the late 1990s, the Greek Orthodox population of Istanbul fluctuated between 2,500 in the winter and 5,000 in the summer months.

The Greek Orthodox of Imbros and Tenedos

Between November 1912 and September 1923, the Aegean islands of Imbros and Tenedos remained under Greek administration. Like the rest of the Aegean islands, they had overwhelming Greek majorities. Indeed, in the case of Imbros, the entire population was Greek. Because of Turkish strategic concerns voiced at Lausanne, the islands were handed over to Turkey in the wider terms of reference of the Lausanne Treaty. In it the Turkish government was required to implement a regime of local self-administration for the Imbriots and Tenediots. Article 14 of the Lausanne Treaty reads:

> The islands of Imbros and Tenedos, remaining under Turkish sovereignty, shall enjoy a special administrative organisation composed of local elements and furnishing every guarantee for the native non-Muslim population in so far as concerns local administration and the protection of persons and property. The maintenance of order will be assured therein by a police force recruited from amongst the local population by the local administration above provided for and placed under its orders.[6]

Even though the Turks refused to comply with the provisions of Article 14, the Greek islanders managed to preserve their local Aegean ethno-religious character until 1970 (Alexandris 1980: 27). According to the 1927 Turkish census, the population of Imbros was exclusively Greek Orthodox and numbered 6,762. Between 1951 and 1965 they maintained eight churches and ten Greek-language schools (ibid.). The much smaller island of Tenedos had 1,631 inhabitants, the great majority of whom were Greeks. From 1926 to the present day, a high-ranking bishop (Metropolitan) representing the Greek Orthodox of the two islands has been sitting at the Holy Synod of the Ecumenical Patriarchate, while from the 1950s onwards a number of Imbriots rose through the Phanar ecclesiastical hierarchy to achieve the highest possible positions in the Greek Orthodox Church. Both the incumbent of the Ecumenical Throne, Patriarch Bartholomeos I, and former Archbishop of America Iakovos are natives of Imbros.

During the late 1960s and early 1970s, a series of legal and administrative restrictions relating to minority education and cultural matters coupled with an extensive programme of expropriations forced the local Imbriot and Tenediot Greek Orthodox to abandon their native islands en masse and find refuge in Greece, western Europe, the United States and Australia (Aziz 1973: 104; Tenekidis 1986: 128–44). Reflecting the demographic changes imposed, Imbros was renamed officially as Gökçeada in 1970 (Law No. 5442 and decision 8479/29.7.1970). Interestingly, the first Turkish mosque in the islands was built in 1965 on an expropriated Greek Orthodox *vakıf* (communal property) in Panagia (now renamed Çınarlı), the capital of Imbros, and was given the name *Fatih Camisi* (the Conqueror's Mosque). Today there are about 10,000 residents in Gökçeada, of whom only about 300 are Greeks, the rest being Anatolian migrants brought in after 1964. The Greek presence in Tenedos/Bozcaada has almost disappeared with only a handful of the native Greek Orthodox remaining (Alexandris 1980: 5–31).

Greek Orthodoxy and the Turkish state

Of great importance to the deeply religious Orthodox minority in Istanbul and on the islands was the fate of the Ecumenical Patriarchate. After a long debate at the Lausanne Conference, the institution was maintained in Turkey. In accordance with the compromise reached, the Patriarchate remained in its historical seat in the Fener (Phanar) district of Istanbul as a purely religious and spiritual establishment, and as a result waived all political and temporal authority over its Greek Orthodox flock in Turkey. The ecumenical spiritual competences of the Patriarchate were not affected or curtailed by the Lausanne compromise (Giannakakis 1956: 10–26, 1957: 26–46; Agnides 1964: 12; Spatharis 1964–1965: 74–80).

Although the Turks have honoured their pledge at Lausanne to allow the Ecumenical Patriarchate to stay in Turkey, the perception that the Greek Orthodox Patriarchate 'was and continues to be the custodian of the Hellenic Great Idea' is still deeply rooted among Kemalist and nationalist Turks (Kıbrıslıoğlu 1967; Şahin 1980: 124ff). By means of legal and bureaucratic impediments, the Turks have limited the effective functioning of this internationally respected institution. In accordance with a special Turkish decree (*tezkere* 1092/6) of December 1923, eligibility for the office of the Patriarch was restricted to the Greek Orthodox clergy with Turkish citizenship who exercised their ecclesiastical duties in Turkey. Electors were also required to meet the same conditions. Moreover, the closure of the historic Theological Seminary of Chalki (*Heybeli Ruhban Okulu*) in 1971 has meant that for the last thirty years the Greek Orthodox cannot train their clerics, with serious repercussions for the survival of this minority as a distinct religious community in Turkey. Equally critical was the shutting down of the patriarchal printing house in 1964. Since then the Patriarchate has been unable to publish any printed religious material.

As of 1923, the goal of Ankara has been to reduce the Ecumenical See to the status of an ordinary Turkish minority religious institution simply catering for the Greek Orthodox in Turkey. The traditional school of thought on the question of the Greek Orthodox Patriarchate, adhered to by the military, the foreign ministry bureaucracy and nationalist politicians, is that the ecumenical character of this institution is to be viewed with great suspicion because of its potential to increase Greek influence in Istanbul (Sofuoğlu 1996: 207–30; Çelik 1998: 31–38;). Thus, the Turks interpret their Lausanne pledge for allowing the presence of the Phanar in Istanbul in the narrowest possible sense and, in the words of Suat Bilge, a former diplomat and academic, Ankara should 'leave the existence of the Fener Greek Patriarchate to the passage of time', i.e., let it wither away (Bilge 1998: 34).

According to patriarchal sources, there remain just over twenty bishops (metropolitans) with Turkish citizenship, many of whom are in their late seventies or early eighties (*Imerologiou* 2001: 559–60). Under the circumstances, and given the legal obstacles for recruitment of Greek Orthodox bishops from abroad, the Ecumenical Patriarchate will find it extremely difficult to function in the future since there will be too few Greek Orthodox with Turkish citizenship to enter the ranks of the Church, and those few who are qualified will not be able to benefit from the proper training because of the closure of the Theological Seminary of Chalki.

However, a growing section of informed Turkish public opinion, especially European-oriented Turkish academics, lawyers, human rights acitivists, journalists and businessmen, has been campaigning for a more tolerant attitude towards the Patriarchate and the Greek Orthodox. Such a change in the traditional Kemalist policies towards minorities is seen as part of the wider process of democratisation and Europeanisation (interview of lawyer Murat Cano in *Turkish Daily News*, 9 and 10 February 2001). Unlike mainstream Turkish politicians and bureaucrats, this section of the public recognises the global significance of the Ecumenical Patriarchate and points to its benefits for Turkey's international standing (see articles in *Hürriyet* by Deringil [17 March 1995], Uluengin [4 July 1995] and Çandar [26 September1995]). Recently, two younger scholars – a Muslim Turk and a member of the minority Rum Orthodox community – produced a balanced book on the Patriarchate, free from the traditional biased accounts that abound in post-1950s Turkish bibliography (Benlisoy and Macar 1996: 53–56).

Amongst Turkish politicians, it was the far-sighted Turgut Özal who recognised the importance of preserving the Patriarchate in Turkey and took some positive steps to ease long-standing restrictions on it. During the 1980s, the Özal government issued long-withheld building permission for the reconstruction of the section of the Patriarchate destroyed by fire in September 1941, and in 1991 Patriarch Bartholomeos was elected without Turkish government interference. In fact, the election of this enlightened senior Phanar cleric reversed a tradition of government interference in the patriarchal elections (1924, 1925, 1936, 1948 and 1972). A staunch advocate for Turkey's accession to the European Union, Patriarch Bartholomeos has also cooperated closely with Mehmet Nuri Yılmaz, President of Religious Affairs of Turkey, in organising international conferences promoting religious tolerance and understanding (February 1994 and May 2000).

Muslims of Thrace[7]

According to an Anglo-French census taken on 30 March 1920, 86,793 Muslims were living in Western Thrace, accounting for 40.8 percent of the total population (Mitrany 1936: 224–226). However, by the time of the exchange, the Lausanne Mixed Commission issued 106,000 exemption documents to Muslims, who all received Greek citizenship. A few years later, the 1928 Greek census recorded 103,175 Muslims living in the region, made up of 85,585 Turkish-speakers, 16,740 Pomaks, and 850 Roma.[8]

Religion constitutes one of the most significant unifying factors among the various Muslim ethnic groups in Thrace, where under Greek administration a moderate non-political form of Islam has flourished (Balic 1979: 32). A total of 287 mosques and 460 Muslim clerics are testimony to the intensely religious character of the Thracian minority. Religious education is provided in two higher-grade Koranic schools, known as *medrese*, in Komotini and Echinos. The religious circles in Komotini publish their own newspaper *Hakka Davet* or *Yeni Hakka Davet*. Apart from the majority Sunni Muslims, Sufi groups like the Bektashi and Kizilbashi orders are also present in Thrace (Zenginis 1988: 245–46).

The survival of the Islamic-Ottoman traditions in Greek Thrace is largely due to the mufti system, operating since 1923. Two muftis (Komotini and Xanthi) and an assistant mufti (Alexandropolis) offer spiritual guidance to the Muslims, but in their capacity to apply Islamic law they are also salaried judicial functionaries. Between 1923 and 1990, muftis were chosen by the Muslim leadership, that is to say, politicians, clergymen and local dignitaries. Following this selection, the Greek government proceeded officially to endorse the election and to appoint the new muftis (Minaidis 1990: 322, n.556; Soltaridis 1997: 77ff). This arrangement appeared to be acceptable to all parties until the 1980s when minority activists supported by Ankara campaigned vigorously for the election of muftis by popular vote. It was as a result of such circumstances that Greece, fearing the prevalence of political Islam within Greek borders, proceeded to regulate the mufti issue. According to the Mufti law 1920/1990, a committee of eleven Muslim clergymen and laymen proposes a list of qualified persons eligible for the post. After formal consultations with the religious leaders, the mufti is selected from the list by the Greek authorities, on the basis of personal qualifications (university degree, experience, etc.) He is subsequently appointed by ministerial decision for a ten-year term (Tsourkas 1981–82: 587; Georgoulis 1993: 3; Soltaridis 1997: 86ff). Present-day muftis Hafız Cemali Meço (Komotini) and Mehmet Emin Şinikoğlu (Xanthi) were appointed in accordance with law 1920/1991. The official muftis strongly oppose fundamentalist tendencies and political Islam, preferring to develop links with Muslim countries like Saudi Arabia, from where they apparently receive financial assistance.

A section of the minority opposed the system of officially appointed Muslim leaders, and, with support from Turkey, proceeded to elect rival muftis themselves. Thus, in the absence of any established procedure or practice for popular mufti elections – in Greece, Turkey or anywhere else – both İbrahim Şerif in Komotini and Mehmet Emin Aga in Xanthi were elected in 1990 by a simple show of hands. Owing to this procedure, the so-called elected muftis are known as *parmak müftüleri* (finger or hand-picked muftis), while the Ankara-backed militants describe the official muftis as 'muftis of the Christians' and 'puppet [*kukla*] muftis' (Akgönül 1999: 106; Küçükcan 1999: 62). In support of the Turkish activists' position, the Turkish government blacklisted the muftis appointed by Athens, barring them from visiting Turkey (ibid.: 213–215). In Thrace, the Ankara-backed muftis challenge the authority of their

government-appointed counterparts, accusing the Greek government of inter-
fering in their religious affairs. Greek courts have convicted the 'elected' muftis
of usurping the authority of the official muftis, who in their capacity as Muslim judges are also Greek civil servants. These court decisions attracted much
adverse publicity outside Greece, including a negative ruling by the European
Court of Human Rights which, however, carefully avoided pronouncing any
judgment on the question of the legal status of the muftis (December 1999). In
any case, it would have been an extremely difficult task for a European Court
to take a position in a matter involving antiquated judicial authorities
bestowed upon Muslim religious leaders in Greece. Such competences are
based on Islamic law and are neither prescribed by Lausanne nor applied by
any European, or for that matter moderate Islamic, state.[9]

Turkish-speaking Muslims of Thrace

Turkish is the most frequently used language amongst the members of the
Muslim minority (Sella-Mazi 1999: 33–48). In accordance with official Greek
data, by the early 1990s about 56,000 Muslims identified themselves as turkophones, either by birth or through acculturation. Turkish-speaking Greek
citizens adopt Turkish names, publish numerous local newspapers, operate
their private local Turkish-language radio stations, watch Turkish satellite television broadcasts, converse freely in Turkish and use Turkish in Greek courts.
Those members of the Muslim minority who are of Turkish ethnic background
are permitted to describe themselves, individually, as being of Turkish descent.
 While denying the presence of a national Turkish community in Thrace,
Greece recognises the existence of a smaller group with Turkic ethnic origins
(*Türk asıllı*) within the larger family of the Muslim religious minority.[10] Thus,
on the individual level ethnic identity is a matter of self-ascription in Greece.
In an effort to obviate any confusion between ethnicity and nationality, the
Greeks address the Turkic section of the minority as *tourkogenis* (of Turkish
descent, culture and linguistic affiliation), as opposed to *Tourkos* (Turk), a term
which has national connotations since it defines the citizens of the Republic
of Turkey. The Turks see things differently. In accordance with the Gökalpian
nationalist ideology, all Balkan and Anatolian Muslim populations sharing a
common Ottoman-Islamic cultural heritage (Kurds, Lazes, Bosnians,
Torbeshes, etc.) belong to the larger Turkish national family.[11]
 The Muslims of Thrace maintain their own Turkish-language minority
schools, which, numbering almost 280, catered to a total of 7,019 elementary,
606 secondary and 159 high-school students during the academic year
1999–2000. Since 1920, Turkish-speaking Muslim deputies have represented
the minority in the Greek Parliament, often acting as intermediaries between
the minority and the Greek political elites, but also as intermediaries with the
Turkish consulate. Although the great majority of the Turkic Muslims in
Thrace are moderate and ready to work and prosper as citizens of the Greek
state, a small group of ethnocentric activists are not.

Undoubtedly, the most prominent figure of Thracian turkophones has been
Sadık Ahmet (1948–1995), a medical doctor, who was elected twice to the
Greek Parliament as an independent, in the elections of June 1989 and again in
April 1990. A Turkish ethnic nationalist, Sadık Ahmet was the protégé of Turkish Foreign Minister Mesut Yılmaz during the late 1980s, and developed close
ties with ultra-nationalist Turkish organisations, participating regularly at various
Pan-Turkic events (Aarbakke 2000: 389ff). In March 1990, the ultra-nationalist
federation of Turkish Hearths (*Türk Ocakları*) in Turkey awarded Sadık Ahmet
for his struggle to preserve Turkism in Thrace, while the Thracian activist
pledged allegiance to the Turkish nation (*Kıbrıs*, 26–31 March 1993). By contrast,
although extremely proud of his Turkic ethnic background and critical of restrictive measures imposed during the 1970s and 1980s, İbram Onsunoğlu, a Turkic
Muslim psychiatrist and politician, has been advocating Muslim loyalty to the
Greek state. Likewise, the former deputy of left-wing *Synaspismos* Mustafa
Mustafa has been a staunch advocate of the full-scale integration of the minority in Greek political and economic life (Aarbakke 2000: 408–9).

Pomak Muslims of Thrace

Down the centuries, the Pomaks, a largely slavophone Balkan Muslim ethnic
group, have been affected and shaped by many and diverse cultural influ-
ences (Popovic 1986: 169ff; Turan 1999: 69–83). The Pomaks have a long
presence in both Greek and Bulgarian Thrace. When Bulgaria annexed most
of the Rodopi area in 1912, the Pomaks were regarded as Bulgarian Muslims.
Nevertheless, while their ethnic origins remain obscure, Pomaks continue to
speak their native tongue and have managed to maintain their particular
ethno-cultural characteristics, distinguishing them from the rest of the Balkan
peoples (Seyppel 1989: 42). Presently, the Pomak population lives in small
settlements in the mountainous Rodopi regions of Thrace near the Bulgarian
border, with the biggest concentration situated in the Xanthi province where
they form 63.4 percent of the Muslim population (Dalégre 1997: 233).

As citizens of Greece and members of the largely turkophone Muslim
minority, it is essential that the Pomaks know Greek and Turkish. As for their
own language, they use it mainly within the family or for colloquial interaction with friends and acquaintances. Indeed, there is a great deal of
evidence showing that the Pomaks of Thrace are passing through a period of
identity crisis, serious enough for ethnographer Tatjana Seyppel to characterise them as an 'endangered Balkan population':

> Factually, no Pomak can think of himself as Greek … Nobody wishes to be Bul-
> garian, in spite of all linguistic relationships. Now and then they claim to be
> Turkish, but what they actually mean seems to be that they are Muslim. Their
> relationship to Turks may be generally described as that of a client who seeks help
> and assistance from a stronger organisation that is recognised to a certain extent
> by law – whereas they, the Pomaks, are not. When asked as to their identity,
> Pomaks tend to hesitate. Some people prefer to utter the word 'Pomak' only in a
> subdued manner, just like the word 'Gypsy' or 'Jew' elsewhere (1989: 46–47).

Certainly one major reason for the current Pomak identity crisis is the integration over the last forty years of Pomak children into a Turkish-language minority education system that includes no reference to Pomak language and culture. Having become Turkish-speaking, many Pomaks also feel an affinity towards Turkey. According to a social anthropologist, Yannis Frangopoulos, who conducted research in the Pomak villages of Thrace, 'L'ethnicité pomaque et, d'un autre côté, la religion musulmane, suivie par un nationalisme turc émergeant, se trouvent en interaction constante et même en relation antagoniste' (1994: 153).

In addition, a feeling of exclusion from the benefits of the state has further driven the Pomaks to identify with the larger ethnic Turkic group. It should be remembered that the Turkish-speakers in Thrace, particularly those in cities, enjoy a certain respect among the members of the minority as the descendants of the Ottoman imperial tradition. It is also this group that, enjoying the privileges that come with proximity to the Turkish Consulate in Komotini, forms the minority's elite. One of the two deputies in the Greek Parliament, Galip Galip should be considered as a successful example of an acculturated turkophone of Pomak origin who over the years succeeded in maintaining a privileged relationship with both the local Greek political establishment (he is a deputy of PASOK, the Panellenic Socialist Party) and Turkish consular circles.

In fact, some of the most nationalistic minority figures in Thrace are of Pomak and Roma descent. A key figure in this respect is Mehmet Emin Aga, a politician and former acting mufti of Xanthi. The son of the late mufti of Xanthi Mustafa Hilmi Aga (1905–1990), he has played a pivotal role in the campaign for the turkification of the Pomaks in Thrace during the last forty years. In an interview for an Athenian daily newspaper during the early 1980s, Aga rejected his Pomak origins and declared that his mother country was Turkey and warned the Greek authorities that 'if Greece does not solve our problems in Western Thrace, we will resort to the mother country Turkey in order to get a satisfactory solution' (*Ta Nea*, 12 March 1984).

However, the rampant Kemalist infiltration in Thrace since the 1930s has provoked a backlash by the still-predominant conservative religious circles, especially among the rank and file Pomak population. In the inter-war years powerful organisations like the Union of Muslims in Greece (*İttihat-ı İslam Cemiyeti*) and the Islamic Teachers' Association (*Müslüman Muallimler Birliği*) stressed the religious character of the minority and remained loyal to the Greek state (Aydınlı 1971: 369–75; Özgüç 1974: 71–74; Minaidis 1990: 249–51). More recently, signs of self-assertion have coincided with a tendency in Athens to lay emphasis on the separate ethno-cultural identity of the Pomaks. Leading Pomaks, such as the present-day muftis Hafız Cemali Meço (Komotini) and Mehmet Emin Şinikoğlu (Xanthi) and Xanthi councillor Raif Sabuncu have become exponents of such sentiments (*Eleftheros Typos*, 20 August 1993).

In an attempt to give substance to the Pomak ethnic identity, a group of Thracian Muslim teachers[12] published the first Pomak–Greek, Greek–Pomak dictionaries (Karahoca 1995), and a Pomak-language newspaper, *Zagalisa*, has been circulating in Komotini since October 1997. Another newspaper, *Gazete Pomaci*, followed in Xanthi a couple of months later. Such initiatives mark what could be considered the first steps in recording Pomak, one of the last oral languages of the European Union (Syrigos 1995: 8–9). These initiatives were taken under the auspices of the Centre for Pomak Studies in Komotini, whose president Ömer Hamdi expressed publicly his discontent with Turkish pressure for assimilation and called upon the Greek government to take positive steps to protect Pomak ethnicity and culture in Greek Thrace (*Macedonian Press Agency*, 25 August 2000). Such efforts, however, have been piecemeal; much more serious and scholarly research has to be undertaken, possibly, as one observer suggested, at the University of Thrace (Syrigos 1999–2000: 43–84). Meanwhile, the Turks brush away these expressions of defiance as Greek propaganda, and they brand those who emphasise their Pomak identity as 'tools of the Greek administration'.

Muslim Roma (Gypsies) of Thrace

Another ethno-cultural group whose presence in Thrace dates back to the pre-Ottoman period is the Roma (Zenginis 1994: 13). The Greek Gypsies professing Islam are known as the *Horahane* Roma and speak a variation of Romany, the language of the *Athingani/Çingene*. The Horahane Roma are concentrated in the Evros prefecture and at Ifestos, the Gypsy quarter of Komotini. During the last twenty years, a considerable number of Roma Muslims have moved to the urban centres of Greece. They are to be found in high concentrations in the working-class suburbs of Athens, such as Elefsis and Liosia. Today, the Roma are one of the fastest growing groups in Greece. According to Efstathios Zenginis, there are almost 24,000 Roma Greek citizens in Thrace (ibid.: 53–69).

Whether Christian or Muslim, the Roma have historically remained at the bottom of society both because of their colour and their nomadic mode of life. Like the Muslim Pomak population, the Horahane Romany are passing through a period of identity crisis. Certain Muslim Gypsies, headed by Ahmet Faikoğlu, have already identified themselves with Ankara, and are in close cooperation with the Turkish Consulate of Komotini. Others, however, have remained faithful to their Romany background, staying loyal to the Greek state. This is particularly so in Alexandroupolis and Didymoteicho, where the majority of the Muslim population is of Roma origin.

The Muslim minority and the Greek state: a new direction

The Muslim population of Thrace – and in particular those of Turkic descent – have been affected by bad relations between Greece and Turkey. During the forty-year period between 1924 and 1964, successive Greek governments chose to ignore the presence of the Muslims in Thrace, and the traditional policy towards the minority was one of benign neglect. Athens displayed a similar lack of interest in the Christian population of Thrace. This resulted in a massive wave of out-migration both to the large urban centres or Greece and abroad, especially in the 1950s and 1960s. With the escalation of anti-Greek measures in Turkey during the Cyprus crisis, successive Greek governments, but especially the military junta (1967–1974), reciprocated by applying certain restrictive measures in Thrace. However, at no time did the measures carried out in Greece acquire the harshness or heavy-handedness to which the Turkish government subjected the Greek Orthodox in Istanbul and Imbros/Gökçeada. In particular, Athens did not resort to such extreme measures as massive deportation of minorities or the instigation of destructive anti-minority riots.

The events in Cyprus in 1974 and Turkish claims in the Aegean did not make matters easier for the Muslim minority in Thrace. The perception that Turkey harbours expansionist designs against Greece is deeply embedded in Greek public opinion. During the 1970s, 1980s and early 1990s, a defensive nationalism and sentiments of mistrust towards those members of the Muslim minority who exhibited strong Turkish sympathies prevailed among Greeks, who feared that Ankara might be tempted to follow the Cyprus precedent in Greek Thrace.

However, the combination of Greece's entry into Europe and an increasing international sensitivity to questions of human and minority rights in the post-Cold War era prompted Athens to pay closer attention to matters involving its minorities, as a result of which it became more responsive to the wishes of its Muslim citizens (Whitman 1992; Kottakis 2000: 197–203). This coincided with a growing confidence due to Greece's membership in the European Union and its enhanced role as a stabilising force in the conflict-torn Balkans. In the political sphere, Athens committed itself to adhere fully to the principles of *isonomia* (equality before the law) and *isopoliteia* (equality of civil/civic rights) for all Greek citizens irrespective of religion or ethnic origin. A televised panel discussion including the leaders of the three major Greek parties on 12 March 1990 can be considered a turning point in this direction. Regarding the Thracian issue, Andreas Papandreou (PASOK), Constantine Mitsotakis (New Democracy) and Charilaos Florakis (Communist Party of Greece) agreed that: 'Greece's policy [in Thrace] must be based on the economic and cultural development of the area. We have done nothing to develop the region. There must be strict observance of the principle of equal treatment' (*Athens News Agency*, 13 March 1990).

Greece has slowly but steadily revised its policy towards the Thracian minority, a move supported by the Mitsotakis government between 1992 and 1993, and given new impetus by the present Simitis government. A more positive attitude towards the Thracian minority can be traced to August 1992, when Michalis Papakonstantinou was appointed foreign minister. The practice of subjecting the minorities to retaliatory and punitive measures on a tit-for-tat basis with Turkey has gradually been abandoned. In this context, plans to establish an agricultural prison in Thrace similar to that set up decades earlier by the Turkish government in the Greek-inhabited island of Imbros were abandoned.

Since the mid-1990s, a new school of thought has emerged in Greece that demonstrates greater readiness to tolerate a Turkic ethnic entity in Thrace so long as there is no questioning of its loyalty to the Greek state and to the inviolability of the Lausanne Greek–Turkish borders. Headed by influential personalities such as Professor Christos Rozakis, Vice President of the European Court of Human Rights, the late Yiannos Kranidiotis, and Professor Nikos Mouzelis of the London School of Economics, a vocal section of Greek public opinion advocates the eradication of any remnants of prejudicial attitudes towards minority ethnic, linguistic and religious groups (Rozakis 1997: 20–22; Tsitselikis and Christopoulos 1997: 435–46; Kranidiotis 1999: 389–407; Heraclides 2001: 312–15). Such circles enjoy the endorsement of the modern-minded section of the Simitis government and especially of Foreign Minister George Papandreou, who has publicly reaffirmed the right to individual self-identification by every Greek citizen regardless of ethnic background (interview of G. Papandreou for Flash Radio, 29 July 1999).

However, a large section of Greek public opinion and particular factions of both major Greek political parties, PASOK and New Democracy, continue to view such ideas with apprehension so long as the Turkish Kemalist establishment remains antagonistic towards Greece. Such apprehensions are articulated by Komotini deputy of New Democracy Evripidis Stylianidis (his article suggesting a new approach to the minority issue appeared in *Ependytis* 27.2.1999) and are shared to a large extent by the PASOK deputy of Xanthi, Panayiotis Sgouridis (2000). Nevertheless, there is a consensus in Greece that past policies towards the Muslim minority were short-sighted and counterproductive. To redress this situation, measures have been taken to integrate the minority into mainstream Greek life, particularly in the economic sphere from the early 1990s. Large amounts of European Union money earmarked for Greece under the European Union programmes for structural aid are already being spent on projects to improve infrastructure, including motorways linking Thrace with the rest of Greece and Bulgaria. Furthermore, between 1995 and 2000 restrictions and official permits for entering the controlled military zone along the Greek–Bulgarian border were gradually lifted, making conditions better for forty villages inhabited predominantly by Pomaks (*Pomakohoria*). As Muslim Pomak Greek citizens of the Rodopi region benefit from the increased economic activity in Thrace, signs of a greater willingness to integrate into Greek society are already visible.

In 1997, Greece's signing of the Council of Europe's Framework Convention for the Protection of Minorities prompted the Simitis government to accelerate the pace of reform in Thrace. Under this convention, Greece is held solely responsible for providing high-quality education for the Muslim minority. Responding to these responsibilities, the Greek government has begun to apply a bilingual Greek–Turkish education programme in Thrace, and already a number of such schools operate in the Rodopi district. In tandem with this, a policy of positive discrimination to expedite the entry of

Muslims into the Greek higher-education establishment has been introduced, and a quota system ensures that Muslims are employed in the Greek banks. Furthermore, controversial Article 19 of the Greek citizenship law has been revoked and Muslims can now freely buy immovable property in Thrace.

The right of members of the Muslim minority to form Turkish organisations with a clearly ethno-nationalist agenda has been a highly controversial issue, particularly during the 1980s. The existence of such associations can be traced back to the late 1920s. The Turkish Youth Associations (*Türk Gençler Birliği*) in Xanthi and Komotini were formed in 1927 and 1928 respectively. In 1936, the Association of Turkish Teachers of Western Thrace (*Batı Trakya Türk Öğretmenler Birliği*) was founded. The main focus of such associations was to promote Turkishness and Kemalism among the members of the Muslim minority as well as to act as a counterbalance to organisations that emphasised the religious identity of the minority, such as the Muslim Teachers Union (*Müslüman Muallimler Birliği*). During the post-1974 period, a number of minority organisations was constituted, including the Consultative Association of the Turkish Minority (*Türk Azınlığı Danışma Kurumu*) and the University Graduates Society of the Turkish Minority of Western Thrace (*Batı Trakya Türk Azınlığı Yüksek Tahsilliler Derneği*). Some of these associations soon fell victim to intra-minority rivalries while others, such as the Union of Turkish Associations of Western Thrace, were outlawed in 1986. However, a combination of the recent change of approach towards minority issues together with the High Court's reversing of a previous restriction on the operation of the Turkish Union of Xanthi (*Eleftherotypia*, 12 December 2000) has served to alleviate tensions in this area.

Modernists in Greece argue that the integration of the Muslim minority into the Greek political, economic and cultural apparatus will eliminate any possibility of a future eruption of inter-communal tensions such as witnessed in Komotini in January and February 1990 (Heraclides 1997: 11ff). In this context, religious leaders have a pivotal role to play. A dialogue similar to that ongoing between Patriarch Bartholomeos and the Muslim spiritual leadership in Turkey should be inaugurated by local religious heads of both religions in Thrace. The visit of the Greek Orthodox Metropolitan Panteleimon of Xanthi to the official residence of Mufti Mehmet Emin Şinikoğlu during the Muslim religious festival in January 1998 is to be considered a step in the right direction. Such gestures go some way to assuaging the Muslim-Christian animosity aggravated by clerics such as Mehmet Emin Aga and İbrahim Şerif, as well as by some local Greek Orthodox church leaders and Greek ultra-nationalist groups. Fortunately, though, with the recent improvement in Greek–Turkish relations, such extreme nationalists from both groups appear to have been marginalised, while a tendency to favour coexistence and cooperation between all ethno-religious groups is gaining ground. In the long run, the benefits of belonging to the economically prosperous and politically democratic European family of nations are likely to starve agitators of ethnic or religious antagonism of support.

Conclusions: towards new multilateral minority protection instruments

Concluded eighty years ago, the old Lausanne arrangement still remains in force, and still constitutes a reference point in Greek–Turkish minority issues. Yet, to a large extent this arrangement failed to safeguard the rights of the minorities as is amply attested by the almost complete disappearance of the Greek Orthodox community of Turkey. Given the pre-existing tensions between Greece and Turkey, it is natural that the historical, religious and cultural affiliations to respective 'mother countries' proved detrimental to the relations between minority and majority groups. In the situation that ensued, and against a backdrop of international indifference, the minorities had to rely on the idea of reciprocity, but this was doubly flawed: in a fundamental sense in that reciprocity more often than not meant retaliation, and in a practical sense in that although numerically similar the two minority communities were not symmetrical at all. On the one hand was a prosperous, well-educated, cosmopolitan and high-profile minority in Istanbul; on the other, an introverted rural community of devout Islamic character and backward Ottoman ways, one that until the 1980s lacked a vocal elite. In diplomatic terms, the Greek side had much less room to manoeuvre given the greater stakes involved with the Constantinopolitan Greek Orthodox minority and its especial vulnerability.

In this atmosphere of enmity and mistrust, even narrowly focused and technical agreements between Greece and Turkey, such as the protocols of 1951 and 1968 regulating minority education, failed to promote the interests of the minorities. In Thrace, these protocols produced a structure of Turkish education that might at best have prepared students for Turkey, but certainly not for Greece. Nor did they safeguard Greek Orthodox minority education in Imbros/Gökçeada, or the functioning of the Theological School of Chalki. It is for these reasons that the Lausanne bilateral approach to minority issues appears to be receding as Greece and Turkey sign up to a number of international minority rights documents and conventions.[13]

This development offers new opportunities to the minorities in Greece and Turkey by enabling them to escape the strict bilateralism imposed by Lausanne. With access to global legal redress, these minorities should experience better protection of their rights. Indeed, in the context of its participation in the European Union, the Greek government has already initiated a process aimed at facilitating the full enjoyment of equal rights and opportunities by the Muslims of Thrace. On the other side of the Aegean, a genuine convergence with the European Union principles of democracy and respect for minority and human rights would greatly benefit the Ecumenical Patriarchate and the remaining Greek Orthodox. Above all, if these two Aegean neighbours are to cooperate within an European Union context, historical enmities and suspicions must be replaced with understanding and tolerance. In this regard, the minorities themselves have a constructive role to play, in that they are the only groups that have a clear understanding of both cultures. Such an understanding is extremely valuable, for although neighbours, contemporary Greeks and Turks know very little about each other. In this manner the minorities' contested identities could be transformed into valuable assets in promoting Greek–Turkish understanding and goodwill. If Greek–Turkish friendship is to take root, the Lausanne minorities and their institutions must be seen not as a burden but as rare commodities.

Notes

1. *League of Nations Treaty Series* (1923): 29–35.
2. In this essay the author, himself a member of the Greek Orthodox minority of Turkey, expresses personal views which are based on extensive research of primary and secondary sources regarding Greek–Turkish minority issues.
3. *Lausanne Conference on Near Eastern Affairs*: 320–33.
4. Various Turkish observers have adopted the official Ankara view that the Greek nationals in Istanbul were in Turkey solely as a result of the 1930 treaty (Bölükbaşı 1992: 43–44) and prefer to ignore the fact that these people were natives of Istanbul who, between 1922 and 1930, remained in Turkey as non-exchangeables under the terms of the Treaty of Lausanne.
5. The Hellene Greek Orthodox were 12,000-strong in the early 1960s. Of these only 500 elderly were allowed to remain in Istanbul, while another 2,000 who used to move between Istanbul and Greece were denied permission to return to Turkey. The remaining 9,500 were deported to Greece during the years 1965 to 1967.
6. *Lausanne Conference Treaty Series*: 21
7. The Norwegian researcher Vemund Aarbakke has recently produced an extensive and comprehensive study of the Muslim minority in Greek Thrace. This doctoral thesis, submitted at the University of Bergen, has a thorough grasp of internal minority politics and developments (Aarbakke 2000).
8. *Statistika Apotelesmata Apografis tou Plythismou tis Ellados 15$^{\underline{η}}$–16$^{\underline{η}}$ a·°ô~ 1928 [Statistical Data of the Population Census of Greece, 15–16 May 1928]*: 280f.
9. A debate regarding the judicial authority of the muftis was initiated by the Pan-Hellenic Greek Association of Lawyers which in June 1992 concluded that these competences are unconstitutional and incompatible with the secular European legal order. They therefore proposed the revision of Article 5 of the Mufti Law (no. 1920/1991) that lays down the competences of the Muslim religious leaders in Thrace (Vroutsis 1999–2000: 85–88).
10. I consider the term Turkic as the most appropriate for the members of the minority who are turkophone or of Turkish racial descent. This term rightly draws a clear distinction between ethnic and national identity. Like the Turkic Uzbeks, Uygurs or Azeris, the Turkic inhabitants of Thrace can be considered racially akin to the Turks of Anatolia but without any political or irredentist affiliation or loyalty to the Turkish Republic.
11. For the views of the Turkish nationalist philosopher Ziya Gökalp see his pioneering work, *Türkçülüğün Esasları [Principles of Turkism]* Istanbul, 1987, 3rd ed.
12. Rıdvan Karahoca, Aydın Mumin and Muzaffer Cemali Kapıca.
13. Of these the most far-reaching are the provisions for minorities in the documents of the Conference on Security and Cooperation in Europe concluded in Vienna (1989), Copenhagen (1990), Moscow (1991) and Helsinki (1992). They contain detailed political commitments regarding minorities and significantly strengthen existing provisions for their fair treatment in Europe (Heraclides 1993a, 1993b; Stavros 1995: 6). Furthermore, the United Nations and the Council of Europe have adopted a series of conventions regarding the status and the protection of minorities.

10

Inter-war Town Planning and the Refugee Problem in Greece

TEMPORARY 'SOLUTIONS' AND LONG-TERM DYSFUNCTIONS

Alexandra Yerolympos

Introduction

In the quest for the optimum outcome of spatial arrangements, the task of the town planner involves unemotional, 'scientific' calculations and long-term provisioning. The populations involved in these plans are treated as abstract human categories, and a considerable length of time is necessary before the planning strategies result in specific schemes and programmes of action. However, in the context of 1920s Greece thousands of homeless refugees were urgently in need of shelter, and to them, with their lives and personal prospects at stake, time was of the essence. In such circumstances, arguments favouring speedy ad hoc decisions are not easily dismissed, but there is nevertheless a widely acknowledged need for well balanced and thoroughly researched programmes. I was well aware of this dilemma when examining the problems of refugee settlement during the inter-war period in Greece. As a result of eighty years' distance and hindsight, the critical questions of the time can now be approached more dispassionately, and, moreover, the consequences of the so-called solutions that were adopted are apparent for all to see.

The influx of 1.2 million destitute people into a small state with a population of only five million would inevitably and profoundly affect the country's overall pattern of urban settlements, as well as individual settlements themselves. Here we will concentrate on three areas: the procedures designed to control and manage urban expansion in the nascent Greek state;

the main principles governing urban planning immediately prior to the compulsory exchange of populations between Greece and Turkey in 1923; and the ways in which these principles were implemented, showing how the urgent need to house the massive wave of refugees led in practice to planning principles being diluted or even abandoned altogether.

Control and management of urban expansion in pre-Lausanne Greece

In the small state that emerged in the nineteenth century in devastated areas of the Peloponnese and the southern Greek mainland, the establishment of a network of properly functioning towns capable of eventual expansion was an urgent priority. Immediately, great efforts were made to reconstruct existing settlements and to found new cities. There was a need to attract new inhabitants – internally displaced as well as peasants – in order to promote urbanisation and the interior colonisation of what was then still a predominantly rural and sparsely populated country. Since the first National Convention of 3 June 1831, and almost up until the 1910s, the general outline of the programme was as follows: land would be offered gratis as an incentive to those 'wishing to construct cities or suburbs on land currently derelict, or on any other land they wish, provided only that a *plan* is submitted' (emphasis added). The legislation included more specific stipulations too: the surface of the individual plots would not exceed six hundred square metres; space in the area to be developed should be reserved for public and municipal buildings; building on land grants should commence within one year of the grant; and sale of the land was not permitted.

The aim was to stipulate a regular design as a model pattern for the modern Greek city, i.e., to lay down a set of criteria for the selection of a suitable site, which should enjoy good access, adequate transport networks, fertile farming land and an adequate water supply.[1] If networks did not exist, the eventual cost of establishing them had to be considered. As far as location was concerned, the legislation expressed a preference for sea coasts, rivers or south- or east-facing hill slopes. A town plan was to be drawn up, for which an orthogonal grid was recommended;[2] it should be oriented with its four corners to the four points of the compass. Streets were to be constructed to a prescribed width, and supplemented by the construction of sidewalks, arcades and alleyways. Several squares, not overwhelmingly large, should be distributed symmetrically around the city. Public and religious buildings, such as the church, town hall, school and hotel, should be constructed around a large free space in order to form a city centre. Cemeteries, hospitals, lunatic asylums and prisons, however, should be located on the outskirts of the city. Noisy or dirty workshops, factories, slaughterhouses, tanneries, etc.,[3] were also assigned to special areas.

Similar planning initiatives were under way at the same time in the neighbouring Balkan countries of Serbia and Romania. The strategies involved in the building of new towns – the offering of free land, the legal procedures employed and the urban design adopted as a standard pattern – were almost identical in the newly formed Balkan states; they all expressed the same desire to colonise large areas of land and to urbanise rural populations (Yerolympos 1996). In almost all cases the planning model adopted was the chessboard plan, which involved the allocation of empty blocks to public buildings and open space, the distribution of equally sized building lots (which could be distributed by lottery without invidious differences in the size of plots), accessibility, and the flexibility of design that allowed for future expansion. The idea is extremely old; it goes back to the standard plan of Roman and mediaeval towns. It is intended to help the inhabitants settle down and resume economic activity as rapidly as possible, and constituted a rational solution for dealing swiftly with large-scale problems of settlement, only possible, of course, in a centrally administered nation-state. Yet in Greece, rather than creating properly conceived urban configurations, the planning instruments put forth served only to divide up and privatise the land, creating a series of semi-rural housing settlements.

It was only towards the end of the so-called period of rural colonisation (Panayiotopoulos 1980), after the 1870s, when substantial inward movement from the countryside to the city began, that the search for methods to control urban expansion in Greece started. The issue was given added urgency by the arrival of the first refugees in the years leading up to 1920 [4](for later rural-urban population shifts see Table 10.1). It was stimulated and enriched by the growing international interest in the new discipline of town planning, which involved wide-ranging debate and exchange of experiences between different countries. In general terms, the techniques and operational parameters involved in town planning were now enhanced by a social concern that could not be met by planners merely seeking the best possible spatial design for a city. Increasingly, there was also an interest in the community life of the citizens, the redistribution of the added value of the land accruing from development, and the improvement of living conditions for the city's new inhabitants. Population growth and expansion were no longer regarded as desirable purely in themselves.

Demographic developments in Athens and Piraeus illustrate the problem vividly. Until 1923, the two cities were still separate entities, but with rapidly growing populations – a combined population of 242,300 in 1907 rose to

Table 10.1 Proportion of Greece's population in urban, semi-urban and rural environments, 1920–1940

	1920	*1928*	*1940*
urban (cities of more than 10,000 inhabitants)	22.9%	31.1%	32.8%
semi-urban (settlements of 2,000–10,000 inhabitants)	15.2%	14.5%	14.8%
rural	61.9%	54.4%	52.4%

Source: Greek National Censuses

453,000 in 1920 (see Censuses). Although Athens had grown in size from 272 hectares in 1860 to 2,162 hectares in 1916, there was still no provision for public spaces, transport and infrastructure. In 1920 Athens, population density had fallen from 171 individuals per hectare to 75, but at the same time the housing conditions of low-income groups in the centre and on the outskirts of the city had deteriorated. According to research conducted by the National Finance Ministry in 1920, the number of inhabitants per dwelling ranged from 10.75 to 13 (Guizeli 1984). Parallel studies concerning the incidence of tuberculosis as a cause of death show that in 1920, 18 percent of the male population died of the disease, but that the proportion rose to 38 percent among the working-class population (ibid.). A similar study of Jewish neighbourhoods on the outskirts of Thessaloniki, conducted by the Jewish community in 1897, reached equally depressing conclusions on the living conditions of the impoverished groups pouring into the city (Yerolympos 1994). In all these cases, the main reason for wretched living conditions was the city's lack of readiness to provide the infrastructural support necessitated by rapid expansion.

New principles of town planning after the First World War

Fuelled by the absence of a proper legislative framework in the previous century, the debate was made all the more urgent after the Balkan Wars by the incorporation of the new territories (*nees chores*) in the north. Following the departure of the Muslim Ottomans and other ethnic groups (mainly Bulgarians), both small and large cities in this region that had developed their own individual character now found themselves in need of extensive restoration and regeneration. The large-scale war damage inflicted on many of the cities (e.g., Serres 1913, and market towns and villages of eastern Macedonia 1913–1918), and the great fire of Thessaloniki in 1917, provided the opportunity for sophisticated planning initiatives, ready for full implementation by the beginning of the 1920s. In a climate favouring social reforms and original political initiatives, the newly acquired territories were viewed as a field for experimentation that could attract international interest and support and also secure the social and cultural assimilation of the various ethnic groups through universally accepted ideals of human progress.[5] This assimilation had to be achieved, of course, with the consent of the groups involved. Under the direction of the reformist Minister of Communications, Alexander Papanastasiou (at the time responsible for the Town Planning Reform in Greece), field research on the living standards and local economic and social conditions of the inhabitants was undertaken. This was followed by legislation and programmes that respected the specific features of the area, and even involved the participation of different social groups in the drafting of particular measures (Hadjimichalis et al. 1988).

For 170 devastated settlements in eastern Macedonia, the proposal was for a network of rural settlements that could serve as a model for similar arrangements on a national scale. Modern settlements breaking with traditional patterns of life were established, and enforced agrarian reform was introduced, encouraging the inhabitants to organise in cooperatives. The designs that were produced by foreign (mainly British) planners testify to their knowledge of contemporary standards of layout, and are reminiscent of designs for garden suburbs: the streets have an organic pattern and follow the topography of the site; there is ample provision for public space, sanitary facilities and infrastructure networks; civic buildings are suitably located; and there is careful design of both private lots and collective spaces, which combine to form interesting and lively neighbourhood units (Kafkoula 1992: 4–10).

The redesign of multiethnic Thessaloniki, whose centre was almost completely destroyed by fire in 1917, was the showpiece of the Liberal government. Here, all the major themes of twentieth-century planning appeared: civic centre, urban parks, university campus, garden suburbs, workers' housing, residential neighbourhood units, industrial zones, etc. Implementation of the plans involved sophisticated techniques and marked a clean break with the nineteenth-century planning tradition. The main objective was to put an end to individualistic practices in the making of urban space and, in their place, to resuscitate the territorial unit (the *quartier* or neighbourhood) as the basis of social solidarity (Yerolympos 1995). Thus, cooperative movements and building societies were to be encouraged and new types of community units were to be introduced so that inhabitants could break away from traditional ethnic and religious affiliations.

It is clear that this kind of discourse reflected the major themes of reformist thought of the time, as well as the concomitant faith in social engineering. Through city planning procedures and proper urban layout, urban dwellers would eventually adopt more socially-aware attitudes, public interest would prevail over individual rights, and land speculation would be adequately controlled in the best interest of lower-income groups and the whole community.

The 1923 Planning Act 'on the planning of cities, towns and settlements, and the construction thereof' draws heavily on all these reformist concepts, incorporating them in a single legal text. However, the massive influx of refugees was to undermine this idealistic project, despite the vehement objections of its authors, who strove in vain to implement their vision throughout the 1920s.[6]

Today it is easy to dismiss the unshakeable certainties of the planners of the early twentieth century – including their conviction that social harmony could be achieved through town planning – as naïve or unsophisticated. However, the multiple coincidence in time of the approval of the Planning Act, the arrival of the refugees and the new legislation[7] regulating their settlement was extremely unfortunate.

Implementation of refugee settlement

The urgency of the settlement problem and the extent of colonisation envisaged entailed the immediate implementation of mechanisms for central planning, design and construction, yet regrettably the comprehensive programme of the refugee settlements was not coordinated with the planning of cities. The autonomy of the various agencies involved (Refugee Settlement Commission, welfare services, etc.) meant that each operated independently of the other. Thus, although this was the first operation of organised social housing on Greek soil – and on a very large scale – the opportunity for concerted large-scale planning was missed. Firstly, the selection of sites itself was limited by the scarcity of public land; thus from the outset a full range of options was not available. Secondly, in execution, the layout of both rural and urban refugee settlements was rudimentary. The law concerning the settlement of refugees stipulated that each settlement be 'laid out according to a simple plan and divided into lots'. The result was that variations of simple orthogonal designs were employed, often repeating just one basic type of layout. The public spaces and amenities were kept to a minimum, often in the form of an empty block supplying only the most basic amenities: school, church and city square, and this despite the fact that the refugee settlements were planted amidst unbuilt space on the outskirts of the cities. This poor provision of public space meant that even in the future the new districts would not be able to develop other community functions. As for the urban settlements, typically their distance from the city (due to the random availability of public land) created a lack of cohesion and made it difficult for the new settlement to be assimilated into the existing urban context.

The problems are well illustrated in northern Greece where a dense network of rural settlements was established as well as a series of refugee districts on the outskirts of the main cities. Although the state had already prepared, tried and amended a plan of action to meet Greece's planning needs, it suddenly found itself compelled to resort to even more primitive expediencies than the practices of the nineteenth century.

A typical victim of these developments was the programme of Alexander Papanastasiou for the reconstruction of eastern Macedonia (see above). The settling of the refugees after 1922 meant that the numerous plans that had been prepared – and in some cases that had been approved and were awaiting implementation – were simply abandoned. The settlements remained in their first location, following a pattern established ad hoc by newcomers arriving and former residents returning, and were legalised after the event by the allocation plans of the Ministry of Agriculture. Indeed, developments after 1923 are characterised by the widespread application of demonstrably makeshift and crudely standardised plans, which when compared to the original 'experimental' and exemplary programmes of action, are seen to involve critical compromises and simplifications (Kafkoula 1990, 1992).

Between 1923 and 1927, the Ministry of Communications (responsible for town planning) persevered to preserve the coherence of overall policy. It bombarded the Ministry of Public Works, the Ministry of Health and Welfare, prefectures and police departments with letters in the hope of achieving at least some coordination of the various activities. In its circulars, the Ministry reminded the agencies that the founding of a refugee settlement next to a town or city corresponds exactly to an extension of the city, and that such development must be carried out in accordance with the new urban plan because 'otherwise serious problems will arise'. The Ministry also had to intervene and admonish when areas set aside as free public spaces in the new plans were occupied by the local authorities and earmarked for refugee housing. Such land was only to be developed in exceptional cases and 'only in the form of temporary wooden constructions', 'of modest dimensions' and 'at points away from the centre' so as not to 'offer any impediment to circulation or cause nuisance to the other residents or landowners'.[8] Sadly, however earnestly the Ministry urged that development should not be allowed on such areas, its pleas fell on deaf ears.

This absurd tug-of-war continued until 1927, when planning and construction of refugee housing was explicitly and categorically removed from the remit of the Ministry of Communications and ceased to come under the provisions of the 1923 Planning Act. From this point onwards, refugee housing would be regulated by special laws and orders in council. For the next four years, responsibility for the construction of refugee dwellings and settlements, as well as schools, churches, manufacturing and other relevant facilities was transferred to the Ministry of Health 'without compliance with the legislation on the planning of cities or with any related legislation or provisions'.[9] At the end of this period, the powers to override the town-planning legislation were extended for a further two years.[10]

Although in theory an Act of Parliament in 1934[11] confined the permitted deviations from planning law to the areas within the bounds of the then-existing refugee settlements, in practice a situation of planning anarchy was perpetuated, with innumerable cunning deviations being allowed. 'It should be noted that the explicit exemptions had a more widespread and adverse effect on town planning in the large urban centres,' declared a disenchanted A. Dimitrakopoulos, director at the Ministry of Communications in 1937. At the same time, the Ministry made every effort to alert other government and social agencies to the problems that would be created in the long term by the planning anarchy and the total lack of properly researched plans for urban development. It insisted that no design or initiative could prove effective unless 'the planning aspect of the settlement of the refugees was subjected to the general laws of the State ... and the administration was left free to impose checks on unauthorised construction outside the city plan'. However, the Ministry's crusade proved fruitless and 'political interest prevailed'. The consequences for the Greek city have since then been evident for all to see.[12]

Evaluation

Questions may arise as to the reasons for this total divorce of tasks between town-planning services and agencies on the one hand and the refugee settlement committees on the other. In addressing this question, consideration must be given to the fact that the urgent need to provide for large numbers of refugees arriving in successive waves made it almost impossible to devote the necessary time to preparation of detailed plans, to optimisation of objectives and to training of staff in local offices. In order to allow speedy procedures of expropriation and to facilitate negotiations with the fewest possible individual land owners, important decisions had to be taken instantly for the acquisition of large pieces of land with clearly defined property status. As early as October 1922 (in immediate response to the Smyrna catastrophe) the Refugee Settlement Treasury, a non-governmental agency, was set up to provide assistance, relief and shelter. Drawing from the model of the French programme of reconstruction after the First World War,[13] the Refugee Settlement Treasury was an autonomous body with unlimited power of decision. The Refugee Settlement Commission, which replaced it one year later under the auspices of the League of Nations, was also completely autonomous and had final power of decision over all procedures relating to the research, financing and implementation of settlement programmes. In 1930, when the Refugee Settlement Commission was dissolved, 147,000 families had been settled in rural areas and 125,000 families in urban areas (Pelagidis 1997: 235–296).[14] It is certain that if 'regular' planning procedures had been followed, numerical results would have been much poorer, while the desired 'quality' of settlements would remain to be proven. It should also be borne in mind that in 1922 Greece was in dire financial straits; the settlement of refugees relied on massive foreign loans extended under strictly defined conditions relating to management, 'efficiency' and type and modality of expenditure. The task was indeed massive. Its magnitude is borne out by the figures of the 1928 census:

- Athens, Piraeus and Thessaloniki each received between 100,000 and 130,000 refugees.
- Several northern Greek cities received more than 10,000 refugees each, in some cases more than doubling the population. For instance, in Kavala 29,000 refugees were added to the existing population of 23,000, in Drama 22,000 refugees were added to the existing population of 17,000, in Serres 15,000 refugees to 15,000, in Xanthe 15,000 to 16,000, and in Komotini 11,000 to 21,000.
- In ten more cities, the refugees constituted 20 to 60 percent of the inhabitants in 1928. For instance, refugees accounted for 48 and 58 percent of the total populations in Katerini and Giannitsa, 59 percent in Alexandroupolis, 43 percent in Veroia, and 40 percent in Edessa. Kilkis which had lost almost its entire population of 5,700 in 1913 had increased its population to 6,800 by 1928.
- In general, the urban population in all Greek cities with more than 20,000 inhabitants consisted of three almost-equal groups: natives (35 percent), internal migrants (33.3 percent), and refugees (31.7 percent).

Equally impressive are the numbers of the new rural settlements created for refugees. Altogether they totalled 1,954 small villages and towns: 1,047 in Macedonia, 574 in Thrace, and 331 dispersed all over Greece.

The figures make it quite plain that the cities and towns of the country, and especially those of northern Greece, were exposed to significant population upheaval. When considered together with the changes involved in integrating the cities and towns into the Greek state just a few years before, the pressing need for new planning measures becomes all the clearer. Although the other agencies continued to ignore or find some way around its regulations, the Ministry of Communications persevered in promoting its overall planning objectives. It prepared plans for all the cities and towns with major refugee settlement, mainly in northern Greece, as well as for the cities of Chios, Mytilini and Crete, which had also received large numbers of refugees. The plans had to undergo repeated adaptation and, once again, functioned merely as a framework in which the already existing refugee settlements could be cloaked in a mantle of legality.

A combined study of plans and aerial photographs of three cities from the inter-war period together with the relevant census figures permits an evaluation of the planning programmes as implemented. In the 1920 census, Drama was found to have 16,755 inhabitants and, according to the plan of 1916, the historic city extended over an area of 75 hectares. Thus in 1920 it had an overall population density of approximately 223 inhabitants per hectare. The census of 1928 recorded 32,186 inhabitants, 22,601 of them being refugees. The census data alone demonstrate that only some 10,000 inhabitants were indigenous, meaning that 6,000 to 7,000 had departed in the exchange of populations. The town plan, approved in 1930 and extended in 1933, did no more than legalise the existing ad hoc refugee settlement. Aerial photographs taken in 1932 show building development sparsely scattered and the city sprawling along the road arteries to take in the new developments. In 1932 the city extended over 200 hectares, with a population density of just 160 inhabitants per hectare.

In the 1920 census, Komotini was recorded as having 21,294 inhabitants, and it covered an area of twenty hectares. The overall population density was 177 inhabitants per hectare. By 1928, the population had risen to 31,551, of whom 10,745 were refugees. The 6,000 Muslims who left in the population exchange had been replaced by internal migrants. The new layout of Komotini was approved in 1932, and by the time its aerial photograph was taken later that year it was already under construction. By this point, the sparsely developed town spread over an area of some 180 hectares, and the population density had fallen to approximately 100 inhabitants per hectare.

Finally, the same pattern can be seen in the expansion of Alexandroupolis. The population increased from 6,963 in 1920 to 14,019 in 1928, of whom 8,262 were refugees. The 1929 extension to the urban plan included the refugee settlements in an overall area of 135 hectares (104 inhabitants per hectare), and left the city with a pattern of sprawling development without any focus on urban features, public buildings, or community spaces and services.

Conclusion

From its establishment in the early nineteenth century, the modern Greek state's need to provide housing for migrants and refugees was caught up in a curiously shifting relationship with the emerging discipline of town planning. A study of Greek planning history shows that serious interest in making the process of urban development an orderly and rational one always existed. However, the specific measures and policies generated by this interest inevitably proved too weak to withstand the ever more pressing need to provide housing for massive numbers of newcomers. Planning measures collapsed under the strain of demand in exactly the circumstances where they most needed to be implemented without dilution or adulteration.

Despite the protests and well-documented analyses of planners at the Ministry of Communications, the country-wide situation that arose was one in which the approved plans served exclusively individual needs (whether justified or not) on the basis of private ownership of individual housing. At the same time, the process of urbanisation – finally imposed by the force of circumstances – extended and perpetuated the rural character of the urban centres. The disadvantages of this type of 'solution' need hardly be discussed: while offering a privately owned house aimed at the social integration of the refugees, the so-called solution ultimately produced formless space that often led to an absence of collective spirit and to socially isolated quarters – 'handicapped' areas[15] as regards poverty, unemployment, and reputation.

The result was uncoordinated and unsustainable, and did not live up to the original objectives. Under the pressure of urgent need, the ambitious intentions of the socially aware technocrats of the Liberal Party government of the time were implemented only after having been stripped of their long-term perspective. Their aspiration to produce urban plans that would combine developmental goals and modern spatial and functional requirements within a reformist approach were never fulfilled. The modern Greek city was thus turned into a home-owner refugee settlement – a *prosphygoupolis.* The saddest consequence, perhaps, is that a scale of priorities for town-making was consolidated which scars the Greek landscape up to the present day.

Notes

1. See the Planning Act of 1835.
2. The orthogonal neoclassical design was welcomed because it fulfilled the requirements for a new order while at the same time it was considered a product of ancient Greek planning tradition (the Hippodamean plan).
3. The efficacy of these general guidelines has been demonstrated repeatedly in the history of urban planning: in the New World since the sixteenth century; in Russia in the eighteenth century; and in other countries undertaking large-scale internal colonisation, e.g., during the eighteenth century the Prussian colonisation in Silesia or the Austrian colonisation in Banat, where chessboard plans were also used. See Bunin 1961: 110–11;Gutkind 1964: 125–127; Reps 1965: 29–32.

4. In the first twenty years of the century Greece accepted 150,000 refugees from Asia Minor and Thrace, the Black Sea region, Bulgaria, and the Caucasus. Of these, 100,000 settled in Macedonia, 22,000 in Attica and 11,000 in Western Thrace, while the remainder were dispersed throughout the country. As is evident, the northern Greek region received the greater number by far. See *Statistical figures from the Greek census of 1928. Actual and legitimate population, refugees* (1933) (Athens: National Press).

5. The reference point in classical antiquity, so dear to the nineteenth century, was replaced by powerful arguments in favour of a universally applicable pattern of life, sharing similar cooperative movements, cultural models and the goal of industrial development.

6. The fate of an attempt to secure the planned development of Athens from 1918 to 1929 is characteristic, described in Dimitrakopoulos 1935 and Biris 1966.

7. Legislative Decree 'concerning rural resettlement of refugees' (Government Gazette, 6–11 July 1923) and Decree 'on the planning of cities, market towns and public housing settlements, and the construction thereof' (Government Gazette, 16 August 1923).

8. Circulars of the Ministry of Communications to various recipients, no.s 63703/1924, 63704/1924, 68810/1924, 81003/1925, and 30540/1926.

9. Legislative Decree 'on the organisation of the services of the Ministry of Health, Welfare and Assistance' (Government Gazette 156A, 22 July 1927), see in particular article 20. See also Legislative Decree of 10 August 1928 'on the organisation of the services of the Ministry of Health, Welfare and Assistance' (Government Gazette 165A, 16 August 1928) and Act 3714/1928 which ratifies the above.

10. Legislative Decree of 29 September 1931 (Government Gazette 345A, 3 October 1931) and Act 5309 (Govrenment Gazette 27A, 1 February 1932) which ratifies the decree.

11. Act 6076 'on the urban resettlement of refugees' (Government Gazette 77A, 21 February 1934).

12. Quotations from Dimitrakopoulos 1935.

13. See report of the Refugee Settlement Treasury director E. Harilaos, a well known Greek financier, entrepreneur and ex-minister, in Morgenthau 1929.

14. Pelagidis draws from official reports of the Refugee Settlement Commission to the League of Nations and offers a detailed account of procedures and financial funding of the settlement of the refugees in urban and rural areas, as well as an overall assessment of the RSC activities in urban areas. After 1930, the programme was taken over by the Venizelos government.

15. See Hirschon 1998[1989] (chs. 3, 4) for a description of the urban refugee quarters, and Kokkinia in particular.

11

When Greeks Meet Other Greeks

SETTLEMENT POLICY ISSUES IN THE
CONTEMPORARY GREEK CONTEXT

Eftihia Voutira

Introduction

History, in E.H. Carr's felicitous phrase, is a continuous dialogue between the past and the present. In this chapter, I examine the legacy of the exchange of populations in contemporary Greece, beginning with an analysis of how a long-term memory of the 'successful' adaptation of the 1.2 million Asia Minor refugees was formed. I then examine how this interpretation of the inter-war refugee experience has become a source of legitimacy and inspiration in formulating current state policies towards the new 'co-ethnic' immigrants from the Former Soviet Union (FSU). Finally I analyse the role this memory has played in social relations between the Soviet Greek newcomers and the members of the host Greek state.

As shown below, the term 'refugee' has attained positive connotations in Greece and is used as a term of honour, unlike contemporary constructions of the term based on negative stereotypes that cast refugees as a burden and a state liability. This positive connotation is largely due to the collective perception of the successful integration of Asia Minor refugees and their contribution to modern Greek economic, social and cultural development. Specifically, the meaning of the term 'refugee' in modern Greek is informed and mediated by the collective memory of the Asia Minor refugees as a national asset, i.e., as *integrated* refugees, *after* their rehabilitation in, and adaptation to, modern Greek society. This particular form of anachronism is an essential component of collective social memory construction and one that, as Paul Connerton has noted, depends on the regular repetition and reaffirmation of the past in the present through commemorative narrative enactments of significant events that mark the identity of a society (1989:12).

Whether the reception of the Asia Minor refugees was truly a success depends not only on the timeframe of assessment (long- versus short-term), but also on whose criteria are being applied and whether, to the extent that any received wisdom is sought to be reapplied elsewhere, the success is transferable to other cases of refugee settlement in other regions or in the same country at a later historical time. My main concern is not to make such an assessment, but rather to show the longer-term impact of the Lausanne Convention as it pertains to lessons learnt from Greece's refugee past and as applied in the case of Soviet Greek newcomers. The majority of these are close relatives of the Asia Minor refugees that came from Pontos in the period between 1918 and 1923, an element that has relevance in the way these recent arrivals construe their own 'refugee' identity, which they promote through their cultural associations as an essential component of their financial expectations from the Greek state.

Focusing on the post-1989 arrivals from the FSU, I provide examples of the newcomers' preference for being called, and using as a term of self-ascription, 'refugees', rather than 'repatriates' (*palinostountes*) or 'returnees' (*epanapatrizomenoi*) as they have been labelled by various Greek state agencies. The term 'repatriates' (*palinostountes*), as used in the modern Greek context, refers to the more recent arrivals of Soviet Greeks by distinguishing them from the Greek political refugees from the Greek civil war, who had fled to the communist countries and were granted the right to return to Greece (as *epanapatrizomenoi*) after the end of the military junta (1974). As such, the term has particular social connotations and political implications: it refers to the East-West migration phenomenon that consists of a reshuffling of populations along ethnic lines across the old Cold War divide, allowing specific populations to return to their putative historical homelands (e.g., ethnic Germans, Greeks, Poles, Jews), an immediate result of the liberalisation policies of the late Soviet regime and eventual disintegration of the FSU (Voutira 1991, 1996, 1997, 1997a). Thus, Soviet Greeks, like the other ethnic minorities of the FSU that have a 'place to go' in the West, have been granted the right to return. The debate as to whether the newcomers are refugees or repatriates is paradigmatic of the problem that is addressed by the main hypothesis of my paper, namely, that the collective perception of the 1923 rural refugee settlement as a success case has shaped Greek state policy towards the new immigrants and coloured the relations between the newly arrived Greeks and those who had settled in the country earlier (whether 'earlier' means ten, seventy or hundreds of years previously). I conclude that, primarily because the Greek host-state of 1989 was not that of 1923 and because the substance of state policy did not match its rhetoric, the policies intending to duplicate the success of the 1923 case, or at least the policies moulded in its image, led to false expectations on the part of both the hosts and the newcomers, which have led, in turn, to mutual disillusionment.

The received wisdom about Greece's refugee past

State policies towards the refugees

The immediate consequences of the Lausanne Convention involved the settlement of some 1.2 million Asia Minor Greeks within the newly expanded borders of Greece. The challenge was immense at the end of the Asia Minor Catastrophe in 1922; Greece was fraught with civil strife, class, ethnic and regional cleavages. The large influx of newcomers, a potential national liability, however, was transformed into a socio-economic, political and cultural asset. Meeting the challenge became the core of, what I will call, Greece's refugee past; as such, it was deemed to be a success primarily due to the attitude and approach of the Greek state to this settlement. As noted by a number of scholars, the Asia Minor refugee settlement represented a unique achievement of Greek domestic policy (e.g., Psomiadis 1968: 106–8; Petropoulos 1989: 462–3; Mavrogordatos 1992: 10–11). The criteria of success were defined in terms of the *magnitude* of the challenge, the *speed* of rehabilitation and the meeting of the desired end state: cultural homogeneity of the population.

What made this successful resettlement unique? First was the magnitude of the population movement: some 1.2 million people arrived within a space of four years (Hirschon 1998 [1989]: 36ff). Secondly, it was the speed with which they were accommodated: 'In three years, from 1923 to 1926, the largest part of the refugee resettlement had been accomplished' (Mavrogodatos 1992: 10). Possibly the most important dimension was the way in which refugees were used to serve the multiple political and economic interests of the Greek state. One of these was the creation of a culturally homogeneous population: before the arrival of the refugees from Asia Minor, the population of the region of Macedonia was 42.6 percent Greek; by 1926, that figure had risen to 88.8 percent (Pentzopoulos 1962: 134).

To achieve these ends, the Greek state employed a strategy of investment in the impoverished rural economy and imposed the revolutionary measure of radically redistributing the land in central and northern Greece where most rural refugee settlement took place. The historical particularity contributing to the so-called success, then, was the quasi-feudal political economy of Greece (combined with the government's willingness to take the risk of redefining the institution of property by expropriating the rural lands for distribution to the refugees). As Mavrogordatos has shown, this particular policy of land redistribution involved, in fact, a type of social revolution *from above* , which undermined the possibility of a revolution *from below*; the introduction of these radical measures was not done by the refugees, it was done *before* them, and *for* them, by the Greek state (1992: 12).[1] On the political level, the allocation of land titles to the newcomers was part of the government's aim to create the conditions for the formation of a small landholding class of peasants with an interest in maintaining liberal democracy against the threat of communism (Mavrogordatos 1992: 11; Karakasidou 1997: 168); in this sense the state policies deployed in the interest of the refugees' economic self-sufficiency coincided with the political end of undermining the threat of communism.

In order to appreciate the uniqueness of this historical case and the value assigned to the 'refugee factor' in modern Greek thinking, it is important to identify the three main factors that differentiate the 1923 case from contemporary refugee situations.

(i) The exchanged population, who were labelled refugees upon their arrival in Greece, were *not* perceived as a temporary phenomenon. Due to implementation of the Lausanne Treaty, they were forced to move to Greece and were unable to return or be returned (Petropoulos 1989: 385).

(ii) The refugees were not seen as dispossessed 'others' who, having crossed international boundaries, remain, a 'categorical anomaly' in a world of nation-states (Malkki 1990: 48). Rather, their membership and citizenship status vis-à-vis the new nation were preconditions of their arrival in Greece. This unrestricted allocation of citizenship rights worked, eventually, to the mutual benefit of the state and the refugees. For the state, the investments made in the refugees, supervised by the Refuge Settlement Commission, were in the long-term interest of the national centre (Dritsa 1989: 47ff). For the refugees, the manner of assistance given required their engagement *as social actors* in the reconstruction of their livelihoods, an additional factor facilitating their long-term socio-economic integration.[2]

(iii) Venizelos displayed the charismatic leadership required to transform the demise of Greek irredentism in the Asia Minor Catastrophe into a national state policy that placed the issue of refugee rehabilitation at its core. It is in this sense that the whole long-term process of refugee settlement became identified in the public view as a national struggle and victory, which is one of the ways in which the Asia Minor Catastrophe, and its aftermath of compulsory exchange of populations, have come to 'dominate the modern Greek consciousness as the fundamental event which has transformed the form and character of the contemporary history of the nation' (Kitromilides 1972: 372).

Constructing and reinforcing the modern Greek collective memory of the refugee past

Greece's refugee past does not typically constitute part of textbook knowledge of modern Greek history. There is, however, a remarkable consensus among scholars, politicians and the refugees concerning the success of the 1923 settlement. In Greek academic writing, the case is often used as an example in disciplines such as international relations, history and economics (e.g., Psomiades 1968: 106; Tenekides 1980: 15; Kostis 1992: 31–33; Mazower 1992: 119) and as such has contributed to the social construction of knowledge and the modern Greek collective memory regarding Greece's refugee past. The memory of the refugee past as a story with a happy ending is typically encapsulated in popular discourse by the often repeated evocative phrase: 'The Asia Minor refugees managed despite all odds to tame their fates and inject new blood in the old Greece' (Yiannakopoulos 1992: 28). Assuming a culturally homogenous state as a major political end, Kitromilides notes: 'The whole effect of cultural evangelism of community construction worked out so well that Greece, after absorbing the Greek populations of Asia Minor and Thrace following the exchange of populations in 1923, emerged as one of the most ethnically homogeneous states in Europe' (1989: 50).

The term 'refugees' has been affirmed as positive on the level of modern Greek collective representations. In one such affirmation, Leonidas Iasonides, a Pontic Greek refugee who repeatedly served as a member of the Greek Parliament with the *Komma Phileftheron* (Venizelos' party) stated:

> Many times, it is said that we finally should stop being called refugees since after thirty years we are all now natives, children of the same Greek homeland [*patrida*]. ...This may indeed be so, yet, it is also the case that in order to get a piece of land one should still prove that one is a refugee; for a deferment of military service, one has to prove that one is a refugee; and after all, the word refugee is an honourable term for us... Because as refugees, as displaced persons [*ektopismenoi*], uprooted from our lands, we carried an ancient civilisation and we injected new blood in the Greek one, and because we have so totally hellenised northern Greece so that the League of Nations also acknowledged that through the refugee input – Pontic Greeks, Asia Minor Greeks and Thracians – today northern Greece is 97 per cent Greek... Therefore, the term 'refugee' is a term of honour and we must insist on it. And not only we, the true refugees [*alethes prosphyges*] but the children of our children as well. [1954 speech in *Pontiaki Estia*] (Iasonides 1983: 84).

As encapsulated in Iasonides' speech, the impact of the Asia Minor refugee experience on the meaning of the term 'refugee' as a hereditary entitlement and term of honour has great relevance for understanding some of the contemporary expectations of newcomers and hosts in Greece. Such ideas have found resonance among the more recent Pontic Greek newcomers from the FSU, many of whom feel that they, also, are the descendants of what Iasonides refers to as, *alithes prosphyges*, 'true refugees'.

A hard act to follow: 'repatriation' of Soviet Greeks in the shadow of the refugee past

Differing state policies in a new era of East-West repatriation

In contrast to the determination and purposefulness with which the Greek state approached the forcibly exchanged population in the wake of the Lausanne Convention, Greece appeared unprepared for the influx of immigrants that were increasingly arriving at its borders from the disintegrating Soviet Union. Although immigration from the East was not a new phenomenon in Greece,[3] post-1989 ethnic migrations from the FSU have been larger, longer-lasting, and far more complex than any earlier migrations. Since 1989, people of Greek ethnic origin arriving from the FSU have comprised Greece's largest category of immigrants and have largely contributed to Greece's shift from an emigration to an immigration country (Lazarides 1996). The dominant approach adopted by the Greek state has been to address this immigration wave as an instance of a 'national crisis'. As articulated by one of the government officials responsible for the management of the policy response:

> The mass influx of immigration from the Soviet Union was something unknown to Greece for two generations. Greece had no institutions to handle such a crisis. Various thoughts and proposals were presented, considered, tried, tested and failed. In the beginning it was left to relatives and Pontian associations. Subsequently, charitable institutions and local authorities were involved, then ministries started doing their share. By the end of 1989 when arrivals reached 1,000 per month and our embassy in Moscow sent us a 'storm warning' on the possibility of further significant increase of arrivals, the need for centrally coordinated action became obvious (Kokkinos 1991b: 314).

By 1990, arrivals of Soviet Greeks had reached 1,500 per month. From its initial ad hoc approach, Greece eventually adopted policies that sought to replicate some of the measures adopted in the early 1920s, particularly vis-à-vis rural settlement. In January 1990, it established the National Foundation for the Reception and Resettlement of Repatriate Greeks (EIYAPOE or 'National Foundation'), originally as a branch of the Ministry of Foreign Affairs and nine months later as an independent organisation, to address the 'immigration crisis' by planning and coordinating the reception of Greeks from the FSU.

The National Foundation adopted the strategy of using EU and state funding to design and implement a rural settlement plan in the region of Thrace, known as the 'National Settlement Plan', to which Greeks from the FSU would be channelled. The state policy operated with a particular image of the newcomers that attempted to fit them more easily into the Asia Minor rural refugee settlement mould:

> The repatriates are people with low economic claims and demands, and therefore they can accept without any kind of complaint even the most difficult form of life in the border regions. (EIYAPOE, Annual Report, 1992: 8).

> Their presence in these regions will be able to create in and of itself an economic revitalisation and this will generate the 'pull' for a return migration among the local population that has emigrated. (EIYAPOE, Annual Report, 1991: 6).

The rationale for targeting the region of Thrace was originally articulated in non-ideological terms: that Thrace offered available space, resources and a means of preventing further congestion in the urban areas to which self-settlement tended (Athens and Salonika were attracting 38 and 35 percent of such settlement respectively) (ibid.: 12; cf. Apostolides 1992: 313–330). The second annual report of the National Foundation, however, provided a more ideological justification for the particular rural settlement plan in Thrace,[4] namely, revitalising this vulnerable region in terms of demography, economics and security (EIYAPOE Progress Report, July 1992: 2–4).

By 1992, the mass immigration influx from the FSU began to be presented in the press and public forums as a major political issue that could, in the manner of the 1923 model, be transformed into an asset in order to solve the 'national issue of Thrace' (*to ethniko zitima tis Thrakis*) or 'our national development issue in Thrace' (*to zitima tis ethnikis mas anaptyksis stin Thraki*)[5] (e.g., *Eleftherotypia* 3 October 1992, 5 June 1993; *Ta Nea* 6 June 1993; *Thessaloniki* 8 July 1994). In these different press accounts, largely in concert with state policy, the general expectation articulated was that the settlement of 'our kith and kin' from the FSU in Thrace would revitalise the underdeveloped region by creating a flourishing labour force, would reverse the demographic imbalance between the Muslim and Christian populations, and would transform the political constituencies thereby undermining the newly formed Muslim party 'Equality, Friendship and Peace' that had unified the ethnologically diverse (Turk, Pomak, Gypsy) minority population under a single-issue political umbrella and had won a seat in the parliamentary elections of April 1990 (cf. Christides 1997: 160–61).

The Greek state was attempting to turn (what it at least perceived as) a liability into an asset, as it had in 1923, yet the concrete strategies adopted to effect such a transformation proved deficient. As originally proposed, the National Settlement Plan involved integration through housing, language and employment. However, language training and subsidised employment schemes met with limited success, while only a fraction of the housing planned was built. The newcomers' efforts to find jobs were hindered both by widespread unemployment in the region and by the job market's division among various Muslim groups that had already created their own economic niches. Integration through housing was to be achieved with the help of additional funding that had been allocated 'for housing programmes in most of central and northern Greece *with the rationale that these areas are the poorest and the most underpopulated*' (Kokkinos 1991a: 399, emphasis added). The housing developments were to be kept small – one hundred houses or less – 'to ensure integration in communities and [better] human living conditions' (ibid.: 399). However, the first five-year assessment of the National Foundation's performance revealed that only 604 houses had been constructed or bought, mainly in Thrace, accommodating 2,753 individuals, and that 2,988 apartments had been rented, housing 11,146 repatriates (EIYAPOE, Annual Report, 1996). These figures may be contrasted with the goal, as set out in the 1990 plan submitted to the Council of Europe's Social Fund, of constructing 13,000 urban or semi-urban houses and 2,000 rural houses (Kokkinos 1991a: 399). Possibly the greatest problem with the settlement policy was that it only managed to attract some 14,000 out of the 140,000 ethnic Greeks (*omogeneis Ellines*) who had arrived in Greece from the FSU since 1989 (Kamenides 1996: 4ff). The delay in housing construction for the newcomers and the makeshift solution of rented accommodation increased tensions between the newcomers and their hosts.

Over time, Greece's policy with respect to the Soviet Greeks continued to change, departing from the 1920s policy of making the refugees resources for national development. By implication, it also departed from the original goals of the policies of the early 1990s. Since 1994, the official Greek policy has been one of containing, rather than encouraging, immigration from the diaspora in the FSU, as a result of which it has been less generous in granting citizenship to Soviet Greeks in the mid and late 1990s. From 1996 onwards, more than half of the estimated 140,000 newcomers from the FSU were formally illegal immigrants either because they outstayed their tourist visa or because they have acquired their documents illegally on the black market.

Five years after the implementation of the National Foundation Resettlement Plan (*Programma Apokatastasis*) in Thrace, there was a progressive realisation that the plan was deficient: not only was it ineffective in completing housing construction projects, but also the vast majority of the newcomers *preferred* to settle in urban areas due to greater employment opportunities there. In the wake of this realisation and pressure from civil society organisations, another body, the General Secretariat of Returning Diaspora Greeks, undertook to redress the settlement issue. Established in 1990 under the auspices of the Ministry of Macedonia-Thrace, it was only set in operation in 1994. In his Memorandum of 20 May 1996 to the Ministry of Macedonia-Thrace, the General Secretary of the Secretariat of Returning Diaspora Greeks, Mr. Kamenides, explicitly referred to Greece's refugee past:

> While the European Greece of 1922 with protagonist Eleftherios Venizelos was able to rehabilitate, in a short time and effective manner, a far greater number of refugees, today's relatively prosperous Greece has as yet to manage much vis-à-vis the repatriates from the FSU, even though eight years have already gone by...The new tragedy of the Pontic Greeks – their uprooting [*o kserizomos*] from their new homelands [*nees esties*], the FSU – should have been perceived as a gift from god [*doro theou*] for contemporary Greece, which has a huge demographic problem and faces multiple national problems from the east and the north, [in that it could use them] to fortify its vulnerable regions of Thrace and Macedonia and to contribute more effectively to national development (1996: 23).

Substantively, the General Secretariat adopted recommendations that harkened back to the spirit of the 1923 settlement policies, or that otherwise recognised the National Settlements Plan's deficiencies:

> Full citizenship status to be allocated to all Soviet Greeks considered to be illegal immigrants, because as co-ethnics [*omoethneis*] they may have come on a tourist visa but they desire to settle here permanently.
>
> The creation of a new programme of self-settlement [*aftostegasis*] to be put in place and promoted in rural and urban areas of Northern Greece (ibid.).

Perceptions and differing expectations among 'old' and 'new' Greek refugees: the effect of Greece's refugee past on social relations

The majority of the Soviet Greeks (as I have called them for the sake of simplicity) arriving in Greece in the early 1990s did not speak modern Greek and, prior to leaving the FSU, had little understanding of their co-ethnics inside Greece. The older generations arriving from central Asia, Georgia and southern Russia still speak the Pontic Greek dialect, which they refer to as *Romeika* (Mackridge 1991).[6] The rediscovery of an ethnic past inside the FSU coincided with liberalisation policies introduced in the late *perestroika* years. Elements of such 'ethno-genesis' were evident, for example, in the establishment of Greek festivals, including some dedicated to traditional dancing and singing. A more politicised form of this phenomenon was seen at the 1991 meeting of the All-Union Greek Congress (Vsesoiuznogo s'ezda Grekov SSSR), a forum of the thirty-four Greek cultural associations that had begun burgeoning in 1988 in the different republics of the FSU. The congress took place in the town of Yelendzhik, southern Russia and was attended by numerous state officials invited from Greece. At the congress a decision was taken (by 71 to 65 votes) to define the cultural associations' agendas in future in terms of cultural rather than territorial autonomy.[7] Similarly, the Greek Executive Committee (*National'nie Palata*) in the FSU formed a strategic plan to promote the cultural representation of the Greek minority at the All-Union level in the *National'nii Soviet*. Evidently, the dissolution of the FSU at the end of 1991 stifled many of these political aspirations and further reinforced the emigration trend towards Greece.

The people in Greece had somewhat unrealistic expectations of the newcomers, often mediated by collective perceptions about the country's refugee past. The formal encounter of the two groups began with a certain euphoria of 'rediscovering their long-lost brothers'. The media and politicians in Greece hailed the newcomers as members of the Greek nation, as 'our own':

> Pontic Greeks from the Soviet Union... coming [to Greece are] an amazing... unique, a glorious case... [Y]ou feel proud when you think of how these people have maintained their Greekness, their traditions, their language under the Soviet regime, how they fought like demigods in order to remain pure Greeks, and how today...they fight without forgetting and without losing their Greekness [*choris na afellinizontai*]! (*Eleftherotypia*, 6 July 1988).

Those Soviet Greeks who in the early 1990s faced the dilemma of either staying in the FSU or going to Greece (Voutira 1991; 1997a) formed high expectations of their 'historical homeland'. Maintaining a distinct Greek ethnic identity under the old Soviet regime had often exacted high costs, the incentive to do so usually being ties to a 'fatherland' abroad. The stronger the Soviet Greeks felt disillusionment with their Soviet past, the greater their fear of economic and physical insecurity and the more seriously they perceived the threat that minority rights would be undermined as nationalist discourses emerged in central Asia, Georgia or southern Russia, the more they came to expect from Greece.[8] Talking with prospective repatriates in the FSU during the period 1991–93, I often heard sentiments expressed such as:

> Gamsakhurdia said that all foreigners are guests in this land [Georgia]. We have been here for five thousand years but now we are being thrown out from our homes. Greece will help us construct new ones…When Mitsotakis came [in 1992] he promised us new houses in Thrace…
>
> [I]f Greece wants us they must help us get there. They should minimise the costs of repatriation [i.e., visa applications, transport, export taxes for household goods]… When Stalin deported us here to Kazakhstan, he put us in trains and brought us for free!
>
> The government has made teaching of the Koran part of the required education curriculum: we can't stay here and see our children learning to be Muslims. We have to go to Greece for the sake of our children so that they can still remain Greeks.
>
> There are no jobs for us anymore. Everyone who is not Kazakh is leaving – the Germans, the Jews, now the Russians, and the Poles. We are also leaving to find a better life in our *patrida*. There are no prospects here for the Greeks anymore.

The Soviet Greeks not only had higher expectations of their hosts than did their counterparts in the 1920s, but they were also less suited to rural living and agriculture. Once inside Greece and dissatisfied with the treatment they encountered in their putative homeland they were mobilised by Pontic Greek associations. The newcomers began to use the language of 1920s policies in order to further their own cause, and, aware of its positive connotations, they seized upon the term 'refugees' as their self-ascription in an attempt to achieve greater entitlements. The president of the Association of Pontic Greek Refugees from the FSU (*Syllogos Pontion Prosphygon apo tin teos Sovietiki Enosi*) in Salonika argued in an interview published in a bilingual Soviet Greek newspaper:

> Everyone knows about the exchange of properties as part of the Lausanne Treaty and the exchange of populations. Land property was distributed then to those refugees including those who arrived gradually from Russia until 1930. To be sure, four thousand of those refugees [who came from Russia] were left outside the pool and received nothing. This, however, does not mean that until today, the whole lot has been distributed (*Epistrophi*, October 1992: 4).

The further elaboration of the Soviet Greek self-ascription as 'refugees' is particularly telling:

> [W]e, the Pontic Greeks from the FSU are not merely repatriates [*palinostountes*]: we are refugees [*eimaste prosphyges*]. [Because]… if we, or our ancestors, were able to catch the boats and come to Greece in 1920 then we would have had the right to the lottery for land distribution. In fact, however, the Soviet Union, by closing its borders, deprived us of the right to resettle in Greece [*na metoikisoume stin Ellada*]. Since the Pontic Greeks were not able to leave the

Soviet Union – not out of their own fault, but because of coercion – they must now be considered by Greece as refugees from Turkey via the Soviet Union, which had in the meantime closed its borders. If not, it follows that the one who was able to arrive in Greece during the period 1920–30 from Turkey is a refugee while the one who by fleeing death and fell into the trap of the Stalinist regime is not a refugee (*Epistrophe*, October 1992:4).

In their multiple petitions to different national and international bodies, the Soviet Greek associations criticised the existing National Settlement Plan (known as the 'National Plan', *to ethniko programma*) and the use of the label 'repatriate'. In an official petition to the European Court of Human Rights, the president of the Association of Greek Refugees from Sokhumi articulated both disillusionment and a scathing critique of the plan:

The basic cause of the Pontic Greeks' forced flight from their three thousand-year primordial place of residence in Sokhumi was the destruction of the monolithic communist regime, and its aftermath, which was the fight for national self-determination... Now that we have come to Greece *as refugees* in a wave of more than 100,000 Greeks from the former Soviet Union, we suddenly find that we have escaped the clutches of red communism and entered into the even tighter grip of the Greek bureaucracy, by the name of the National Foundation. ... Just the salaries spent on the staff come to approximately $200,000, and the staff are those who destroy the dreams of all the people who have lost their homeland and arrived in their historical homeland – Greek Thrace. The Greek state received money from the European Union specifically in order to accommodate those people who came as refugees. ... However, they label these newcomers not 'refugees', but 'repatriates' [*palinostoudes*]. Definitely, this label is legally inaccurate, because, as it is well known, the term 'repatriate' refers to a person who has left and is now returning to his homeland, yet to call someone a repatriate who is returning to his homeland thousands of years after he has left is indeed ridiculous. However, we think that this is an intentional misuse of the term 'repatriate' in the place of 'refugee', which is what we think we are.[9]

Also insisting on the use of 'refugee' as a term of self-ascription, other associations centred their criticism on the inefficient and ineffective manner in which assistance, mainly in the form of relief, was allocated to them by the state, and in a manner that marginalised and dehumanised the recipients. In his presentation to the International Committee of Pontic Hellenism on 4 March 1994 in Thessaloniki, the president of the Pontic Greek Association *Mavrothalassites*, Mr. Yannis Karypides, from Tbilisi, Georgia articulated his criticism as follows:

We don't need dried food and tinned fish, we need loans to build our own houses and cultivate our own fields... Never in our history have the Pontic Greek people been so marginalised as they are now upon their arrival in their homeland in Greece; even when they were exiled in central Asia, they were able to build their own houses and live well. We are claiming what belongs to us (Karypides 1994: 6).

The newcomers from the FSU also offered their own alternative, based on a self-settlement model of refugee assistance. It was compatible in spirit with the 1923 rural settlement plan that mobilised the refugees as key actors in the rehabilitation programme:

> If in the reception centres every refugee costs the National Foundation 5,000 drachmas [£10] per day then a four-member family would cost 7,000,000 million drachmas per year. If the state provides land and building materials to the tune of half this amount, then unquestionably, using our personal labour, after one to two years new settlements and new communities will be built and the deserted villages of Macedonia and Thrace will be revitalised (Karypides 1994: 4). ... [The National Foundation] remains a self-serving organisation that pays its personnel large salaries while the refugees have to survive in the worst living conditions in the hospitality or reception centers, which they call ghettos. ... We are asking for a National Foundation of Refugees, which would be staffed *by us, the refugees*, i.e., by people who know our problems and who will help us solve them. Most of us have degrees and experience in construction – we can design and build our own homes (Karypides 1994: 6).

The Pontic Greeks' articulation of their demands encountered resistance from both state agencies and the local population, who expected the newcomers to conform to the host population's received wisdom concerning the 1923 refugees. Both policy-makers and the locals tended to view the immigrating Soviet Greeks in a less favourable light than those who had been subject to the forced exchange of populations. Despite the nationalist and religious concerns facing the Soviet Greeks in the FSU, and what has been described by some as 'forced flight', they were often perceived by their hosts in Greece as 'only' economic migrants. At an intra-group level too, differentiations are made. Many of the Soviet Greeks who arrived in Greece earlier in the 1980s insist: 'Those who come now are not real Greeks suffering under the Soviet regime; they are capitalists. They only come here to trade and make a better living.' Equally, among the third generation of Asia Minor refugees in Thrace, the disillusionment with the newcomers is voiced in terms of a comparison with their own perceptions of their grandparents' experiences of settlement and the way they 'tamed their own fates' through personal sacrifice and labour:

> When our families came from Asia Minor they had nothing and it was only through their hard work and sacrifices that they were able to succeed. ... They worked and worked until they would get juice from the stones [*na vgaloun zoumi apo tis petres*]...but these people who are coming now from Russia are lazy [*tembelides*]. They don't like to work – they prefer to sit, drink and wait or to get money from the state through the EU-subsidised professional qualification programmes (Author's interviews with locals in Thrace, 6 October 1995).

Disillusionment with the newcomers was similarly voiced by a government official in Athens: 'When we planned their resettlement we thought that these people would be appreciative of all the material assistance and the training programmes we were devising for them. But unfortunately we found them to be choosy and ungrateful towards the Greek state' (former Secretary of State,

V.Tsouderou in an interview with the author, 6 June 1995). The president of the National Foundation, Mr. Georgios Iakovou, former Secretary of State of the Republic of Cyprus drew the following comparison:

> In Cyprus the refugees from the northern regions were war refugees and they were received by the local people as the victims of that war, which was seen as a collective national struggle. Here in Greece the newcomers from Russia are not refugees – they come voluntarily to improve their lot, they are economic migrants, they don't speak the language, they have a different culture but they are officially ethnic Greeks so they share the same rights as other Greeks in terms of employment, protection and political rights. Yet what is still lacking is social solidarity with the native population (interview with author, 3 October 1995).

Conclusion

Greece's refugee past has been used by both the hosts and the newcomers to promote their own interests and to support competing claims in the present. People or actions in the 1990s have been identified with those of the 1920s even when they are often acknowledged to be different.

Using the past to legitimise the present is an essential component of what anthropologists have referred to as the 'invention of tradition', and one that 'depends on the capacity to use *collective memory* about the past in order to ascribe a moral ontology to the present' (Humphrey 1992: 378). It is the activity of referring to a 'collective past' that serves to legitimise the past's authority and the policies it is called upon to support. Of course, differences in the form of engagement with that past, and in the assumptions of the speakers and audience engaging in it, must be overlooked.

In Greece, the refugee past, a story remembered with a happy ending and repeated by members of the nation over the generations, is a story of cultural homogeneity. Modern Greeks learn that the creation of modern Greece as a culturally homogeneous nation was one of the main achievements of the 1923 Asia Minor refugee settlement story. What I have tried to show in this paper is how Greece's refugee past has been codified in modern Greek long-term memory and how it is being mobilised and used among mainland and diaspora Greeks in their contemporary interactions.

We have yet to determine how the national plans for the settlement of Soviet Greeks will be assessed and how Soviet Greeks themselves will be remembered. Such assessments will no doubt be influenced by the wider processes of globalisation and Greece's membership in the European Union currently undermining the notion of cultural homogeneity of the Greek nation, a crucial notion on which the 'success' of Greece's refugee past was built.

Notes

1. This strategy was part of a wider agricultural reform policy that had begun in 1910, including land expropriation of large Ottoman *chiftlik* estates in Thessaly and Macedonia (Petropoulos

1989: 462; Karakasidou 1997: 165; Kontogiorgi this volume). The policy was partially enacted through state legislation on 18 November 1917 and implemented after the revolutionary decree of 14 February 1923 which called for land expropriation in those regions (Pentzopoulos 1962: 108). This in turn allowed for the transfer of some 500,000 hectares to be used by the Refugee Settlement Commission with a view to making the refugees economically self-sufficient (Kontogiorgi 1992: 48–49; cf. Petropoulos 1989: 463ff). A similar argument for the catalytic role of the refugees on the land redistribution issue in Macedonia during the inter-war period is made by Karakasidou (1997: 164ff), who argues that the refugees' presence affected the allocation of land titles to the local population as well as precipitating the government's aim of creating a small landholder class, irrespective of origins. The long-term socio-economic consequences of the land allocation policies in Macedonia have also been addressed by Agelopoulos (1994, 1997).

2. Admittedly, the state's allocating citizenship rights to the newcomers was not sufficient to give rise to a collective identification of the people as members of one nation. On the local level, 'assumed cultural unity' sometimes gave way to opposition, which manifested itself in the newcomers' and older residents' denying each other's Greekness (eg., Mavrogordatos 1983: 182; Hirschon 1998 [1989]: 30–31; Voutira 1997b: 119–20). Such opposition, widely documented in the literature, demonstrates that the settlement of refugees was not necessarily perceived as a success at the time it was occurring by those immediately involved. The Greek state attempted to combat such opposition with strategies aimed at inculcating a collective sense of membership in the nation, including, for example, the creation of an official enemy in inter-war Greece, namely, communism.

3. Previous waves of immigration include some 150,000 Greeks from the FSU in the period 1928–40, approximately 15,000 in the 1964–66 period, and some 90,000 communist Greeks from the Greek civil war who were allowed to repatriate after the restitution of democracy in Greece after 1974.

4. The national importance of the region for Greek state policy is also intimated by the fact that, quite exceptionally, the whole region of Thrace falls under the jurisdiction of the Greek Ministry of Foreign Affairs. It is also worth quoting the most recent (1991) population censuses: Greek Orthodox 231,000, Muslims (Turks, Pomaks, Gypsies) 114,000. In the District of Rodopi, the Muslim population has a clear majority (62,000) over the Christians (42,000). According to a report of the District Commission on 7 July 1993, published since the inauguration of the Soviet-Greek resettlement project in 1991, the Greek Orthodox population has increased by 9,000, raising the total of the Christians to 51,000 (quoted in Thrakiotis 1993: 25). For a short but comprehensive review of the main issues in the Greek state's relations with its Muslim minority in Thrace, see Christides 1997.

5. A comprehensive collaborative study, *The Development of Thrace: Challenges and Prospects* (1994) published by the Academy of Athens, identifies the geopolitical and national significance of the region and calls for political will and coordination across party lines as a precondition for effective implementation of a long-term, sustainable national development plan in Thrace (161–168). While most of the analyses and proposals seek to situate the region of Thrace in wider European development policies, the language used is couched in the idiom of our 'national priorities'.

6. Not all Soviet Greeks are of Pontic Greek origin, but to date this group remains the most numerous and, since the 1990s, the most visible of the different categories of Greeks from the Soviet Union. In terms of their own self-identification they called themselves *Romaioi*, or used *Greki* as their formal Russian ethnonym. The adoption of the regional qualifier *Pontios* as a term of self-ascription only became possible after the arrival of, and/or their encounter with, Pontic Greeks from mainland Greece. As one of my informants in the FSU put it: 'We didn't know we were Pontic Greeks [*Pontioi*] before 1991. When Pontic Greeks from mainland Greece came here to the First Greek All-Union Congress in Yelendzhik we found out that we were not *Romaioi* but that we were *Pontioi*.' Since then there have been attempts to introduce the so-called regional category 'Pontic Greek' (*Pontiiskei Greki*) in Russian-language publications by drawing a distinction between this category and the general category of 'Soviet Greeks', e.g., *Entsiklopediia Sovetskikh Grekov*, F. Kessidi (ed), Progress Publications, Moscow

(1994) as compared with 'Pontiiskei Grekii', in *Studia Pontocaucasica*, I. Kuznechov (ed), Krasnodar (1997).

7. The proceedings of the congress were published the same year: Materialy I Vsesoiuznogo s'ezda Grekov SSSR, Yelendzhik 1991.

8. See Kassimati et al. 1992 for a sociological study made in Greece examining the expectations of the newcomers from the FSU about reception and resettlement, both before and after their arrival, with special reference to the groups that arrived in Greece between 1985 and 1989.

9. Politides, *Ypomnyma sto Evropaiko Dikastirio Anthropinon Dikaiomaton* (Memorandum to the European Court of Human Rights), Refugee Association of Greeks from Sokhumi, Dioskourias, 20 March 1994, mimeo: 3.

III

Social and
Cultural Aspects

12

Housing and the Architectural Expression of Asia Minor Greeks Before and After 1923

Vassilis Colonas

Introduction

When the relationship between the individual and the environment is fraught with contradictions and inadequacy, he becomes discontent and strives to transform it in his own image in order to satisfy his personal desires and dreams. The purpose of architecture is not merely to provide man with a roof over his head, but to allow him, through the type and form of residence that he chooses, to express both his cultural identity and his social and economic standing. Man needs an environment that will facilitate the creation of images. He needs neighbourhoods with their own individual character, with roads and passageways that lead somewhere, and with focal points that reflect a specific and appealing identity (Norberg-Schulz 1977: 431).

The most direct and fundamental consequence of the Lausanne Convention was a violent interruption in the continuity of human presence in space. More than just the dwellings of the hundreds of thousands of uprooted people were lost: also lost were the architectural expressions of identity and purpose that had been built into their communities, that had made them meaningful homes. Of the Christians forced out of Turkey to Greece, some took over properties left by the Muslims, but with a total influx of over one million refugees these could never be enough. Indeed, even with government provision of thousands of new, hastily built houses, many refugees were left no choice other than to erect makeshift lean-tos with whatever scrap material came to hand. In such circumstances, disorientated and trapped in poverty, the continuing manifestation of architectural expression that this paper uncovers is testament to the Asia Minor Greek community's resilience in the face of adversity.

Architectural expression before 1922

From 1839 onwards, the Ottoman Empire underwent an intense phase of economic and socio-political transformation aimed at the modernisation of the old system. In order to recover from economic crisis and technological under-development, a series of social and institutional reforms based on western models was introduced. One of the main initiatives under the Tanzimat reforms was the granting of civil rights to all subjects of the empire, regardless of faith or ethnicity. In addition, subjects were granted the right to dispose of and develop immovable property as they wished, within the empire's borders.

The granting of equal rights constituted a significant step forward for the non-Muslims. They were better prepared than the Muslims to adapt to the new situation and to embrace and exploit the process of westernisation, and this provided them with the opportunity for rapid advancement and develop-ment. Thanks to the close connections that they had developed in European countries, they became agents of new ideals, understood how to exploit the new financial conditions and became a vehicle for innovations in the fields of education, social provision and community planning. From this point onwards, public and domestic architecture flourished in the Greek-speaking Orthodox communities of Asia Minor, especially in the coastal cities. As agents of modernisation, the members of the Greek Orthodox communities introduced new types of building, employed experienced architects and invested in the building sector in general.

Neoclassicism was the architectural style most widely used: it reflected the influence of contemporary state–sponsored architecture in Greece, as well as the ideological link that the community maintained with the Greek metro-polis, Athens, the capital of the new state. Besides differing from previous types and forms, the buildings in which neoclassicism was used presented an impressive morphological similarity. In choosing neoclassicism as a style, consideration was not given to the particular function of buildings, rather, their significance as powerful landmarks was underlined, reflecting the new image of a modernised community. The consistent use of neoclassicism was indicative of the unity of style demanded by the community, while at the same time it served to differentiate new buildings from those born of other architectural trends favoured by the various ethnic-religious communities or the Ottoman state.

Like all artistic movements, neoclassicism underwent a popularisation in style. Popular neoclassicism – the product of reciprocal influence between sophisticated style and local architectural tradition – was to determine the appearance of provincial towns both within the borders of Greece itself and in cities abroad where Greek communities prospered. The most interesting aspect of this latter phenomenon is found in Smyrna and Aivali where the new architectural trend was adopted before it subsequently spread to other districts of Asia Minor, even as far afield as Cappadocia (Figure 12.1).

Figure 12.1 A house with a Greek inscription in Cappadocia.

The typical urban house of Smyrna

By the beginning of the twentieth century, the Greek urban house of Smyrna was one of the most characteristic features of the city. However, introducing the new style was no easy task. From the outset, the architects and the serious craftsmen and contractors who preceded them faced great resistance to change, and had to make strenuous efforts before finally succeeded in moving on from the old styles. In contrast to the new urban house, the post-Byzantine and Frankish styles were fortress-like in appearance: iron doors, tiny windows set high in thick walls and a further high surrounding wall, access through which was gained by an iron gate with enormous handles. The new urban house also replaced the old style of Turkish house. Built from wattle and daub walls around a timber frame, they were characterised by low ceilings, wooden jetties and lattice windows. Despite all the praise one hears for their picturesque qualities, they were dull and unhealthy dwellings. Thus, to quote F. Phalbos, 'We come to the new urban European type of house, the kind we lived in until 1922, which is still to be seen in Smyrna at those points where the fire was unable to complete its work of destruction, at the Quais, Pounta and elsewhere' (1957: 160).

In the mid-nineteenth century, as soon as the French had finished constructing the Smyrnan waterfront, the new type of urban house started to be built in the Quais. From there, it began its advance towards the interior of the city, first to the Paralleli[1] and then on to the small streets in the northern and eastern parts of the town. It was there that the new city of Smyrna was being built, a clear departure from the more established quarters to the south and west, which included the Christian neighbourhoods of Apano Machala, Agios Georgios, Servetadika, etc., the French quarter (Frangomachala), and the Turkish, Armenian, and Jewish districts. The new type of house consisted of four levels: a basement, the ground floor (three or four steps above street level), the first floor and a roof terrace or *domas*. Particularly characteristic features were the roof terrace itself, the mezzanine, which housed the services, and which was referred to in the local dialect as the *entresol* or, in a Hellenised form, the *entresoli*, and the beautiful, practical and sanitary Smyrnan closed wooden balcony that adorned the facade of the house, providing a small but valuable amenity in the daily life of the family (ibid.: 161–2) (Figure 12.2).

Figure 12.2 A street in the Greek quarter of Smyrna, 1919.

Summer houses

Residential architecture was also flourishing in the garden suburbs of Smyrna, along the coast in Karantina, Karatas, and farther along in Butza, where members of the Greek Orthodox community began to build their summer houses. In these areas, in contrast to Pounta and the Quais, one would see the full range of contemporary European models, such as the Italian villa, the Swiss chalet, or even specimens of a colonial revival architecture. According to Paraskevopoulos in 1898, some of these villas were of a 'mixed Moorish' style, while others looked like a 'Phalerian villa' (Michelis 1992b: 299). In her book *Matomena Chomata* (*Bloodstained Earth*) the Greek novelist Dido Sotiriou gives a description of such a villa:

> Seitanoglou had a house like a palace, no pasha's seraglio was bigger. All in marble, surrounded by gardens of palm trees, bougainvillaea, roses, lemon trees and flower beds full of flowers. It had a tennis court, a stable for the horses, an artificial lake and a whole forest of trees, in whose shade the sons of the master and their wives would lounge and read. The first floor had sitting rooms, studies, a whole room lined with bookcases, dining rooms with Persian rugs and furniture from Venice. The walls were panelled in walnut and hung with tapestries; ancestral portraits looked down from golden frames...(1962: 62–63)

Other areas of Asia Minor

The architecture of Smyrna was imitated throughout the main urban centres of western Asia Minor. The same architectural features were used to emphasise neoclassical lines in the Greek neighbourhoods of Vourla, Tsesme, Moschonisi, Dikeli, Pergamon, Phokaia, Nymphaio, and Aivali, which at the turn of the century had become a model Greek town. Greek key patterns, palmette designs, capitals, door knockers, classical pediments, Corinthian semi-columns, Greek inscriptions and the initials of the owner on the lintel over the door of the house or shop, the date of the building worked into the wrought iron of balconies and gates – all these features are to be found in this coastal region.

At the same time, however, other social groups were using their limited resources to display an anonymous, vernacular architecture that was closely connected with traditional forms similar to those seen on the Aegean islands, where, just as the natural landscape harmonises beautifully with the sea, so the character of the architecture conforms with that of the island shores opposite. Most of the houses in the area of Erythraia are white, and so are those on Chios across the water. As far as architectural continuity is concerned, there does not seem to be a dividing channel of water between the islands and the coast of Asia Minor: there is colour on the walls of Mytilini buildings, and colour opposite too, in the towns of Aiolida. Colour is also a common factor uniting Aivali, Moschonisi, Magnesia, Nymphaio, Mainemeni, the popular quarters of Smyrna, and Pergamon. It is the colour celebrated by the poet Seferis: 'The mauve houses of Pergamon / In the July twilight...' (quoted in

Michelis 1992b: 303). The red samousak stone (from Samousak, near Aivali) and the inventive use of colour gave and still give a theatrical quality to the Greek houses of these cities (ibid.: 302–3). Many of the buildings mentioned above can still be seen in the coastal cities of Asia Minor, while their impressive silhouettes remain among the most significant of the cityscape.

The exchange and after

In pre-exchange Turkey one of the functions of architecture for the Christians was to differentiate themselves from their Muslim neighbours and compatriots. Of course, once these Christians had fled or been expelled to Greece such a function no longer made sense. It was this factor, along with the refugees' impoverished condition, that formed the parameters in which future architectural expression in their new homeland was to develop. While many were proud of their Asia Minor roots – or clung to them for political reasons – the emphasis shifted from differentiation from the majority to social assimilation with it; at the same time, severely limited means restricted what the refugees could in practice hope to achieve.

Housing provision

In the years 1922 and 1923, in excess of one million refugees from Asia Minor poured into Greece. Housing was recognised to be one of the most urgent problems, and the danger of social tension obliged the government to take action. The requisitioning of unoccupied real estate, a measure adopted by the revolutionary government of N. Plastiras, proved insufficient, and on 3 November 1922 the government decided to set up the Refugee Relief Fund, which, together with the Ministry of Health and Welfare, was tasked with constructing dwellings for the refugees. However, most refugees used what means they had in order to house themselves. Huts built of cheap materials, planks and tin sprang up in streets and squares, on the outskirts of towns, next to workers' houses, and around the settlements constructed by state organisations (Figure 12.3).

Despite the fact that the majority of the dwellings erected by the Refugee Relief Fund were nothing more than makeshift wooden sheds roofed with tarred felt, the Fund made a noteworthy contribution in initiating the housing of thousands of people throughout Greece, and especially in Athens, where it opened up the districts of Kokkinia, Kaisariani, Vyronas and Nea Ionia (Yiannakopoulos 1992: 32–35). However, it was not long before it became apparent that the colossal task of settling the refugees could not be carried out without foreign aid. On 29 September 1923, Greece and the League of Nations signed a protocol establishing the Refugee Settlement Commission (RSC), an autonomous, independent organisation through which aid would be channelled. By the end of 1929, the sum of £12.5 million had been placed at the disposal of the RSC, and 8.4 million *stremmata* (about 2.1 million acres)

Figure 12.3 The first phase of settlement. (L. Michelis, Archive).

of land were made available to it, most of it property owned by the Muslims who were part of the exchange.

The RSC threw its weight into rural settlement, which could be achieved more quickly and economically than urban settlement, and moreover without requiring a reorientation of the Greek economy, which had always been based on agriculture. Rural settlement involved granting a plot of farming land and a dwelling, and supplying the farmers with animals, seeds, etc. By the end of 1928, the RSC had created two thousand rural settlements in the Greek countryside, three quarters of which were attached to existing villages. Approximately 150,000 families were settled in these settlements, the majority in Macedonia (87,084 families) and Thrace (41,828 families) (Yiannakopoulos 1992: 34–35; see Kontogiorgi this volume).

In a report on rural resettlement written in July 1923, three basic criteria were proposed to ensure that the settlement operated successfully and with lasting effect:

(i)   the settlement of members of one family, or of a family circle, in the same place
(ii) the re-creation of individual populations as they had lived together in Turkey (the idea being that they would already be linked by moral and social ties that would be of invaluable help in making the settlement a lasting success), and
(iii) the settlement of refugees in a natural environment (e.g., mountain, plain, coast) similar to that which they had abandoned in Turkey.[2]

The bulk of the refugees were settled in Macedonia. Since the abandoned Muslim and Bulgarian houses were insufficient to accommodate all the refugees, as early as 1924, the Macedonian Resettlement Directorate commissioned ten thousand new dwellings from the Sommerfeld-Dehatege company, almost all of which were completed by May 1925. The contract did not include external and internal plastering or the installation of wooden ceilings and floors: this supplementary work was carried out by the RSC itself. Since contracting out the construction work to a large company had proved very expensive, the RSC decided to entrust the work to small, local companies for the further fifteen thousand rural dwellings to be built in Macedonia, or, where possible, to the refugees themselves, who would work as paid labourers under the control of the Commission's technical department.

Most of the houses built included stables and storerooms for agricultural produce. In the tobacco-growing areas space was added for storing tobacco. There was also great variety in construction materials. Many of the rural dwellings had a wooden frame filled in with bricks, while others were of concrete or stone. A common feature of all the houses built was the tile roof (Pelagidis 1997: 238). The houses that the RSC adopted for rural dwellings in Macedonia can be classified into types (Figures 12.4 and 12.5):

I, II: Sommerfeld houses (D.H.T.G.) consisting of one unit of accommodation per house. The company built the stone foundations, wooden frame and tiled roof, while the refugee himself was expected to fill in the walls with whatever material he chose.

Figure 12.4 Different types of houses adopted for rural settlement in Macedonia by the RSC.

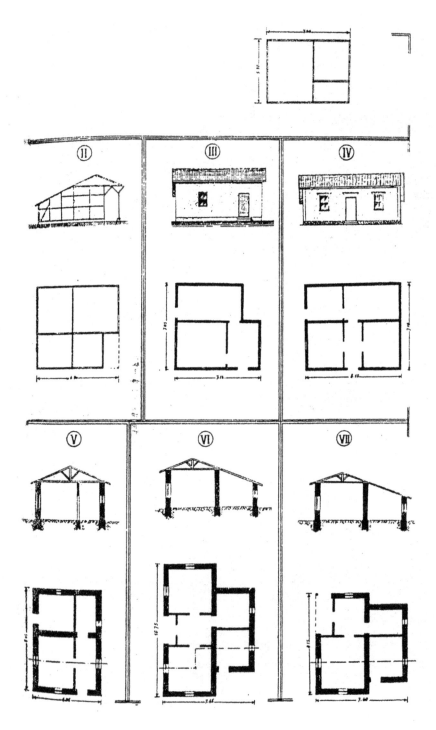

Figure 12.5 Types of houses for rural settlement presented in the 27th Report of the RSC (1930).

III: Standard type of accommodation for one family, with stone foundations and three rooms, one of which was a stable.

IV: One-family accommodation, with stone foundations and four rooms, one of which was a stable. Cost: 17,000 Drs.

V, VI, VII: Standard types of dwelling for a family of farmers, with stone foundations and walls, and a tiled roof (Pelagidis 1997: 244–5).

By 1930 the RSC had built 52,000 houses in addition to the 13,500 built by the state between 1922 and 1924 and the 64,000 abandoned by the departing Muslims (ibid.: 242). Commenting on the work of the RSC, Professor Jacques Ancel of the Ecole des Hautes Etudes Internationales wrote enthusiastically about the transformation that took place within a period of six years: 'Those miserable Turkish hamlets ... are now replaced by large cheerful villages... All around one sees sheaves of maize, fields of tobacco, kitchen gardens, orchards and vines. What a miracle!'(quoted in Pentzopoulos 1962: 111). In his book 'La Macédoine', the same writer often refers to the contrast between the old 'mean and crumbling' Turkish villages and the new settlements 'which can be made out from afar, with the regularity of their streets and uniformity of their houses, their white walls and red roofs' (Ancel 1930: 187).

Despite its initial reservations, from the beginning of 1924 the RSC started to promote urban settlement. The Commission was assigned land that was to be made available for the construction of urban districts, and it assumed ownership of the houses erected by the Refugee Relief Fund that were in need of repair. It abandoned the temporary solutions implemented in the previous period and instead pursued a policy of final rehabilitation, which was essential if the refugees were to be assimilated into Greek society. Over time, we therefore see a gradual but steady move towards durable and 'permanent' construction materials, towards blocks of concrete and bricks replacing planks and other forms of timber. In total, the Commission constructed about 24,000 urban dwellings in fifty-nine districts throughout Greece, but urban 'rehabilitation' essentially consisted of nothing more than simple settlement – refugees were given no help in making a living (Yiannakopoulos 1992: 35; see Hirschon 1998[1989]: 39–42; Kontogiorgi this volume).

When the RSC began its work on urban house-building there were four as yet unfinished settlements in Athens, and three in the provinces. Its first task was to decide upon the type of house best suited to the various special characteristics of the population. The Commission had no experience of such a problem and, as there were no precedents to draw on, it was obliged to improvise. In the first year of construction, the norm was for two separate units each housing four families to be built adjoining one another. On one side would be a single-storey unit with accommodation for four families all on the same level; on the other, a two-storey unit with two sets of living quarters on each floor. Generally, the single-storey units were built with sun-dried brick or mud, pebbles and straw, and the two-storey units with regular masonry, usually fired bricks. Each family unit typically had an area of some thirty-six square metres, organised into an entrance passage, sanitary facilities and two rooms of equal size, one to be used as a kitchen.

A second and third type of house was introduced, constructed respectively between 1925–1927, and 1927–1930 (Figure 12.6). In Athens and Piraeus many such houses were built in the districts of Kokkinia, Kaisariani, Nea Ionia and Vyronas. On the one hand, they included buildings similar in design and materials to what had preceded them, only now housing just two families. However, much larger units housing seven families were also introduced. This latter type of house was built on two floors with regular masonry from fired bricks. By 1926, Charles Howland, president of the RSC, felt able to write that 'the large refugee districts in Athens and Piraeus are real cities with fifteen, twenty, even twenty-five thousand inhabitants' (cited in Guizeli 1984: 192). Indicative of the official perception of these settlements is a description of Kokkinia in the Refugee Journal of the same year:

> Kokkinia may not have marble palaces and asphalt roads, but it does have 10,000 well-built dwellings following all the rules of hygiene, housing 45,000 refugees. And what smart and well laid out housing it is! It is a sign of the developments of the future. Little wooden houses, painted, bright as a new pin. If you offered the people here a palace to live in, they wouldn't leave. The old houses here are well cared for. The new ones, of reinforced concrete, are rising proudly everywhere you look.

The writer becomes almost lyrical as the paragraph closes:

> Kokkinia is simply a dream. Constructed with an appreciation of plastic beauty. Its town planning has made it a masterpiece. Roads one and a half kilometres long – both parallel to one another and perpendicular. To the little birds flying above, the little houses must look like lines of little soldiers. What a beautiful sight! (cited in Michelis 1992b: 182).

However, the aforementioned variations in design evolved in an overall context of monotonous uniformity (Guizeli 1984: 192–4). Indeed, in 1928 the RSC itself declared: 'Whatever the truth of the matter is, we have to admit that of the charges laid against our settlements, the best grounded is that of their uniformity, both in town planning terms and in the construction of individual dwellings (cited in ibid.: 197). The Board decided that the issue of uniformity could best be addressed by the introduction of varied road layouts and house designs, including the materials from which they were built. However, while the latter brought about variations in the desirability of dwellings, overall, uniformity prevailed (ibid.: 197–9).

Although the interests of the RSC did not really extend to the more affluent class of refugees, it nevertheless founded two communities of houses for this very group, in Ymittos and Nea Philadelphia. However, while some financial aid was offered, it was the refugees themselves who supervised the building, and they also made significant financial contributions from their own funds. The houses constructed resembled small villas. At Ymittos five hundred and fifty houses were initially built, not with timber or fired masonry but with fine local stone. 'Ymittos is as beautiful as an English suburb,' wrote

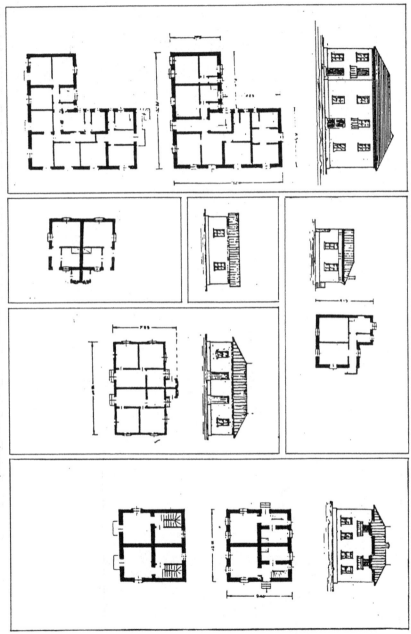

Figure 12.6 Types of urban houses presented in the 27th Report of the RSC (1930).

the papers of the time (cited in Michelis 1992a: 149). The development in Nea Philadelphia was occupied mainly by refugees from Constantinople who had arrived with some modest means of their own. Built between 1925 and 1927, the houses are on two floors, have verandas and balconies, and were divided from one another by avenues and squares decorated with flowers. Their occupants were successful merchants, manufacturers and office workers. They, with the inhabitants of Nea Smyrna and Ymittos, constitute the most privileged group among the refugees (ibid.: 149).

The houses of Nea Smyrna are a class apart from all other refugee dwellings. According to the New Plan for Athens drawn up by the P. Kalligas committee, twelve thousand plots of land were given to families who had the means to build their houses without help. Thought to be astute investments offering high returns, plots were soon being bought and sold on the open market. Refugees sold to other refugees, and even, remarkably, to Athenians (ibid.: 150). What resulted was magnificent: a host of small villas, giving the area the look of an attractive suburb.

Modifications and extensions

The refugees were faced with adapting their previous way of life to a harsh new reality, to new 'receptacles of life'. In order to reestablish continuity in space, they would have to become involved in the organisation and planning of their physical communities, having recourse to and building upon the memory of the way of life that they had left behind in Turkey.

Within just a few months of settlement, visitors observed the first changes and modifications in the endless, uniform lines of houses: plants in coloured tins, whitewashed channels for water to drain away and fresh paint on the walls. Colours were bright, diverse and everywhere: ochres, blues, greens and pinks, painted benches, porches – all underlined the occupants' desire for a better quality of life. According to H. Morgenthau: 'These mean little houses were, however, clean and almost cheerful in appearance: decorated here with a piece of embroidery in lively colours, there with hand-made curtains at the windows and always at least one geranium or basil in a tin, decorating the entrance' (cited in ibid.: 134). Dido Sotiriou gives an insight into the refugees' undiminished sense of pride about their homes:

> The refugees would put up their own shacks, using mud bricks, tins and packing cases. First of all they arranged their flower pots in neat rows and planted in them tiny anaemic bushes. 'To make ourselves feel at home,' they would say, 'to have a little green.' And they would even ration their drinking water, to make sure the plants didn't go thirsty. They whitewashed the shack they had built, so small that even the children's feet would protrude when they were lying down, and put some indigo in the whitewash to make the little house look clean and blue, as blue as the clear new sky above their heads. And in the evenings the women would embroider little curtains for the windows (1978: 217).

In this passage, attention is drawn to the complementary roles of men and women. In the Asia Minor Greek communities, decorative elements of the house and upkeep of the local environment are in the hands of the women. Not only is great effort made to maintain a clean and tidy house, but even the pavement and street outside the house is regularly swept, for an untidy or dirty house reflects badly on the character and worth of a woman, and her social prestige would suffer as a result (Hirschon 1985: 15–21).

Neighbourhood life in the newly built settlements is essentially an extension of the private life of the individual. Reflecting this, private built spaces are clearly connected to the overall environment of the neighbourhood. Of particular interest are the intermediate spaces between the private and the public, for these features transcend the limits of the purely constructed environment. Such areas of the house are spaces of a transitional character between the individual and the collective, spaces that ensure, in the context of the social life of the individual, a harmonious movement back and forth between the private and the social (Guizeli 1984: 118). Various studies in aesthetic morphology have highlighted the innumerable devices employed by the inhabitants to accomplish this harmonious transition between open-air areas and the inner spaces of the house – devices including hallways, courtyards, covered passageways, tents, and furnished living areas on terraces or verandas. Both interior and exterior at the same time, these features make up one of the richest chapters in the anonymous vernacular architecture of Greece.

The focal point of all these intermediate areas is the courtyard, placed at the centre of the building or to one side, open to the street. Perhaps a development of the atrium of ancient times, the courtyard is the space where privacy disappears, since activity there is exposed for all to see. Readily accessible, it becomes a meeting place for neighbours and a logical extension to a walk in the neighbourhood. The gate opening on to the street – if indeed there is one – is never locked; neighbours come and go freely to wish the household good day, and children can use the yard as a space for their games (ibid.: 118). It is ironic then that the courtyard area was often built over in the face of urgent need for extra space.

The modifications made to their houses by the residents of the new settlements were not confined to cosmetic and easily reversible changes. In her study of the district of Germanika in Kokkinia, Hirschon examines the changes that have been made in spatial organisation. These include not only functional changes of original space, but also the creation of completely new additional living space. Not only have refugees built on the exposed area of the courtyard, they have also built underground, excavating beneath the prefabricated structure in order to create basement rooms. Consequently, the overall increase of built space in this community has been 117 percent (Hirschon and Thakurdesai 1970: 194). Various reasons exist for these modifications, among them overcrowding, the need to provide a dowry (with kitchen) and legal impediments to ownership (see Hirschon 1998 [1989]: 117–128, 249–253).

Conclusion

In *The Image of the City*, Lynch wrote: 'We need an environment which is not simply well organised, but poetic and symbolic as well. It should speak of the individuals and their complex society, of their aspirations and their historical tradition, of the natural setting, and of the complicated functions and movements of the city world' (Lynch 1960: 119). Of course, in the shantytowns that sprung up on the edges of the cities, and in the organised settlements that the RSC established, a house was less a medium of architectural expression than a necessity for survival. However, even in conditions like these, the need for cultural expression through architecture is still present, even if forced to confine itself to the secondary features of the house, those features that the refugees could afford. Of little intrinsic value, such features nonetheless have vital symbolic importance as conspicuous and accessible bearers of recent cultural memory; it is this function which makes them the principal symbols in the iconography of the new settlements.

On an individual level, even though their house may have been no bigger than a garden shed of today, the refugees strove to create homes: 'There, at the end of the garden, was our little house. Perhaps no larger than this little cabin, but built with dry stone, not with brick, with packing cases and tins. Well plastered inside, a whitewashed hearth, a roof of tiles, not of tar-paper' (Politis 1988: 140). Individuals – often women – made modifications to the impersonal space in order to feel they had in some way made it their own, in order that their own small area be distinguished in some way from that of their neighbour. Thus each person's individuality, transcending all the shared features of ethnic descent and economic class, would be plain for all to see in the changes made to the uniformity of the original living space. In this way, each individual refugee family's identity was differentiated on a symbolic level from the original collective identity (see Hirschon and Gold 1982: 63–73).

The architectural symbolic system permits the individual to enjoy the experience of an environment endowed with meaning; it helps one find a new basis for life, to experience a new reality. In short, architecture's most essential function is over and above any physical structure: it is to contribute to giving meaning to human existence. All its other benefits – those that merely meet the physical needs of man – can perfectly well be achieved without it (Norberg-Schulz 1977: 433).

Notes

1. One street back from the seafront.
2. Archive of the Ministry of Foreign Affairs, file 1923/A5/VI/13, report of the Ministry of Agriculture: Direction of Resettlement, to the Ministry of Foreign Affairs, in Pelagidis 1997: 74.

13

Space, Place and Identity

MEMORY AND RELIGION IN TWO CAPPADOCIAN GREEK SETTLEMENTS

Vasso Stelaku

Introduction

Two groups of Cappadocian refugees who came to Greece in 1924 as a result of the Exchange of Populations Convention are the subject of this chapter. It examines some ways by which these displaced people adapted their past cultural identity to the new environment in Greece.

With respect to space, time, culture and communication, the disruption involved in the uprooting of people usually gives rise to significant disorientation. The uprooted lose their homeland, power and symbols, which together provide indices of their identity. They leave 'everything' behind, including many components of their former identity, especially their spatial and environmental heritage. In essence, they lose their 'home', where home, to quote Scudder and Colson, 'refers to community in the widest sense, as well as to the surrounding landscape, especially where it is incorporated into origin myths, historical accounts, and religious symbolism' (1982: 270; cf. Downing 1996). As a consequence, they lose the feeling of belonging.

Uprooted people, refugees 'withdraw into a narrow present' (Lynch 1972: 132). Their memories, their experiences and their lifestyle reflect the familiar past, one with which they are often obsessed. Reasons for this obsession can include the present being perceived as a stage of temporariness; a refusal to identify themselves with the disorderly and unfamiliar present, which tends to be out of their control; and a conscious effort to give continuity to their history and to reconstruct their identity. Alongside a process of remembering, refugees attempt to adapt their symbols to the new environment in the host country; in this way, they replicate their culture and they reclaim their past. As a result, one characteristic phenomenon of refugee communities is the preservation of the past. Usually this involves the formation of the new built environment to approximate the one they had shaped over generations in their homeland. In the case of the Cappadocian refugees, perhaps the most striking manifestation of this process is the considerable enterprise shown in the provision for their churches, which are the key markers of religious and cultural identity.

This chapter first examines how the Cappadocian refugees' past conditioned and was conditioned by refugeehood, and second, how an unfamiliar 'space' in Greece was transformed through the process of symbolic reorientation into a 'home place'. This was manifested in the emphasis on continuity achieved through the preservation of sacred relics, the retention of the church as a focal point, the reconstitution of the community, and the choice of name for the settlement.

The setting

Under the terms of the Lausanne Convention, signed on 30 January 1923, an approximate total of over 1.2 million Turkish nationals of the Greek Orthodox religion were exchanged for 354,647 Greek nationals of Muslim religion (Pentzopoulos 1962: 52, 69). As part of the final phase of this agreement, 44,432 Greek Orthodox Cappadocian refugees were expelled from Turkey and came to Greece as exchanged persons in 1924 (Merlier 1963: xix). Since they had not fled under conditions of military conflict, the experience for them was different from that of the earlier waves of refugees who arrived in Greece in 1922. In this chapter, I describe two Cappadocian settlements: New Karvali in eastern Macedonia, northern Greece, and New Prokopi in central Greece, on the island of Evia (Figure 13.1).

In choosing to study these particular settlements two factors proved decisive: their name and their cultural significance. Both settlements were named after places left behind in Cappadocia, with the addition of the word 'New'. This represents a key aspect of the adjustment process, namely the personalisation of the unfamiliar space as well as an expression of the refugees' need for continuity with the past. Belief in the miraculous power of the sacred relics that the refugees brought with them from Cappadocia in 1924 has spread, and both settlements have become well known religious centres that attract pilgrims from all over the country (Efpraxiadis 1974: 362; fieldwork notes 1996).[1]

The heritage of the past

Cappadocia is located in central Anatolia, and lies on a plateau between 1,000 and 1,500 metres above sea level. The landscape is extraordinary: it is

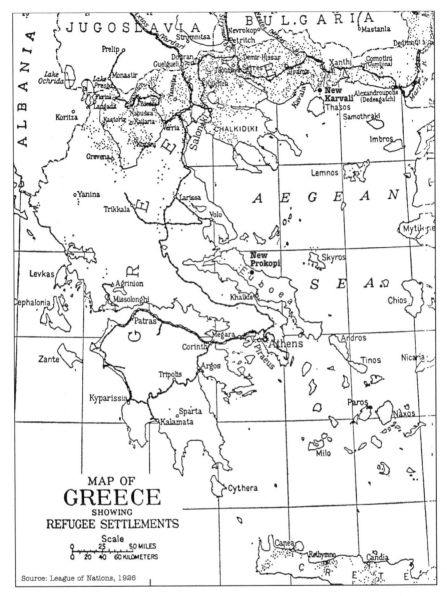

Figure 13.1 Refugee settlements in Greece, showing New Karvali and New Prokopi. (League of Nations, 1926 in Pentzopoulos 1962: 106).

dominated by cone-shaped rocks which were formed when successive layers of ash, cinder and lava were deposited over the countryside after volcanic eruptions. The plateau is enclosed by rocky hills and two extinct volcanic mountains (Panteleaki 1991: 8–9).

The relationship between the built and the physical environment of Cappadocia is particularly strong. Since the rocks are soft but not brittle, they are easy to hew. Over the centuries, Cappadocians took advantage of this with the result that the area is now scattered with churches, dwellings, and caves carved out of the rocks. Not only did these caves serve as ordinary dwellings, but they also provided a place of sanctuary for Christians during times of persecution (Texier and Pullan 1864: 38; Efpraxiadis 1974: 17). Accordingly, Ozkan and Onur note that, 'The geography of the region has permitted it to remain off the main routes of movement, and mountainous tracts of land have facilitated protection and seclusion for people seeking a place of refuge or religious retreat' (1975: 97).

Cappadocia was the centre of an early and great monastic tradition. From ancient times, the district of Prokopi had been a religious centre. In the third century A.D., the district converted to Christianity and the temples changed into Christian churches (Efpraxiadis 1974:19). During that period, the inhabitants were called 'osioi' (saints) because most of them were devoted to God (ibid.: 26). In the thirteenth century, about eighty thousand Christian monks and hermits lived in the caves in the district of Prokopi (ibid.: 40). As far as Karvali is concerned, at the beginning of the third century, the settlement was one of caves and chapels carved out of the rocks. Until the beginning of the seventeenth century, the area was inhabited only by hermits and by Christians of the surrounding districts who took refuge there to avoid islamisation (Akakiadis 1928: 23–24). The name Karvali itself derived from a corruption of 'Kellivara', the name of a local monastery (ibid.: 21) (known today in Turkish as Gelveri). Cappadocia was the centre of religious activity in the early Christian period and the home of some of the most renowned Church fathers, Saints Basil the Great, Gregory Nazianzus, and Gregory the Theologian, 'whose theological and philosophical originality sealed the entire history of Christian thought' (Zizioulas 1985: 24). A further factor that enhanced the Cappadocians' sense of religious conviction was that Caesarea (today's Kayseri), the most important ecclesiastical region in Asia Minor, fell within the region of Cappadocia. Its Metropolitan Bishop was given the title 'The Supreme of the Supremes and the Exarch of the Entire East', a title given to the commanders of this region during the Byzantine era (Skalieris 1990: 280).

More significantly, the fact that most of the Cappadocian Christians spoke the same language as the Muslims, i.e., Turkish, made them all the more inclined to focus on the Orthodox Church as a symbol of their distinctive ethnic identity. Balian emphasises that 'the ideological basis that contributed to the survival of Cappadocia's Orthodox populations was their religious identity' (1991: 38). Thus the Church became the vehicle through which the Cappadocians preserved and expressed their cultural differences.

One of the main reasons for the use of Turkish among the Orthodox Cappadocians was that large numbers of them migrated to major cities where, because of the use of so many different local dialects, the lingua franca was Turkish. Indeed, so pervasive was the use of Turkish that for commercial reasons journals and magazines were published in *Karamanlidika*, i.e., Turkish in Greek characters (Efpraxiadis 1974: 61–62). But in contrast, in the small villages of Cappadocia, the corrupted Greek language was spoken (Zampidis

1954: 16; Efpraxiadis 1974: 62; Mavrohalividis 1990: 284). In many Greek villages in the district of Budak Ova, Greek linguistic idioms were spoken right up until 1924 (Kostakis 1990: lxxi). Balian notes that 'The Cappadocian linguistic idiom, because of their centuries-old isolation from the evolution of the new Greek language, had conserved pure elements of the medieval Greek language' (1991: 32).

Petropoulou shows how a unique sense of identity was created through the Orthodox Church in that it cultivated the linguistic awareness and the religious consciousness of its flock side by side, using each to reinforce the other (1991: 43). As regards education, Mavrohalividis notes that, until the middle of the nineteenth century in Axo of Cappadocia, the priest assumed the role of teacher in the village. The old women called him the 'school priest' and the pupils 'children of the priest' (*papadopaidia*) (1990: 163). In Prokopi, schoolchildren were taught prayers in music lessons because the teacher used to prepare the pupils to be cantors. From 1880 the curriculum in Prokopi schools, as well as in other Christian schools in the Ottoman Empire, was set by the Ecumenical Patriachate in Constantinople, while schoolteachers had to be graduates of the high schools of Constantinople, Trapezus and Caesarea (Efpraxiadis 1974: 287–91). An insight into that curriculum is provided by Kostakis who notes that the pupils in Anaku in Cappadocia were taught the '*Psaltiri*' and '*Oktoicho*', prayers of the Greek Orthodox Church, as well as mathematics, Greek history, grammar, music, and Greek mythology. The ancient texts were translated into the puristic Greek language (*katharevousa*). As for the Turkish language, because the teachers were not conversant with the complicated system of writing in Arabic script and because the Ottoman state did not make it compulsory to teach it, it only started to be taught in 1895 (Kostakis 1963: 140–41).

The Cappadocian refugees in Greece

The case of New Karvali

In 1925, three hundred refugee families from Karvali, Cappadocia were settled in northern Greece on an unpopulated area by the sea, ten kilometres east of the city of Kavala. Between 1925 and 1926, three hundred refugee houses – all very similar to each other – were built on this site by the Greek Government. In 1926, the refugees named this area New Karvali.

According to the census before the exchange of populations, the population of the original Karvali totalled '4,500 Greeks' and '400 Ottomans' (Akakiadis 1928: 21). In 1991, the population of New Karvali totalled 2,100 (National Census 1991). The composition of the population, according to statistical data taken from the village's register in 1996, was: 1,894 inhabitants of Cappadocian origin; 56 people from Lefki[2] and 150 Pontic Greeks from Russia.

In fact, the current urban organisation of New Karvali is a result of government rather than refugee-led intervention in space. Moreover, today only fifty-four so-called refugee houses remain (fieldwork notes 1996). However, the refugee past makes its presence felt and it is this which ascribes identity to the settlement. Several factors are conducive to this. Firstly, the urban plan follows the pattern of the original one. Secondly, buildings related to the refugee cultural tradition, i.e., the church and the New Karvali Cultural Centre, dominate the settlement. Thirdly, the shopping area that has developed along the central road contains various enterprises selling traditional goods, especially sweetmeats and pastries. (Inhabitants run bakeries selling items following Cappadocian recipes.) Finally, the inhabitants themselves ascribe identity to the settlement by keeping the past alive in their memory, and the settlement's change and development are revealed through their narratives.

One building in particular is central to the organisation of the settlement and determines its identity: the church of Saint Gregory the Theologian. The church constitutes both a landmark and a node of activities related to the refugees' past, their place of origin, religion, and cultural tradition. The site of the church, its size and magnificence and above all the refugees' bond with it serve to emphasise the refugees' sense of 'place' (Figure 13.2).

The inhabitants go to the church for various reasons, not only to attend the liturgy but also for what the church offers: a place very familiar to them and intimately involved in their everyday life. The church constitutes a point of reference and a meeting place, and is a symbol of the refugees' culture, which simultaneously is embodied in the church itself. It stands for a formalised and unchanging belief, and the perception of stability that that gives rise to, and it also promotes a sense of security and creates a feeling of belonging. Indeed, on the flag flying over the churchyard is the symbol of Byzantium itself, the double-headed eagle.

It is not by chance that the settlement is often called Saint Gregory instead of New Karvali. The most celebrated calendar event in the settlement is the

Figure 13.2 The church of Saint Gregorios Theologos, New Karvali.

Festival of Saint Gregory the Theologian on 25 January. Strong belief in the miraculous power of the relic of the saint has spread all over Greece, it has become a place of pilgrimage, and great numbers come to visit it. Saint Gregory the Theologian is the patron saint of the settlement, and the refugees frequently turn to him for help. The fact that all the refugees call Saint Gregory the Theologian 'our saint' (*o agios mas*) or 'the saint' suggests a deeper level of attachment. Not only do such names reflect their familiarity with the saint, but they also serve to emphasise the special regard in which the Cappadocians and their ancestors held him, a tradition that the inhabitants of New Karvali have continued.

Located just behind the church is another building related to the refugees' tradition and culture, the Cultural Centre of New Karvali (*Stegi Politismou Neas Karvalis*). Established in 1995, it is here that the Centre for Cappadocian Studies and the Historical and Folklore Museum operate. The Cultural Centre of New Karvali constitutes a direct link between, and continuation of, the educational association 'Nazianzos' originally established in Constantinople in 1884 by Karvalian merchants. Among the museum items on display are documents, books, and photographs brought from Cappadocia. The Cultural Centre also comprises a library, halls for festivals and conferences, and a department for training students in traditional art. The Cultural Centre's Board of Governors has built an open air theatre, organised a 170–strong group of folk dancers, and established the International Folk Festival, 'Sun and Stone'. It also edits a magazine called 'Code' (Iosiphidis and Tsiriktsidou 1996: 2).

Characteristically, the inhabitants frequent the Cultural Centre not only in order to visit the museum or to attend a conference, but mainly because they relate to it as their 'home' – they are drawn to it naturally. The visit is part of their everyday walk, for the Cultural Centre represents the 'place' they are used to go to: it symbolises the past and consequently the collective memory. In addition, it also represents a place where the past is revived. Many refugees contribute to the work of the Cultural Centre, either by supporting it financially, through personal work or in teaching the young people traditional dances and weaving skills. In this way, the Cultural Centre is both a symbol and agent of continuity: through it, the Cappadocian refugees' culture has passed down to the younger generation.

The refugees stress that the creation of the settlement is the result of their desire to be together and so to recreate their community in Greece. To this day, memory and common origin continue to hold the community together. A first-generation refugee (born in Cappadocia) says, 'I am on good terms with my neighbours. All of them come from Gelveri [the Turkish name for Karvali]. As you can see, the key is in the door. Sometimes I leave it there, even all night long.' Nowadays, the profile that the inhabitants present reflects a feeling of 'being at home', a fact that is the result of adaptation and personalisation of space.

The case of New Prokopi, Evia

The refugees from Prokopi arrived in Greece in four shipments. The first went to Corfu; the second, carrying with them the holy relic of Saint John the Russian, to Halkis, the main town of Evia; the third to Skyros; and the fourth to Nafplion. When, at the end of 1925, 220 refugee families from Skyros and Halkis found their final refuge in Ahmet Ağa, they encountered a host population who worked as tenant farmers on Lord Baker's farm (Enotiadis 1994: 48). The conditions that confronted them were so harsh that they left Ahmet Ağa the same year to go to Athens, to Salonika, or to Halkis, Makrimali, and Psachna in Evia (Efpraxiadis 1974: 352). Between 1927 and 1928, two hundred refugee houses were built, though the refugee families that remained were very few (Enotiadis 1994: 56). According to one informant, Efthymios Sophoulis, the families who had remained were only fifty in number.[3] As in New Karvali, the refugee houses were similar to each other and had only two rooms (fieldwork notes 1996).

When at the end of 1925 the refugees settled in Ahmet Ağa, which they later renamed New Prokopi, their first priority was the transportation and installation of the relics of Saint John the Russian, from a church in Halkis where they had temporarily left them, to an existing church in Ahmet Ağa, that of Saint Constantine. Work was started in 1930 on the New Prokopi church, but only finally completed in 1951 (Figure 13.3). The consecration of the church of Saint John the Russian took place on 27 May 1951, the Saint's festival day (Enotiadis 1994: 362).

The population of Prokopi in Cappadocia (today's Ürgüp) totalled '12,000 Turks' and '7,000 Greeks' in 1919 (Efpraxiadis 1974: 30). The liturgy was cel-

Figure 13.3 The church of Saint John the Russian, New Prokopi.

ebrated in Greek, even though the language of Prokopi was Turkish. Only the Epistles and Gospels were read in Turkish, but after 1910 the whole liturgy was performed in Greek. In 1991, the population of New Prokopi in Evia totalled 1,127 inhabitants, and the number of families was 420 (National Census 1991). Only twenty-five of those families were of Cappadocian refugee origin (fieldwork notes 1996). Nowadays, the refugee quarter does not exist. Except for a few remaining refugee houses, New Prokopi presents the image of a new settlement. Only twenty-one refugee houses are left, of which just four are occupied by Cappadocian refugees. Seven others are occupied by members of the host population or by refugees from other parts of Asia Minor (fieldwork notes 1996). However, the refugees' past and the culture of the settlement are reflected in the church, the two guesthouses, and the shopping centre where traditional goods are sold. That past and the cultural heritage, as with New Karvali, is also related through the refugees' narratives.

The Festival of Saint John the Russian on 27 May is a great event. People come from all over Greece to venerate the relics of the saint for their miraculous power (Efpraxiadis 1974: 351–52, 361; Hirschon 1998[1989]: 222–24; Enotiadis 1994:25). Refugees are 'on close terms' with the saint, and his relic is a symbol of the refugees' past in Cappadocia as well as of the continuity and revival of their history and culture: 'I am a neighbour of the saint and I have decided to stay here for ever. I want all my property to remain in New Prokopi' (fieldwork notes 1997). The refugee who says this intends to bequeath all his property to the settlement (the quintessence of which is the saint) as he would bequeath it to his descendants. He stresses, 'The Saint is for me a way of living. I think of him as a member of my family. He is a part of me.'

Although the living conditions are very hard – nowadays unemployment is the main problem and 60 percent of the population work on a part-time basis – the refugees maintain that they continue to live in New Prokopi because of their saint, who himself is a refugee, and with whom they belong, being of the same 'race' (*ratsa*). In the refugees' testimonies, characteristically the concept of place is identified with the saint. 'When someone asks me, "Where are you from?" and I reply that I am from New Prokopi, sometimes they do not know Prokopi, but they know the saint. I am deeply touched because he is in our blood, in our roots...' (fieldwork notes 1997). In fact, New Prokopi is better known by the name of the saint than by its proper name. On the road leading to New Prokopi, there are signs 'To Saint John the Russian', instead of 'To New Prokopi'. In effect, the saint has become synonymous with the settlement's identity.

Like the church of Saint Gregory the Theologian in New Karvali, the church of Saint John the Russian in New Prokopi constitutes both a landmark and a node. In addition, due to widespread belief in the miraculous power of the relic, the economy of New Prokopi is dependent on it. It was what made possible the building of the two guesthouses where pilgrims stay when they visit New Prokopi, and it stimulates demand for the traditional food, icons, and mementoes of the saint that form the stock and trade of many of the shops on the central road of the settlement leading up to the church.

New Prokopi and New Karvali: a shared heritage

When the Cappadocians came to Greece as refugees they faced natural, built, and human environments that were alien to them. Other factors also served to aggravate the disruption of their former identity: the loss of their 'place'; the ambiguous identity of being a refugee; for the turkophone majority the fact that they were no longer in a Turkish-speaking environment; and for others, that the host population was not familiar with their particular linguistic idiom.

Although the mother tongue of most of the Cappadocians was Turkish, it ceased to be so for the generations who grew up in Greece. For those who spoke an idiom of Greek particular to their place of origin in Cappadocia, their mingling with the indigenous population and with refugees from other areas contributed to its disappearance (Pentzopoulos 1962: 215; Kostakis 1977: 539). Apart from these obvious practical reasons, the Cappadocians also found themselves subject to other pressures. The refugees from Cappadocian Prokopi stress that in Skyros the locals abused them (Enotiadis 1994: 47) and even prevented them from entering the church because they were speaking Turkish. One informant relates: 'The locals did not want us. "Go away. You are Turks. Go back to Turkey," they would shout at us. "We originate from Alexander the Great. We know the Gospel by heart, perhaps better than you do," we would tell them. Often they would abuse us with the word *tourkosporoi* [seeds of Turks]' (fieldwork notes 1996, 1997). Such treatment only compounded their sense of loss and disorientation in Greece.

It is noteworthy that the turkophone Greek Orthodox did not have an auspicious introduction to Greek in their homeland of Cappadocia. As one refugee says, 'An additional hindrance for the Turkish-speaking students was that the Greek taught in school was not the spoken [*dimotiki*] language but the puristic [*katharevousa*] one' (Stamatopoulos 1985: 51). A refugee from Sinasos describes the situation in the Greek school of Prokopi:

> They were aware of being at a disadvantage compared to me, speaking Greek with that horrible Greek–Turkish accent ... They could neither speak fast enough, nor find the appropriate words to express themselves. Greek for them was a torment. Being Greeks as they were, they refused to be taught Turkish in school and the Turkish they already knew was fluent and beautifully spoken. We, on the other hand, were being taught the 'ancestral' language in our village school, but we also knew our people's language and thus, once we left school and went to the Greek center, we were able to speak it perfectly and very easily forgot our 'ancestral' one. In contrast, those unfortunate Turkish-speaking students, after leaving school, very easily forgot their ancestral language and spoke their mother tongue – the Turkish language ... And when they spoke Greek with their heavy accent and the half-forgotten words of the 'ancestors' which came out with difficulty through clenched teeth, we laughed ... they tried as much as possible to speak less of the Greek they didn't know well, and more of the Turkish which they really felt was a part of them (ibid.: 51–52).

These people had been forced to learn the purified form of Greek in Cappadocia while preferring to speak their mother tongue, Turkish. When they arrived as refugees in Greece, they were forced to give up Turkish and speak a form of Greek with which they were entirely unfamiliar. If they wanted to assimilate in Greece they had no choice but to use the language.

When the irreversibility of their fate and the impossibility of return to Cappadocia were comprehended, most of the refugees forced themselves to adapt. This involved, amongst other things, the rejection of their mother tongue. However, many illiterate refugees never managed to learn Greek, and so passed the rest of their lives in this new motherland without ever speaking its language. Consequently, outside their family environment these people felt and remained alien, living in constant dependence on others.

A significant contrast is that whereas the Cappadocian perception of Greece was of 'a distant country where "their brothers" of the same nationality lived' (Mavrohalividis 1990: 369), a symbol of prosperity and force, the Cappadocian refugees were perceived by the host society, the government, and various agencies as 'different' and 'alien', despite their shared ethnicity. As a consequence, the refugees' experience in Greece was one of rejection. The label 'refugee' or 'Turk' affected their lives from the day they arrived (Enotiadis 1994: 47; fieldwork notes 1996, 1997). The continued feeling of being 'other' and 'alien' both reinforced their dependency and insecurity, and perpetuated the state of confusion into which refugeehood had already plunged them. The processes of social and economic integration were delayed as a result.

Nonetheless, it is a remarkable fact that all the refugees are proud of their Cappadocian and refugee origin: 'I feel a refugee … I am very proud of it … My parents come from Asia Minor … Should I ever claim being from here?' (fieldwork notes 1996). In addition, the refugees proudly tell how they gave their settlements in Greece the same name their villages carried in Cappadocia, a fact symbolising the starting point of their adaptation to a new life in Greece. However, although the label 'refugee' is used by the Cappadocians to prove their origin as a matter of pride, this same label reflects the marginal and disadvantaged position faced by a refugee in the host country (Hirschon 1998[1989]; Zetter 1995). In fact, the label 'refugee' is established upon important misconceptions aiming to form, transform and manipulate an identity 'within the context of public policy' (Zetter 1991: 40). Indicative of these disadvantages is the fact that refugees from Cappadocia tended to change the ending of surnames that betrayed Asia Minor origins. Most of the Asia Minor refugees' surnames ended in the Turkish '-oğlu' (-son), e.g., Karamanoğlu, Kazanzoğlu, etc., but they changed them instead to various endings, such as '–idis' or '-opoulos'. 'With a surname ending in -oğlu, you could not find a job. So, many of us changed the ending of our surnames' (fieldwork notes 1996). In this way, they tried to conceal their Cappadocian origin and thus simultaneously – even if unconsciously – they denied their identity. By adopting a new surname in order to survive in Greece the refugees suffered further psychological trauma.

Identity, space and place

The main elements that were influential in the process of the refugees' adaptation to the new environment were their past, their memory, and their culture. Tuan stresses that 'awareness of the past is an important element in the love of place' (1974: 99). Once uprooted from the place of their birth and upbringing, refugees lost the security that their 'place' could provide for them. However, the symbolic power of the image of their homeland which they carried with them informed the present, and it was adapted to it through their vivid memory (Carter et al. 1993). In other words, the refugees experienced the concept of 'place' both in familiar symbols and culture carried as a heritage from their homeland, and also through the past that they relived in the new homeland. These elements became embodied in the new space, and thus ascribed meaning to it and transformed it into a familiar 'place'. The refugees could be identified with a recognisable 'place', and they acquired a sense of belonging. That 'place' constitutes the physical space of the collective memory's reflection, for the concept of place has a double character: on the one hand, it represents a site where certain events have happened, but on the other it constitutes an event in itself (Eisenman 1982: 7). The relation of those two parameters became, for the refugees, the concept of the 'appropriated space', that is, the place imbued with the memory, history, and past. In this sense, the refugees' adaptation processes were determined by a process of 'remembering'. As Hirschon puts it, 'In order to reconstitute their lives, memory becomes a critical link, the means of a cultural survival, a kind of capital without which their identity would be lost' (1998[1989]: 15).

The main tools through which the new space was transformed into 'place' were the refugees' religious sense and the close bonds between the refugees themselves. Given that most of them were Turkish-speaking, for the Cappadocian Christians religion had constituted the basic element of their sense of ethnic identity and social cohesion, as well as the main component of place identity. In Greece, however, instead of the church being a symbol of difference it was used to reassure the hosts that they – the refugees from Cappadocia – were also Greeks and Orthodox Christians. Hirschon has noted that 'The sense of identity of the Asia Minor refugees was rooted in a shared heritage which centred on their religious affiliation' (ibid.: 17, 18–22)

The churches of New Karvali and New Prokopi constitute 'landmarks' and 'nodes' (Lynch 1960: 47–48) both because they are in close relation with the refugees' history and because they form not only the hub of many activities, but also the most important element in the economic and urban evolution of the settlements. The saints themselves became symbols not only for the memory of the Cappadocians' lost homeland but also for the refugees' adaptation to the new space. In this sense, the churches and the other buildings related to the refugees' religion and culture embody the concept of symbolism not merely as elements of memory of the past but actually as purposive action, i.e., an intentional revival of the past. Those cultural elements – mainly the presence of the relics of the saints – are transformed into elements of the material culture 'carried' from Cappadocia in order that refugees can reclaim their history and past. They are not merely character-istic elements of a settlement, but they also characterise it (Lynch 1960: 46; Rossi 1982: 21).

Aside from the religious dimension, the other main factor that helped the Cappadocian refugees transform their settlements from 'space' into a meaningful 'place' was that many of them were settled as communities and were not broken up and dispersed. This allowed the transplanted people to name their settlements in Greece after their villages in Cappadocia. This practice constituted a symbol of continuity emphasising their links with their past and further strengthening the concept of 'place'. In the case of the refugees who were brought together from diverse parts of Asia Minor and were settled in Kokkinia, Piraeus, Hirschon notes the importance of place names in creating a 'meaningful environment' (1998[1989]: 25).

In the case of the Cappadocians, the notion of keeping a discrete refugee community together as one unit in the settlement process played a significant role in the refugees' process of adaptation. By settling near relatives and their fellow villagers from Cappadocia, these refugees were encouraged to re-create their neighbourhoods. The presence of the community personalised the unknown and unfamiliar space. Refugees settling with their co-villagers recre-ated the sense of belonging to a community with shared traditions and experiences, facts that also encouraged the development of a collective mem-ory. In stressing the power of the culture, a refugee from New Prokopi says: 'I would not say that the refugees have lost a lot of things because, except for the loss of their property, they have not lost their "mentality" (*nootropia*). They managed to transplant it here, to their new homes' (fieldwork notes 1997).

Conclusion

I have described here the ways in which the refugees from Cappadocia sought continuity with their cultural heritage and imprinted it on their new environment in Greece. I examine how the Cappadocian refugees appropri-ated the new environment and how they changed the inaccessible and unknown 'space' into a familiar and recognisable 'place'.

Having lived in an extraordinary physical and built environment, the Cap-padocians were used to being actively involved in constructing their dwellings themselves. When they settled in Greece, it was the first time that they were forced to live in houses that others had provided for them. Thus they lost a sense of autonomy in the refugee context and they sought to recap-ture this by superimposing an identity on to their churches and communities. In other words, they tried to reconstruct a sense of belonging as an embodi-ment of their settlements.

Though over eighty years have passed, the Cappadocian refugees still recall their 'old' homeland, and the memory continues to be vivid, not only for the first-generation refugees but also for their descendants who have been brought up with Cappadocia's history and culture. Furthermore, for many of the first- and even second-generation refugees, the concepts 'here' and 'there', or Greece and Cappadocia, comprise the concept of homeland. Most refugees, especially from the first generation, stress that they feel they now have two homelands and that in the early days of their settlement in Greece they were – in their own words – 'daydreaming about', 'imagining' and 'longing for' return home. Zetter points out that: 'Alienation, persecution and forced migration are amongst the most profoundly disturbing human experiences ... The traumas of mass exodus confront those who are excluded from societies at times of acute political crises or rapid and fundamental redefinition of their economic, social and ethnic identity' (1991: 1). Indeed, a third-generation refugee from New Prokopi says: 'A refugee is a person who has no homeland, who has been uprooted. This is the crucial point. The refugees lose their contacts' (fieldwork notes 1997).

Notes

1. The fieldwork research is based first on testimonies taken from and interviews conducted with refugees in 1996/97, and second, on visual and cartographic recordings of the settlements' morphology.
2. A village near New Karvali that has been integrated into it.
3. See unpublished material by E. Sophoulis in the *Archeion tou Kentrou Mikrasiatikon Spoudon* [*Archives of the Centre for Asia Minor Studies*] Athens, recorded in 1954.

14

Lessons in Refugeehood

THE EXPERIENCE OF FORCED MIGRANTS IN TURKEY

Tolga Köker
(in collaboration with Leylâ Keskiner*)

Introduction

Of the hundreds of thousands of Muslim refugees that Turkey received under the 1923 Convention this paper concentrates on those who came from Greek Macedonia to Muradiye and Menemen, two small towns near Izmir.[1] Focusing on issues of identity, memory and adaptation, it draws lessons from their experiences, including their encounter with a new environment, their reception in Turkey, lost hopes about repatriation, and the reconstruction of their everyday life. The paper concludes by placing these experiences in the broader context of refugee studies.[2]

Much of the paper is based on the fieldwork of Leylâ Keskiner, who in June 1998 made repeated visits to the *muhacir* (refugee) community in Muradiye and Menemen, interviewing individuals born before or immediately after the population exchange about their personal experiences, memories and what it meant to them to be *muhacirs*.

Throughout the paper two Turkish words are used to describe a newcomer to Turkey: *muhacir* and *göçmen*. While certainly one of the meanings of both words is 'migrant', to give precise and exhaustive definitions is made difficult by the fact that their meaning has changed over time, and from place to place. However, two points are beyond doubt: firstly, only muhacir can have connotations of flight, and secondly, göçmen is a neologism that did not exist at the time of the exchange. Interestingly, while Leylâ Keskiner was gathering information in Muradiye Town Hall, the employees had a discussion about who is a muhacir and who is a göçmen. A so-called göçmen employee insisted that there was no difference, the word muhacir being a borrowing from Arabic and göçmen being the modern Turkish substitute; whereas a so-called muhacir employee claimed that the difference lay in the period of arrival: muhacirs being the immigrants of Atatürk's presidency (1923–1938) and göçmens those of İnönü's (1938–1950). The naming of the main muhacir quarter of the town after Atatürk, and the göçmen quarter after İnönü, reflects this view. For these reasons, in this paper muhacir is used for refugees who were expelled from Greece in accordance with the Lausanne Convention, while göçmen is the term used for later immigrants to Turkey, particularly from the Balkans.

Muradiye: a new homeland?

Before the exchange, Muradiye had been a purely *Rum* (Greek Orthodox) settlement. Therefore, when the muhacirs took up residence they formed the entire population themselves. This makes Muradiye an interesting and rare case in that the refugees remained in relative isolation until a second wave of new arrivals – the göçmens – came from the Balkans in 1939. Even then, the göçmens were settled in different parts of the town and created their own quarters. In direct contrast, the bigger town of Menemen bore witness to contact both between refugees and locals and between established groups of refugees and newcomers.

Muradiye is a small town located ten kilometres west of Manisa. The town itself is composed of three quarters or *mahalles*, all named after Turkish national heroes: Fevzi Çakmak Mahallesi, Atatürk Mahallesi and İnönü Mahallesi. The last is also commonly known as Yeni Mahalle, meaning new quarter, the name given to the göçmens' quarter by the more established muhacirs. Most of the muhacirs live in Fevzi Çakmak and Atatürk Mahallesi.

There are 582 residential buildings in Fevzi Çakmak Mahallesi of which 127 are unoccupied; in Atatürk Mahallesi there are 1,373 residential buildings, 304 unoccupied. The new quarter, İnönü Mahallesi, has 878 residential buildings of which 167 are unoccupied. The population of the town is almost static. According to the 1980, 1990 and 1997 censuses, the population was 5,695, 5,700 and 5,760 respectively. This suggests that there are fewer than three persons per household. However, there are also households with more than thirteen occupants, whom employees of the Municipality noted must be of Kurdish origin.

Due to the agricultural nature of its economy, most of the younger people leave the town to pursue a higher education or to work. Manisa attracts most of the migrants from Muradiye because of its growing manufacturing industry and close location. However, in Muradiye there are approximately five hundred people who work in small shops and the manufacturing or service sectors. This number includes the police, the employees of two banks, namely, state–owned Ziraat Bankası and semi-private İş Bankası, health personnel, and the staff of the three schools. The largest employers are the municipality, with forty-one employees, and Maksan Kola Fabrikası (a soda-pop bottling factory) with forty workers.[3]

There are two mosques in the town. One is called *Bizim Cami* (Our Mosque) by the muhacirs, and the other is known as *Göçmen Camii.*[4] The tea houses are another place to socialise. In all, there are twenty-two tea houses in Muradiye, distributed equally between the three quarters. Several of them are close to the mosques; old men sit around the tables, chat and socialise while waiting for the call to prayer.

Muradiye has been a municipality (*belde*) since 1952. The electorate has a tendency to vote for a centre-right party both in local and general elections. Only one mayor, Hamdi Altıok, has come from a social democratic party. He served two terms representing the People's Republican Party, from 1964 to 1968 and from 1973 to 1977. Furthermore, except for the three appointed mayors during the military takeover from 1980 to 1984, of the nine mayors in its history, only one mayor has come from the göçmen community. He was Sait İlbay, a candidate from the Justice Party, serving between 1968 and 1973.

The older generation cling to their memories and traditions, and work on small parcels of land to earn a living. While some built new apartment buildings, most of the muhacirs still live in the old houses assigned to them on their arrival (Figures 14.1 and 14.2). Indeed, nine out of the fourteen interviewees have stayed at their original settlement allocation. Little change has been made to the houses, especially in the plumbing systems. The houses that the interviewer saw still only had bathrooms in the courtyard. Although nobody remembers the exact date, the informants talk about how they carried gas-lamps in the streets while making house visits to their neighbours. According to the personal accounts of the informants, electricity must have been connected in the late 1950s; the telephone came a little later.

The older generation appears conservative, but behaves tolerantly towards the younger generation. For example, older women cover their hair and wear a long coat (*manto*) before leaving the house, but do not complain when the young do not. Although most of the older generation are understanding about it, they are also bitter about the fact that their sons, daughters and grandchildren want to leave the town to settle in a larger city.

For the older men, there is not much to do in Muradiye but go to the mosque. The muhacirs seem to be very devout Muslims, not skipping any of the prayers and referring to the prayer times frequently in their daily discourse. Interviews had to be arranged according to the prayer times: the first interview took place after the Friday prayer, and there were times when men being interviewed checked their watches so as not to miss going to the mosque. However, male muhacirs never hesitate to talk to women, or to give their hands to be kissed. (It is a sign of respect to kiss the hand of an older person.)

Figures 14.1 and 14.2 Former Rum houses allocated to Muslim families after the 1923 exchange (photos: Levent Sarcını).

Coming to the new lands

Some informants remember how in Greece they first heard about the news of the population exchange from the village imam, who had read about it in the newspaper, but most do not really remember how they first heard.[5] However, almost all of them remember the arrival of the Asia Minor refugees, for this, more than anything else, must have given them an inkling as to their own destiny.[6]

The picture that comes from the interviews about the final phase of their life in Greece is touching. In general, accounts state that the Muslims were living peacefully and happily, busy with their daily lives. However, there were also some unpleasant instances. For the most part, the informants tend not to talk about them much, but as they tell their stories information sometimes slips out, such as about schools and mosques being closed, bodies being secretly buried at night (interview with Sümbül Gür), and Greeks looting Turkish houses (interview with Sakine Günaydın). There is a repeated story about why local Greeks did not resort to much cruelty: supposedly Atatürk sent a message warning Greek officials about any cruelty directed against the Turkish, i.e., Muslim, population. One version has it that Kemâl made the following threat to the Greek authorities: 'Let me hear you've harmed a single Turk, and without taking my boots off, I'll be in Salonica.' (*Duyayım bir Türke eziyet ettiğinizi, çizmelerimi çıkartmadan Selanik'teyim.*) (Interview with Sümbül Gür). All of a sudden, though, Christian refugees from Asia Minor arrived at their courtyards; the local Muslim population were forced to open their houses, share their crops and feed the newcomers. The refugees wore the fez and spoke Turkish beautifully.[7] Christian mothers warned their children against singing jingles against Kemâl Paşa: 'Stop making naughty remarks against Kemâl. Come to your senses, Gire! We've got through the cruelty. God gave us cruelty. Let God make Kemâl's one day a thousand days.'[8] The newcomers were so content with the way that they were treated by the local Muslims in Greek Macedonia that they advised the Muslims where to go and settle in Turkey. Some even offered the gold coins that they had carefully hidden:

> That infidel told my mother, '*İnşallah* you will go to Kütahya. There is a new bridge there. Across the bridge there is a house with new doors. Settle in that house. That house is ours. Go inside, go into the room. There is a cabinet behind the door, on the wall. Open the cabinet, search for a hidden door in it. We have hidden a pot full of gold coins there. Take the coins. I give them to you freely! [*Helâl olsun!*]' But it was not our fate to go there.[9]

While the accounts from informants suggest that there was a great deal of good will, the situation was by no means accepted willingly by all. Haşim and Baki Akçasoy's grandfather, Kara Osman, wanted to stay in Greece, without changing his religion. It was not only he, but also his Greek neighbours who wished him to stay. However, his grandson, Baki Akçasoy, stated that other Muslims put about the rumour that if he stayed he would indeed convert to Christianity, and that under the subsequent social pressure applied by the Muslim community he changed his mind and decided not to remain after all.

All the informant muhacirs were shipped to Anatolia.[10] First, those who had not already gathered there had to be moved to the ports. There they waited to board the ships that would take them to the port nearest to their final destination. The deportation took from a couple of days to five to six weeks. Those who were able to pay the fare did so; for the rest, the Turkish government provided subsidies to the Turkish Maritime Company (*Türk Vapurcular Birliği*). The only informant stating that her family paid for the trip was Sakine Günaydın. She said: 'They [her family] paid the fare. They traveled in the ship's cabin not in the *ambar* [lower deck]. My father even paid for our relatives.'

None of the informants remembers any accounts of death during the sea passage, except for İsmail Özcan:

> It was a big ship. They had boarded nine villages onto it – animals and everything. They had carried the animals with machines: they had tied belts around the animals and lifted them up to the ship. It was so crowded they had to put some of the people down in the ambar. We stayed on the very top, on the deck. The wife of our village imam had died. They brought her up. There was a belief that if there was a corpse onboard, the ship wouldn't go. Superstition! Does the ship know? It was probably so that the body shouldn't smell. They didn't wash the body. They tied two pieces of iron rod this thick [about 10cm] and this long [about 50cm] here [showing his arm pits]. They tied the two iron rods, tied so that they would stay on her. They threw her to the sea, for the fish to eat her. I was so scared. I was scared to get sick and die. If I died they would have done the same thing. Thank God we didn't. We landed at Mersin [on the eastern Mediterranean coast of Turkey]. The trip lasted for nine days and nights. We were finally in Mersin.

The official number of deaths of muhacirs while being transported is relatively low. According to Turkish parliamentary minutes: 'Some 269 died on the way, nine died upon landing and 870 died in the tents and *baraka*s [huts]. The number totaled 3,819 including those who died after being settled' (cited in Arı 1995: 93). This may be the major reason why our informants do not remember such an event. Another factor could be their short trip: most of the informants said that it took a day or two for them to land at Izmir. However, almost all have some relatives who died immediately after arriving and settling in Asia Minor.

Most of the informants remember landing at the ports of Izmir or Urla (near Izmir) where they were put under quarantine and vaccinated.[11] Once released, a few informants managed to find relatives and stayed with them for a while. Those relatives were either early arrivals who had already found buildings to stay in, or officials of the Turkish government residing near the ports. Sümbül Gür remembers her mother recognising a relative within the crowd and staying with them for a couple of days before returning to the barakas. Sakine Günaydın's father's maternal uncle was the Director of Settlement (*İskân Müdürü*) in Izmir, who put the family up until they found their own place.

Resettlement and the first contact with locals

Muhacirs were assigned land and property abandoned by the Rum refugees. The official criteria for resettlement were based on where the newcomers originated from and the type of agriculture with which they were familiar. However, in practice it was quite different (cf. Aktar, Keyder, Koufopoulou this volume).[12] Those who came to Muradiye had to learn how to manage the vineyards and olive orchards. They were not familiar with the land, climate or the type of agriculture. It was the first time they had met with olive trees, and according to Haşim Akçasoy, muhacirs cut them down because they thought the fruit was inedible. He says that the locals complained as a result of which the government stopped allotting olive orchards to the muhacirs. Ahmet Kumrular also confirms this. Although he does not make mention of a complaint by the locals, he states that the government stopped allocating olive orchards to muhacirs and even reclaimed the ones that had already been distributed.

According to the Lausanne Convention, households had to provide property-ownership documents and title deeds in order to receive the equivalent of those possessions in Turkey. However, most informant muhacirs stated that the compensation provisions were not honoured by the Turkish government and that each household was given only two *dönüms*[13] of vineyard and two dönüms of field per person (regardless of sex and age) and a house. The basic grievances of the muhacirs are rooted in this (similar problems existed on the Greek side, cf. Kontogiorgi this volume). All of them, with the exception of Sakine Günaydın, say that the government did not even look at the documents they provided. The Günaydın family was lucky, maybe because they had a relative working in the settlement office. For her part, Sakine Günaydın said that her family had fifteen title deeds and were rightly compensated for them all. She says that there are rumours about her father bribing the officials to get property, but she denies them, saying that her family was very rich before the exchange and got what they deserved afterwards. However, Kaniye Karaorman stated that they were neighbours back in Florina and that the Günaydın family was not as rich as Sakine Günaydın claims.

Even though the Turkish Grand National Assembly had established the Ministry of [Population] Exchange, Public Improvement and Settlement,[14] the informants claim that the government did not provide any material or monetary assistance at all. None of our informants volunteered any information about governmental assistance, and when the interviewer asked them about it directly almost all answered, 'As if there was a government to assist.'[15] Shaw provides an extensive account of governmental assistance to a previous influx of Muslim refugees, those who came between 1918 and 1923, and he states that these policies were incorporated into the Exchange of Population Convention (1998: 90). Arı also describes an account of material assistance (items and their worth) and the civil initiatives for helping the needy immigrants (1995: 100–104). Despite having these official documents, however, our informants insist that they endured hard times because they were not given the animals and farming tools they needed, and instead had to buy them slowly as they saved money.

The houses that the muhacirs took over had previously been looted by the local population. They usually describe the houses as 'four walls, that's all' (*dört duvar, o kadar*). Those who arrived first stayed in tents while waiting for the local occupants to leave the houses. The local people who lived around the town had moved to Muradiye, and occupied the houses left by the Rums. Hacı Ahmet, a local from Karaali village, told the story of how the Greek army had set Manisa on fire and left all their property in cinders:

> There was nothing left. My father started crying. We'd become refugees. We came to Muradiye. Around the region, all whose houses had burnt down took over the evacuated Rum houses. Muradiye did not burn down. It was all the Turkish houses [on fire]. The people of this quarter came down to Muradiye. We entered Muradiye on the fourth day of the [Manisa] fire. The people of this village [Karaali] stayed for a year. We stayed here for two and a half years. My father got permission from the state. Timber and tile were given to those living in the nearby villages [so that they could mend their houses] and they were sent back to their homes. Then the exchanged people came. [The government officials] forced us to leave. My father asked for permission. [He didn't get it.] They [the muhacirs] landed on ready-made houses and lands. They cut down those beautiful vineyards left from the infidels and used them as wood. They devastated this plain. Now they treat vineyards and olive as gold. Now they've learned.

Ahmet Kumrular remembers coming to Muradiye a week after staying in Izmir.

> AK: We came here with our documents. We couldn't find what we had expected. We stayed in the tents here. We came here very wretched – one mattress, one sheet. The locals had occupied the houses. We stayed in the tents ten to fifteen days while the houses were evacuated.
> Int.: Did they feed you while you were in the tents?
> AK: Who had the bread to give to whom? Turkey was shattered. They were creating a new order. The government helped some. It distributed the houses, two dönüms of vineyard and two dönüms of field per person. Twelve people – 24 dönüms vineyard, 24 dönüms field. [The land that was given] was not clustered together, rather a parcel here, a parcel there.

Sooner or later, empty or not, all the muhacir families found a house. It was the amount of land they received which then became an issue. The families with fewer members received less land, which was regarded as a very unfair practice. The Kara Osman family (later named Akçasoy) came as nine people: a father, one unmarried son, one unmarried daughter and two married brothers with their wives and infants. (The infants were Haşim and Baki Akçasoy.) They all lived in a single house with three rooms and a separate room in the courtyard. Baki Akçasoy's nuclear family shared one of the chambers in the house. After him, his mother gave birth to five more children, but since they were born after the population exchange the family was not entitled to any more land. Eight people were feeding on six dönüms of vineyard and six dönüms of fields. The informants said that most of the older people who had enjoyed a better life in Macedonia 'could not survive the misery, and died soon after'.

In general, the local population was unfriendly. They called muhacirs names such as 'lousy muhacir', 'dirty muhacir' and 'naked muhacir'.[16] Some even said openly that they wished the ships had sunk so that the muhacirs could not have landed in Anatolia.[17] Upon being asked about their relationships with the locals, almost without exception the old people immediately said, 'We were on good terms,' until the interviewer asked, 'Didn't they call you names?' Without exception, they all started laughing at this question and the information came out: 'Yes, they were not that good in the beginning.' They even had petty fights like children. They did not pay visits to each other's homes. Most informants recall that neither the muhacir community nor the local population of Karaali village let a member of the other community cross the railroad line, which was regarded as the border.

In the muhacirs' eyes, the locals were cold, unfriendly and did not like *misafirs* (visitors, houseguests). One of the informants said: '[The locals] were so clean that they lived in their kitchen. They thought the misafirs would dirty their homes.'[18] They also thought that the food the locals cooked was different, almost inedible. A local informant remembers an occasion when a muhacir working in neighbouring fields was offered some food. He said how the muhacir could not swallow the food. He explained that it was because the muhacirs were not used to eating olive oil.[19] Afi Alev Akçasoy-Köker, who was present at all the interviews, said that the older generation could not eat food with olive oil because muhacirs were used to cooking with butter.

Divided families, divided communities

As if coming to strange lands as forced migrants was not enough, families and communities often faced the additional trauma of being allocated inappropriate land, the consequences of which could be grave. Leaving one's allotted plot meant giving up one's property rights altogether, but often there was no alternative. Such was the case with İsmail Özcan. He was originally located at Niğde, Aksaray in central Anatolia.

> They chucked us in a mountain village. The land was worthless. A clump of vines here, a clump of vines there. A few bunches of grapes on them. We could not stay. We escaped. I stayed there for three years. I came here because a fellow villager of mine was here. Here the land is fertile. Here a vine yields three times more grapes.

In cases where the allocation of land meant splitting up communities, some did not want to take up their assigned lots at all. Sakine Günaydın's family did not want to stay in Karşıyaka, Izmir, and moved to Menemen; Ahmet Uncu's family did not want to move to Turgutlu, Manisa, and moved to Muradiye. Necmiye Öğreten's family first moved to Küçükköy near Ayvalık, Balıkesir, but her maternal grandfather was in Muradiye. When they wanted to move to Muradiye they had to leave their property behind. She said that the judge scolded her mother when she asked to be given property in Muradiye in exchange for that in Ayvalık. Ceylan Ödül's original village was in Bursa, but later he came to Muradiye to be with his maternal uncle.

Ahmet Yalınç's story is extraordinary. When his family came to Muradiye his father looked around and decided to leave, whereas his mother decided to stay with the other members of her family. Ahmet Yalınç's father eventually settled in Bursa, where he found a new wife. Ahmet Yalınç remembers his father sending a message to his mother saying that he had found a new wife and advising her to find a new husband. When she did, her new husband did not want to be father to the young Ahmet Yalınç, so the toddler was de facto adopted by his grandparents. Ahmet Yalınç says: 'So my grandfather took over as my father and my grandmother as my mother. From Mustafa and Ayşe my parents became Hüseyin and Kerime, and my mother became something of a sister.' Maybe it was because of this confusion that he only got his land fifteen years later. In the meantime, he had to work hard to earn a living, doing many different jobs. He worked in a restaurant and in a tea house, he bought and sold cars, worked as a woodcutter, engaged in illegal wood-cutting, sold ice cream in the mountain villages, and sold tobacco on the black market. Since he had no land and property, no muhacir had wanted his daughter to marry him.

Arrival of the göçmens

Shortly before the outbreak of the Second World War, Turkey witnessed an influx of immigrants from the Balkans, some of whom found their way to Muradiye.[20] Even though Turkey remained neutral until the end of the war it was another period of hardship for its population. The muhacirs did not welcome the göçmens whom they were forced to feed: they treated the new arrivals very similarly to the way they themselves had been treated at the hands of the locals when they first arrived.[21] The göçmens were lucky, the muhacirs thought, because they had chosen to come and were able to sell their property so that they had enough money to settle in the new lands. Since they were not caught unexpectedly they were able to bring their animals and tools as well as all their personal belongings. In addition, the Turkish government discriminated against old muhacirs by providing the newcomers with more land. The göçmens were given ten dönüms of field per person and an extra one dönüm of land on which to build their house.

The newcomers were very hardworking people. The muhacirs talk about this characteristic of the göçmens with envy and admiration. They say that the göçmen people work from age four to ninety.[22] Their women also work in the fields, which was not the case in the muhacir community. The muhacirs say it is a matter of great shame to let women work, that their place is in the home as homemakers and raising the children. For this reason, they did not want their daughters to marry göçmens, especially in the early days. However, they were always willing to take göçmen brides.

Remembering the past and creating a closed community

The stories of the muhacirs are strikingly similar, and indeed are reinforced by the stories in Kemal Yalçın's (1998) *Emanet Çeyiz: Mübadele İnsanları* (Entrusted Trousseau: the People of the Exchange). The wealth possessed before the exchange has become the stuff of myth, and the past, in which the 'homeland' has become almost utopian, is glorified. Almost all the informants talk enthusiastically about their homelands, and about how peaceful, wealthy and happy they were there: 'We were farmers. The land was so fertile. You could grow anything. There was an abundance of everything. There were two lakes, one to the west one to the east. My uncle was a hunter. Geese, ducks, their eggs, fish: there was an abundance of food. Here, we found nothing. There, we had a lot of food.'[23] However, as they were interviewed further it was revealed that in Macedonia they grew crops of just a single variety whereas in Turkey they had actually learned to grow a greater variety of fruits and vegetables. They learned about figs, olives, and about other edible plants, such as *hardal otu* (mustard green), *börülce* (green black-eye beans) and *kereviz* (celery). In fact, they felt nostalgia more for the sheer scale of their land in Greece: 'Of course I miss my homeland. Most of all I miss my land. There we had 2,500 dönüms of land. Here they gave us two dönüms per person. We were four people – two sisters, my mother and I. They say property is the core of one's being [*Mal canın yongasıdır, derler*].'[24]

Most remember their fathers or grandfathers saying, 'One day, we will return.' Haşim and Baki Akçasoy are cousins. In Turkey, they lived in the same house with seven other members of the household. They both recall finding sacks full of Greek currency (which was no longer in circulation). They both claim that this was evidence of their grandfather's will to return to their lands in Greece. There are exceptions, however:

> We were on the border of Bulgaria and Greece. We were smugglers. We saw a lot of cruelty – a lot of cruelty. Thank God we are on Turkish lands, on Muslim lands. Who wants to live in the land of the infidels? Infidels cannot be friends. Thank God we are here. May God not make us re-live the things we went through. May God deliver us from those days. The things we suffered... (interview with İzzet Burgazlı).

Upon being questioned whether he misses or would like to visit his land of origin, İzzet Burgazlı finally lets down his defences and says, 'Yes, I do miss it,' and concludes: 'I want to go back but I cannot. [Now] those are the lands of the infidels.'

Lessons of the muhacirs' experience

The first generation of refugees is the one that suffered most. The harsh repercussions that they had to endure Scudder and Colson refer to as physiological stress, 'best measured by increased morbidity and mortality rates following the removal' (1982: 269). In the absence of comparative studies for the period before and after the Lausanne exchange[25] it is impossible statistically to prove that morbidity and mortality rates were aggravated among muhacirs. However, the interviewees repeatedly said that their elderly relatives died relatively young, because of 'misery and broken hearts'. The muhacirs' belief in this regard is very similar to that of other relocatees, for instance those of the Favela removal in Rio de Janeiro, of the Najova and Yavapai tribes of North America, and of Sudanese Nubians.[26] There is no evidence of similar physiological stress among the göçmens who immigrated to Turkey of their own free will.

The experience of the population exchange on the Turkish side clearly shows how such a process should not be executed.[27] Fearing that the agricultural season would be disrupted if there were any delays, the parties were in a rush to start the exchange (Arı 1995: 2), meaning that the Rums and Muslims were compelled to emigrate without any proper notification. The Muslim expellees were forced to travel under inhumane conditions, with no international agency helping them once they had left for Turkey, and when they landed in Anatolia they received only limited health assistance from the Turkish Red Crescent.

Since the muhacirs were not moved as social units, communities were broken up and they lost pre-existing social networks and local forms of organisation. For example, half the population of Kayalar and Eleviş in Greek Macedonia were sent to the Aegean coast, and the other half to the Black Sea region.[28] The division of families and communities increased the impact on behavioural patterns, worsened the damage to economic practices and institutions, and speeded the loss of common symbols. The result was a major reduction in the muhacirs' cultural inventory, and hence their social capital.

No effort was made to minimise the distance between the areas left and the areas to which expellees were relocated. Moreover, some muhacirs were located in central Anatolia and on the Black Sea coasts of Turkey where the habitat is completely different from the Aegean basin. Tobacco farmers were allocated vineyards, and vine cultivators were given olive orchards (cf. Aktar this volume). The arbitrary assignment of refugees to unfamiliar habitats eventually led to the degeneration of agricultural and natural resources: grazing land was denuded, water resources depleted, and the landscape deforested. Later, self-settled göçmens chose to settle in habitats familiar to them, and consequently had a more beneficial effect on the environment compared with the muhacirs.[29]

Most muhacirs lost their property as a result of the exchange. They brought their title deeds from Greece with the assurance under the terms of the 1923 Convention that they would be compensated with comparable property in Turkey. However, one of the biggest problems in settling the forced immigrants was the de facto occupation of abandoned Rum property by the locals. In addition, the jurisdictional uncertainty between the Ministry of Finance (*Maliye Vekâleti*) and the Commission of Immigrants (*Muhacirin Komisyonu*) on the right of possession created confusion (Arı 1995: 117).

Although the immovable property left by the Rums was supposed to be distributed to the newcomers through the Commission, the Ministry had already disposed of much of it through public auction or through leases to locals, army officers and state employees. Furthermore, the reallocation mechanism was overtly political, especially in urban areas (Keyder 1987: 82). It was as a result of such a system that large muhacir families were allotted only a limited amount of land.

The departure of the Rum population from all over Anatolia had left a shortage of skills and under-capacity in the Turkish economy (Arı 1995: 2). It was expected that this vacuum would at least be partially filled by the arrival of the Muslims, but instead the poorly organised and ill-planned resettlement programme only aggravated the situation.[30] The combination of this incompetence, the lack of any international assistance and the shattered state of Turkey's economy meant that the muhacirs were left to fend for themselves in often wretched, alien and hostile conditions.

Conclusion: refugee experiences in retrospect

One of the main reasons for the compulsory exchange was the creation of a 'homogenous population', which was regarded as a prerequisite for nationhood.[31] However, as Bernard Lewis points out, some of the refugees could not even speak Turkish. He goes on to argue that 'this was no repatriation at all, but two deportations into exile – of Christian Turks to Greece, and of Muslim Greeks to Turkey' (1961[1968]: 348–349).[32] Similarly, William Ramsey writes that the Cretan Muslims were 'obviously of Greek origin' (1916: 21). Of this last group, Mackridge writes that it was ironic that they were exchanged for the Christians of Ayvalık because the two were virtually identical except for their religion (1986: 75–76). Moreover, even today, some native Anatolians regard the descendants both of muhacirs and of other latecomers as 'outsiders'. For example, in a discussion about Turkish politics a native Turk told Afi Alev Akçasoy-Köker, the locally born daughter of a muhacir from Macedonia, 'You did not die [in the 1919–22 war] for this homeland [*vatan*] so you have nothing to say on this matter.'

Demonstrably, turning minorities into refugees does not guarantee the formation of 'homogenous national homes', which itself is one of the many failures of modernity. This fact is reflected in the discourses of the forcibly displaced from both sides of the Aegean. Implicitly condemning European-born nationalism, they often say that it was the Great Powers who brought the hatred, and the 'stupid politicians' who made them hate one another.[33] In her novel, *Matomena Chomata (Bloodstained Earth)*, Dido Sotiriou (1985)[1962] also gives air to such views, highlighted by the closing words of the book: 'Damn those responsible.' If only one conclusion can be drawn from this paper, let it be that forced migration and involuntary resettlement cause too much human suffering. They are not inevitable, and should be prevented. The search for long-term stability shows us that 'prevention is a key – and that the only way to attempt to prevent flows of refugees is to attempt to cure the causes of their flight' (Thorburn 1996: 122). If one concedes that no political dilemma – regardless of its 'complicated' nature – is unresolvable, then the argument that forced migration is a way of saving lives is unsound.

Appendix: details of fieldwork

Tolga Köker has lived in Menemen for six years and he has visited Muradiye several times before and after the fieldwork. Before Leylâ Keskiner went to Muradiye and Menemen, Afi Alev Akçasoy-Köker had informed her elder brother, Baki Akçasoy, about their arrival and had asked him to tell his friends about Leylâ's' intention to interview them. Leylâ arrived in Muradiye on 19 June 1998. The interviewees were informed, and times were agreed in advance. Baki Akçasoy served as a contact and go-between. That day four interviews were held: Baki [Akçasoy] (b. 1922, Eleviş, Florina-Manastır), Haşim [Akçasoy] (b. 1922, Eleviş, Florina-Manastır), Ceylan [Ödül] (b. 1909, Peteska, Florina-Manastır) and Ahmet [Uncu] (b. 1919, Noylan, Salonica). On 22 June Leylâ went to Menemen to interview two local informants: Ayşe-tete-[İnan] (b. 1333 [app. 1918], Divrik, Sivas) and Mustafa Naci Ertuğ (b. 1926, Menemen, İzmir), and two muhacirs: Sakine [Günaydın] (b. 1337 [app. 1922], Florina, Manastır) and İzzet [Burgazlı] (b. 1328 [app. 1913], Drama, Salonica). Sakine Günaydın resisted telling her and her family's story that day. The next day Leylâ and Afi Alev Akçasoy-Köker went to Muradiye to interview three more muhacirs: Ahmet [Yalınç] (b. 1334 [app. 1919], Langaza, Salonica), Ahmet [Kumrular] (b. 1331 [app. 1916], Eleviş, Florina-Manastır) and İsmail [Özcan] (b. app. 1913, Kesiriye, Manastır). On 26 June Leylâ went back to Menemen and Muradiye to interview Sakine Günaydın (details above), Kaniye [Karaorman] (b. app. 1913, Florina, Manastır), Sümbül [Gür] (b. 1329 [app. 1914] immigrated from Serbia to Salonica after the Balkan Wars of 1912–13) and Necmiye [Güneş-Öğreten-Taşçıoğlu] (b. app. 1922, Salonica). One day later, she went to visit Karaali village to conduct interviews with *yerli*s (natives).

Notes

I should like to express my gratitude to Afi Alev Akçasoy-Köker and Baki Akçasoy for arranging the interviews on which this paper is based. I also thank Muhittin Acar, Laurie Brand, Didar Erdinç, Ferdan Ergut, Julia Havelin, Hakan Yavuz, Onur Yıldırım, and Nasır Yılmaz for their helpful comments. This paper has also benefited from the comments of conference participants, of whom a special thanks goes to Renée Hirschon for her encouragement and insight. This article is dedicated to the refugees of both Asia Minor and the Balkans, particularly İzzet Burgazlı and Sümbül Gür who died just after contributing to this research.

* Leylâ Keskiner: Freelance researcher, M.A. in history (Indiana University, Bloomington, USA).

1. Tolga Köker's mother's family belongs to these communities.
2. This paper is one of the rare works on such communities in Turkey. Some studies exist focusing on Muslim refugees in Anatolia prior to 1924. See, for example, McCarthy 1993: 87–111 and Shaw 1998: 58–90. Attention is also drawn to Yıldırım 2002.
3. The information about the town was gathered through an interview with the employees of, and documents prepared by, the Municipality of Muradiye.
4. Hülya Oğuzel, a third-generation muhacir born in Muradiye, said that until recently she thought that Bizim Cami was the Göçmen Camii because it is closer to her family's house. This is one of many manifestations of continuing refugee experience.
5. Interview with Baki Akçasoy.
6. During the Lausanne negotiations, some Muslim religious leaders in Macedonia expressed their objections to a forced exchange in writing to the Greek government (personal communication, Onur Yıldırım). However, it is doubtful that the lay Muslim population foresaw a forced exchange.
7. Interview with İsmail Özcan.
8. Interview with Necmiye Öğreten. The jingle in Turkish goes something like: *Yaşa Kemâl Paşa, yaşa ... Boktan yaşa!* ('Long live Kemâl Paşa, long live ... Long live like shit!') The girl's name who sang the jingle was Gire. The mother's words in Turkish were: *Gire, Gire aklını başına topla. Biz zulümü aştık. Allah bize zulüm verdi. Kemâl'in bir gününü Allah bin etsin.*
9. Interview with Necmiye Öğreten. Similarly, Sakine Günaydın and Sümbül Gür said that the Asia Minor refugees advised their families to go to Menemen and Manisa.
10. For the shipping arrangements, see Arı 1995: 36–43.
11. See Arı 1995: 43–49. The Red Crescent Association of Turkey (*Hilal-i Ahmer Cemiyeti*) carried out vaccination and provided limited health care services to the refugees.
12. Arı writes that it was planned for some 4,000 tobacco farmers, 20,000 vine cultivators and 40,000 olive farmers from the regions of Zeytüncü, Drama, Kavala and Salonica to be relocated to Manisa, Izmir, Menteşe and Denizli (of western Anatolia). He also points out that the reallocation in practice turned out to be quite different (1995: 52–53).
13. One dönüm is equal to one thousand square meters, or one-fifth hectare, or almost a quarter acre.
14. *Mübadele, İmar ve İskân Vekâleti.*
15. '*Hükümet mi vardı kızım, da yardım etsindi.*'
16. '*bitli muhacir*', '*pis muhacir*' and '*çıplak muhacir*'.
17. Interview with İsmail Özcan.
18. Interview with Sakine Günaydın.
19. Interview with Ahmet Yardımcı, a native from Karaali village.
20. In its 1995 country study of Turkey, the Federal Research Division of the Library of Congress points out that: 'Between 1935 and 1940, about 124,000 former residents of Bulgaria and Romania immigrated to Turkey. Between 1954 and 1956, about 35,000 immigrated from Yugoslavia. Between 1923 and 1980, an average of 23,764 immigrants arrived in Turkey annually. Of these, 36 percent came from Bulgaria, 30 percent from Greece, 22.1 percent from Yugoslavia, and 8.9 percent from Romania.' See http://lcweb2.loc.gov./cgi-bin/query/r?frd/cstdy:@field(DOCID+tr0040). These figures definitely increased after 1980 with the arrival in Turkey of refugees from Bulgaria in the late 1980s and Bosnia in the mid 1990s. There are also some refugees in Turkey from Afghanistan, Iran and Iraq.
21. For example, İsmet Akçasoy, a göçmen bride married into a muhacir family, recalls being called a 'dirty göçmen' (*pis göçmen*) as a child by the muhacirs (interview with İsmet Akçasoy).
22. Interview with Ahmet Yalınç.
23. Interview with Ahmet Kumrular.
24. Interview with İsmail Özcan.
25. However, Cernea provides some statistical evidence of increased morbidity and mortality after forced migration among relocatees in Ghana, Sri Lanka, Thailand and Indonesia (1996).
26. Documented in studies by, for example, Fahim 1973, Scudder 1979, Perlman 1982, Khera and Mariella 1982.

27. See also the literature on the resettlement of development-induced displacement, for example, Cernea 1988, Cernea and Guggenheim 1993, Cernea 1993, Downing 1996, Cernea and McDowell 2000.
28. Interview with Alev Akçasoy-Köker.
29. For arguments supporting self-settlement, see Jacobsen 1997, especially pp. 30–34.
30. For an analysis of how the deportation of minorities negatively affected Turkey's economy, see Keyder 1981: 21–23. For the effect of the departure of minorities on the social fabric in Turkey, see Keyder 1987, especially chapter 4, and this volume. See also Aktar this volume.
31. It has also been argued that in pushing for an exchange the operative concern of the Turkish delegation at Lausanne was to stifle Greek irredentism in Turkey and to put an end to foreign interference in the country's internal affairs (Dark 1998, Göçek 2002).
32. Geoffrey Lewis also makes a similar point regarding the exchange (1974: 88).
33. For quotations of this type among Asia Minor refugees, see Hirschon 1998 [1989]: 30. The author has observed the same discourse among Balkan immigrants to Turkey from Albania, Bulgaria, Greece and the former Yugoslavia, as well as among Turkish Cypriots.

15

Muslim Cretans in Turkey

THE REFORMULATION OF ETHNIC IDENTITY IN AN AEGEAN COMMUNITY

Sophia Koufopoulou

Identity issues

The Lausanne Treaty has been a subject of inquiry in many and diverse disciplines, ranging from demography to international law, from economics to social and political geography.[1] However, what much of this work has in common is its focus on the national and international, whereas relatively little research has been published examining the Treaty's consequences for individuals and communities.[2] Relying on oral, genealogical and other data collected during extended fieldwork in the 1990s, I focus here on how the implementation of the Convention, the actual population exchange, affected the lives of the Muslim Cretans, a group that was forcibly relocated to the Turkish island of Cunda.

Various terms have been used to denote this group.[3] In this chapter, I use the terms 'Muslim Cretans' and '*Kritiki*' ('Cretans' in Greek). I use Muslim Cretans when discussing the situation on Crete before and during the exchange in order to distinguish between the Muslim and Christian inhabitants of that island; I use the term Kritiki in the post-exchange context, for that is how the current inhabitants of Cunda describe themselves when speaking Greek, the language in which interviews took place.[4]

When the islanders talk of their removal and resettlement as a result of the Lausanne Convention, they do not – unlike the majority of Muslims that were expelled from Greek territory – refer to themselves as *muhacir*s (immigrants, refugees, in Turkish), but rather as *mübadeleci*s (exchangees). This distinction came to my attention when I tried to explore whether their experiences had been similar to the experiences of the refugees who fled to, or were relocated in, Greece, and for whom a sense of separate refugee identity developed during the twentieth century (Hirschon 1998 [1989]). Objections to forays into this subject were subtle, consistent and firm, and usually constituted variations of the response, 'We are not muhacirs, we are mübadelecis. When we came here we brought our money and our property – muhacirs brought nothing.' Whereas the term muhacir is associated with poverty and misery, and with various other ethnic groups in Turkey (see Köker, this volume), the term mübadeleci allows the Kritiki to differentiate their ethnic identity, and strengthens the Cretan refugees' claim of being superior to the refugees who came from other areas of Greece.

Just as there are various terms for the members of this community, there are also various names for the island itself. The original name of the island is Moschonisi (Bibelas 1956). Nowadays, this name is used to describe the island by local inhabitants for the benefit of Greek tourists, and also by some local intellectuals.

Officially, the island is called Alibey Adası, the name given to it by the Turkish government as part of its nationalistic effort to turkify all Greek place-names. It was chosen to honour the Turkish general who conquered the island in 1922 during the war between Greece and Turkey. This name is used – at least it was in my presence – by bureaucrats, Turkish tourists (referred to as *xenoi*, i.e., foreigners, by the Greek-speaking locals) and local residents with strongly nationalistic agendas. The third name, Cunda, is the most frequently used by the Turkish mass media and intellectuals (Çiçekoğlu 1992; see articles in *Milliyet* by Gönültaş, 1 October 1991) and also by the local residents. The origin of the word is unknown, but the locals support the idea that it is a Greek word, and they have created a variety of myths associated with it, mainly harking back to their own Venetian, Ottoman, and Greek past. Indeed, the inhabitants of the island have created a strong sense of Cundalı identity, the expression of which is frequently apparent in their confrontations with the neighbouring people of Ayvalık. In this paper, I will use Cunda when I refer to the island after the settlement of the Kritiki people, and Cundalı identity when I refer to that community's local identity.

The principal objective of this paper is to show how a people's identity has been recast by the imposition of an institutional legal arrangement, in this case the Lausanne Convention. To this end, I examine a number of factors, including the effect the exchange has had on the Kritiki's livelihood, their language, shared ideas and symbols, their religious beliefs and practices, and other cultural indicators such as gender roles and gender relationships.

Initially, I recall an episode that occurred at the very beginning of my field research, one that to me perfectly encapsulated the feeling of multiple ethnic-local identities so evident among the people of Cunda. One of my key informants, an elderly lady in whose *pension (pansiyon)* I stayed during my fieldwork, was one of those forcibly relocated to Turkey from Crete in the 1920s. In the presence of a visitor from Istanbul, my landlady was recounting how difficult it was for her to do the household's weekly washing. She had washed the clothes in a manual washing machine, but out of fatigue had left the wet clothes sitting in a basin for almost twenty-four hours without rinsing them. The visiting lady offered to help rinse and hang out the clothes. My landlady politely refused the offer but acknowledged that she herself ought to rinse the clothes immediately so they would not get an *oturmak myrodiası*. Literally translated, this means a 'sitting smell', which refers to the stale smell associated with damp. This phrase and its context constituted for me what Fernandez (1986: xi-xii) labels a 'revelatory incident', a notion based on the micro-sociological methods of Geertz' idea of 'thick description' (1973). Firstly, linguistically, my landlady had revealed herself by using her pidgin language, a combination of Greek and Turkish, with Turkish being dominant. She used the Turkish word *oturmak*, which means 'sitting', in combination with the Greek word *myrodia*, which means 'smell', and she made a compound of the two nouns using the Turkish convention of attaching the possessive suffix –sı to the second noun. Secondly, this key phrase *oturmak myrodiası* metaphorically represented for me the situation of these relocated people in that the refugees' identity could, in a very real sense, be equated with the 'sitting smell' that the Kritiki acquired after the 'washing cycle' of the relocation mandated by the Lausanne Convention.

The 'washing cycle': some background information

In accordance with the terms of the Lausanne Convention, most of the Muslim population of Greece (with the exception of approximately 110,000 Muslims living in Western Thrace) was forcibly relocated to Turkey (Dakin 1972).[5] However, it would be a mistake to assume that this entire group was homogenous. One major characteristic distinguishing the Cretan Muslims was their language: they spoke a particular dialect of Greek called Kritika[6] (Andrews 1989). This dialect itself has sub-dialects such as Haniotika and Rethymniotika.[7]

Before the exchange, the Muslim Cretans lived mainly in Hania, Rethymnon, and Heraklion-Kastros, with a small number living in the province of Lasithi. According to the census of 1881, there were approximately 75,000 Muslims on the island, as compared to 200,000 Christians (Stavrakis 1890). In 1898, due to Crete's newly won independence from the Ottoman Empire (Dakin 1972), Muslim inhabitants of the island emigrated in large numbers to other Ottoman domains, including Istanbul, Izmir, Bodrum, Antalya, Syria and Lebanon (Mansur 1972; Ozbayri and Zakhos-Papazakhariou 1976; *Adesmephtos* 5 April 1999). Although some returned to Crete later, the overall effect was a large reduction in the Muslim population of the island. Indeed, it is estimated that by the time of the exchange, the Muslim population on Crete was between 23,000 and 40,000.[8]

The official policy of the new Turkish government was to settle the exchanged people in the communities that had just been vacated by the

Christians who had either been forcibly relocated or had fled because of their fear of Turkish reprisals. One such locality was the island of Moschonisi (now Cunda), in Edremit bay, north of Izmir and opposite the Greek island of Lesvos. My fieldwork data indicate that by 1925 almost 4,500 Kritiki had arrived in Edremit bay. The ˜washing cycle', that is to say their relocation, was implemented mainly through the use of Turkish boats, and the trip to 'their fatherland' has been described by key informants as more of a 'cruise' than as a painful refugee experience.[9] This contrasts sharply with the narratives of the Asia Minor refugees who were forcibly relocated to Greece (KMS 1980; KMS 1982).

The 'rinse cycle' and its implementations

With the 'rinse cycle' and the end of the so-called cruise came a new and alien environment, a new culture and, of course, the ordeal of the obligatory quarantine period. (Quarantine periods were adopted by both the Greek and Turkish governments as a precaution against major infectious diseases.) The following description indicates how strange the Kritiki found their new society and culture: 'When we arrived, the locals were waiting for us with welcoming music – but it was a strange, wild music. They had big drums [*daoulia*] and we, the children, were frightened. We had never seen *daoulia* or heard these sounds before. We knew only the music of the *lyra* [fiddle] and *mandolino*' (İsmet Teyze, informant from Cunda). Despite the external and landscape similarities between Crete and Cunda, the latter was still viewed as a strange and rather alien place by the forcibly exchanged Cretans. One particular complaint among the first generation of Kritiki concerned the differences in climate. Compared with Crete which is in the southern Aegean, Cunda, located in the northeastern Aegean, has a much cooler climate, especially during winter. However, notwithstanding climate differences and related difficulties, the Aegean coastline of Turkey is ecologically similar to that of Crete. In both regions, large areas are given over to the cultivation of olive trees, and in both areas sheep and dairy farming are prevalent.

Another characteristic common to both Cunda and Crete is their similar architecture and building styles and technologies. Given the pre-1920s economic prosperity in both areas many beautiful houses and buildings had been constructed in the neoclassical style. The Cretans in Cunda have built myths and stories around these houses. For example, the locals told me that one of the most beautiful houses on the seashore, which today is an orphanage, was once the house of Venizelos' daughter. However, we know that Venizelos (the renowned Greek statesman and politician) did not have a daughter and never visited Moschonisi.

I feel that these physical and ecological similarities between the two locations suggest that the process of assimilation of these refugees into mainstream Turkish life was likely to be neither fast nor fluid. Given the recurrent visual reminders of their former residence and the similarity in landscape between their old and new communities, Cretans did not have to change their attitudes and lifestyles as dramatically as they would have done if they had been relocated to a completely different environment. This similarity allowed them to live and identify themselves much as they had done in the past. Indeed, Cunda and the nearby town of Ayvalık is described in terms of their landscape, architecture and general planning and construction as 'sleepy Greek towns' in the 1989 Insight Guide.

Economic consequences

Even allowing for the fact that in the individual and collective memory of refugees the past is often 'beautified' and previous status tends always to be elevated higher than current status, from the testimony of the Kritiki it nevertheless appears that the economic consequences of the exchange were quite devastating. Almost all of the interviewees referred to the superior socio-economic status of their lives in Crete compared with their lives in Cunda, especially after they first arrived on the island. This phenomenon was most pronounced in individuals whose families were described as middle-class city dwellers. Not only had they enjoyed high status relative to the farming community on Crete but they had also had to bear the additional shock of moving from an urban to a rural area. Furthermore, in Cunda there was a lack of employment opportunities in industry and the crafts. Still, it was very interesting that during my fieldwork some speakers insisted that they were able to preserve their socio-economic status in the new country. These were mainly rich Muslim Cretans who had enjoyed prominent roles in Crete's olive farming, and who were able to continue in the same business in Cunda. Significantly, because they were prepared for the exchange, which did not occur until 1926, they were able to bring much of their money and belongings (including furniture, linen, silver and porcelain). In addition, when the Muslim Cretans moved to Cunda, they were able to take advantage of the existing infrastructure for the production of olive oil and related commodities which had been abandoned by the former Christian inhabitants of the island when they were forced to leave abruptly. The Mytilinii (Muslim refugees from the island of Lesvos) who first settled in Cunda described the situation graphically: 'When we first came to Moschonisi, we were surprised to find that on the tables were dishes of food, some of it already on forks ready to be eaten.'

The great majority of the newcomers gradually left the initial reception area, usually to seek better economic opportunities in urban areas. According to Stavrakis' statistical analysis (1890), and reinforced by observations from my fieldwork, many Muslim Cretans were artisans, manufacturers, professionals and industrial workers. The expulsion of the Rum bourgeoisie class and the destruction of the vibrant economic triangle between the island of Lesvos, the Ayvalık area and Smyrna had significantly reduced economic opportunities in the region (Sifnaiou 1996).[10] Consequently, although some professionals did remain on Cunda, the vast majority of Kritiki who stayed on were peasants, farm-workers, sailors, fishermen and shepherds. The occupations of the Muslim Cretans did not change greatly after their relocation. They continued to work in the olive groves, at the olive press or in the creameries producing cheese, butter and yoghurt. Furthermore, the necessity to learn Turkish was not pressing because the vocabulary and language required for occupational and professional purposes remained essentially unchanged. (The same did not apply to those people who moved outside the area.)

However, the major problem for the Kritiki was not language, but the absence of a sizeable and sustainable market to absorb the product of their labour. Since the old trade networks had been lost due to the expulsion of the Rum bourgeoisie who had controlled them (Sifnaiou 1996), the Kritiki had either to create or re-establish them. In this regard, their knowledge of Greek proved very useful. Those Kritiki who spoke both Greek and Turkish had the greatest opportunities because they became the intermediaries between their own community and both the Turkish state and the Mytilinii. Even though the Mytilinii were Turkish-speaking Muslims and had arrived first, compared with the Kritiki very few of them managed to exploit their Turkish-language advantage in the political arena, no doubt because those Kritiki who spoke both languages were highly educated and could exploit the wily skills that they had already honed in the political circles of Crete. In fact, my fieldwork suggests that despite the fact that the Mytilinii had originally been more wealthy than the Kritiki, it was the latter who in the resettled communities became the more prosperous.

General economic deterioration forced many of the poorer Kritiki to adopt fishing as their primary means of support, which has now developed into a strong industry. Starting around the 1960s, this economic involvement in fishing became another factor in the reinforcement of the Kritiki's identity and dialect. The isolated nature of fishing fostered cohesiveness and solidarity within the group, and given the fact that a weak local market meant that most of the catch was exported to Greece and Italy, it was not as important to speak Turkish. Given the sustained demand for fish and its stable and competitive price structure, Kritiki fishermen also embarked on smuggling their fish to the Greek island of Lesvos. Other enterprising Greeks, mainly from Salonica, learned of these smuggling networks and began to organise the Kritiki fishermen into companies that would sell exclusively to them. During the 1990s, fish was moved on an everyday basis to Salonica, from where it was exported to Italy. Recently, though, the Kritiki have established their own direct contacts with buyers in Italy.

One of the most interesting effects of what I call 'the 'rinsing cycle' has been the development of the tourist industry. During my research, I encountered a number of locals who openly declared that it was actually the effects of the Convention that elevated their socio-economic status: as a result of their Cretan origin and being native Greek-speakers, the Kritiki were uniquely placed in a niche market. Until the late 1980s, Greek tourists formed the predominant international tourist group in Turkey, coming as pilgrims to their grandparents' homeland, and it was to their interests that the

Kritiki were perfectly qualified to cater. Indeed, it was largely because of these tourists that Cunda and Ayvalık were able to develop a fledgling tourist industry in the first place. However, after several Greek tourists were attacked in the early 1990s, tourism from Greece declined, but the industry has now successfully reached out to a wider European market.

Religious consequences

Because they spoke Greek, the Cretans were treated by the other Turkish ethnic groups as foreigners, especially by the Sunni Turks and the Mytilinii Muslims, and were called *gavur fidanı* (infidel saplings). This reaction is similar to that experienced by the Turkish-speaking Christian population relocated to Greece who were labeled *tourkosporoi* or *tourkomerites* (Turkish seeds) by the Greeks (cf. Stelaku this volume).

In their effort to become accepted and to prove their national and religious credentials, the Kritiki became more religious, in much the same way as some of the Asia Minor refugees who settled in Greece (Hirschon 1998[1989]: 30–33). A number of the original Kritiki, particularly those living in urban areas, had been Bektashi and Alevi Muslims. Gradually some of these people abandoned their own religious practices and 'converted' to Sunni Islam. The rationale behind their conversion was, first, that the socio-political climate of Turkey under Atatürk did not encourage or support their original religious practices and, second, that conversion to Sunni Islam was thought to ensure greater acceptance by, and equality with, other Turks in general.[11] However, the majority of Kritiki have preserved the religious practices and customs that were incorporated into their Muslim faith through a process of religious syncretism between Christianity and Islam. For example, during Easter the Greek Orthodox dye eggs red (symbolically representing the blood of Christ) and they make a special sweet bread called *tsoureki*. The Kritiki in Cunda do exactly the same thing during the Muslim *Hıdrellez* celebration of the Prophet Ilias, and moreover, they recognise that they adopted this practice from the Christian Greeks.

Gender consequences

Among the Muslims in Crete, the men were the breadwinners and the women filled the traditional role of home-keeper, responsible for childcare and domestic and family chores. However, regular contact with the Christian Orthodox and Europeans in general, especially in urban areas, led to the increasing secularisation and modernisation of their traditional Muslim way of life. This influence can be discerned from their stories of travels in Greece, and from photographs and oral descriptions of their clothes, houses and lifestyle in general in Crete.[12]

When they moved to Cunda, the Cretan women were shocked because the Mytilinii, who were mainly from rural backgrounds and had had less contact with the Christian Orthodox communities, still wore traditional clothing and maintained a traditional, peasant way of life. While in the process of redefining their own identities, which included adopting the Europeanising reforms of Atatürk, the Kritiki began to develop something of a feeling of superiority towards other displaced Muslims. The women followed Atatürk's radical encouragement that they participate in the labour force or open their own businesses, and they placed a very high premium on education. The legacy today is that many of the third- and fourth-generation female Kritiki are well educated and work in the formal service sector of the Turkish economy.

It is noticeable that the Kritiki women support every effort of the Turkish government to encourage gender equality, and it is reflected in the way husbands and wives participate equally in decision-making in the household. This is not to say that equality between the sexes in the western sense has been applied uniformly in their everyday lives. There is still a strong division of labour, and usually the husband is the primary wage earner. A certain degree of segregation between the 'female' and 'male' worlds exists, and the social life of women is more intense than that of males in the sense that women have much more free time to spend being involved in the community (Koufopoulou 1992, 1993). As breadwinners, men spend approximately eight to ten hours at work outside the home. Women, in contrast, can complete their domestic tasks and still find time to engage actively in social relationships and in establishing and preserving social networks through regular and expected visits to the homes of friends and relatives. This social behaviour is a longstanding norm among Muslim women (Tapper and Tapper 1987). Notably, however, within their own ethnic communities, their status as females is much higher than that of women in other ethnic groups (Abadan-Unat 1981, 1986; Kandiyoti 1990). In short, the perception of gender equality among Kritiki can be characterised as being similar to Gökalp's ideas on women's status and their role in the Turkish family (Duben and Behar 1991).

Although the Kritiki women are the gatekeepers of their Cretan identity, at the same time they try to incorporate into their everyday lives every western attitude that Turkey imports. This is reflected not only in their style of dress but, significantly, also with regard to food and cuisine. In order to maintain and preserve their characteristic Cretan diet, the Kritiki cultivated vegetables extensively. Eventually, the Kritiki became well known throughout Turkey for their culinary expertise, variety and innovation. In particular, the Kritiki introduced broadbeans, artichokes and various herbs (Psilakis 1995), and their fondness for herbs and a wide variety of vegetables and greens became renowned throughout Turkey, mentioned even in travel guides (Atlas 1993; Gezi Traveller 1997). The first joke that locals tell regarding their diet is that once upon a time the *za* (domestic animals) took the Kritiki to court to sue them because they were eating all their food. Nowadays, of course, their diet is perceived as being very healthy, particularly as it incorporates the use of much olive oil, a fact that does not go unexploited by Kritiki women, who say that this proves that their cuisine is sophisticated and cosmopolitan.

In the same way, referring to their dress code, female interviewees often repeated the expression 'black is the colour of a Cretan woman'. The fact that black is also chic and fashionable probably plays no small part in the motivation for making this statement, and is yet another indication of the Kritiki women's innate sense of a more outward-looking European identity.

Cultural consequences

Having been uprooted from their homeland, the Kritiki have created a culture out of being refugees. *Kriti mou omorpho nisi, to phioro tou Levanti* (Crete, my beautiful island, the flower of the Levant) is a *mantinada*[13] known even among the younger generations about homesickness for Crete (Magrini 2000). In the case of the Kritiki, as with all refugees, the expatriation was deeply traumatic, but this did not prevent them from attempting to recover or from trying to recreate their past lives in their new homes – their strength emanated from their desire to survive.

In Crete, the Muslim part of their identity was pronounced in their confrontations with other Greeks, whereas after their displacement, their Cretan identity became the central focus of their interaction with other Turks. This explains why in references to their lives in Crete they call themselves Turks, but when they talk about themselves today they use the word Kritiki. In other words, the exchange of populations changed the critical feature of their ethnic identity rather than leading to ethnic assimilation. Their Kritiki dialect is still used among the third generation, but it is beginning to fade away among younger generations. Within the fourth- and fifth-generation Kritiki, the Cretan dialect has almost disappeared entirely, largely as a result of vigorous state efforts to promote homogeneity in education, but also because of the effect of the mass media and nationalist propaganda in general. However, in the face of such difficulties, there are a number of fourth- and fifth-generation Kritiki who have recently rediscovered the Cretan language, either for intellectual enrichment (there is an intellectual movement that favours the Greek language) or for economic and business reasons (young people involved with tourism). Ultimately, the Cretan dialect is only one of a number of cultural elements that promote Kritiki ethnic cohesiveness and solidarity. These include food (selection and preparation), the dress code and, most importantly, their innate sense of Europeanness based on their Cretan past.

The Kritiki, like many refugee groups, re-created their past by retaining certain key elements of their culture (cf. Hirschon 1998[1989]). Other parts of their cultural heritage have vanished or diminished in importance, in particular their Cretan music. When they were first moved to Turkey, the Cretans continued to entertain themselves by singing mantinades, and by playing the Cretan lyra. However, modern Greek and Turkish music took precedence for later generations, and the older, more traditional forms of entertainment faded in importance (cf. Williams 2003).

Conclusion: the absence of an 'automated spinning cycle'

This case study reveals how an institutional decision and process – the forcible exchange of populations between Greece and Turkey – promoted a unique Cundalı identity. The Kritiki's very existence as a discrete social group is based on their compulsory displacement. Their relocation enabled them to restructure their past and to use it for their successful present, while their key phrase, *biz de Avrupalıyız* (we too are European) is an example of their expression of this new identity, and a justification of their acceptance of everything western and modern. This is not to say that there is no official process of assimilation (an 'automated spinning cycle') in this community. On the contrary, the Turkish state tried to assimilate these people through education, the mass media and other institutional mechanisms, and for a period of time the Cretan language could not be spoken publicly or in the presence of Turkish officials.

The Cretans' resettlement in Cunda assisted them in spinning their new identity in a number of ways. Its many similarities with Crete made it easier for the Kritiki to establish a continuity of the present with the past, and to this day it allows for the perpetual creation and re-creation of their Cundalı identity. Also of central importance in this creation is the fact that this is a border area. Numerous studies have emphasised the impact of borders on community life in terms of the preservation of double or multiple national and ethnic identities (e.g., O'Dowd and Wilson 1996). In the case of Cunda, there is considerable smuggling across the Greek–Turkish border. This smuggling activity began in the 1930s and continues to this day and involves regular and sustained, if clandestine, contact between elements of the two border communities (Koufopoulou and Papageorgiou 1997). Secondly, Greek tourism to Cunda and Ayvalık has flourished since the 1980s and has necessitated that the third- and fourth-generation Cretans revitalise their Greek-language skills so as to be effective in this industry. Thirdly, being so close to Greece, the Kritiki have been able to view Greek television and listen to Greek radio. To do so was especially popular until the early 1990s, at which point the number of Turkish television and radio stations greatly increased. In the old manual electric washing machines like the one my landlady used in the village, the absence of a spinning cycle leads to the accumulation of water and residues in the actual washing load. That is why my landlady was obliged to squeeze out the water manually – unsuccessful efforts could lead to the development of mildew and an unpleasant odour. Similarly, in the case of the Cundalı Kritiki, an 'automated spinning cycle' that might have led to full assimilation of the *mübadeleci* was absent, and consequently a certain odour or *myrodia* was left. This can be discerned in various contexts in the interplay of the Kritiki's multiple identities: national (Turkish), local (Cundalı), and ethnic (Cretan). In the absence of an automated system, the people became responsible for 'spinning' their own fate. By rediscovering their past and successfully adapting it to the present, they have formulated a new Cundalı-Cretan identity. In so doing, like other immigrant and refugee groups in the Balkans and the Middle East, they have constructed a contemporary identity based upon a shared Ottoman past.

Notes

1. See for example Ladas 1932; Pentzopoulos 1962; Davidson 1974; Kolodny 1974; Svolopoulos 1977; Koufa and Svolopoulos 1991; McCarthy 1983; Kitromilides and Alexandris 1984–85; Kolodny 1995; Barutciski this volume.
2. Exceptions are Salamone 1987; Hirschon 1998[1989]; Antoniou 1995; Tsimouris 1997, and chapters in this volume by Köker and Stelaku. Also Erginsoy 1998.
3. In the anglophone literature, they are variously described as Greek-speaking Muslims or Cretan Muslims (Danielsen 1989), as Muslim or Muslim Cretans (see Millas' this volume) or simply as Cretans, with the associated connotation of Turkish refugees from Crete (Mansur 1972). In the francophone literature, they are usually labeled either as *Turcocretois* (Turko-Cretans) (Kolodny 1995) or as *Cretois Musulmans* and *Turcs d'origine Cretois* (Özbayri and Zakhos-Papazakhariou 1976). In the Greek literature, they are usually named either as *Tourkokritiki* (Hidiroglou 1972) or as *Kritotourkoi* (Agelis 1998). Finally, in the Turkish literature, they are usually referred to as *Giritli*, which is the Turkish word for *Kritiki* or Cretan. The group's self-designation is usually Kritiki when they use Greek and Giritli when they speak Turkish (Yorulmaz 1997).
4. The researcher is Greek and the entire research was usually conducted in *Kritika*, a Cretan-Greek dialect.
5. See Appendix for Article 2 of the Lausanne Convention, signed on 30 January 1923. Later, a second exception was made for Albanian Muslims living in Epirus (Dakin 1972).
6. Despite the current, fertile discussion among linguists and sociolinguists about the usage of the terms dialect and sub-dialect and their possible replacement with the term language, I prefer the term dialect. My preference is reinforced, and indeed informed, by the seminal work of N. F. Kontosopoulos (1988) on the Cretan language, in which the term dialect is preferred.
7. I arrived at this conclusion through my own fieldwork, during which I studied both Haniotes (Muslim Cretans from the city of Hania and its suburbs) and Rethymniotes (Muslim Cretans from Rethymnon).
8. Kolodny (1995) suggests that 23,000 people were actually relocated. Özbayri and Zakhos-Papazakhariou (1976) state that the figure was much closer to 30,000. Through extrapolations of data collected during my fieldwork, I think the number exceeded 30,000 and was closer to 40,000.
9. This designation comes from some of my key informants when they described the details of their voyage from Crete to Moschonisi.
10. Smyrna was one of the major economic centers of the eastern Mediterranean. Through Smyrna, Aivali and Lesvos olive oil and various products generated from olive oil production were exported to the western Mediterranean centre of Marseilles and to other European trade centres.
11. During my fieldwork, I attended many female religious gatherings (Mevlut readings) and I was 'adopted' by the female organiser of them. In all of these religious gatherings there was a clear-cut line of distinction between the Giritli and the Mytilinii women on the one hand and the Kurdish Alevi women who settled in Cunda in the 1930s on the other.
12. A good source of information is various pictures dating from the beginning of the twentieth century photographed either by Greeks, Europeans, or Ottoman photographers such as Behaedin.
13. A genre of extemporary lyrical singing based on rhymed distichs.

16

The Exchange of Populations in Turkish Literature

THE UNDERTONE OF TEXTS[1]

Hercules Millas

In spite of the reciprocal aspect of the exchange of populations between Greece and Turkey, the event is reflected differently in the literary texts of the two countries. In this analysis, I concentrate on Turkish novels and short stories related to the forced exchange, with only occasional references to Greek literature in order to highlight the differences. Of those differences the most striking is the limited appearance of the event in Turkish literature. I maintain that this is mainly owing to political reasons. In addition, the way the two societies perceive themselves also plays a role. In Turkish literature the predominant sense is that of belonging to a strong and sovereign central state. This contrasts with Greek literature in which the sense of a motherland – closely associated with a family home, personal memories and the 'space' of a small local community – is more keenly expressed.

Silence: the exchange in the Turkish novel, 1923–1980

This study is based on 290 randomly selected novels and 60 volumes of short stories of 105 Turkish writers published in the years between 1923 and 1998.[2] The analysis shows that in the years from 1923 to 1980, and especially until 1960, the references to the exchange are very few and mostly indirect. The event was also interpreted in different ways according to the political ideology of the writers.

The first case in which the departure of the Greeks is encountered is in the novel by Aka Gündüz (1886–1958) *The Star of Dikmen (Dikmen Yıldızı)* published in 1928. The snobbish young girl Nazlı complains that after the great fire of Izmir in 1922 the city had lost its beauty, implying that she does not approve of the changes that took place after the departure of the Greeks. The heroine Yıldız is furious and she even doubts the ethnic purity of her former friend. Yıldız is happy that the old city has been burned down: 'Our torn-down hearts were built up again together with the flames, as the flames tore down those houses.' Yıldız would like even the foundations of the walls to be removed in order to save the city from its old, i.e., Greek, appearance (ibid.: 199–201). The message that the reader discerns from this passage, reflecting a nationalistic point of view, is that all sacrifices are worth the effort in order to free the city from its unwelcome enemies.

In his novel *Panorama* (1953) Yakup Kadri Karaosmanoğlu (1889–1974), another nationalist writer and one who in general portrays Greeks as negative characters,[3] even portrays a Muslim immigrant, Fazlı Bey, negatively because he resembles the Greeks.[4] Fazlı Bey, one of the exchanged from Ioan-nina/Yanya, seizes the property of poor peasants and then exploits them with exorbitant usury. He is not liked by the villagers. The members of his family still speak Greek amongst themselves, which reminds the locals of the Greek invasion of 1919. Fazlı Bey is a clever and shrewd businessman, 'like all the immigrants from Rumeli' (ibid.: 66–76).

However, these writers represent only one particular ideological approach in Turkish literature. A second approach is seen in *Ateş Gecesi (The Night of Fire)*, a novel by Reşat Nuri Güntekin (1889–1956) published in 1942. Gün-tekin is the forerunner of a humanist approach. In *The Night of Fire*, Greek-speaking Muslim immigrants who came to Turkey from Crete before 1923 are portrayed living in a predominantly *Rum* environment in Milas, a town on the Aegean coast. These grecophone Christians (the Rums) are full of life; they are honest, pleasant, generous, industrious and so on. The Turk-ish hero Kemal meets a Muslim family who had immigrated from Crete. They carry a Greek family name: Sklavaki. The main theme is Kemal's love affair with their daughter, Afife. All the members of the family speak Greek amongst themselves – their Turkish is very poor – but it is their language and accent that Kemal likes most. Afife prefers to use the Greek name Fofo for herself. She likes to spend her time with the Greek girls of the town and she even enjoys going to the church with them. This Muslim family is exalted as honest, patriotic and considerate. One can even think that it is the 'Greek' part of them that makes them so charming. At the end of the novel, Kemal remembers with great nostalgia these Greeks whom he had loved so much (ibid.: 248).

Some Marxist writers pursue a slightly different approach, concentrating less on the 'ethnic' aspect of the exchange, and more on class-oriented criti-cism against the state. For example, in *Çirkince* probably the first short story concerned with the exchange published in 1947 in a book of short stories entitled *Sırça Köşk*, Sabahattin Ali (1907–1948) emphasises the exchange's economic consequences. The Turkish hero twice visits a small town near Izmir called Çirkince, with an interval of several years. On the first visit, the town is inhabited by Rums and on the second by Muslim immigrants who came as part of the exchange. The difference is striking. When the Rums lived there the town was almost a paradise. The Rums were competent and lovely people, and the town used to be alive and neat, and had clean streets and many beautiful fountains. The people were healthy, cultivating their figs and olives by day and in the evenings playing the mandolin and enjoying themselves, men and women all together, nicely dressed. The town had four primary schools and two high schools. However, the town undergoes a trans-formation – for the worse – after the arrival of the Muslim immigrants from Xanthi/Iskeçe. On the second visit, naked and dirty children play in muddy streets. Weeds have spread everywhere, and the houses have collapsed. In them men and animals live together. Manure and garbage are all around. The hero asks an old man, a local, whom he knows from his previous visit, 'Is this what will happen to every piece of land that we get hold of?' As the hero talks to the old man, the reason for this change comes to light: economic factors and the mistakes of the dignitaries[5] have caused the decline. The peas-ants of Xanthi (in Greece), who used to cultivate tobacco, are not accustomed to figs and olives. Worst of all, two local feudal chieftains (*derebeyis*) have seized the land of the newcomers. 'The state too is controlled by these feudal chieftains.' The profits are not reinvested but are spent on consumption goods elsewhere. 'This is the reason for the decay. Do not think that the infi-del is divinely inspired and the Muslims are guilty!'

After 1960 a few more passages appear in the literary texts of some leftist-cum-Marxist writers. In his memoirs, *Efkâr Tepesi (The Hill of Worries)* and in the chapter entitled *Cevizlideki Kilise (The Church in Cevizli)*, Fakir Baykurt (1929–1999) narrates how the gendarmes pull down an imposing church left by the Rums in order to use the stone for new army quarters. The writer praises the old times when the area was rich, whereas now 'one cannot help making comparisons'.

Zaven Biberyan (1921–1985), an Armenian activist in the Turkish socialist movement, also refers to the emigration of Christians in his novel *Yalnızlar (The Lonely Ones),* published in 1965. The author presents an illiterate nationalist who hates the Christian minorities of Istanbul and who asks with surprise how it is that these minorities are still to be found in Turkey since, as he has heard, all 'infidels', such as Greeks (*Yunanlıs*) and Russians, were expelled (ibid.: 75). In his novel *Ateş Yılları (Years of Fire)* (1968), Hassan Izzettin Dinamo (1909–1989) presents the Turkish-speaking Orthodox Chris-tians as 'Turks', implying that it was a mistake that they were exchanged (ibid.: 228). In *Savaş ve Açlar (War and the Starving)* (1968) he presents a class-based explanation for the war: the forced migration of the Armenians and Greeks (Rums) in 1915 was a means used by certain members of the Com-mittee for Union and Progress (CUP) to dispossess these people and seize their land (p. 134). In *Kurt Kanunu (The Law of the Wolf)* (1969) another leftist writer, Kemal Tahir (1910–1973), describes how the land and houses left behind by the Rums have been unevenly and unjustly distributed among the Turks (ibid.: 115). In his novel *Homeland Hotel (Anayurt Oteli)* (1973) Yusuf

Atılgan (1921–1989) presents the hotel as a luxurious former Rum house. In this novel the Rums are mentioned briefly as 'fugitives' or 'killed people', in whose houses others were now lodged (ibid.: 122).

Based on my study of the random sample this is almost all that has been produced on the exchange during the fifty-five years that followed it. In essence, mention of the event is taboo.[6] During the same period in Greece, however, many novels and short stories were written about the experience of the Christians who were part of the exchange. The common themes usually involved the motherland left behind or the new life in Greece.[7] Apart from a tendency to be silent on the exchange, two additional traits appear in Turkish literature (discussed below). Firstly, the life of the immigrants does not form a narrative in its own right but is used rather as a means to develop political arguments. Probably the only exception is R.N. Güntekin, whose humanistic approach is not part of a nationalist or socialist political discourse. Secondly, there is an almost complete absence of descriptions of the life of the immigrants in their former homeland, i.e., in Greece.

The 'discovery' of the exchange after 1980

Since 1980 growing Turkish interest in the exchange has become evident. A number of publications on the exchange have started to attract the public's attention. For example, several articles have appeared in the history journal *Tarih ve Toplum*, and in 1997 an exhibition on migration in Turkey was organised by the Foundation for Economic and Social History in Istanbul.[8] In addition, lines of communication have opened between Turks and Greeks: immigrants have begun to visit their former homes, with visits often being reciprocated, conferences have been organised where the 'two parties' discussed both the period of coexistence before the exchange and the exchange itself,[9] surveys in the form of oral history have appeared, and for the first time articles and memoirs have been translated and appeared in both Greece and Turkey.[10] During this period, the exchange started to appear more frequently in Turkish literature, and after 1992 there are even some novels dedicated solely to the topic. First, I will outline these texts, especially the three novels on the exchange itself (which are all products of leftist writers) and then I shall discuss the understanding of 'motherland', 'state' and 'citizenship' found in them.

In 1985, F. Otyam (1926–) published *Pavli Kardeş (Brother Pavli)*, half memoir half novel, based on the friendly relationship of the author with a Rum, Pavli, who in the story has recently left Istanbul for Greece. Pavli, the hero, insists that he is a Turk and that he hates the Greeks. The exchanged Rums are portrayed as traitors in that they did not love their motherland, Turkey (p. 154), and so it follows that it was a good thing that they were expelled from 'our' country. According to the author, Pavli is a 'positive' Rum, apparently because he is a Turk and not a Greek (*Yunanlı*). The principle of loyalty to the Turkish state seems very important in determining this Rum's identity.[11]

In the short story *'Karagedik'* in *Es Be Süleyman, Es (Blow Suleyman, Blow)* published for the first time in 1980 and published again in *Savrulup Gidenler (Gone with the Wind)* in 1987, Salim Şengil (1913–) presents the departure of the Greeks as a sad incident and only briefly touches upon it. Mario Levi (1955–), a writer of Jewish origin, also presents the exchange as an unfortunate event. In his book *En Güzel Aşk Hikâyemiz (Our Most Beautiful Love Story)* (1992) he calls the migration of the Istanbul Greeks, who are portrayed melancholically, as a 'forced' one. The theme of people expelled 'from the land of their birth' is also encountered in his *Madam Floridis Dönmeyebilir (Madame Floridis May Not Return)* (1990). Mehmet Eroğlu (1948–), in his novel *Yürek Sürgünü (The Exile of the Heart)*, published in 1994, gives the theme of migration and exile a new dimension: ethnic Turks leave Turkey due to their conflict with the state authorities and seek political asylum in Greece (ibid.: 170). He also tells of the elderly Turks who break the law by going to the island of Chios/Sakız to see their old friends, the Greeks (Rums) who had left their villages forty-two years ago. In a short but very nostalgic paragraph, some try to find their old lovers (ibid.: 319).

The novel *Suyun Öte Yanı (The Other Side of the Water)* by F. Çiçekoğlu (1951–) published in 1992, marks a new beginning in Turkish literature. It is the first book which has as its main theme the migration and exile of Greeks and Turks. The author presents a Greek who had moved of his own volition to the island of Cunda/Moschonisi to escape the Greek military regime of 1967–74. Cunda is now inhabited by Greek-speaking Muslim immigrants who had come from Crete in 1923 (cf. Koufopoulou this volume). There is also a Turk who faces a similar dilemma when he runs into trouble with the military forces of Turkey, which, like those of Greece, have intervened in politics to take control of the country. The Cretan Turks speak Turkish with a Greek accent and sing Greek songs. However, state officials prohibit the 'foreign' language and the singing in Greek. Notably, this is the only mention of the prohibitive attitude of the state towards the Muslim immigrants in any Turkish literary text from my sample. However, the violence that both ethnic groups were subjected to is described, including bloody incidents and torture. The walls of the houses abandoned by the Greeks are covered in blood. The reader is led to feel pity for the people who had to leave their home country.

As if this novel opened the way, two further novels appeared in 1997 and 1998, the main theme of which is again the exchange of populations. In his novel *Savaşın Çocukları (The Children of War)* (1997) Ahmet Yorulmaz (1932–), a second-generation immigrant from Crete, narrates the lives of the Muslim Cretans in the years before the exchange, and the events that led up to it. He also relates some instances of the immigrants' life in their new country. The Muslim Cretans suffer a great deal since the Greeks use violent means to annex the island. Still, there were times when relations between the two communities were good. In this respect, Vladimiros and his wife, an old Christian couple, are especially noteworthy for they looked after Aynakis Hasan, the hero, as if he were their own son.

The sovereignty discourse is deeply embedded in the novel. To whom do these places belong? According to a wise Greek character, it is only the ancient Greeks who were real expansionists and invaders. It was they who captured Anatolia, reaching as far as Afghanistan. Only the arrival of the Turks from Asia drove the Greeks back from these lands (ibid.: 78). The Turks captured Crete from the Venetians: the Greeks came later (ibid.: 30). While the Venetians may have a right to claim these lands, it is a 'great injustice' that they are controlled by the Greeks (ibid.: 32). He gives reasons to prove that the Muslim Cretans are really Turks: they resisted all the efforts that 'others' exerted in order to convert them to Christianity (ibid.:12), and they refused to fight against the Ottoman Empire during the First World War when they served in the Greek army, even though they faced the death penalty for not doing so (ibid.: 13). However, most important of all, the hero (the author) explains that Anatolia is the motherland of his ancestors. He therefore thinks it strange to feel nostalgic towards Crete in his own home country (ibid.: 19). For him, then, the criterion for being a Turk is Anatolian origin, an argument that necessarily makes the Muslims in Crete outsiders. The author goes on to develop two terms in order to explain the dilemma regarding 'his land': Crete is his 'land', his 'country' (*yurt*) and Turkey is the 'motherland' or 'home country' (*anayurt*). Thus he writes, 'I set out for my home country leaving my land for good' (ibid.: 133) and again, 'I lose my land and I go to my home country' (ibid.: 134, the last page).[12] The term *anayurt* is frequently encountered (ibid.: 104, 120, 121) and will be discussed below. However, it is of interest at this point to note that the boundaries of the home country are not defined: its reference is simply Anatolia. The question is why should Anatolia be more a home country than Crete? Historically both have been captured by force and, moreover, the hero was born and brought up in Crete. Is Anatolia a motherland because the Turks are in a majority or is it because the Turkish state's sovereignty is assured there?

The second novel to raise similar questions, published in 1998, was written by the internationally acclaimed author Yaşar Kemal (1922–). Its subject is the exodus of the Greeks. *Fırat Suyu Kan Akıyor Baksana (Look, the River Fırat is Flowing in Blood)* is the first of a trilogy. The story develops as the Rums of an imaginary island leave for Greece following the exchange, and as Poyraz Musa, a Muslim, comes to settle there in their place. Vasili, a Rum, stays behind and intends to kill the first Turk who sets foot on the island. Eventually, though, he treats Poyraz well. The past is explored as the two men recall various incidents.

There is a distinction in the book between Greeks and Rums. The Rums are presented as a population that lived in 'these lands' for three thousand years (ibid.: 50, 59, 73, 222, etc.). It is the Greeks (*Yunanlıs*) who burned down Muslim villages and raped and killed Muslims during the war years between 1919 and 1923 (ibid.: 59). The relations between Rums and Turks are idyllic on the island – it is as if nationalism had never existed in Anatolia. The Rums with whom the reader becomes acquainted have a very strong attachment to the Ottoman state. They do not want to migrate to Greece, not only because they are attached to the island but also because they do not feel

Greek. As one Rum explains, they are treated very badly in Greece because they are considered to be Turks (ibid.: 222). Most of these Rums speak perfect Turkish. An interesting aspect of this attachment to the Ottoman/Turkish state is the military one. Repeatedly the Rums are shown to have taken part in the wars that the Ottomans fought (ibid.: 51, 54, 57, 293). The Rums take pride in these sacrifices. Lena, for example, explains how her sons fought together with Mustafa Kemal against the Greeks (ibid.: 222).

In the novel, everybody – the Rums themselves, the Turks in the area, the civil servants and the military dignitaries – would prefer the Rums to stay (ibid.: 74). This becomes clear in a scene in which a Turkish officer comes to announce the people's fate under the exchange and does everything possible to delay their deportation. Milto, a civilian, but one who has apparently served in the Turkish army, faces the officer as a soldier at attention. Milto answers like a dedicated soldier, 'Yes, sir!' (*Evet komutanım!*) and both the officer and Milto decide that the Rum is a born soldier and should face the situation bravely.[13] Throughout the book, however, there is no mention of the 'other side', the Muslims that come to Turkey.

Forced migration and contrasting concepts of the 'home country'

There are two clear differences in the way the exchange of populations is presented in Turkish and in Greek literature, which in turn are indicative of certain conditions found in the two countries and their ethnic communities. The first difference is the relative lack of interest that the Turkish side shows in the exchange, almost entirely ignoring its occurrence until very recent years; the second is the special understanding of 'home country' encountered in certain novels.

The Turks were not as keen as the Greeks to record and preserve the memory of the lands left behind. In Greece, one finds many societies, foundations, etc., with the express aim of keeping the memory of the 'exodus' alive and of recording the memories of a 'home' or of a town that has been left behind or 'lost'. The term 'lost homelands' (*chamenes patrides*) is well known in Greece, and there are hundreds of villages and suburbs that carry the names of these former homelands, mostly with the prefix 'New' (see Stelaku this volume). In Turkey this is not the case, and the relatively limited interest in the exchange is reflected in the country's literature.

There are certain historical, demographic, economic, and political factors that help to explain the Turks' limited interest in the exchange. Firstly, while the Greeks would be justified in perceiving the event as the result of a military defeat and hence as a blow to their pride, the Turks see the exchange as the outcome of a military victory: for them it is less traumatic. Secondly, a much greater number of immigrants moved to Greece than to Turkey: approximately 1.2–1.5 million Christians compared with some 450,000 Muslims.[14] In relative numbers the difference is even greater: the immigrants who settled in Greece comprised approximately 20 percent of the population whereas in Turkey the corresponding figure was only 3.8 percent.[15]

Moreover, 90 percent of the Muslim immigrants moved to Turkey under controlled conditions after the Lausanne Convention had been signed, whereas only 8 percent of the Christians had this opportunity, the great majority fleeing from Turkey without protection or supervision (Arı 1995: 8, 88, 92). For most Christians the experience of the exchange was one of chaotic flight from Anatolia in the wake of the Greek army's defeat there. This caused a greater impact on the Christians than the more controlled conditions did on the Muslims. In addition, the Turks might well have been more accustomed to the phenomenon of immigration, for the Ottoman Empire received more than 400,000 refugees from the Balkans alone in the years between 1912 and 1920 (Behar 1996: 62).

The socio-economic make-up of the refugees is also important. Compared with the exchanged Muslims, a greater proportion of the exchanged Christians were from towns, which would suggest higher rates of literacy and a stronger likelihood of able writers emerging from their number. Also, any talented Turkish writers that did emerge would have felt the pressure of one of the paramount ideological aims of modern Turkey, namely, to create a national identity based on the 'Turkishness' of Anatolia. In this environment, all irredentist rhetoric and hence references to 'lost motherlands' was prohibited, or at least discouraged. However, with the issue being politicised *ab initio*, it was very difficult for writers to make literary references to the exchange without connecting it to some kind of political criticism, directed either at the idea of forced exchange itself or at the practical consequences of its implementation.[16] Almost all the authors who wrote about this issue were left-wing intellectuals who were to varying degrees in opposition to the state. However, from 1925 until the 1950s there was strict censorship in the Turkish media. With restrictions on producing texts that alluded to settlement problems or the shortcomings of the government, this period was not a favourable one for writers.[17]

Further to these observations, textual analysis of the exchange as it appears in Turkish literature enables one to reach some conclusions concerning the understanding of national identity, citizenship, motherland, the state and also of the exchange itself in Turkish society. One point of view that often emerges is that the exchange was beneficial for the Turks since it enabled the state to attain national homogeneity. A contrasting understanding is that the Rums were faithful Turkish subjects who actually belonged to the country. Underlying these opposing views are two different understandings of nation and citizenship: the ethnic and the civil approach. According to the ethnic approach 'Turks' are only those that are ethnically so. In the civil approach, however, it is argued that Anatolia is the locality of the 'country', and all its inhabitants are Turks.[18] The latter constitutes a major difference with respect to Greek literature in which Turks and those Muslims that took part in the exchange are seen definitely and without doubt as members of a distinct nation.

This difference regarding the definition of 'our nation' is a major one and reflects the degree of ethnogenesis (nation building) attained in the two countries. In Greece there is a higher degree of consensus regarding national identity; it has, after all, been an independent nation-state since 1830. In Turkey, the 'identity issue', as it is called, still gives rise to heated debates. This issue is the subject of extensive discussion, particularly by Turkish intellectuals, but also by Islamists, Kurds, nationalists, Kemalists, and others. In Turkish literary texts, the Greeks, sometimes as the negative 'other' and sometimes as 'an Anatolian and one of us', are used by writers of various ideologies to define their version of the 'nation'.[19]

As was seen both in A. Yorulmaz's and Yaşar Kemal's novels, the ethnicity and citizenship of the individuals are closely associated with their loyalty to the state.[20] Loyalty and 'Turkishness' are often expressed in terms of actual participation in the military operations of the state, or as a willingness to do so. At first glance this understanding seems to correspond to the modern French definition of citizenship. On closer examination, however, it is seen that this loyalty is not evaluated on an individual basis but on a communal (*millet*) basis, as it was in the Ottoman period. In these texts the Rums are either loyal or disloyal to the state in their totality, as a group. The behaviour of the individuals determines an evaluation of all the members of the millet.

More important than citizenship, however, is the definition of country and motherland. A. Yorulmaz seems to perceive the motherland or the home country as the place where there is Turkish sovereignty, where the Ottoman or the Turkish state dominates. When this state does not control the lands then only a 'country' is perceived. This is probably another main difference between the Greek and the Turkish communities. For the Greeks, the land in which one is born and brought up and in which one lives is his or her home country, irrespective of the 'state'.[21]

The Greeks and Turks have probably adopted these different understandings of motherland owing to centuries of divergent historical experience. For the subjugated Christians in the Ottoman Empire, sovereignty was inconceivable, in the same way that absence of sovereignty was for the Muslims who were their overlords.[22] In addition, it should be noted that the traditional Islamic view perceives two distinct worlds: on the one hand the areas controlled by Muslim forces where Islam is dominant, and on the other hand, the rest of the world, where Islam is not dominant. The first is called the 'the lands of Islam' (*dar al-Islam*) and the second 'the lands of war' (*dar al-harb*). The first is perceived as the place where the Muslims live in peace and harmony whereas in the second the inhabitants are called *harbi*, i.e., people of war. The Islamic forces are supposed to be in a state of strife with this outer world.

Common to many Turkish texts is the importance and the centrality of the state. Indeed, the ethnic character of the state determines the ethnicity of the people, not the reverse. Thus, the Greeks and Rums of Anatolia were part of Turkey not because they were born there and lived there, but rather, as one is constantly reminded, because they were serving the state. Loyalty to the state is to be valued even if the state is misguided.[23] This understanding is clearly seen in *Fırat Suyu Kan Akıyor Baksana (Look, the River Fırat is Flowing in Blood)* by Yaşar Kemal, a leftist writer critical of the practices of the state (see above). Actually, almost all leftist writers have chosen to direct their criticism against the state – in that respect too the state is central. It is not individuals who are accused of wrongdoings but the state; the state acts, and the people suffer or prosper as a result. The concept of a civil society does not come through in these texts.

This lack of the concept of civil society may constitute an additional reason why the exchange of populations was not treated as an important event in Turkish literature: within the Muslim communities the sense of a land or of a 'space' to which one belongs was associated with a Muslim state and Muslim sovereignty. Historically, settlements were planned by the Ottoman state. The Muslims moved to newly captured lands and, following state directions, moved away again when these lands were lost as a result of a military defeat. However, the motherland was always present: it was the Muslim central state that was there all through the centuries. If this is so, then the loss of 'country' was not as real a disaster for the Muslims as long as 'their state' was victorious in this last war against the Greeks.[24]

Bibliography of literary works

Aladağ, E. (1987). *Sekene, Türkleşmiş Rumlar / Dönmeler* (İstanbul: Belge and Marenostrum).

Ali, S. (1975) [1947]. '*Çirkince*' in *Sırça Köşk* (İstanbul: Bilgi).

Atılgan, Y. (1974) [1973]. *Anayurt Oteli* (Ankara: Bilgi).

Baykurt, F. (1960). '*Cevizlideki Kilise*', in *Efkâr Tepesi* (İstanbul: Remzi).

Baysal, F. (1972) (1944). *Sarduvan* (İstanbul: Tel).

Biberyan, Z. (1966). *Yalnızlar* (İstanbul: Öncü).

Cumalı, N. (1986) (1976). *Makedonya 1900* (İstanbul: Makedonya).

—— (1998) (1995). *Viran Dağlar* (İstanbul: Cumhuriyet Kitap Kulübü).

Çiçekoğlu, F. (1992). *Suyun Öteki Yanı* (İstanbul: Can).

Dinamo, H.İ. (1968). *Ateş Yılları* (İstanbul: Yalçın).

—— (1969). *Savaş ve Açlar* (İstanbul: May).

Eroğlu, M. (1994). *Yürek Sürgünü* (İstanbul: Can).

Gündüz, A. (1928). *Dikmen Yıldızı* (İstanbul: Semih Lütfi).

Güntekin, R.N. (1970) (1942). *Ateş Gecesi* (İstanbul: İnkilâp & Aka).

Karaosmanoğlu, Y.K. (1987) [1953–1954]. *Panorama* (İstanbul: İletişim).

Kemal, Y. (1998). *Fırat Suyu Kan Akıyor Baksana* (İstanbul: Adam).

Levi, M. (1990). *Madam Floridis Dönmeyebilir* (İstanbul: Afa).

—— (1992). *En Güzel Aşk Hikayemiz* (İstanbul: Afa).

Otyam, F. (1985). *Pavli Kardeş* (İstanbul: Kaynak).

Şengil, S. (1987). *Karagedik*, in *Savrulup Gidenler,* (İstanbul: Can). (First publication in 1980 in the collection of stories titled *Es Be Suleyman, Es*).

Tahir, K. (1969). *Kurt Kanunu* (İstanbul: Bilgi).

Yorulmaz, A. (1998) [1997]. *Savaşın Çocukları* (İstanbul: Belge).

Notes

1. This chapter is based on the findings of my Ph.D. thesis. See Millas 2000, 2001.
2. A list of all literary texts referred to in this paper appears at the end of this chapter.
3. For Karaosmanoğlu and his image of Greeks, see Millas 1991 and 1996.
4. In present-day Turkish two terms are used for the grecophone Christians: *Yunanlı* and *Rum*. *Yunanlı* refers to those with Greek nationality, while *Rum* is used for those of Turkish or other nationalities. The Turkish-speaking Orthodox Christians, better known as *Karamanlıs*, are also *Rums*. In Turkish literature, especially after 1912, *Yunanlıs* and *Rums* are mostly presented as belonging to the same ethnic group and are portrayed with similar (negative or positive) characteristics (Millas 2000).
5. I use 'dignitaries' as a catch-all word for those people in the novel who are variously described in the Turkish as a vague and menacing 'they', or as '*bey*' or '*ağa*'. No doubt the author had in mind the 'bourgeoisie' and those who controlled the state and directed the exchange.
6. It is of interest that Faik Baysal (1919–) begins his novel *Sarduvan* (1944) by saying that the village he is going to write about was once inhabited by Rums – who have by this point left – but that in any case he intends to write about other things.
7. See, for example, I. Venezis, *To Noumero 31328, Galini, Lios, O Apogonos tou Eksomoti, Akif,* and *Oros ton Elaion*; S. Doukas, *Istoria Enos Aichmalotou*; S. Myrivilis, *To Prasino Vivlio*; K. Politis, *Stou Hatzifrangou*; F. Kontoglou, *To Aivali, i Patrida mou*; D. Sotiriou, *Oi Nekroi Perimenoun, Matomena Chomata*; L. Nakou, *I Kyria Doremi, i Istoria tis Parthenias tis Despoinas tade*; P. Prevelakis, *To Chroniko Mias Politeias*; Y. Theotokas, *To Chroniko tou 1922, O Leonis;* N. Kazantzakis, *Oi Adelphophades*; M. Loudemis, *Synephiazei*. Recently, other writers have produced such novels e.g., Ch. Samouilidis, *Oi Karamanites*; A. Nenedakis, *Oi Voukephaloi*; Y. Andreadis, *Tamama*; M. Veinoglou, *To Megalo Ploio*. The term 'lost homelands' (*chamenes patrides*) is well known in Greece, and is used to denote the lands the expelled population left in order to migrate to Greece.
8. For a list of publications and academic studies on this subject by Arı, Arıkan, Berber, Çapa, Tekeliö and Yerasimos, see bibliography in Arı, 1995.
9. See for example, the International Symposium of Foça, August 1996, in Foça, Turkey, and the meeting 'Exploration of a Cultural Heritage: Turkish and Greek Communities in the Ottoman World', April 1997, at Boğaziçi University, Istanbul (see Preface).
10. See for example the memoirs of T. İzbek (1997: 68–77) a third-generation immigrant from Crete living in Cunda/Moschonisi, whose moving account of the exchange appeared in Greek in Crete. See also Balta and Millas (1996) and Millas (1998), a study on Venezis and his image of Turks. Extracts from the archives of the Centre for Asia Minor Studies, Athens were published in Turkey in 2001 as *Göç* (Migration) by İletişim publishers.
11. Other authors who wrote novels in this spirit include Cevat Şakir, better known as Halikarnas Balıkçısı (1886–1973), Kemal Tahir (1910–1973), Hasan Izzettin Dinamo (1909–1989), and Yılmaz Karakoyunlu (1935–). According to these writers, a Rum is 'positive' to the extent that he is distanced from the ethnic, cultural, and ideological characteristics of the Greeks, and to the extent that he is politically loyal to, and performs military service for, the Turkish state (see Millas 2000).
12. The term 'motherland' (*anayurt* or *anavatan*) is used in Turkish instead of fatherland. There are also other words in use, e.g., *memleket* (close to 'country') and *vatan* (like the French *patrie*).
13. The wording, which is repeated three times, is actually *asker doğmuş bir toprağın çocuğu* which conveys the idea of 'child of a soldier land'. This phrase is redolent of the popular Turkish saying *Türk asker doğmuş* ('Turks are born soldiers') meaning that the Turks have an innate capacity for successfully serving the state in the army. The overall effect is one of likening this Rum to a Turk.

14. The generally accepted figure for the number of Muslims exchanged is 350,000 (see chapter 2, p. 14), but according to other official sources the number that came to Turkey is 456,720, some 50,000 of whom came of their own initiative (Arı 1995: 92).

15. In 1923 the population of Greece was about five million and of Turkey about thirteen million. Alternatively, the impact of the Exchange can be viewed in terms of population 'loss'. In such terms both countries lost approximately 10 percent of their original inhabitants.

16. Ottoman/Muslim writers who were born and/or lived in various 'lost' Ottoman lands, such as Şemşettin Sami (1850–1904) and Ahmet Mithat (1844–1912) did not write about their 'homelands'. However, Ömer Seyfettin (1884–1920) did write some short stories about the Balkan town where he lived. N. Cumalı (1921–) seems one of the exceptions in that he wrote a novel in 1995 about the life of Turks in Macedonia, *Viran Dağlar (Deserted Mountains)*. He has also had published (in 1976) short stories about the lands where his parents had lived, *Makedonya 1900*.

17. A law known as the 'regulation of silence' (*takrir-i sükûn*) was passed in 1925 after the Kurdish revolt of the same year, enforcing censorship on news related to this uprising. However, the law was used to suppress almost all political opposition. An additional development that discouraged reference to the arrival of 'outsiders' was the effort within Turkey in the 1920s and 1930s to develop a theory presenting the Turks as composed of a pure race (Keyder, Aktar this volume. See also Oran 1998: 158).

18. An extreme case of identifying Turkish identity with Anatolia is encountered in E. Aladağ's book *Sekene (The Inhabitants)* (1997). It is not included in this study since it is less a literary work than a narration of imaginary events accompanied with analysis and interpretations. A Turk talks to a young Greek woman who is from a family that migrated from Anatolia and who visits Turkey. He calls her more Turk than himself 'since she is an Anatolian' (ibid.: 104). The woman also calls herself a Turk since, she says, her ancestors were 'from these lands' (ibid.: 100).

19. The 'other' in Greek and Turkish literature and its role in expressing national identity is a complex issue and will not be discussed here. For more details see Millas 2000, 2001.

20. The same understanding is also encountered in F. Otyam's memoir-cum-novel mentioned above. The equating of loyalty to the state and hence 'Turkishness' with participation in military operations is encountered in other Turkish writers and also in texts that are not directly related to the exchange. Tarık Buğra and Kemal Tahir are two well-known authors who share this approach.

21. This view seems to be confirmed in other chapters in this volume. Stelaku explains, referring also to Hirschon's work, that the Greek refugees acquired a sense of belonging in their new homelands based on familiar symbols which were 'carried' with them. Koufopoulou stated that the Cretan refugees in Cunda (Turkey) never expressed any desire to return to Crete, in contrast to the Greek refugees who openly advocate this preference. Köker's chapter notes (a) that some immigrant Turks refuse to talk to those Turks who did not fight in the army ('you did not die for the *vatan*'), and (b) that some Turkish immigrants made it clear why they did not want to go back to their homes: 'We are [now] on Turkish lands, on Muslim lands. Who wants to live in the lands of the infidels?'

22. For a contemporary parallel in Cyprus, see note 24.

23. The central role of the state in Turkish society can be seen indirectly in various fields of public life. Professor Hikmet Şimşek, speaking on Turkish state television, for example, said that the Turks survived throughout history because they feared two things, God and the state, and that 'this respect towards the state should not end' (TRT 1, 10:00, 15 November 1998). An unusual and quite vague pronouncement on the Turkish understanding of homeland is found in Volkan and Itzikowitz 1994: 192: 'In the Ottoman Empire, the concept of the state was so overwhelming that the concept of homeland appeared only in the late nineteenth century with the advent of the Young Ottomans...'. Late appearance of the concept of homeland was followed by its late consolidation.

24. A practical consequence of a more recent conflict in Cyprus is the ongoing discussion about the meaning of 'motherland' among Turkish Cypriots. The terms used are *vatan* (home country/*patrie*/motherland) and *yavru vatan* ('baby' home country/*patrie*/motherland). Some

Turkish Cypriots see Turkey as the motherland and Cyprus only as its 'baby'; others perceive Cyprus as their motherland. Notably, the first group usually argues that it is almost impossible for the Turkish Cypriots to live together with the Greek Cypriots due to the 'circumstances', whereas the second group, those who identify more with 'space', i.e., Cyprus instead of Turkey or Anatolia, seem more attached to their physical homeland than to the entity that is the sovereign state, and are more inclined to try to coexist. Thus the political problem seems to involve a facet of identity and a perception of the territory to which one belongs.

17

The Myth of Asia Minor
in Greek Fiction

Peter Mackridge

For the political and intellectual leaders of Greece from the end of the War of
Independence in 1829 until 1922, Asia Minor was Greece's other half. There
had been a Greek presence in Asia Minor, with demographic fluctuations,
since at least 1000 B.C., spanning the Ancient Greek, Roman, Byzantine and
Ottoman periods, while, according to official Ottoman statistics, in 1910 Asia
Minor counted among its inhabitants more than 1.7 million Orthodox Christians. The political and intellectual leaders of Greece considered these people
to be Greeks. If we bear in mind that the total population of Greece in the
same year numbered only 2.6 million, we realise the importance, even in
purely demographic terms, of Asia Minor to Greece at that time.

The Treaty of Lausanne, however, placed a barrier between the western
and eastern halves of the Greek world – a partition similar to that between
India and Pakistan, or between East and West in the days of the Iron Curtain.
Since then, Asia Minor has been a prohibited zone for the Greeks, a site of
desire that has been physically unapproachable (or at least uninhabitable)
and for that reason a space on which fantasies can be projected. Asia Minor
before the coming of war in 1914 is both another place and another time, not
only for those Greeks who have lived there, but also for those (especially
their descendants) who have not. It has become a dream-world that can be
imagined as the opposite of the waking world of the here-and-now, a semi-
real, semi-imaginary landscape where it is possible to take the world and
'Re-mould it nearer to the Heart's Desire'.[1]

The focus of this chapter is the presence of peacetime Asia Minor in Greek
fiction. 'Asia Minor' in Greek fiction is of course an invention, a mental construction. By 'the myth of Asia Minor' I mean a set of mental images
articulated through language, rhetoric and representation concerning a num-

ber of particular places, which are defined in terms both of their internal coherence, ambiguities and paradoxes and of their relations with, and oppositions to, other places. What we read in the relevant novels and stories is not necessarily 'untrue'; yet it is written (and intended to be read) as literature, that is, as a form of discourse with its own conventions and its own coherence, irrespective of the extent to which it is 'true to reality'.

Although there was considerable Greek literary activity in Asia Minor (particularly in Smyrna and Trebizond) before 1922, none of the texts produced there has had any lasting impact on modern Greek literature, and none of them in any way contributed to what I call the myth of Asia Minor. By contrast, a significant number of widely read and influential novels and short stories concerned with Asia Minor and what Greeks call the 'Asia Minor Catastrophe' have appeared since 1922. Some of these texts are central to the canon of modern Greek literature. Their importance should not be underestimated, for they are among the texts primarily responsible for instilling the myth of Asia Minor in the Greek consciousness.

It is possible to distinguish three main periods in the output of these texts. The first ends during the Axis occupation of Greece in 1943 with the publication of the novel *Aioliki Gi (Aeolian Earth)* by Ilias Venezis.[2] This novel represents the culmination of the process of mythologisation of Asia Minor as a *locus amoenus* or 'place of comfort' in Greek fiction. Whereas other novels present life in Asia Minor in largely realistic fashion, narrating events in more or less chronological order, Venezis's novel presents a timeless world of myth that has been destroyed by history.

This first period of activity was followed by two decades during which the political situation in Greece (Axis occupation followed by civil war and repressive right-wing government) seems to have pushed the Asia Minor theme into the background. However, the fortieth anniversary in 1962–3 of the Greek military defeat and the Treaty of Lausanne was marked by the publication of two major novels by writers from Asia Minor, *Matomena Chomata (Bloodstained Earth)* by Dido Sotiriou and *Stou Hatzifrangou (At Hadzifrangou)* by Kosmas Politis.[3] The intervening experiences of these two authors – both representatives of the defeated Left in the Greek civil war – clearly coloured their view of the period before 1922.

The third period, dating from the fall of the military dictatorship in 1974, has witnessed the continued production of novels and somewhat fictionalised memoirs concerning Asia Minor,[4] most of them by writers who never lived there, the majority being the sons and daughters of refugees.[5] To some of these more recent writers the departure of the Greek–Cypriots from northern Cyprus as a result of the Turkish intervention and military occupation in 1974 has suggested parallels with the expulsion of the Orthodox Christians from Asia Minor.[6] We sometimes find in these recent novels references to the Turks as the eternal enemy of the Greeks, whereas such expressions are hardly ever found in the earlier novels.[7]

Asia Minor is a major theme in modern Greek fiction. There are three thematic strands in these novels and stories, each text concentrating on one or more of them: peacetime life in Asia Minor before the Catastrophe;[8] the experience of war, captivity and/or expulsion; and finally the resettlement of the refugees in Greece, with the economic, social and psychological diffi- culties that this entailed. To deal adequately with the Asia Minor theme in Greek fiction would require a book-length study.[9] For this reason, while the experiences of the Orthodox Christians of Asia Minor during the turbulent period from 1914 to 1922 and the resettlement of the survivors in Greece have formed the subject matter of a number of novels and short stories, this chapter will confine itself to the first of these themes, namely peacetime life in Asia Minor. However, before I analyse the myth of Asia Minor in Greek fiction, it will be helpful if I give a brief sketch of the backgrounds of the three authors I have already named.

Ilias Venezis was born in Ayvalık (in Greek, Aivali) in 1904. His family sought refuge in Mytilini during the First World War, after which they returned home. In September 1922, after the cessation of hostilities, the eigh- teen-year-old Ilias was taken as a hostage in Ayvalık by Turkish forces and along with the other Orthodox Christian menfolk aged between eighteen and forty-five was sent on a forced march to a labour camp in the interior. He was held in captivity for fourteen months before being reunited with his fam- ily in Mytilini. He later claimed that of the 3,000 men from Ayvalık and the nearby island of Moschonisi (now Alibey or Cunda) captured by the Turks, only twenty-three survived and found their way to Greece (Venezis 1974: 48–49).[10] Soon afterwards he began to write a harrowing chronicle of his experiences as a captive under the title *Tò Noumero 31328* (*Number 31328*), which he published in an incomplete early draft in a local newspaper in Mytilini in 1924. In 1931 he published the full text in book form in Athens, revising it in subsequent editions; this book – the only one written by an Orthodox Christian about his experiences as a captive of the Turks after Sep- tember 1922 – has been constantly in print for several decades. His second novel, *Galini* (*Tranquillity*), (1939), tells the story of a community of Greek refugees from Phocaea (Turkish Foça) who settle at Anavyssos in Attica and struggle to carve out a new life for themselves from this arid, salty soil. *Aeo- lian Earth* (1943), which forms one of the focuses of this chapter, was his third novel. Venezis's first three novels, then, deal with peacetime life in Asia Minor, captivity at the end of the Greco-Turkish war, and resettlement in Greece (though not in that order).

Dido Sotiriou was born in 1909 in Aydın, where her father was a success- ful businessman (he owned a soap factory). At the end of the First World War her family moved to Smyrna. Shortly before the Turkish army entered the city on 9 September 1922, she sailed to Greece. Although the whole family survived, they lost all their wealth, and her father worked as a docker in Piraeus. She had a career as a journalist and Communist activist, and it was not until the age of fifty, in 1959, that she published her first novel, *I Nekroi Perimenoun* (*The Dead Await*), which tells the story of a woman growing up in Asia Minor and moving to Greece. Her second novel, *Matomena Chomata* (*Bloodstained Earth*) (1963), which I shall discuss below, was based on the autobiographical account of a Greek from western Asia Minor.[11] According to a survey conducted in the summer of 1997 *Bloodstained Earth* was still one of the best-selling novels in Greece.

Kosmas Politis (*nom de plume* of Paris Taveloudis) is the oldest of all the writers referred to in this chapter. He was born in Athens in 1888. His father was from Mytilini and his mother from Ayvalık, and the family moved to Smyrna in 1890. Politis remained in Smyrna until 1922, working as a clerk in various banks from the age of seventeen. His first publication, the novel *Lemonodasos* (*The Lemon Forest*), appeared in 1930 when he was already forty-two. He published three more novels until, at the age of seventy-five, he produced *At Hadzifrangou*, the first of his works to refer to Asia Minor.

In addition, there were novelists who were not from Asia Minor but who nevertheless wrote about it and contributed to the formation and propagation of the myth. Foremost among these was Stratis Myrivilis, who was born in Mytilini in 1892 and fought in the Asia Minor campaign in 1919–22. In his novel *I Panagia i Gorgona* (*The Mermaid Madonna*), published in an initial version in a newspaper in 1939 and in its definitive form in 1949, he makes it clear that before 1922 Mytilini formed a single cultural area with the mainland opposite, an area inhabited by both Christians and Muslims who to meet their economic needs moved freely back and forth between island and mainland across a narrow channel.

As is to be expected, bearing in mind the places where the novelists were born and/or brought up, the part of Asia Minor that they present in their work is mostly confined to the western coastal strip. We can roughly divide the components that constitute the myth of Asia Minor into those that concern the setting, and those that concern human inhabitants.

It is a commonplace in Greek fiction that Asia Minor is an *evlogimeni gi* (blessed land).[12] Sometimes it is also referred to by the Biblical phrase *gi tis Epangelias* (Promised Land) (Myrivilis 1985: 26). The connotations of these two phrases are obvious: Asia Minor is a land blessed by God and granted in His infinite bounty to its inhabitants. Significantly, the phrase *gi tis Epangelias* began to be applied to Asia Minor only *after* the Greeks had been expelled; the implication is that, paradoxically, they only realised it was their Promised Land after their sojourn there had ended. These phrases also bring to mind another Biblical parallel, namely the expulsion of Adam and Eve from the Garden of Eden after they had committed the original sin.

The fertility of Asia Minor is constantly stressed in these texts, usually in contrast to the barrenness of the Greek islands and mainland. In an early story, published in 1928, Venezis depicts characters who have come from the offshore island of Lemnos to work at the wheat-harvest on a big estate on the mainland because 'their country is dry and they travel to us in the East [*Anatoli*, i.e., Anatolia], which is full of *evlogia* [blessing]' (Venezis 1928: 105). Interestingly, it is Myrivilis, born and bred in Mytilini and not from Asia Minor, who not only provides some of the most vivid and evocative descriptions of this land of plenty, but also suggests that what he is describing draws from folk-tale, dream and fantasy. In his novel *The Mermaid Madonna*, which tells the story of a community of Asia Minor Greeks who are settled on the east coast of the island of Lesbos, in sight of their lost homeland, he says of Anatolia, from the viewpoint of the island, 'Over there, you see, everything's big, just as the mainland of Anatolia itself is big – both its bounty and the storms that lash it' (Myrivilis 1985: 13). The islanders themselves used to travel '*pera*' (over yonder), 'to Anatolia, the *ftochomana* [literally, 'mother of the poor'; figuratively, a place where the poor are able to live]'. From there they brought 'livestock, cheese, butter, and the bounty of Abraham': some of the villagers of Mouria in Mytilini even had their own farms there (ibid.: 25). In this 'Promised Land' the mountains are so high that the snow never melts, and people bring it down to make sherbets with honey and rosewater; there are golden seas of wheat that feed the poor throughout the winter, the great rivers flow with rose-sugar and milk, and the bunches of grapes hanging from the vines are as big as babies' (ibid.: 26). Yet, Myrivilis's narrator tells us that: 'One day, suddenly, the blessed mainland cut loose and drifted far, far away. So distant did it become from Skala [the harbour on the island] that people began to see it from this beach as if it were a foreign land – like America, say' (ibid.: 25). Now, Myrivilis's narrator continues:

> it's as if everything was brought to life there by some magic complicity, and it may all dissipate and disappear from sight like multicoloured scented smoke – like a city that's no longer there, but once existed in folk tales and dreams and remained there, painted by the imagination, so men would remember it in their sleep, think of it in their waking hours and refer to it in their conversations like a folk tale (ibid.: 26).

In the past, when Anatolia was still nearby, if the islanders suffered a poor harvest because of drought, they would bring olives and grain from over yonder, where 'the huge mountains with their dense forests attract the rain and fields are watered'. Now, however, as the narrator puts it later in the novel, 'wars have made frontiers with ditches of blood' (ibid.: 402).

Myrivilis goes on to narrate how, when the refugees tell the locals what they used to possess and what they have now lost, their nostalgia exaggerates everything: their neat little houses come to have two or three storeys, while their little back yards with a little bitter-almond tree and a few aromatic plants in whitewashed oil cans become olive-groves and orchards full of flowing waters and singing birds. The locals, who know that these people used to be poor fishermen, listen to their tales with compassionate indulgence (ibid.: 34f.). Here Myrivilis acutely reveals the origins of the myth of Asia Minor, in which nostalgia, fantasy and frustrated desire play a significant part.

Venezis, personifying natural phenomena in his characteristic way, begins his novel *Aeolian Earth* with a description of the island of Lesbos (Mytilini) rising from the sea, harmonious and silent. The mountains of Anatolia, the Kimindenia, see her and retreat inland, leaving a 'place of tranquillity' in Aeolia as a counterpart to the island (Venezis 1969: 23f.). Translated into geopolitical terms, this image suggests that, far from the island being an extension of the mainland (as Turks may see it), the coast of Anatolia is an extension of the Aegean island. Chapter 4 of Venezis's novel is devoted to the story of old Joseph, who left his poor native island of Lemnos in his youth 'to find sustenance in the rich land of Anatolia'. Before leaving, Joseph had told his fiancée Maria:

> of a rich land with tall trees and fertile [literally 'fat'] soil. You cast one seed into it and it gives you back five hundred or a thousand. The mountains, they say, are full of innumerable flocks and herds, let alone the wild animals, the deer and the bears and the wild boar that live in the untrodden places. That is the most blessed land in the world (ibid.: 54f.).

The word that sums up the bounty of Anatolia, and which recurs in most of the novels we are discussing, is *bereketi* – characteristically a Turkish word (*bereket*) that combines the meanings of abundance and fruitfulness with divine blessing (Tessi 1981: ch. 1; Sotiriou 1983: 24; Myrivilis 1985: 264). In several of the texts it is said that Anatolia provides such abundant bounty that there is enough there for everyone, whether Christian or Muslim, Greek or Turk, implying that no group should have believed that it could have an exclusive right to it.

The title of Venezis's novel, *Aeolian Earth*, makes it clear from the outset that there is an indissoluble bond linking the inhabitants with the soil and the other natural elements of Anatolia. Unlike old Joseph from Lemnos, the ancestors of the novel's autobiographical hero, Petros, have lived in Anatolia since time immemorial. Petros's family owned a large farm under the Kimindenia mountains, where his ancestors had worked the land for generations and where his mother had spent her childhood. (Petros's immediate family – his parents and their children – spend their winters in the town, while his mother takes the children to spend the summers on the estate, which is run by his grandparents.) Contrary to other versions of the myth, the land beneath the Kimindenia mountains is not especially fertile, for it has sea-water beneath it, and the farmers wage an unending struggle to keep their crops growing. The grandfather, who governs his peaceful domain serenely and according to an age-old ceremonial, is able to hear the secret voice of nature that foretells the weather, following the 'humble, solid, sacred ... experience' that he has inherited from his 'simple forebears' (Venezis 1969: 67). As for the children, from whose point of view Asia Minor is experienced and evoked in the novel, their imagination is in contact with the secrets of the natural processes of this land and of the legendary beings – both human and non-human – that inhabit it. At the end of the novel, when the family leaves the farm, the grandfather takes a clod of his native soil in which he will grow a basil plant in exile.

The characters' bond with the earth is also stressed in Politis's novel *At Hadzifrangou*. Most of the action of this book is set in a Greek working-class quarter of Smyrna in 1901–2. However, the main action is interrupted in the middle of the novel by an interlude in which, sixty years later, i.e., in 1962, we meet Yakoumis, who had once been a market gardener in Smyrna, where he had owned a plot of land that he had inherited from his father. Now, in Athens, Yakoumis is a hired labourer employed to tend a rich industrialist's garden, and his one ambition in his old age is to acquire his own tools, i.e., his own means of production. Yakoumis suffers from a four-fold alienation: geographical, cultural, psychological and economic.[13]

In Politis's novel it is not a natural environment that is evoked but a city: the city of Smyrna, whose memory is so sacred that its name is not pronounced anywhere in the book, even though specific streets and other locations in the city are mentioned by name. *At Hadzifrangou*, named after a working-class quarter of the city, is a spatial novel, its episodes linked chiefly by their connections with the place where they occur. As with Venezis's novel, the focus of experience is largely placed on children. Politis's characters, whether children or adults, spend much of their time walking through the city, which gives the novelist the opportunity to describe buildings, streets and neighbourhoods as he remembers them, with their characteristic sights, sounds and smells.

According to these novels, most of the denizens of the blessed land of Asia Minor are simple, humble folk. While the narrator's family in *Aeolian Earth* are clearly prosperous, though undoubtedly hard-working, farmers, Venezis, like the other Greek authors who depict life in Asia Minor, focuses especially on the poor, honest folk who are the unselfconscious bearers of tradition. This depiction in fiction contrasts with another version of the myth of Asia Minor that we find outside literature, namely a picture of the Greeks of Asia Minor as financially successful, highly educated and cosmopolitan. All four novelists (Venezis, Myrivilis, Politis and Sotiriou) more or less ignore the rich and famous, stressing that the vast majority of Orthodox Christians in Asia Minor were simple labourers.

The linguistic particularities of Asia Minor are stressed to a greater or lesser extent by the various writers, and all the novels and stories about Asia Minor are full of toponyms of Turkish origin that are exotic and evocative for the Greek reader. Even though Venezis seems to play down linguistic differences, writing in a fairly standardised demotic, he nevertheless quotes a number of Turkish phrases used by Turkish characters, for which he provides translations in footnotes. Other novelists stress the spatio-temporal distance between the contemporary Greece in which they are writing and the Asia Minor of the past by the use of the so-called 'popular style', which attempts to imitate the vocabulary, morphology, syntax and speech patterns of the uneducated characters whose stories they are narrating. It is significant that the regionalisms of vocabulary and grammar that characterise the language and style of Politis's *At Hadzifrangou* and of Sotiriou's *Bloodstained Earth* are nowhere to be found in their other novels – even in Sotiriou's earlier *The Dead Await*, which is also partly set in Asia Minor. Sotiriou's narrator–hero in *Bloodstained Earth* is a turcophone Christian for whom Greek is his second language, and his Greek speech has what the author takes to be a strong Turkish colouring. Sotiriou is obliged to resort to footnotes to interpret many of her narrator's regionalisms, while she leaves many others uninterpreted, as though their function is to contribute to the exotic atmosphere rather than to be clearly understood. As for Politis, he employed such a large number of words characteristic of the region that he felt obliged to append a lengthy glossary to the end of his novel, in addition to the footnotes in which he interprets phrases spoken by Turkish characters.

These novels generally provide a wealth of local colour, documenting not only the language but also the exotic dress, food, and music of the inhabitants of Asia Minor. As for music, Artemi, the sister of Petros, the narrator of *Aeolian Earth*, is unable to relate to the western music which their Scottish neighbour Doris plays on the piano; Artemi compares these unfavourably to 'the tunes of our land' played on the *zurnas* [pipes], *davuls* [drums] and *gaydas* [bagpipes] that accompany the smugglers, 'the heroes of Ayvali', when they dance (Venezis 1969: 202). Here Venezis is making an explicit contrast between the Anatolian Greeks, who share their Turkish neighbours' taste in music, and the family of westernised Athenians into which Doris has married.

Venezis is one of the chief creators of what the critic Stamatis Philippidis has called 'the mythology of Greek *levendia* [heroism]' (1997: 81). By the time Venezis came to write *Aeolian Earth* (published in 1943), the Axis Occupation of Greece was well established. In this novel, written in the midst of foreign occupation, violent repression and material deprivation, Venezis's narrator, Petros, evokes the summers he spent on the farm in Asia Minor until 1914, when the tranquil rural idyll was brought to a violent end by the outbreak of the First World War, and his family left to seek refuge in Mytilini from the roaming bands of armed Muslims who themselves had been expelled from areas of the Balkans that had recently passed from Ottoman rule to the predominantly Christian nation-states of the region. Like Myrivilis in *The Mermaid Madonna*, Venezis repeatedly talks of war as a phenomenon that reaches his characters from elsewhere, brought by fate, and no blame is attached to anyone; war is viewed as a natural disaster, like flood and earthquake.

Venezis develops his 'mythology of Greek heroism' in *Aeolian Earth*, especially in the long passages devoted to Andonis Pagidas, 'the epic leader of the smugglers' (Venezis 1969: 100). The smugglers are the greatest local heroes; they chiefly smuggle tobacco between the Anatolian coast and the Greek islands, defying both the Ottoman authorities and the French-run *Régie Turque* (in which way they are unwittingly patriotic). The smugglers always act 'crazily and thoughtlessly', spending all their gains on parties and women; their 'playing with fire' is done 'with no practical goal'. The smugglers have a keen sense of honour, they never steal, but give protection to those who kill, whether these be Greeks or Turks (ibid.: 249ff.). They become legends in their own lifetimes, and the local people live these legends with them. Petros listens to the smugglers recounting the exploits of a timeless legendary hero, who turns out to be none other than their own leader. Conversely, when the smugglers tell stories of the legendary Byzantine hero Digenis who dares to fight a duel with Charos (Death), they consider him to be 'one of us' (ibid.: 283). Thus present and past are fused in a timeless and unchanging tradition. When two smugglers quarrel and prepare for a shoot-out, Petros sees them as the two most renowned figures in 'the epic cycle of heroism of Ayvali' (ibid.: 257), while everyone knows that they are about to witness a moment that will become a folk tale and a legend (ibid.: 276). The farm labourers and the many wayfarers (Jews, Armenians,

Turks and Christians) to whom Petros' grandfather offers hospitality are continually telling fairy tales, legends and true stories (ibid.: 75). Interestingly, the squalid violence and economic oppression that play a large part in the two stories from Venezis' 1928 collection that are set in peacetime Anatolia are completely absent from *Aeolian Earth*. The atmosphere prevailing in Venezis's novel is one of beauty, joy, folk tale, legend, epic and magic – the antithesis of German-occupied Athens in which the author was living at the time.

In most of the Greek novels and stories about Asia Minor the Turkish characters tend to appear merely as part of a colourful background to life in Anatolia. Venezis's description of the nomadic *yürüks* from the mountains near Kozak arriving with their caravan of camels laden with fruit in the *alan* [square] at Ayvalık at the beginning of his 1928 story 'Manolis Lekas' sets the tone for later depictions: 'the Kozakians, Turkish villagers with short breeches ending above their knees, coloured cummerbunds more than half a cubit in breadth, the camels foaming at the mouth, covered with bells' (Venezis 1928: 4).[14] It is characteristic of Greek novels and stories about Asia Minor that these Turks are not depicted as talking or interacting with the characters who are at the centre of the story. These Greek writers tend to display a Hellenocentric view of their homelands. Similarly, in *Aeolian Earth*, some aspects of the 'exotic Orient' are depicted through the eyes of a foreign character who arrives from Scotland to settle near Petros' family farm. Doris is to all intents and purposes Scottish, even though she has a Greek grandmother and has recently married a Greek neighbour of Petros' family, whose parents are themselves from Athens. Doris witnesses a camel fight, a primitive ritual that is said to manifest 'the dark deity of the Orient' (Venezis 1969: 173), and before the contest she is entertained by *zeybeks*[15] in short breeches playing *davuls*. Here traditional local Turkish culture is viewed by an outsider as a colourful backdrop to the life of an Orthodox Christian community in Asia Minor.

Turkish characters play a slightly more important – though sometimes purely symbolic – role in some of the other novels. The Smyrna of Politis's *At Hadzifrangou* is basically a Greek city, but it is ideologically significant that the elderly local Turkish policeman, who is an entirely sympathetic character, is himself a refugee from Thessaly in Greece. In Sotiriou's *Bloodstained Earth*, the narrator, Manolis, a member of a turcophone Christian farming family living near ancient Ephesus, has a Muslim childhood friend named Şevket, a slightly older shepherd-boy from a nearby village. Later, during the First World War, Manolis often thinks of Şevket, who is by now in the Turkish army pursuing Christian deserters whom the under-age Manolis is helping to conceal. Eventually, at the end of the novel, as Manolis is sailing to Samos following his escape from captivity after September 1922, he bids a lyrical farewell to Anatolia and its Turkish inhabitants, and in particular Şevket, whom he has not seen since the beginning of the First World War.

While Venezis and Myrivilis, after socialist beginnings, came to identify with the conservative ideology of the bourgeois Greek state, Sotiriou, like Politis, was committed to the Left. The whole tenor of Sotiriou's novel is that Christians and Muslims have lived for centuries as brothers in Asia Minor,

and it is Greek and Turkish nationalism, stirred up by the European powers
and 'foreign capital', that has turned otherwise peaceable people into violent
fanatics; Manolis's closing words in the novel are (first in Turkish, then in
Greek), 'Kahrolsun sebep olanlar. Damn those responsible!' Sotiriou, like
some of the other Greek novelists who write about Asia Minor, frequently
stresses that differences of social class and wealth are more significant than
those of race and religion: in many of the novels and stories, Greeks and
Turks are shown to be united by poverty. Manolis, in *Bloodstained Earth*,
shows his contempt for the rich Greek merchants and landowners he sometimes works for, preferring the company of 'honest' smugglers. Nevertheless,
Manolis claims – somewhat disingenuously on the author's part – that the
Turks have been happy to allow the Greeks to control the economy (Sotiriou
1983: 63).

It is true that many Greeks today still assume that Asia Minor (like Constantinople) is Greek, both by virtue of ancient history and because of the fact
that more than one and a half million Orthodox Christians lived there before
the First World War. As far as the first of these claims is concerned, the novels and stories frequently mention the ancient Greek past of Asia Minor, of
which the characters become aware not only through the existence of ancient
ruins in their neighbourhood, but also through the teachings of local school-
masters. Manolis, for instance, the narrator of *Bloodstained Earth*, is taken
around the ruins of Ephesus by his schoolteacher, who tells him about 'our
near neighbour Homer' (ibid.: 22), while the characters of Politis' *At Hadzifrangou* are equally conscious of living in Homer's birthplace. But it should
be stressed that these assertions concerning the Greekness of Asia Minor are
never translated into any kind of threat against the territorial integrity of
Turkey. The Asia Minor that the Greeks have in mind is a mental construct
that exists purely in history, memory and the imagination. This is made clear
in a passage of lyrical nostalgia for Smyrna from Politis' *At Hadzifrangou* – a
passage that recalls Myrivilis's evocation of Anatolia quoted earlier:

> In the summers of our mind's eye, blithe, unruly, barefoot urchins and rascals
> roam around the alleyways and vacant lots of the great city, which now reclines
> on its ashes like an immense grey phantom, like a haze of transparent, crys-
> talline smoke that has taken its definitive shape and form in your mind, with all
> its details, in all its length and breadth, so that, starting from the harbour wall,
> you can make out, one behind the other, through the successive transparent
> layers of crystal, the cobbled streets and the pavements with their rows of
> houses, and beyond all these the greenery of the gardens and orchards, with
> their wells and their potting-sheds, all gleaming in the sun (Politis 1988: 238).

Some Greek literary texts about Asia Minor

What follows is not a bibliography or list of references, but a representative
list of literary texts that are wholly or partly about peacetime life in Asia
Minor before 1914. While almost all of the texts were originally written in

Greek, the list also contains two texts written by Greek authors in English. The list gives the dates of first publication and (where appropriate) references to English translations.

Chrysochoou, I. *Pyrpolimeni Gi [Scorched Earth]* (Athens 1973).
—— *Martyriki poreia [March of Martyrdom]* (Athens: I. Zacharopoulos, 1974).
Domvros, A. K. *I Proikonnisos: anamesa stin Aspri kai sti Mavri Thalassa [Proikonnisos: between the White and the Black Sea]* (Athens: Nea Synora, 1997).
Doukas, S. *Istoria Enos Aichmalotou* (Athens 1929). English translation: *A Prisoner of War's Story* (Birmingham: Centre for Byzantine, Ottoman and Modern Greek Studies, University of Birmingham, 1999).
Grigoriadou-Soureli, G. *Kaftes Mnimes apo ti Smyrni [Burning Memories from Smyrna]* (Athens 1985); 2nd ed. entitled *Mnimes tis Smyrnis [Memories of Smyrna]* (Athens: Patakis, 1997).
Harvey, J. *Familiar Wars* (London: Michael Joseph, 1987).
Kazan, E. *Beyond the Aegean* (New York: Knopf, 1994).
Kondoglou, F. 'Archaioi Anthropoi tis Anatolis' [Ancient People of Anatolia] and 'Alithina Paramythia' [True Fairytales], in *To Aivali, i Patrida mou [Aivalı, my Homeland]* (Athens: Astir, 1962).
Myrivilis, S. *I Panagia i Gorgona* (Athens 1949). English translation: *The Mermaid Madonna* (London: Hutchinson, 1959); reissued by Efstathiadis, Athens 1993.
Politis, K. *Stou Hatzifrangou. Ta Sarantachrona mias Chamenis Politeias [At Hadzifrangou. A Forty-Year Commemoration of a Lost Town]* (Athens: Karavias, 1963).
Psathas, D. *Gi tou Pontou [Land of Pontus]* (Athens: Phytrakis, n.d. [1966?]).
Sotiriou, D. *Oi Nekroi Perimenoun [The Dead Await]* (Athens: Kedros, 1959).
—— *Matomena Chomata [Bloodstained Earth]* (Athens: Kedros, 1963). English translation: *Farewell Anatolia* (Athens: Kedros, 1991).
Tessi, E. *Anatolika t' Archipelagous [East of the Archipelago]* (Athens 1981).
Venezis, I. 'O Manolis Lekas' [Manolis Lekas], in *O Manolis Lekas ki Alla Diigimata [Manolis Lekas and Other Stories]* (Athens 1928); revised version in *Anemoi [Winds]* (Athens 1943).
—— 'To Lios' [Lios], in *O Manolis Lekas...*; revised version in *Aigaio [Aegean]* (Athens 1941).
—— 'Ston Kampo, katou ap' ta Kimintenia' [On the Plain beneath the Kimintenia], in *O Manolis Lekas...*; revised version entitled 'Ta Kimintenia', in *Anemoi [Winds]* (Athens 1943).
—— *Aioliki Gi [Aeolian Earth]* (Athens 1943). English translation: *Aeolia* (London: Campion, 1949, and Denver 1951), reissued as *Beyond the Aegean* (New York: Vanguard Press, 1956).

Notes

I would like to thank Margaret Alexiou and Renée Hirschon for their valuable advice in the final stages of the preparation of this paper.
1. Khayyám 1904: 32 (stanza 73).
2. Passages quoted in this paper are in my own translation.
3. A Turkish translation of Sotiriou's novel appeared in 1970; for an English translation see bibliography. Politis's novel has been translated into Turkish (see bibliography), but not into English. For details on Politis's novel, see my introduction in Politis 1988.

4. It should be pointed out that the division between fictional and factual narrative has never been considered significant in modern Greek literature.

5. See, for example, the entries for Domvros, Grigoriadou-Soureli and Tessi in the list of books at the end of this chapter.

6. The 'lost homelands' of northern Cyprus have become in turn an analogous theme in Greek–Cypriot literature; but that is a topic for another paper.

7. It is not untypical of Greek literature about Asia Minor that the epigraph at the beginning of Stratis Doukas's 1929 novella *Istoria Enos Aichmalotou* (*A Prisoner of War's Story*), in which the narrator tells of his capture by the Turks in 1922 and his hazardous escape to Greece, reads: 'Dedicated to the common *martyria* [literally 'martyrdoms', figuratively 'sufferings'] of the Greek and Turkish people[s].' In the 1958 edition of his book, however, the author altered the epigraph to 'Dedicated to the common sufferings of the peoples'.

8. By contrast, there is very little in Greek literature about the life of Muslims in what became Greece. Exceptions include Ilias Venezis, *Akiph* (1944), Stratis Myrivilis, *Vasilis o Arvanitis* (1943), both set on the island of Lesbos; and Pandelis Prevelakis, *Tò Chroniko mias Politeias* (1938), and Nikos Kazantzakis, *O Kapetan Michalis* (1953), both set in Crete.

9. The only book-length study of the Asia Minor theme in Greek fiction is Doulis 1977.

10. Venezis was released from captivity in November 1923, more than nine months after the Turkish–Greek Agreement on the Extradition of Civil Hostages and on the Exchange of War Prisoners (part of the Lausanne Convention, signed 30 January 1923).

11. In this, as in the supposedly Turkish colouring of the narrator's Greek, Sotiriou follows Doukas, who presented *Istoria Enos Aichmalotou* (1929) as a literary adaptation of the oral narrative of another real-life turcophone Anatolian Christian.

12. For example, '*evlogimenos topos*' (Politis 1988: 77). Fotis Kondoglou uses the adjective *vlogimenos* three times on a single page when he evokes the Ayvalık of his childhood (1962: 79). Kondoglou closes the same text with the words, 'All those who are born in Anatolia are blessed – Greeks and Turks.' In general, Kondoglou's evocation of Ayvalık, which is not explicitly fictionalised, is very similar to that of Venezis and Myrivilis, with whom he collaborated, from the 1920s onwards, in the development of the myth of Asia Minor.

13. Politis's epigraph to his novel expresses his own alienation: 'They have managed, in my own country, to give me the sense of being a *raya*.' He feels more alien in modern Athens – not only as a refugee but as a Leftist – than he ever did as a *raya* [non-Muslim subject] under Ottoman rule.

14. There is a similar description of *yürüks* in Myrivilis 1985: 26–8.

15. Swashbuckling heroes of south-western Anatolian villages.

18

Between Orientalism and Occidentalism

THE CONTRIBUTION OF ASIA MINOR
REFUGEES TO GREEK POPULAR SONG,
AND ITS RECEPTION

Stathis Gauntlett

Asia Minor refugees are widely credited with having first introduced into Greece the *bouzouki,* now the national instrument, and the internationally popular type of Greek song known as *rebetika.* Curiously, the refugees themselves and their descendants have been at pains to abjure these attributions as mischievous and offensive. This paper explores the cultural politics behind the fabrication and perpetuation of what are indeed false attributions. It finds at the core of the issue a contest over modern Greek cultural identity, one of whose principal arenas from the 1880s to the 1980s was Greek popular song. Although it is now celebrated as one of the most sophisticated achievements of modern Greek culture, popular song in Greece has regularly been declared to be in crisis, periodically of such gravity as to incur official censorship, not just of lyrics, but also, remarkably, of music.

The attested presence of Anatolian musicians in Greece dates from some fifty years before the Asia Minor Catastrophe of 1922 (Gauntlett 1991b: 13). Their influence on the popular music of metropolitan Greece was reinforced in the first two decades of the twentieth century by gramophone recordings which they made in the Ottoman Empire (Kounadis and Papaioannou 1981: 295f.). It was thus only to be expected that in their new capacity as refugees in Greece, Anatolian musicians should continue to be prominent as professional performers. One measure of their prominence is the fact that in the evolution of rebetika, one of the principal genres of Greek popular music, the era 1923–32 is commonly referred to as the 'Smyrnaic period' (Petropoulos 1979: 17). Indeed, refugee musicians dominated the commercial recording of popular song in Greece from 1923 until September 1937, when the westernising dictatorship of Metaxas instituted a form of censorship that has been described as 'genocidal' by Kounadis and Papaioannou because it aimed at the elimination of the distinctive musical culture of the Asia Minor refugees (1981: 306).

This censorship of *à la Turca* music in Greece needs to be seen in the context of the cultural priorities of a client state that since its establishment in the 1820s had constantly striven to prove to its patrons (and itself) the continuing validity of its raison d'être, namely, the twin roles of agent for western values and influence in the southern Balkans and, secondly, of custodian of the classical Hellenic heritage, in which the west anchored its humanist tradition. In practice, until recently westerners have tended to explicate the Hellenic tradition with scant regard for the insights of its indigenous custodians, whom they treated as mere guardians of a kind of classical theme-park containing such physical remains of antiquity as could not readily be transported to the West. This attitude intensified Greek endeavours to demonstrate the credentials of a modern nation–state with privileged access to an esteemed heritage. The corollary of these endeavours was the repudiation of the nation's recent Ottoman past and the demonising of the continuing cultural legacy of several centuries of close contact with the Turks.

The westernisation of Greece was thus underpinned by an orientalist discourse (cf. Said 1991[1978]) that pervaded Greek literature, journalism and other forms of cultural commentary from the Enlightenment onwards. Following the Treaty of Lausanne, this discourse served within Greece to subordinate the refugees from the East to the cultural, social and political authority of a westernising Greek establishment.

The definitive literary monument to modern Greek orientalism was composed two decades before the arrival of the Anatolian refugees by the eminent Athenian poet Costis Palamas in the form of a poem entitled 'Orient' [*Anatoli*], first published in 1907 (Palamas n.d.: 202f). In it the Orient is personified as a dangerously seductive harem slave, ever threatening to infect the unwary with incapacitating doses of lethargy, fatalism, lust and a vague, unfocused longing – in unstated, but implied, antithesis to western progress, optimism, decisiveness, enterprise and clean living. Significantly, the vehicle of the Orient's insidious wiles in Palamas' poem is oriental Greek song, the wailing threnodies of the Greek East commonly called *amanedes*, which, by the beginning of the twentieth century and courtesy of travelling bands of oriental café artistes, could be heard right across the breadth of the Greek-speaking world from Yiannena in the western mainland to Constantinople and Smyrna. (The rhythm and rhyme of the original Greek poem, evoking the hypnotic lassitude of the wailing oriental songs, are lost in my translation.)

ORIENT

Songs of Yiannena, Smyrna, Constantinople,
drawling oriental songs,
so sad,
how my soul gets dragged along with you!
It's cast of your music
and travels on your wings.

What gave birth to you and in you speaks
and groans and exudes a heavy aroma
is a mother whose wanton kiss burns
and who trembling worships fate,
a soul all flesh, a slave in a harem –
the lascivious Orient.

[...] if only I could live my life in idle solitude,
dreaming of the sea and sky,
mute, without the ardour of a single care,
with as much brain

as it takes to stand like a tree
and smoking, to knit together
little blue rings;
and occasionally to move my mouth
and revive on it the longing
which heavily torments you

And keeps beginning, returning, never ending.
For a whole race lives and languishes in you
and writhes in bondage its whole life through,
You songs of Yiannena, Smyrna, Constantinople,
drawling oriental songs,
so sad.

This poem can be seen as the poetic epilogue to a public debate spanning the last two decades of the nineteenth century about the directions taken by mass culture in the urban centres of the Kingdom of Greece. The dispute was ultimately about modern Greek identity, but it manifested itself in the high-brow press as a somewhat *nuancé* public duel between advocates of two different forms of imported musical entertainment: on the one hand, the habitués of the west European *cafés chantants*, and on the other, the so-called 'suitors of the Asiatic Muse' (*Ephimeris* 5 October 1876, cited in Hatzipandazis 1986: 29 n. 9) as she appeared in the *kafe-aman* with its *à la Turca* repertoire. Thodoros Hatzipandazis, who brought the documents of this debate to light, sees Palamas' poem 'Orient' as a sympathetic obituary for the songs of the Greek East following their demise into the lowest reaches of popular culture in the 1890s (1986: 107f). It seems to me, though, that for all the narrator's professions of proneness to seduction by Greek oriental song, the manifestly orientalist exoticism of the poem amounts to a high-handed denigration of this form of popular culture.

For present purposes the poem's significance is the fact that it posits popular song as a battleground for the contestation of Greek cultural identity. As mentioned earlier, Greek popular song has retained this role ever since, being discussed earnestly and with impressive regularity in the Greek media for over a century. Greek songs with oriental features have been a perennially contentious issue in Greek cultural politics (Gauntlett 1991b, 1999). Furthermore, if Palamas' poem was ever intended as an obituary for Greek oriental song, it was certainly premature: the westernisers' agenda for the de-orientalisation of Greek popular culture faced a massive challenge in consequence of the Asia Minor Catastrophe of 1922, which brought 'Our East' (*i kath' imas Anatoli*) home to roost in the Balkan peninsula in the form of 1.2 million refugees. They gave a new lease of life in Greece to the plaintive oriental songs of Yiannena, Constantinople, and Smyrna, with the assistance of a burgeoning recorded-sound industry.

The wide range of musical genres that Asia Minor refugees cultivated in Greece can be gauged very roughly from the programme of live performances surrounding the academic conference on 'The contribution of Asia Minor Hellenism to the development of modern Greek song' held in Piraeus in July 1998 under the auspices of Athens University Music Department and the Municipality of Nikaia. Delegates were treated to a remarkably diverse assortment of Greek music and song from Asia Minor, including classical piano compositions by Yiannis Konstantinidis (alias Kostas Yiannidis) of Smyrna, western-style popular music of Smyrna, traditional folksongs of Cappadocia, amanedes or *manedes* (defined below), and rebetika. From this wide range, the conference papers and discussion focused primarily on the last genre, rebetika, reflecting the signal contribution of refugees to the development of this form of song, which, by 1930, was already perceived to enjoy the broadest popular appeal and profitability of all the various types of Greek song.

The role of Asia Minor refugees in the production, distribution, and consumption of rebetika was undeniably immense, both in Greece and in the U.S.A., as has been demonstrated by a host of publications. Most recently Kapetanakis (1999: 477f) and Kounadis (2000b: 56–63) have listed over twenty prolific refugee composers and exponents of rebetika from Smyrna and a dozen from Constantinople, together with the (often conflicting) dates for their birth and death. Several refugee musicians attained a legendary status that survives to this day among the youthful rebetika revivalists of Greece and the global Greek diaspora who imitate their recordings and avidly collect anecdotes about their professional exploits. Among the most revered are Panagiotis Toundas (b. Smyrna 1886) and Spyros Peristeris (b. Smyrna 1900), both of whom served as local repertory managers and orchestra leaders for the Greek popular catalogue of, respectively, the Columbia and Odeon recording companies, testimony to peer acknowledgement of their professional musicianship. Refugee musicians were also prominent in the governance of the professional body Mutual Aid (*Allilovoithia*) established to protect the interests of musicians in Greece (Petropoulos 1979: 350f.).

The specialism of Asia Minor refugees in rebetika is attested to by Edmund Michael Innes, an executive of the British Gramophone Company who visited Greece in 1930 on a trouble-shooting mission. He reported to company headquarters in Hayes, Middlesex that rebetika are:

> Light songs of the low class people, introduced in 1923 by the refugees from Asia Minor. There are old ones of unknown composers and new ones, the best of which are written by Toundas, Vaindirlis, Dragatsis. Our Dalgas also is writing Rebetika, but without any great success up to now. ... Manedes and Rebetika are the most popular and best selling categories of Greek music ....[1]

The old rebetika 'of unknown composers' recorded by Asia Minor musicians – before and after they became refugees in Greece – tend to be loose concatenations of stereotyped couplets telling of urban low-life, machismo, hashish-smoking, gambling and seduction, often set in the 'Upper Districts' of Smyrna or in Constantinople:

> *Won't you tell me, won't you tell me*
> *where hashish is sold?*
> *The dervishes sell it*
> *in the Upper Districts.*
>
> *In Tzavatis' yard*
> *they killed a hashish smoker*
> *and the hashish smokers mourned him,*
> *all of them connoisseurs ...*
>
> *A widow taught me to smoke hashish*
> *and she turned me into a vagabond ...*

(Gauntlett 1985: 235f.)

These songs give signs of improvised formulaic composition, with variant performances comprising different combinations of couplets and variants of stereotyped verses. The verses also contain features of Greek urban dialects of Asia Minor, including many words of Turkish origin, such as *yagini, gulekas, yavuklu, nefesi, damira* (respectively: fire, thug, lover, 'dope', hashish) (Gauntlett 1985: 72).

Other recorded songs were attributed to known composers and seem purpose-designed for the duration of one side of a 78 rpm gramophone record. Attribution of authorship of recorded songs was important because it secured royalties, in addition to performance fees or in lieu of them. Thus Toundas contrived to set his own Greek words to a traditional Turkish tune and copyrighted both as *Hariklaki* (Little Harikleia) (Rovertakis 1973: 20f.).

In contrast to the preoccupation of the literary production of Asia Minor refugees with the loss of their native lands (Politis 1973: 246ff.; Mackridge this volume), their popular songs, to judge by the extant commercial recordings, were only briefly concerned with nostalgia:

> *Smyrna, you were embellished with riches and charm [...]*
> *Smyrna with your environs, blessed city,*
> *Your riches and advantages have been devastated by a storm.*

('Smyrna with your environs', Tambouris n.d.-a: #10)

In some such verses the forlorn hope of return is broached:

> *Cheer up, my refugee girl, forget your misfortune*
> *and one day we shall return to our familiar haunts.*
> *We'll build our nest in our lovely Smyrna*
> *and enjoy my [sic] sweet love and embraces.*

('Refugee girl', Kounadis 1994: #18)

But others contain more realistic demands:

> *I've come from Smyrna to find some comfort,*
> *to find in this Athens of ours some love, an embrace.*

('What is it to you', Schorelis 1977: 126)

Most compositions by refugee musicians resumed and developed the less subdued themes of traditional rebetika: affirmations of prodigality, low-life revelry and erotic rapports. The stylistic and formal characteristics of these personal compositions were initially similar to those of traditional songs, but experimentation with form led to innovation and increasing complexity (Gauntlett 1985: 80f). Some contained licentious allusions, veiled in *double entendre,* which eventually incurred the ire of the Greek authorities in 1936, when a song about the nocturnal 'fishing' exploits of Varvara (Barbara) led to the trial of the composer Toundas and the responsible officers of the recording company (Kapetanakis 1999: 391–6). Another innovation in the compositions of refugee musicians was the depiction of the Orient as exotic, a form of orientalism which will be analysed at greater length below.

As well as rebetika, refugee musicians also specialised in the commercial recording of amanedes or manedes, defined by Leigh-Fermor as 'wailing, nasal, rather melancholy melopees in oriental minor mode' (1966: 106), and rather more fully by Innes as:

[A] sort of lament or wailing song of Turkish origin; there are two kinds and the same singer can hardly sing both: one from Constantinople – heavy, built up on Turkish motives, played on lyra (or violin), kanoun (or santouri) and outi; and another one from Smyrna, lighter, more Greek – more like folk songs, played on violin (not lyra), santouri, and outi; some of them can be accompanied by the accordion. Dalgas sings the Constantinople Manes and only imitations of the Smyrna kind. Nouros [alias Kostas Marsellos] sings Smyrna Manes (1930).

In terms of its lyrics, the *amanes* is typically a single couplet of fifteen-syllable verses, often containing a wry observation on the human condition, e.g.:

> *Open up the graves, spread out the bones,*
> *and let's see if you can tell apart the rich from the poor.*

> (Schorelis 1977: 146)

Each phrase is sung with a great deal of improvised melodic elaboration and interpolation of the expletive *aman* ('mercy!' in Turkish) between the clusters of syllables, which are repeated in strictly defined patterns (Dragoumis 1976).

Asia Minor refugee musicians also recorded songs in Turkish until the late 1930s; these were particularly in demand in Salonika, according to Innes' Report:

> The Salonika Territory. ... while the population has become outstandingly Hellenic, there has been erected [sic] the anomalous situation of many thousands of the new settlers from Asia Minor speaking only Turkish. ... The kind of music predominating consists in Manes and music of Turkish inspiration. This is the market for Turkish records. The Odeon Turkish record is greatly distributed and Columbia have started since one year and a half. Both are in greater favour than our Turkish record, I suppose because of lack of loudness in ours (1930).

Significantly, Innes makes no mention of the instrument bouzouki, neither in connection with refugees, nor otherwise. In the inter-war years the bouzouki was an instrument of low social standing. The resentment of the refugees of 'the Great Catastrophe' and their descendants at the stigma of having its importation into Greece imputed to them is poignantly expressed in a book about the role of refugees in the development of Greek popular song, first published in 1982, the sixtieth anniversary of the Asia Minor Catastrophe. The author, Dimitris Liatsos, dedicates the book to his parents who had sought refuge in Greece from Eastern Thrace 'in the first wave of persecution in 1914', but he seeks to restore the good name of later refugees from Asia Minor in the face of their continued defamation by association with the bouzouki and with what the author deems to be the most 'abject' genre of Greek popular music, rebetika songs. Indeed Liatsos strives to correct what he sees as a threefold popular misapprehension, mischievously cultivated by the mainstream Greek media, that refugees were responsible for importing from Asia Minor not just rebetika and the bouzouki (their accompanying instrument *par excellence*) but also the drug culture that dominated the content and social ambiance of these 'depraved' songs (1982). He claims that the history of all three in Greece predates 1923, and that the wilful vilification of Asia Minor refugees as their importers is part of a sixty-year-old conspiracy on the part of vested interests to undermine the refugees' industriousness and social potential. Liatsos accuses well known figures of contemporary Greek culture, such as the composers Mikis Theodorakis and Manos Hadjidakis, and the film producer Vasilis Maros of complicity in what he sees as degradation of Asia Minor refugees, often in the international media (ibid.: 13–22). He claims they should have known better, particularly a 'progressive' intellectual like Theodorakis whose left-wing ideological affiliations of that time were close to the author's own.

Liatsos is deluded with regard to several aspects of the evolution of rebetika and Greek popular music in general, partly by his ideological prejudice. Thus, for example, he claims that the appearance of partisan songs (*andartika*) during the German occupation instantly stymied the development of low-life rebetika (ibid.: 19, 46–9). His moralistic denunciation of rebetika, and his attempt to dissociate *Smyrneika* (Smyrna songs) and *laika* (popular songs) from them (ibid.: 42–6) are naive and disingenuous given the manifest overlap in themes, form, composers, exponents and consumers.

However, that part of Liatsos' argument that relates to chronology is indeed borne out by even stronger and earlier evidence than he is able to adduce. From the early 1890s there are, first of all, plausible reports of well established hashish dens, doubling as the headquarters of known criminals, in specified locations in Athens and Piraeus, and evidence of the flourishing production of high-quality hashish centred on the Peloponnesian town of Tripolis and destined, paradoxically, for export to Turkey and Egypt (*Akropolis* [Athenian newspaper] 18 May 1891: 2f. and 30 July 1891: 3). There are also repeated appearances of the bouzouki as a local instrument in Athenian literature of the 1890s, most conspicuously in Spandonis' novel *I Athina mas* (*Our Athens*) (1893: 236, 247f.), together with attestations of rebetika, in substance if not in name, in the Athenian review-theatre of the same decade (Hatzipandazis 1986: 85ff. n. 78).

It would therefore appear that such prominence of 'the Asiatic Muse' as might be due to the influx of refugees in 1923 was a question of scale, not of origin. As for the connection with the bouzouki, refugee musicians seem to have connived to keep this instrument out of the Athenian recording studios until the early 1930s (Pappas 1999: 364–6), and the best known refugee exponents of the bouzouki – Delias, Papaioannou, Peristeris – actually learnt to play it in 1930s Greece.

The value of Liatsos' book is as a source of perceptions and sensitivities rather than of hard data on the musical culture of refugees. Likewise Innes' 130-page report to the British Gramophone Company in 1930 is inaccurate in places and clearly influenced by some rather opinionated local sources, but it is highly revealing as regards the self-presentation of Greeks of the time to foreigners. The denigration of the refugees which Liatsos calls persecution and the bias which Innes' questions elicited both need to be seen in the context of the defensive orientalist discourse outlined above.

Moreover, rebetika songs composed and/or performed by refugees for recording in the inter-war period sit in a paradoxical relationship with the orientalist discourse that was stigmatising and marginalising them within Greek society. Their songs are usually conspicuously oriental in their music (based on the *makam* system of modes), in their main dance-rhythms (*zeybekiko*, *hasapiko*, and *tsifteteli* or belly-dance) and in their instrumentation (as Innes noted in 1930, typically comprising *ud* [fretless lute], *santouri* [hammered dulcimer] and a *lyra* or a fiddle). Yet their lyrics can often be seen to represent the East in much the same manner as Palamas' poem, as a fairy-tale setting full of carnal temptations, recreational drugs, and opportunities for enrichment and leisure among compliant hordes of subjugated women. The composers thus appear to be colluding in the demeaning 'orientalisation' of themselves and their refugee compatriots.

A classic example of such 'self-orientalisation' occurs in the song 'In the Turkish baths of Constantinople', composed to belly-dance rhythm (tsifteteli) by the Asia Minor refugee Anestis Delias in 1935:

> *In the Turkish baths of Constantinople a harem is taking the waters;*
> *black guards watch over them and take them to Ali Pasha.*
> *He orders his guard to bring them before him*
> *to get them to dance for him and play bouzouki for him,*
> *so that he can smoke a few hookahs with hashish from Bursa*
> *while the harem-girls dance a gipsy bellydance.*
> *That's how all the pashas of this world live:*
> *with hookahs, bouzoukia, embraces and kisses.*

(Aulin and Vejleskov 1991: 118)

Other such rebetika songs of the inter-war years offer compromising depictions of refugees from the Orient. Refugee women in particular are made to appear seductive, coquettish, but ultimately vulnerable and available, so that their courtship, or rather conquest, becomes a sport for predatory local males, e.g., 'In Athens' by Toundas (Kounadis 1995b: #13):

> *... There are some hanumakia* [Turkish girls, or girls from Turkey]
> *with beautiful eyes,*
> *Refugee-girls from Smyrna*
> *who set hearts ablaze.*
> *I can't live in Athens*
> *without love* [eros].
> *Flocks of girls,*
> *married dolls and lots of widows*
> *make me sigh.*
> *'Dear Moma!' I cry.*
> *Damn them!*
> *They've stolen my mind.*

The tendency to identify such females by the name of their native town now lost in Asia Minor, or by the name of a refugee quarter of Athens or Piraeus, underlines the orientalist dimension, as in, for example, 'The romancer' by Toundas (Kounadis 1995b: #5):

> *... In the Vyron [refugee-] quarter*
> *[I've] a twenty-year old widow*
> *with gorgeous,*
> *sweet, erotic eyes.*
> *... Another one at Peristeri*
> *a beautiful doll from Smyrna*
> *has taken everything I own*
> *and has set me ablaze, mother mine!*

(Cf. 'The connoisseur of suburbs' by Asikis [Georgiadis 1993: 38–39]; 'The Athenian Romeo' by Ogdondakis [Kounadis 1995a: #13]; and 'They're all beauties' by Papazoglou [Tambouris n.d.-b: #2].) Depiction of the vulnerable women of incapable menfolk as ripe for exploitation and subjugation has been a constant element in orientalism since Greek antiquity (Said 1991[1978]: 56).

In some of these songs composed and performed by refugees, a predatory narrator responds to resistance or infidelity on the part of refugee women with threats of violence (e.g., 'A Constantinopolitan woman at Podarades' [Kounadis 1995c: #10]). In Dalgas' 1927 recording of 'Your kerchief, my Smyrna lass' (Kounadis 1995d: #8) the curse 'Death to women from Smyrna!' is shouted. Taken at face value, such recordings by refugee musicians might be seen as evidence of not just collusion in denigration, but as incitement to maltreatment of their own kind.

Refugee composers and exponents also connived in the depiction of male refugees or immigrants from the East as pathetically inadequate competitors in a macho world of quick-witted metropolitan Greeks. Thus Dalgas' song 'A wise guy from Constantinople' (Kounadis 1995c: #3) ridicules one of his compatriots who is no match for local spivs:

> *All the wise guys of Athens*
> *rushed up with their tricks*
> *and they took out of his hands*
> *the hashish that he had brought.*

If this self-orientalisation was intended to ingratiate the composers and exponents with the locals through flattery, it achieved only limited success. Westernising Greeks continued to be scandalised and affronted by the popularity of such songs, describing them as 'overdue exchangees' that should be deported to Turkey under the Lausanne Treaty (Gauntlett 1991b: 14). In the words of Zacharias Papantoniou, one of the most persistent denigrators of Greek oriental music: 'A nation which entrusts the narrative of its passions to such simmering music, is, as we in Europe say, beyond the pale of civilisation' (*Eleftheron Vima* [Athenian newspaper] 3 July,1938).

A small intellectual élite was prepared to argue in the mid-1930s (as another group had in the 1880s) that oriental music was in fact being reintroduced to its land of origin, given that Persians, Arabs, and Turks had originally borrowed it from the ancient Greeks and Byzantines (Gauntlett 1991b: 14). But this argument carried no weight with the Metaxas regime, whose pre-emptive censorship put a stop to the burgeoning oriental-music industry in Greece in September 1937:

> [...] depuis Septembre 1937 nous ne pouvons pas procéder à aucun enrégistrement sans avoir reçu préalablement autorisation d'une Censure de l'Etat (constituée spécialement à ce but) qui examine d'abord la musique et les paroles de chaque titre à enrégistrer. Cette Censure rejette absolument et sans exéption toutes chansons du type *Hariklaki, Hasapiko, Katife* et *Zeybekika*...[2]

Metaxas' censor also rejected verses perceived to be encouraging the trafficking and use of hashish. As Greece had signed international treaties relating to such intoxicants in 1925 (Gauntlett 1985: 100 n. 196) this was arguably overdue. Metaxas' censorship of oriental music, however, is claimed to have been precipitated by rumours from Turkey that the Kemalist regime was banning amanedes as part of its programme of westernisation (Gauntlett 1991b: 14). It would be a cruel irony indeed if competition between two authoritarian, nationalist regimes in a Balkan version of western 'progress' were responsible for this devastating blow to the livelihood of refugee musicians in Greece. By 1937, commercial recording was a prestigious and lucrative medium for the dissemination of popular song, and denial of access to the recording studios – and to the broadcasting studios of the newly established radio service – severely affected the viability of manedes and 'Smyrna-style' rebetika in Greece.

Refugee musicians were further afflicted by the depredations of the three-year Axis occupation of Greece and the ensuing five-year civil war, which between them decimated their ranks in the 1940s, as the dates of death cited by Kapetanakis (1999) and Kounadis (2000b) attest. The Greek civil war also opened the door to cultural imperialism by the superpowers. Both sides distanced themselves from the songs of the Orient, but interestingly, the Left was to accuse the Right of insidiously promoting oriental fatalism and passivity through popular song in order to neutralise the heightened revolutionary fervour of the proletariat (Gauntlett 1991b: 15–17).

The few refugees to survive as professional musicians in Greece in the 1940s had long since entered into collaboration with overtly westernising popular composers. The latter belonged for the most part to a younger and better educated generation that had emerged under Metaxas and exploited their advanced literacy skills to satisfy the censor – and on occasions to outwit him by cloaking daring themes in subtle expression (Gauntlett 1985: 111 f.). This was the second generation of professional bouzouki players, headed by Vasilis Tsitsanis. Tsitsanis claimed to have abominated oriental music since childhood (Gauntlett 1979: 274) and appears to have been one of the chief antagonists of its revival in a modified form in the 1950s.

In the Cold War years, amid growing tension between Greece and Turkey, Greek popular taste for oriental music turned further eastward. Between 1954 and 1968 over 111 Indian films were screened in Greece (Abatzis and Tasoulas n.d.: 13, 63), each film containing over a dozen songs as the protagonists sang of their emotions at key points of the highly lachrymose plots (ibid.: 13f.). Between 1959 and 1968 at least 105 melodies from Indian films were recorded in Greece, dubbed with Greek lyrics of an erotic or pessimistic nature, many complaining of an uncaring, exploitative society. Some of these songs became so popular that they appeared in multiple versions, often transposed for the bouzouki (ibid.: 17). Among the best-selling records were Stelios Kazantzidis' 'Mandubala' and Stratos Attalidis' 'Mangala', both of 1959 (ibid.: 17). The most prolific Greek composer of 'Indo-Hellenic' songs was Apostolos Kaldaras, while their main Greek female exponent was Voula

Palla, whose popularity extended to the Greek diaspora communities of the West (Abatzis and Tasoulas n.d.: 60).

This development in Greek popular music again attracted vehement opposition in Greece, both at the time and in retrospect. Greek recording companies were accused of profiteering at the expense of Greek culture and of importing records from India for Greek composers to copy (ibid.: 66, 68). In 1964 Mikis Theodorakis formally protested in the Greek Parliament at the trafficking of 'musical Indian cannabis' over the airwaves in Greece (Theodorakis 1984: 46). The popular composer Vasilis Tsitsanis denounced the vogue as 'Indocracy' and vilified its exponents alleging that the inspiration for their 'hit' compositions consisted of a visit to a cinema armed with a tape-recorder (Tsitsanis 1979: 41f.). Middle- and upper-class devotees of various kinds of western music branded Indo-Hellenic music 'Turko-Gypsy style' (Abatzis and Tasoulas n.d.: 24).

Seeking an explanation for the exceptional appeal of Indian songs to Greeks in the 1950s, Abatzis and Tasoulas (n.d.: 14–18) offer an assortment of factors, ranging from the similarities between the muddy backstreets of Delhi and those of Thessaloniki in the 1950s, to the common Indo-European roots of Greek and Indian cultures. The political explanation is probably the most plausible: Turkish films became politically unacceptable in Greece in the 1950s following the outbreak of inter-communal violence in Cyprus and persecution of the Greek community of Istanbul. India was a ready alternative source of comparable films for the entertainment of the residual post-Second World War devotees of the Asiatic Muse (ibid.: 15).

The Greek flirtation with the 'Bollywood musical' might also have been a rearguard reaction against the increasing encroachments of western popular music during the 1950s, as Zachos has argued (1980: 250). Parodies of Anglo-American and European music in quasi-rebetika style are further evidence of such sentiments, e.g., '*Rok ent Rol me bouzouki*' (Rock and Roll with bouzouki) by Stratos Payioumtzis (78 rpm record GO 5402) and '*Mambo me pennies*' (Mambo with bouzouki notes) by Vasilis Tsitsanis (Gauntlett 1985: 287). These reactions could be seen as a prelude to the occidentalism which became more marked twenty years later. (Occidentalism is the counter-discourse to orientalism and typically demonises western culture as vulgar, depraved and venal [Chen 1995]).

The period of 'Indocracy' is supposed by Abatzis and Tasoulas (n.d.: 21) to have been stifled in Greece by the military junta's censors around 1968. The junta promoted the heroic folksongs and dances of the robust Greek peasantry, and disapproved of urban song, both of the oriental variety and the new hippy music of 'degenerate' western youth-culture. By predictable reaction, the junta's disapproval provoked a revival of interest in near-oriental song, which was further stimulated by the prison sentence inflicted in 1969 on Elias Petropoulos, the first anthologist of rebetika, for violation of censorship laws (Gauntlett 1991b: 25–27). Another catalyst of popular interest in rebetika was the rapid succession of deaths of veteran exponents of the genre in the early 1970s – Stratos Payioumtzis, Markos Vamvakaris, Yiannis

Papaioannou, Kostas 'Nouros' Marsellos all died in 1971–2. Though most of the deceased had been neglected for many years, commemorative re-releases of their 'greatest hits' now became a lucrative enterprise and helped revive the popularity of rebetika.

The junta's perceived dependence on the CIA and NATO, coupled with their abhorrence of rebetika, caused the songs to be perceived as a means of defiance of both the junta and its western sponsors (Gauntlett 1991a: 88). Anti-western sentiment may therefore be seen to have underpinned the restoration of this genre to popularity in Greece in the 1970s. The last years of that decade saw the widespread emergence of revivalist rebetika bands comprising young enthusiasts who used acoustic instruments to play the rebetika songs that they learned from pre-War 78 rpm records. Their revival-ist zeal often led them to attempt to strip away the layers of 'corrupt' commercialisation and westernisation in order to reach a supposedly pure Greek-oriental tradition. In the process, they sometimes anachronistically over-orientalised songs of the inter-war period (Gauntlett 1991b: 28f.).

Occidentalist discourse in Greece reached its peak in the populist cultural policies of Andreas Papandreou's administrations of the 1980s. Papandreou needed to keep faith at least at the rhetorical level with his initially anti-west-ern platform, while at the same time presiding over Greece's progressive enmeshment in the (then) EEC. These policies originated in the pre-election documents of the late 1970s and promised to emancipate the nation's creative potential from the previous regimes' obsession with the products of western cultural imperialism. The term 'bellydance-ocracy' (*tsiftetelokratia*) was coined to describe Papandreou's style of government (Gauntlett 1991a: 87f.). Rebetika became the signature tune of his 'Panhellenic Socialist Movement' (PASOK) in the 1980s, and Papandreou is reported to have asked to hear rebetika sung by Sotiria Bellou on his deathbed in 1996 (Gauntlett 1997).

In contrast, both the political Right and 'the traditional Left' adopted an anti-oriental posture. On the Right, the straight-laced Karamanlis and Rallis administrations of the late 1970s had censored the re-issue of historic record-ings of offensive songs during the rebetika revival, as did the New Democracy Government under Mitsotakis in 1991. Unreconstructed stalwarts of the 'tra-ditional Left' were also at pains to distance themselves from revivalist tendencies in mass culture. They variously denounced the revival of rebetika as reactionary, as commercially opportunistic, and even as part of an Ameri-can plot to emphasise the common ground between Greek and Turkish cultures as a prelude to political rapprochement and Greek concessions to Turkey in the Aegean and Cyprus (Gauntlett 1991b: 34).

By the 1990s one might have expected the crude binary polarities of both orientalism and occidentalism to have fallen into abeyance under the weight of globalisation, of postmodern pluralistic bricolage, and of multiculturalism, with which even Greece and its ostensibly homogeneous population have increasingly had to come to terms. Yet there have been signs of the contrary from the arena of Greek popular song. For example, in 1994 Stavros Xarhakos staged a highly publicised extravaganza of rebetika songs and dances under the title '*Aman... Amen*' first in Athens Municipal Theatre and then in the AEK sports stadium. The programme, which gave prominence to rebetika composed by Asia Minor refugees, had as its motto: 'We don't belong to the West; the West owes us.'

Such gestures suggest that the distinctive contribution of Asia Minor refugees to Greek popular song continues to be at the centre of a contest for the authority to define and represent Greek cultural identity in a dynamic context of conflicting political and commercial interests.

Notes

1. Unpublished 'Report on visit to Greece April–May 1930' in the EMI Archives.
2. Lambropoulos Frères SA, Athens, to the Overseas Department, The Gramophone Co Ltd, Hayes Middlesex, 7 December 1938, EMI Archives.

References

(Archival and newspaper sources are cited in individual chapters and are not included in this general bibliography).

Aarbakke, V. (2000). 'The Muslim Minority of Greek Thrace' (Unpublished Ph.D., University of Bergen).

Abadan-Unat, N. (1981). *Women in Turkish Society* (Leiden: Brill).

—— (1986). *Women in the Developing World: Evidence from Turkey* (Denver, CO.: University of Denver).

Abatzis, E. and Tasoulas, M. (n.d.). *Indoprepon Anakalypsi* [*The Discovery of Indian-style Songs*] (Athens: Atrapos).

Academy of Athens. (1994). *I Anaptyksi tis Thrakis. Prokliseis kai Prooptikes* [*The Development of Thrace. Challenges and Prospects*] vol. 6 (Athens).

Afentakis, D. N. (1927). 'Macedonia', in *Megali Elliniki Enkyklopaideia* [*The Great Greek Encyclopaedia*] (Athens).

Agelis, N. (1998). *Edepsizika Naklia (Piperata Anekdota) ton Kritotourkon* [Spicy Tales of the Turkocretans] (Athens: Smyrniotakis).

Agelopoulos, G. (1994). 'Cultures and Politics in Rural Macedonia' (Unpublished Ph.D., University of Cambridge).

—— (1997). 'From Bulgarievo to Nea Krasia, From "Two Settlements" to One Village: Community Formation, Collective Identities and the Role of the Individual', in P. Mackridge and E. Yannakakis (eds), *Ourselves and Others: The Development of a Greek Macedonian Cultural Identity Since 1912* (Oxford: Berg): 133–152.

Agnides, T. I. (1964). *The Ecumenical Patriarchate in the Light of the Lausanne Treaty* (New York).

Ahmad, F. (1993). *The Making of Modern Turkey* (London: Routledge).

Aigidis, A. (1934). *I Ellas Choris tous Prosphyges* [*Greece Without the Refugees*] (Athens).

Akakiadis, J. (1928). *H Karvali Nazianzou kai o Vios Grigoriou tou Theologou* [*Karvali of Nazianzos and the Vita of Gregory the Theologian*] (Athens: Tipis 'I Panprosphigiki').

Akar, R. (1992). *Varlık Vergisi* [*Capital Levy*] (Istanbul: Belge Yayınları).

Akgönül, S. (1999). *Une Communauté, Deux Etats: la Minorité Turco-musulmane de Thrace Occidentale* (Istanbul).

Aktar, A. (1996a). 'Cumhuriyetin İlk Yıllarında Uygulanan "Türkleştirme" Politikaları' ['Turkification' Policies in the First Years of the Republic] *Tarih ve Toplum*, 156 (December): 4–18.

—— (1996b). 'Economic Nationalism in Turkey: the Formative Years, 1912–1925', *Boğaziçi Journal, Review of Social and Administrative Studies*, 10 (1–2): 263–290.

—— (1996c). 'Varlık Vergisi ve İstanbul' [Capital Levy and Istanbul] *Toplum ve Bilim*, 71.

Alexandris, A. (1980). 'Imbros and Tenedos: A Study in Turkish Attitudes toward two Ethnic Greek Island Communities since 1923', *Journal of the Hellenic Diaspora*, 7(1): 5–31.

—— (1983). *The Greek Minority of Istanbul and Greek–Turkish Relations, 1918– 1974* (Athens: Centre for Asia Minor Studies).

Alexandris, A. (2001). *To Archeio tou Ethnomartyros Smyrnis Chrysostomou Mikras Asias, Mitropolitis Smyrnis A', 1910–14 [Archive of National Martyr Chrysostomos of Smyrna, Asia Minor, Archbishop of Smyrna A', 1910–14]* vol. 2 (Athens: MIET)

Anastasiadou-Dumont, M. (2000). Interview with Dimitri Frangopoulos, *Sychrona Themata* (special issue on Constantinople*)* (22) 74–5: 88–113.

Ancel, J. (1930). *La Macédoine: Son Evolution Contemporaine* (Paris: Delagrave).

Andreadis, A.M.(ed.). (1917). *I Elliniki Metanastefsis. Phrontistrion Dimosias Oikonomikis kai Statistikis, [Greek Emigration. Seminars on the National Economy and Statistics]*12 (Athens): 61–216.

Andrews, P. A., (ed.). (1989). *Ethnic Groups in the Republic of Turkey* (Wiesbaden: Reichert).

Antoniou, P. (1995). 'H Ellino-Armeniki Koinotita tis Athinas. Ekdoches kai Antilipseis tis Armenikotitas mesa apo ti Symviosi me tin Elliniki Koinotita' [The Greek–Armenian Community in Athens. Expressions and Perceptions of Being Armenian through Symbiosis with the Greek Community] (Ph.D., Department of Social Anthropology, University of the Aegean).

Apostolides, A. (1992). 'Ypodochi kai Apokatastasi Palinostounton Ellinon Pontiakis Katagogis' [Reception and Settlement of Repatriate Greeks of Pontian Origin] *Proceedings of the Third Congress of Pontic Hellenism* (Thessaloniki: Panellinia Omospondia Pontiakon Somateion).

Arı, K. (1995). *Büyük Mübadele: Türkiye'ye Zorunlu Göç, 1923–1925 [The Great Exchange: Forced Migration to Turkey, 1923–1925]* (Istanbul: Tarih Vakfı).

Armaoğlu, F. (1959). '1955 Yılında Kıbrıs Meselesinde Türk Hükümeti ve Türk Kamuoyu Davranışları' [The Behaviour of the Turkish Government and Turkish Public Opinion on the Cyprus Question in 1955] *Siyasal Bilgiler Fakültesi Dergisi*, 14 (2–3) (Ankara).

—— (1963). *Kıbrıs Meselesi, 1955–1959. Türk Hükümeti ve Türk Kamuoyu Davranışları [The Cyprus Question 1955–1959. The Turkish Government and the Behaviour of Turkish Public Opinion]* (Ankara; Sevinç Matbaasi).

Augustinos, G. (1992). *The Greeks of Asia Minor: Confession, Community, and Ethnicity in the Nineteenth Century* (Kent: Kent State University Press).

Aulin, S. and Vejleskov, P. (1991). *Chasiklidika Rebetika [Hashish Rebetika]* (Copenhagen: Museum Tusculanum Press).

Avdela, E. (2000). 'The Teaching of History in Greece', *Journal of Modern Greek Studies*, 18(2): 239–53.

Aydınlı, A. (1971). *Batı Trakya Faciasının İçyüzü [The Inside Story of the Western Thrace Calamity]* (Istanbul: Aydınlı Cagaloğlu).

Azcaraté, P. (1969). *La Société des Nations et la Protection des Minorités* (Genève: Centre Européen de la Dotation Carnegie pour la Paix Internationale).

Aziz, A. (1973). 'Gökçeada üzerinde toplumsal bir inceleme' [A Social Investigation of Imbros] *Siyasal Bilgiler Fakültesi Dergisi*, 28 (1–2) (Ankara).

Bahcheli, T. (1990). *Greek–Turkish Relations since 1955* (Boulder: Westview Press).

Baker, R. S. (1960). *Woodrow Wilson and World Settlement*, vol. III, Original Documents of the Peace Conference (Gloucester, MA: Peter Smith).

Bali, R. (1999) *Cumhuriyet Yıllarında Türkiye Yahudileri. Bir Türkleşme Serüveni, 1923–1945* [Turkish Jews during the Republican Era. A Quest in Turkification, 1925–1945] (Istanbul: İletişim Yayınları).

Balian, A. (1991). 'Cappadocia After the Seljuks' Conquest and the Christian Communities from the 16th until the 18th Century' in L. Evert, N. Minaidi and M. Phakidi *Cappadocia. Travel Across the Christian East* (Athens: Adam): 30–39.

Balic, S. (1979). 'Eastern Europe: The Islamic Dimension', *Journal of the Institute of Muslim Affairs*, 1 (1) (Jeddah).

Balta, E. and Millas, H. (1996). 'Bir Destan ve Sözlü Tarih'[An Epic Poem and Oral History] *Tarih ve Toplum*, (May) (Istanbul): 5–15.

Barkey, K. and von Hagen, M. (eds) (1997). *After Empire: Multiethnic Societies and Nation-Building: the Soviet Union and Russian, Ottoman, and Habsburg Empires* (Boulder: Westview).

Barutciski, M. (1996). 'Politics Overrides Legal Principles: Tragic Consequences of the Diplomatic Intervention in Bosnia–Herzegovina (1991–1992)', *American University Journal of International Law and Policy*, 11 (767).

Behar, C. (1996). *The Population of the Ottoman Empire and Turkey* (Ankara: State Institute of Statistics).

Benlisoy, Y. and Macar, E. (1996). *Fener Patrikhanesi [The Phanar Patriarchate]* (Ankara).

Berktay, A. and Tuncer, H. C. (eds) (1998). *Tarih Eğitimi ve Tarihte 'Öteki' Sorunu [History Education and the 'Other' in History]* (Istanbul: Tarih Vakfı).

Beyani, C. (1997). 'A Political and Legal Analysis of the Problem of the Return of Forcibly Transferred Populations', *Refugee Survey Quarterly*, 16 (10).

Bibelas, P. A. (1956). *Laographika Kydonion (Aivali) Moschonision (Nisi), Genitsarohoriou (Horio) [The Folklore of Kydonies (Aivali), Moschonisia (Nisi), Genitsarohorio(Horio)]* (Athens).

Bierstadt, E. H. (1925). *The Great Betrayal: A Survey of the Near East Problem* (London: Hutchinson).

Bilge, A. S. (1998). 'The Fener Greek Patriarchate', *Perceptions. Journal of International Affairs*, 3 (1) (Ankara) 19–38.

Biris, K. (1966). *Ai Athinai apo ton 19on eis ton 20on aiona [Athens, from the 19th to the 20th Century]* (Athens).

Bitsios, D. S. (1964–1965). 'Vindictive Deportations of Greeks from Turkey Violating International Law and Morality', *International Relations*, 7–8 (Athens).

Bölükbaşı, Ş. (1992). 'The Turco-Greek Dispute: Issues, Policies and Prospects' in C. H. Dodd (ed.) *Turkish Foreign Policy: New Prospects* (Huntington).

Bringa, T. (1993). 'We Are All Neighbours', *Disappearing World Series* (War), Granada TV.

Buğra, A. (1994). *State and Business in Modern Turkey: A Comparative Study* (Albany: State University of New York Press).

Bunin, A. V. (1961). *Geschichte des Russischen Städtebaues bis zum 19 Jahrhundert [The History of Russian Urban Planning before the 19th Century]*.

Calhoun, C. (1998). 'Nationalism and the Contradictions of Modernity', *Berkeley Journal of Sociology*, 42.

Campbell, J. K. and Sherrard, P. (1968). *Modern Greece* (London: Ernest Benn).

Çanlı, M. (1994). 'Yunanistan'daki Türklerin Anadolu'ya Nakledilmesi' [The Transfer of the Turks in Greece to Anatolia] *Tarih ve Toplum*, 130 (October): 51–59.

Carabott, P. (1997). 'Slavomakedones kai Kratos stin Ellada tou Mesopolemou' [Slavomacedonians and the State in Inter-war Greece] *Istor*, 10 (December).

Carter, E., Donald, J. and Squires, J., (eds) (1993). *Space and Place: Theories of Identity and Location* (London: Lawrence and Wishart).

Çelik, M. (1998). *Türkiye'nin Fener Patrikhanesi Meselesi* [*The Question of Turkey's Phanar Patriarchate*] (Izmir).

Cernea, M. (1988). *Involuntary Resettlement in Development Projects: Policy Guidelines in World Bank-Financed Projects* (Washington, D.C.: The World Bank).

—— (1993). *The Urban Environment and Population Reallocation Projects* (Washington, D.C.: The World Bank).

—— (1996). *Impoverishment Risks and Livelihood Reconstruction: A Model for Resettling Displaced Populations* (Washington, D.C.: The World Bank).

—— and Guggenheim, S. E. (eds) (1993). *Anthropological Approaches to Resettlement: Policy, Practice and Theory* (Boulder: Westview Press).

—— and McDowell, C. (eds) (2000). *Risks and Reconstruction: Experiences of Resettlers and Refugees* (Washington, D.C.: The World Bank).

Chatterjee, P. (1986). *Nationalist Thought and the Colonial World: A Derivative Discourse* (London: Zed Books).

Chen, X. (1995). 'Occidentalism as Counterdiscourse', in K. Appiah and H. Gates (eds) *Identities* (Chicago): 63–89.

Christides, Y. (1997). 'The Muslim Minority in Greece', in G. Nonneman, T. Niblock and B. Szajkowski (eds) *Muslim Communities in the New Europe* (Reading: Ithaka Press): 153–160.

Churchill, W.S. (1929). *The World Crisis* (London: Thornton Butterworth).

Çiçekoğlu, F. (1992). *Suyun Öteki Yanı* [*The Other Side of the Water*] (Istanbul: Can).

Clogg, R. (1979). *A Short History of Modern Greece* (Cambridge: Cambridge University Press).

Colson, E. (1999). 'Forced Migration and the Anthropologist's Response' (Unpublished Seminar Paper, *Forced Migration Seminar*, Refugee Studies Centre, University of Oxford).

Connerton, P. (1989). *How Societies Remember* (Cambridge: Cambridge University Press).

Costis, C. (1990). *Economie Rural et Banque Agraire. Les Documents* (Athens: Fondation Culturelle de la Banque Nationale de Grèce).

Cowan, J.K. (ed.). (2000). *Macedonia: The Politics of Identity and Difference* (London: Pluto Press).

Dafnes, G.(1961). *Ta Ellinika Politika Kommata, 1821–1961* [*Greek Political Parties, 1821–1961*] (Athens: Galaxias).

Dakin, D. (1972). *The Unification of Greece, 1770–1923* (London: Ernest Benn).

Dalégre, J. (1997). *La Thrace Grecque: Population et Territoire* (Paris).

Dark, M. (1998). 'The Comparative Politics of the Greco-Turkish Exchange' (Unpublished Conference Paper, *The Compulsory Exchange of Populations between Greece and Turkey*, Refugee Studies Centre, University of Oxford).

Danforth, L. (1995). *The Macedonian Conflict: Ethnic Nationalism in a Transnational World* (Princeton: Princeton University Press).

Danielsen, E. (1989). 'Greek-Speaking Muslims', in P. A. Andrews (ed.) *Ethnic Groups in the Republic of Turkey* (Wiesbaden: Reichert).

Davidson, R. H. (1974). 'Turkish Diplomacy from Mudros to Lausanne', in G. A. Craig and F. Gilbert (eds) *The Diplomats, 1919–1939*, vol. I (New York).

Dawn, E. C. (1973). *From Ottomanism to Arabism: Essays on the Origins of Arab National-ism* (Urbana: University of Illinois Press).

Demir, H. and Akar, R. (1994). *İstanbul'un son Sürgünleri: 1964'te Rumların Sınırdışı Edilmesi [The Last Exiles of İstanbul: The Expulsion of the Greek Orthodox in 1964]* (Istanbul).

Deringil, S. (1998). *Well-Protected Domains: Ideology and the Legitimation of Power in the Ottoman Empire, 1876–1909* (London: I.B. Tauris).

—— (1999). 'Conversion to Islam and Apostasy during the Tanzimat: A Reformulation of State-Subject Relationship' (Unpublished Conference Paper, *Citizenship in the Ottoman Empire,* SUNY-Binghamton).

Dertilis, G. B. (1993). *Atelesphoroi i Telesphoroi; Phoroi kai Eksousia sto Neoelliniko Kratos [Effective or Ineffective? Taxes and Authority in the Modern Greek State]* (Athens).

Dimaras, K. Th. (1978). 'O Telesphoros Syngerasmos' [The Effective Convergence] *Istoria tou Ellinikou Ethnous,* 15 (Athens: Ekdotiki Athinon).

Dimitrakopoulos, A. (1935). 'Schedia Poleon kai Poleodomia en Elladi' [Town Plans and Town Planning in Greece] *Techniki Epitiris tis Ellados [Technical Bulletin of Greece]* (Athens).

Dosdoğru, M. H. (1993). *6–7 Eylül Olayları [The Events of 6–7 September]* (Istanbul).

Doukas, S. (1929). *Istoria Enos Aichmalotou.* (1999) English transl. *A Prisoner of War's Story* (Birmingham: University of Birmingham).

Doulis, T. (1977). *Disaster and Fiction: Modern Greek Fiction and the Asia Minor Disaster of 1922* (Berkeley: University of California Press).

Downing. T. (1996). 'Mitigating Social Impoverishment when People are Involuntar-ily Displaced' in C. McDowell (ed.) *Understanding Impoverishment: The Consequences of Development-Induced Displacement* (Oxford and Providence, RI: Berghahn Books).

Dragoumis, M. (1976). 'Scholio gia ton Amane' [A Comment on the Amanes] *Tram* (September): 151–7.

Dritsa, M. (1989). 'Prosphyges kai Ekviomichanisi' [Refugees and Industrialisation] in T. Veremis and G. Goulimi (eds) *Eleftherios Venizelos: Koinonia-Oikonomia-Politiki stin Epochi tou [Eleftherios Venizelos: Society-Economy-Politics in His Era]* (Athens: Gnose).

—— (1998). 'Pisti kai Viomichania ston Mesopolemo' [Credit and Industry During the Inter-war Period] in G. Mavrogordatos and Chr. Chatziiosif (eds) *Venizelismos kai Astykos Eksychronismos [Venezelism and Urban Modernisation]* (Crete).

Duben, A. and Behar C. (1991). *Istanbul Households: Marriage, Family and Fertility, 1880–1940* (Cambridge: Cambridge University Press).

Eddy, C. B. (1931). *Greece and the Greek Refugees* (London: Allen and Unwin).

Efpraxiadis, L. (1974). *Prokopi Kappadokias. Patrida Mou. Istoria kai Laographia [Prokopi of Cappadocia. My Homeland. History and Folklore]* (Thessaloniki: Typo Ellinismos).

Eisenman, P. (1982). 'The House of Memory: The Texts of Analogue', in A. Rossi, (ed.) *The Architecture of the City* (Cambridge, Mass.: MIT Press).

Enotiadis, C. (1994). *Istorikes Maties [A Historical Review]* (Athens: Adelphotita Prokopieon Athinon–Piraios kai Perichoron 'Osios Ioannis o Rossos').

Erim, N. (1953). *Devletler Arası Hukuk ve Siyasi Tarih Metinleri [International Law and Political History Texts]* vol. 1 (Ankara: TTK).

Erginsoy, G. (1998). 'Sweet as an Almond: from Gliki to Bademli: Tracing the Misfor-tunes of the Imbrians' (Unpublished Conference Paper, *The Compulsory Exchange of Populations between Greece and Turkey,* Refugee Studies Centre, University of Oxford).

Evelpidis, C. (1950). 'Oikonomiki Istoria tis Ellados' [Economic History of Greece] in *Neoteron Enkyklopaidikon Leksikon Iliou [Modern Encyclopaedic Dictionary Iliou]* vol. 7 (Athens: Ellas).

Fann, P. (1996). 'Exiles on Stage: Greek Pontian Theatre 1922–1972', *Journal of Modern Greek Studies,*14: 47–65.

Fahim, H. M. (1973). 'Nubian Resettlement in the Sudan', *Ekistics*, 212 (Athens).

Fairchild, H. P. (1911). *Greek Immigration to the United States* (New Haven: Yale University Press).

Fernandez, J. (1986). *Persuasions and Performances: The Play of Tropes in Culture* (Bloomington: Indiana University Press).

Frangopoulos, Y. (1994). 'La Minorité Musulmane et les Pomaques de la Thrace: Entre Islam et Ethnisme', *Cahiers d'études sur la Méditerranée orientale et le monde turco-iranien,*17 (Paris).

Frangoudaki, A. and Dragonas, T. (eds) (1997). *Ti Ein' i Patrida mas; Ethnokentrismos stin Ekpaidefsi ['What is Our Homeland?' Ethnocentrism in Education]* (Athens: Alexandreia).

Gauntlett, S. (1979). 'Mia Anekdoti Synentefksi me ton Vasili Tsitsani' [An Unpublished Interview with Vasilis Tsitsanis] in E. Petropoulos (ed.) *Rebetika Tragoudia* (Athens: Kedros): 273–5.

—— (1985). *Rebetika Carmina Graeciae Recentioris [Rebetika Songs of Modern Greece]* (Athens: Denise Harvey and Co.).

—— (1991a). 'The Greening of the Greek Blues', in M. Clarke (ed.) *Proceedings of the Fourth National Folklore Conference* (Canberra: Australian Folktrust Inc.): 85–91.

—— (1991b). 'Orpheus in the Criminal Underworld: Myth in and about Rebetika', *Mandatophoros*, 34 (December): 7–48.

—— (1997). 'Sotiria Bellou' [obituary] *The Independent*, 6 September 1997.

—— (1999). 'Pos Asomen epi Gis Allotrias?' [Greek Song and Identity 'Down-under'] *Etudes Helléniques*, 7 (2) (Autumn): 127–36.

Geertz, C. (1973). 'Thick Description: Towards an Interpretative Theory of Culture', in C. Geertz , *The Interpretation of Cultures: Selected Essays* (New York: Basic Books).

Georgiadis, N. (1993). *Rebetika kai Politiki [Rebetika and Politics]* (Athens: Sychroni Epochi).

Georgoulis, S. (1993). *O Thesmos tou Moufti stin Elliniki kai i Allodapi Ennomi Taksi [The Institution of the Mufti in the Greek and Foreign Legal Order]* (Athens/Komotini).

Giannakakis, B. (1956).) 'International Status of the Ecumenical Patriarchate', *The Greek Orthodox Theological Review* (Brookline, Mass.,) 2 (December): 10–26.

—— (1957) International Status of the Ecumenical Patriarchate', *The Greek Orthodox Theological Review* (Brookline, Mass.,) 3 (Summer): 27–46.

Göçek, F. M. (2002). 'The Politics of History and Memory: A Multidimensional Analysis of the Lausanne Peace Conference (1922–23)', in H. Erdem, I. Gershoni and U. Wokoeck (eds) *New Directions in Studying the Modern Middle East* (New York: Columbia University Press).

Gökalp, Z. (1959). *Turkish Nationalism and Western Civilization*, Berkes, N. (ed. and transl.) (New York: Columbia University Press).

Greenfeld, L. (1992). *Nationalism: Five Roads to Modernity* (Cambridge, Mass.: Harvard University Press).

Guizeli, V. (1984). *Koinonikoi Metaschimatismoi kai Proelefsi tis Koinonikis Katoikias stin Ellada, 1920–1930 [Social Changes and the Origins of Social Housing in Greece, 1920–1930]* (Athens: Epikairotita).

Gutkind, E. A. (1964). *International History of City Development*, vol. 1, Central Europe (London: Macmillan).

Güvenç, B. (1993). *Türk Kimliği: Kültür Tarihinin Kaynakları [Turkish Identity: Sources of Cultural History]* (Ankara: Kültür Bakanlığı Yayınları).

Hadjimichalis, C., Kalogirou, N., and Yerolympos, A. (1988). *Voreioelladikoi Oikismoi prin kai meta tin Apeleftherosi. Metaschimatismoi tou Astykou kai Periphereiakou Chorou prin kai meta to 1923* [*Transformations of Urban and Regional Space in Northern Greece, Before and After 1923*] (Thessaloniki: Ministry of Industry, Technology and Energy).

Hatzipandazis, T. (1986). *Tis Asiatidos Mousis Erastai* [*Suitors of the Asiatic Muse*] (Athens: Stigmi).

Hatzivassiliou, E. (1990). 'The Riots in Turkey in September 1955: A British Document', *Balkan Studies*, 31 (1) (Thessaloniki).

Henckaerts, J. (1995). *Mass Expulsions in Modern International Law and Practice* (London: Martinus Nijshoff).

Heper, M. (1985). *The State Tradition in Turkey* (North Humberside: Eothen).

Heraclides, A. (1993a): *Security and Co-operation in Europe: The Human Dimension, 1972–1992* (London: Frank Cass).

—— (1993b). *Helsinki II and its Aftermath: The Making of the CSCE into an International Organisation* (London: Pinter).

—— (1997). 'Elliniki Meionotiki Politiki: I Anachronistiki Stasi kai ta Aitia tis'[Greek Minority Policy: an Outdated Stance and its Causes] *Sychrona Themata* (19) 63:32–5.

—— (2001). *I Ellada kai o eks Anatolon Kindynos* [*Greece and the Threat from the East*] (Athens).

Hidiroglou, P. (1972). 'Simainontes Tourkokrites' [Leading Turkish Cretans] *Kritika Chronika* (Iraklion).

Hirschon, R. (1985). 'The Woman-Environment Relationship: Greek Cultural Values in an Urban Community', *Women and Space in Human Settlements* (special issue), *Ekistics*, 52 (310): 15–21.

—— (1998) [1989]. *Heirs of the Greek Catastrophe: The Social Life of Asia Minor Refugees in Piraeus* [Oxford : Clarendon Press] (New York, Oxford: Berghahn).

—— (2001). 'Surpassing Nostalgia: Personhood and the Experience of Displacement' (Unpublished Lecture, *Elizabeth Colson Lecture in Forced Migration*, Refugee Studies Centre, University of Oxford).

—— (2003). ' "We got on well with the Turks": Christian-Muslim Relations in Late Ottoman Times' in D. Shankland (ed.) *Anthropology, Archaeology and Heritage in the Balkans and Anatolia, or The Life and Times of F.W.Hasluck (1878–1920)* (Istanbul: Isis Books).

—— and Gold, J. (1982). 'Territoriality and the Home Environment in an Urban Greek Locality', *Anthropological Quarterly*, 55 (2): 63–73.

—— and Thakurdesai. (1970). 'Society, Culture and Spatial Organization: An Athens Community', *Ekistics*, 30 (178): 187–196.

Housepian, M. D. (1972)[1966]. *Smyrna 1922: The Destruction of a City* (London: Faber).

Humphrey, C. (1992). 'The Moral Authority of the Past in Post-Socialist Mongolia', *Religion, State and Society*, 20 (3 and 4): 375–389.

Iasonides, L. (1983). *Collected Works* (Thessaloniki: Association Panagia Soumela).

Iosiphidis, K. and Tsiriktsidou, S. (eds) (1996). *Enthymion. 15 Chronia Stegi Politismou Neas Karvalis* [*Memento. 15 Years of the Cultural Centre of New Karvali*] (Kavala: Stegi Politismou Neas Karvalis).

İzbek, T. (1997). 'Dose to Cheri sou Kriti', *Erisma* (Chania) (Spring).

Jacobsen, K. (1997). 'Refugees' Environmental Impact: The Effects of Patterns of Settlement', *Journal of Refugee Studies*, 10 (1) (January).

Janowitz, M. (1965). *The Military in the Political Development of New Nations* (Chicago: University of Chicago Press).

Jelavich, B. (1983). *History of the Balkans: The Twentieth Century*, vol. 2 (Cambridge).

de Jong, F. (1980). 'The Muslim Minority in Western Thrace', in G. Ashworth (ed.) *Muslim Minorities in the Eighties* (Sunbury: Quartermaine House).

Just, R. (1989). 'The Triumph of the Ethnos' in M. Chapman, E. Tonkin and M. MacDonald (eds) *History and Ethnicity* (London: Routledge).

Kafkoula, K. (1990). 'I Idea tis Kipoupolis stin Elliniki Poleodomia tou Mesopolemou' [The Idea of the Garden City in Greek Town Planning in the Inter-War Years] *Academic Register of the Faculty of Architecture*, 12 (4) (University of Thessaloniki).

—— (1999). 'Metamorphoseis tou Agrotikou Chorou: o Epoikismos tis Anatolikis Makedonias kata tis Protes Dekaetieas tou Aiona' (Transformations of Rural Space: the Settlement of Eastern Macedonia in the First Decades of the Century) in *o Kserizomos kai i Alli Patrida: oi Prosphygoupoleis stin Ellada (The Uprooting and the Other Homeland: Refugee Settlements in Greece)* (Athens: Research Society for Modern Greek Culture and General Education).

—— (1992). 'The Replanning of the Destroyed Villages of Eastern Macedonia After World War I: the Influence of the Garden City Tradition on an Emergency Programme', *Planning History*, 14 (2).

Kamozawa, I. (1982). 'Ethnic Minority in Regionalization: The Case of Turks in Western Thrace', *Population Mobility in the Mediterranean World* (Tokyo: Mediterranean Studies Research Group, Hitotsubashi University).

Kandiyoti, D. (1990). *Women, Islam and the State* (Philadelphia: Temple University Press).

Kapetanakis, E. (1999). *Adespotes Melodies [Stray Melodies]* (Athens: Livanis).

Karahoca, R. (1995). *Pomakiko-Elliniko Leksiko [Pomak-Greek Dictionary]* (Komotini).

Karakasidou, A. (1997). *Fields of Wheat, Hills of Blood: Passages to Nationhood in Greek Macedonia, 1870–1990* (Chicago: University of Chicago Press).

Karaosmanoğlu, Y. K. (1991)[1934]. *Ankara* (Istanbul: Iletisim).

Karpat, K. H. (1985). *Ottoman Population, 1830–1914* (Madison: University of Wisconsin Press).

Karypides, Y. (1994). 'Provlimata Stegasis ton Ellinopontion Prosphygon apo tin Proin ESSD' [Housing Problems of the Pontic Greek Refugees from the Former USSR] (Unpublished Conference Paper, *International Committee of Pontic Hellenism*, Thessaloniki).

Kassimati, K. with V. Mao, V.Agdzidis, M. Vergetti, A. Ragousis (1992). *Pontioi Metanastes apo tin Sovietiki Enosi: Koinoniki kai Oikonomiki Entaksi [Pontian Immigrants from the Former Soviet Union: Social and Economic Integration]* (Athens: Ministry of Culture and Panteion University).

Kazantzakis, N. (1953). *O Kapetan Michalis [Captain Michalis]* (Athens). English translation (1956): *Freedom and Death* (Oxford: Cassirer).

Kent, M. (ed.) (1984). *The Great Powers and the End of the Ottoman Empire* (London: Allen and Unwin).

Keyder, Ç. (1981). *The Definition of a Peripheral Economy: Turkey 1923–1929* (Cambridge: Cambridge University Press).

—— (1982). *Dünya Ekonomisi İçinde Türkiye 1923–1929 [Turkey in the World Economy 1923–1929]* (Ankara: Yurt Yayınları).

—— (1987). *State and Class in Turkey: A Study in Capitalist Development* (London, Verso Books).

—— (1994) 'The Agrarian Background and the Origins of the Turkish Bourgeoisie', in A. Oncu, Ç. Keyder, and S.E. Ibrahim (eds) *Developmentalism and Beyond: Society and Politics in Egypt and Turkey (*Cairo: AUC Press).

—— (1997). 'The Ottoman Empire', in K. Barkey and M. von Hagen (eds) *After Empire: Multiethnic Societies and Nation-Building: The Soviet Union and Russian, Ottoman, and Habsburg Empires* (Boulder: Westview).

—— (1999a). 'Port-Cities and Politics on the Eve of the Great War', *New Perspectives on Turkey*, (20) (Spring).

——, ed. (1999b). *Istanbul: Between the Global and the Local* (Boulder: Rowman and Littlefield).

——, Özveren, E. and Quataert, D. (eds) (1993). *Port-Cities of the Eastern Mediterranean, 1800–1914*, (special issue) *Review*, 16 (4) (Fall).

Khayyam, O. (1904)[1859]. *Rubáiyát of Omar Khayyám*, translated by Edward Fitzgerald (London: Arthur C. Fifield).

Khera, S. and Mariella, P.S. (1982). 'The Fort McDowell Yavapai: A Case of Long-Term Resistance to Relocation', in A. Hansen and A. Oliver-Smith (eds) *Involuntary Migration and Resettlement: The Problems and Responses of Dislocated People* (Boulder: Westview): 159–177.

Khosla, G. D. (1949). *Stern Reckoning: A Survey of the Events Leading Up To and Following the Partition of India* (Delhi: Oxford University Press).

Kıbrıslıoğlu, I. (1967). *Patrikhane Köstebekleri, Megali Idea, Türklüğün İmha Planı ve Yerli Rumlarin Rolü [Patriarchal Moles, Great Idea, The Plan to Destroy Turkishness and the Role of the Local Greek Orthodox]* (Istanbul).

Kitromilides, P. (1972). 'Symvoli sti Meleti tis Mikrasiatikis Tragodias: Tekmiria tis Katastrophis tou Ellinismou tis Vithynias' [Contribution to the Study of the Asia Minor Tragedy: Evidence on the Destruction of the Hellenism of Bithynia] *Mikrasiatika Chronika*, 15: 372–398.

—— (1989). 'Imagined Communities and the Origins of the National Question in the Balkans', in M. Blinkhorn and T. Veremis (eds) *Modern Greece: Nationalism and Nationality* (Athens: Sage, ELIAMEP): 23–65.

—— and Alexandris, A. (1984–85). 'Ethnic Survival, Nationalism and Forced Migration: The Historical Demography of the Greek Community of Asia Minor at the Close of the Ottoman Era', *Deltio Kentrou Mikrasiatikon Spoudon [Bulletin of the Centre for Asia Minor Studies]* 5 (Athens: Centre for Asia Minor Studies): 9–44.

Kitromilides, P. (ed.). (1992). *I Mikrasiatiki Katastrophi kai I Elliniki Koinonia [The Asia Minor Catastrophe and Greek Society]* (special edition), *Deltio Kentrou Mikrasiatikon Spoudon[Bulletin of the Centre for Asia Minor Studies]* vol. 9.

KMS (Kentro Mikrasiatikon Spoudon [Centre for Asia Minor Studies]). 1980. *I Eksodos [The Exodus]* vol. 1 (Athens).

KMS (Kentro Mikrasiatikon Spoudon [Centre for Asia Minor Studies]).1982. *I Eksodos, [The Exodus]* vol. 2 (Athens).

Kokkinos, D. (1991a). 'The Reception of Pontians from the Soviet Union in Greece', *Journal of Refugee Studies*, 4 (4).

—— (1991b). 'The Greek State's View of the Pontian Issue', *Journal of Refugee Studies*, 4 (4).

Koliopoulos, J. S. (1994). *Leilasia Phronimaton [A Plunder of Loyalties]* (Thessaloniki: Vanias).

—— (1999). *A Plunder of Loyalties* (London: Hurst).

Kolodny, E. (1974). *La Population des Iles de la Grèce – Essai de Geographie Insulaire en Méditerranée Orientale* (Aix-en-Provence).

—— (1995). 'Des Musulmans dans une Ile Grecque: Les "Turcocretois"', *Mediterranean World*, XIV (Tokyo: Mediterranean Studies Group, Hitotsubashi University).

Kondoglou, F. (1962). *To Aivali, I Patrida mou [Aivali, My Homeland]* (Athens).

Kontogiorgi, E. (1992). 'Agrotikes Prosphygikes Enkatastaseis stin Makedonia: 1923–1930' [Rural Refugee Settlements in Macedonia: 1923–1930] in P. Kitromilides (ed.) *Mikrasiatiki Katastrophi kai Elliniki Koinonia* [*The Asia Minor Catastrophe and Greek Society*] (special edition), *Deltio Kentrou Mikrasiatikon Spoudon/Bulletin of the Centre for Asia Minor Studies*] 9: 47–59.

—— (1996). 'The Rural Settlement of Greek Refugees in Macedonia: 1923–1930' (Unpublished D.Phil., University of Oxford).

Kontosopoulos, N. (1988). *Glossikos Atlas tis Kritis* [*Language Atlas of Crete*] (Iraklion: University of Crete Press).

Koraltürk, M. (1996–97) 'Mübadelenin İktisadi Sonuçları Üzerine bir Rapor' [Report on the Economic Consequences of the Exchange] *Çağdaş Türkiye Tarihi Araştırmaları Dergisi*, 2 (6–7): 183–98.

Kostakis, Th. (1963). *I Anakou* [*Anakou*] (Athens: Centre for Asia Minor Studies).

—— (1977). *To Misti tis Kappadokias* [*Misti of Cappadocia*] (Athens: Akadimia Athinon).

—— (1990). Eisagogi [Introduction] in G. Mavrohalividis, *I Akso tis Kappadokias: Monographia* [*Axo in Cappadocia: a Monograph*] (Athens: Mavrohalividi).

Kostis, K. (1992). 'I Ideologia tis Oikonomikis Anaptyksis: Oi Prosphyges sto Mesopolemo' [The Ideology of Economic Development: the Refugees in the Inter-war Period] in P. Kitromilides (ed.) *Mikrasiatiki Katastrophi kai Elliniki Koinonia* [*The Asia Minor Catastrophe and Greek Society*] (special edition), *Deltio Kentrou Mikrasiatikon Spoudon* [*Bulletin of the Centre for Asia Minor Studies*] 9: 31–46.

—— (1988). 'Agrotiki Metarythmisi kai Oikonomiki Anaptyksi stin Ellada, 1917–1940' [Agrarian Reform and Economic Development in Greece, 1917–1940] in G. Mavrogordatos and Chr. Chatzhiiosif (eds) *Venizelismos kai Astikos Eksychronismos* [*Venizelism and Modernisation*] (Crete).

Kottakis, M. (2000) *Thraki: I Meionotita Simera* [Thrace: The Minority Today] (Athens).

Koufa, K. and Svolopoulos, C. (1991). 'The Compulsory Exchange of Populations Between Greece and Turkey: the Settlement of Minority Questions at the Conference of Lausanne, 1923, and its Impact on Greek–Turkish Relations', in P. Smith (ed.) *Ethnic Groups in International Relations: Comparative Studies on Governments and Dominant Ethnic Groups in Europe, 1850–1940*, vol. 5 (New York: New York University Press): 275–308.

Koufopoulou, S. (1992). 'A Primeval Form of Rotating Credit Association among Turkish Women' (Unpublished Conference Paper, *Women's Use of Rotating Credit Associations Workshop*, Centre for Cross Cultural Research on Women, University of Oxford).

—— (1993). 'Ethnicity and Gender in Turkish Society' (Unpublished Conference Paper, *Women and International Development*, Michigan State University).

—— and Papageorgiou, D. (1997). 'Morphes kai Oria "Perithoriakon" Epikoinoniakon Dyktion ston Aigaiako Horo: I Praktiki tou Lathremporiou sto Aivali kai sti Lesvo' [Borders and Expressions of Marginalised Communicative Networks: The Practice of Smuggling in Aivali and Lesvos] in *Dyktia Epikoinonias kai Politismou sto Aigaio* [*Communication Networks and Culture in the Aegean*] (Athens: Pnevmatiko Idryma Samou).

Koulouri, C. (2002) *Clio in the Balkans: The Politics of History Education* (Thessaloniki: Centre for South-East European Studies).

Kounadis, P. (1994). (Compact Disc) 'Panayiotis Toundas 1' *Archive of Greek Discography – Composers of Rebetika* 2 (ed. P. Kounadis) (Athens: Minos-EMI).

—— 1995a. (Compact Disc) 'Yiannis Dragatsis 1' *Archive of Greek Discography – Composers of Rebetika* 10 (ed. P. Kounadis) (Athens: Minos-EMI).

—— 1995b. (Compact Disc) 'Panayiotis Toundas 2' *Archive of Greek Discography – Composers of Rebetika* 18 (ed. P. Kounadis) (Athens: Minos-EMI).

—— 1995c. (Compact Disc) 'Antonis Diamandides 1' *Archive of Greek Discography – Composers of Rebetika* 22 (ed. P. Kounadis) (Athens: Minos-EMI).

—— 1995d. (Compact Disc) 'Antonis Dalgas 1' *Archive of Greek Discography – Singers of Rebetika* 7 (ed. P. Kounadis) (Athens: Minos-EMI).

—— (2000a). *Eis Anamnisin Stigmon Elkistikon. Keimena yia to Rebetiko* [*In Memory of Alluring Moments. Texts About Rebetika*] (Athens: Katarti).

—— (2000b). *Yeia sou Periphani kai Athanati Ergatia* [*All Hail the Proud, Immortal Workers*] (Athens: GSEE).

—— and Papaioannou, S. (1981). 'A Discography of Rebetika in Smyrna–Constantinople Before 1922', in P. Kounadis, *Eis Anamnisin Stigmon Elkistikon. Keimena yia to Rebetiko* [*In Memory of Alluring Moments. Texts About Rebetika*] (Athens: Katarti): 285–307.

Kranidiotis, Y. (1999). *I Elliniki Eksoteriki Politiki* [*Greek Foreign Policy*] (Athens).

Küçükcan, T. (1999). 'Re-claiming Identity: Ethnicity, Religion and Politics Among Turkish-Muslims in Bulgaria and Greece', *Journal of Minority Affairs*, 19 (1) (London).

Kyriakidou, E. (1892). *Istoria tou Sychronou Ellinismou 1832–1892* [*History of Contemporary Hellenism 1832–1892*] vol. 1 (Athens).

Ladas, S. P. (1932). *The Exchange of Minorities – Bulgaria, Greece and Turkey* (New York: Macmillan).

Lampsidis, G. (1982). *Oi Prosphyges tou 1922: Eksinta Chronia Symvoli stin Oikonomiki Anaptyksi tou Topou* [*The Refugees of 1922: Sixty Years Contribution to Economic Development of the Country*] (Athens).

Lazarides, G. (1996). 'Immigration to Greece: Critical Evaluation of Greek Policy' *New Community*, 22 (2): 335–348.

League of Nations (1926). *Greek Refugee Settlement* (Geneva).

—— (1931). *The Agricultural Crisis* (Geneva).

Legg, K. R. (1969). *Politics in Modern Greece* (Stanford: Stanford University Press).

Lemos, N. (n.d.). 'The Exchange of Populations and Greek Music,' (Unpublished Paper) Refugee Studies Centre (Documentation Centre), University of Oxford.

Leigh-Fermor, P. (1966). *Roumeli* (London).

Lewis, B. (1968) 2nd ed. [1961]. *The Emergence of Modern Turkey* (Oxford: Oxford University Press).

Lewis, G. (1974). *Modern Turkey* (New York: Praeger).

Liakos, A. (1993). *Ergasia kai Politiki stin Ellada tou Mesopolemou* [*Labour and Politics in Inter-war Greece*] (Athens).

Liatsos, D. (1982). *Oi Prosphyges tis Mikras Asias kai to Rebetiko Tragoudi* [*Asia Minor Refugees and Rebetika songs*] (Piraeus).

Llewellyn Smith, M. (1998). 2nd ed. [1973]. *Ionian Vision: Greece in Asia Minor 1919–1922* (London: Hurst).

Loizos, P. (1981). *The Heart Grown Bitter: a Chronicle of Cypriot War Refugees* (Cambridge: Cambridge University Press).

—— (1999). 'Ottoman Half-lives: Long-term Perspectives on Particular Forced Migrations', *Journal of Refugee Studies*, 12 (3): 237–263.

Lynch, K. (1960). *The Image of the City* (Cambridge, Mass.: MIT Press).

—— (1972). *What Time is This Place?* (Cambridge, Mass.: MIT Press).

Macartney, C.A. (1934). *National States and National Minorities* (London: Oxford University Press).

Mackridge, P. (1986). 'The Two-Fold Nostalgia: Lost Homeland and Lost Time in the Work of G. Theotokas, E. Venezis and K. Politis', *Journal of Modern Greek Studies,* 4 (2).

—— (1991). 'The Pontic Dialect: A Corrupt Version Of Ancient Greek?', *Journal of Refugee Studies,* 4 (4).

Magrini, T. (2000). Vocal Music in Crete, CD 40437 (Washington, D.C.: Smithsonian Folkways Recordings).

Malkki, L. (1990). 'Context and Consciousness: Local Conditions for the Production of Historical and National Thought Among Hutu Refugees in Tanzania', in R. Fox (ed.) *Nationalist Ideologies and the Production of National Cultures,* 2 (American Ethnological Society Monograph Series).

Mansur, F. (1972). *Bodrum: A Town in the Aegean* (Leiden: E. J. Brill).

Marrus, M. R. (1985). *The Unwanted: European Refugees in the Twentieth Century* (Oxford, New York: Oxford University Press).

Marshall Brown, P. (1923). 'The Lausanne Conference', *American Journal of International Law,* 17 (290).

Marx, E. (1990). 'The Social World of Refugees: A Conceptual Framework', *Journal of Refugee Studies,* 3 (2): 189–202.

Mavrogordatos, G. (1983). *Stillborn Republic: Social Coalitions and Party Strategies in Greece, 1922–1936* (Berkeley: University of California Press).

—— (1992). 'To Anepanalipto Epitevgma' [The Unique Achievement] in P. Kitromilides (ed.) *Mikrasiatiki Katastrophi kai Elliniki Koinonia* [T*he Asia Minor Catastrophe and Greek Society*] (special edition), *Deltio Kentrou Mikrasiatikon Spoudon[Bulletin of the Centre for Asia Minor Studies]* 9: 9–12 (Athens: Centre for Asia Minor Studies).

—— (1995). 'The 1940s, Between Past and Future', in J. Iatrides and L. Wringley (eds) *Greece at the Crossroads: The Civil War and its Legacy* (Pennsylvania State University Press).

Mavrohalividis, G. (1990). *I Axo tis Kappadokias. Monographia [Axo of Cappadocia: a Monograph]* (Athens: Ekdosi Mavrohalividi).

Mazower, M. (1991). *Greece and the Inter-war Economic Crisis* (Oxford: Clarendon Press).

—— (1992). 'The Refugees, the Economic Crisis and the Collapse of Venizelist Hegemony, 1929–1932', in P. Kitromilides (ed.) *Mikrasiatiki Katastrophi kai Elliniki Koinonia* [T*he Asia Minor Catastrophe and Greek Society]* (special edition), *Deltio Kentrou Mikrasiatikon Spoudon[Bulletin of the Centre for Asia Minor Studies]* 9:119–134 (Athens: Centre for Asia Minor Studies).

—— (1998). *Dark Continent: Europe's Twentieth Century* (London: Allen Lane).

McCarthy, J. (1983a). *Muslims and Minorities: The Population of Ottoman Anatolia and the End of the Empire* (New York: New York University Press).

—— (1983b). 'Foundations of the Turkish Republic: Social and Economic Change', *Journal of Middle Eastern Studies,* 19 (2) (April): 139–152.

—— (1993). 'Muslim Refugees in Turkey: The Balkan Wars, World War I and the Turkish War of Independence', in H. W. Lowry and D. Quataert (eds) *Humanist and Scholar, Essays in Honor of Andreas Tietze* (Istanbul: ISIS Press): 87–111.

—— (1995). *Death and Exile: The Ethnic Cleansing of Ottoman Muslims, 1821–1922* (Princeton, N.J.: Darwin Press).

Mears, E. G. (1929). *Greece Today: The Aftermath of the Refugee Impact* (Stanford: Stanford University Press).

Meindersma, C. (1997). 'Population Exchanges: International Law and State Practice', *International Journal of Refugee Law,* 9 (1): 335–653.

de Mello, S. V. (1977). 'Forcible Population Transfers and Ethnic Cleansing', *Refugee Survey Quarterly*, 16 (vi).

Mendiluce, J-M. (1994). 'War and Disaster in Former Yugoslavia: The Limits of Humanitarian Action', *World Refugee Survey* (U.S. Committee for Refugees).

Meray, S. (1969–1973). *Lozan Barış Konferansı, Tutanaklar, Belgeler [Lausanne Peace Treaty; Proceedings, Documents]* 8 volumes (Ankara: Siyasal Bilgiler Fakültesi).

Merlier, M. (1963). 'Prologos' [Preface] in Th. Kostakis, *I Anakou [Anakou]* (Athens: Kentron Mikrasiatikon Spoudon) xvii–xxix.

Michelis, L. (1992a). *Prosphygon Vios kai Politismos [The Life and Culture of Refugees]* (Athens: Dromena).

—— (1992b). *Astygraphia tis Elassonos Asias [Urban Survey of Asia Minor]* (Athens: Dromena).

Millas, H. (1991a). 'Türk Edebiyatında Yunan İmajı: Yakup Kadri Karaosmanoğlu' [The Image of Greeks in Turkish Literature: Yakup Kadri Karaosmanoğlu] *Toplum ve Bilim*, Winter (Istanbul).

—— (1991b). 'History Textbooks in Greece and Turkey', *History Workshop Journal*, 31: 21–33.

—— (1996). 'The Image of Greeks in Turkish Literature: Fiction and Memoirs', in *Oil on Fire? Textbooks, Ethnic Stereotypes and Violence in South-Eastern Europe* (Hanover: Hahnsche Buchhandlung).

—— (1998). *Ayvalık ve Venezis [Ayvalık and Venezis]* (Istanbul: İletişim).

—— (2000). *Türk Romanı ve Öteki, Ulusal Kimlikte Yunan Imajı [The Turkish Novel and the Other. The Image of the Greek in National Identity]* (Istanbul: Sabancı Üniversitesi Yayınları).

—— (2001). *Eikones Ellinon kai Tourkon [Images of Greeks and Turks]* (Athens: Alexandreia).

Minaidis, S. (1990). *I Thriskeftiki Eleftheria ton Mousoulmanon stin Elliniki Ennomi Taksi [Religious Freedom of the Muslims Within the Greek Legal Order]* (Athens).

Mitrany, D. (1936). *The Effects of the War in South Eastern Europe* (New Haven: Yale University Press).

Moraux, P. (1964). *Bibliothèque de la Société Turque d'Histoire, Catalogue de Manuscrits Grecs* (Ankara: Fonds du Syllogos).

Morgenthau, H. (1929). *I Was Sent to Athens* (New York: Doubleday).

Myrivilis, S. (1943). *O Vasilis o Arvanitis [Vasilis Arvanitis]* (Athens). English translation (1983): *Vasilis Arvanitis* (Armidale: University of New England Press).

—— (1985). 11th ed. *I Panagia i Gorgona [The Mermaid Madonna]* (Athens).

Nur, R. (1967). *Hayat ve Hatıratım [My Life and Memoirs]* 4 vols. (Istanbul: Altındağ Yayınevi).

Norberg-Schulz, C. (1970). *La Signification dans l'Architecture Occidentale* (Paris: Mardaga).

O'Dowd, L. and Wilson, T. M. (eds) (1996). *Borders, Nations and States : Frontiers of Sovereignty in the New Europe* (Brookfield, USA: Avebury).

Ökte, F. (1951). *The Tragedy of the Capital Tax*, transl. by Geoffrey Cox, (1987) (London).

O'Mahony, A. (2003). 'Between Orthodox Christendom and Turkish Islam: Baba Eftim and the Turkish Orthodox Church' in D. Shankland (ed.) *Anthropology, Archaeology and Heritage in the Balkans and Anatolia, or The Life and Times of F.W.Hasluck (1878–1920)* (Istanbul: Isis Books).

Oran, B. (1991). 2nd ed. *Türk-Yunan İlişkilerinde Batı Trakya Sorunu [The Question of Western Thrace in Turco-Greek Relations]* (Ankara: Bilgi).

—— (1988). *Atatürk Milliyetçiliği [Nationalism of Atatürk]* (Ankara: Dost).

—— (2000). *Küreselleşme ve Azınlıklar [Globalisation and Minorities]* (Ankara: İmaj).

Özbayri, K. and Zakhos-Papazakhariou, E. (1976). 'Documents de Tradition Orale des Turcs d'Origine Crétoise', *Turcica*, VIII (1): 292–346.

Özgüç, A. (1974). *Batı Trakya Türkleri [The Turks of Western Thrace]* (Istanbul).

Özkan, S. and Onur, S. (1975). 'Another Thick Wall Pattern: Cappadocia', in P. Oliver (ed.) *Shelter, Sign and Symbol* (London: Barrie and Jenkins).

Palamas, K.(n.d.) *Anthologia Kosti Palama [The Kostis Palamas Anthology]* (Athens: Estia).

Pallis, A. A. (1925). 'Racial Migrations in the Balkans During the Years 1912–1924', *The Geographical Journal,* 66 (London): 315–331.

—— (1927). 'To Prosphygikon Zitima' [The Refugee Issue] *Megali Elliniki Enkyklopaideia [The Great Greek Encyclopaedia]* (Athens).

—— (1937). *Greece's Anatolian Venture and After: A Survey of the Diplomatic and Political Aspects of the Greek Expedition to Asia Minor, 1915–1922* (London: Methuen).

Panayiotopoulos, B. (1980). 'I Viomihaniki Epanastasi kai I Ellada, 1832–1871' [Greece and the Industrial Revolution, 1832–1877] in *Eksychronismos kai Viomihaniki Epanastasi sta Valkania tou 19o Aiona [Modernization and the Industrial Revolution in the Balkans in the 19th Century]* (Athens).

Panteleaki, N. (1991). 'The Physiognomy and History of Cappadocia from the Ancient Era until the End of the Byzantine Era', in L. Evert, N. Minaidi and M. Phakidi, *Cappadocia: Travelling across the Christian East* (Athens: Adam).

Papadopoulos, R. (1997). 'Individual Identity in the Context of Collective Strife', *Eranos Yearbook*: 99–113.

—— (2000). 'Factionalism and Interethnic Conflict: Narratives in Myth and Politics', in T. Singer (ed.) *The Vision Thing: Myth, Politics and Psyche in the World* (London: Routledge).

Papparigopoulos, K. (1976). *Istoria tou Ellinikou Ethnous [History of the Greek Nation]* (Athens: MIET).

Pavlowitch, S. (1999). *A History of the Balkans* (London: Longman).

Pappas, N. (1999). 'Concepts of Greekness: The Recorded Music of Anatolian Greeks after 1922', *Journal of Modern Greek Studies,* 17 (2) (October): 353–73.

Pelagidis, S. (1997). *Prosphygiki Ellada (1913–1940) [Refugee Greece (1913–1940)]* (Thessaloniki: Kyriakidis).

Pepelassi-Minoglou, I. (1988). 'O Venizelos kai to Kseno Kephalaio (1918–1932)' [Venizelos and Foreign Capital (1918–1932)] *Proceedings of the Congress on Eleftherios Venizelos* (Athens).

Pentzopoulos, D. (1962). *The Balkan Exchange of Minorities and its Impact Upon Greece* (Paris: Mouton).

Perlman, J. E. (1982). 'Favela Removal: The Eradication of a Lifestyle', in A. Hansen and A. Oliver-Smith (eds) *Involuntary Migration and Resettlement: The Problems and Responses of Dislocated People* (Boulder: Westview Press): 225–263.

Petropoulos, E. (1979). *Rebetika Tragoudia [Rebetika Songs]* (Athens: Kedros).

Petropoulos, J. A. (1976). 'The Compulsory Exchange of Populations: Greek–Turkish Peacemaking 1922–1930', *Byzantine and Modern Greek Studies,* 2: 135–160.

—— (1989). 'I Ypochreotiki Antallagi ton Plythismon: Ellinotourkikes Eirineftikes Diefthetiseis, 1922–1930' [The Compulsory Exchange of Populations: Greco-Turkish Peace Negotiations, 1922–1930] in T. Veremis and G. Goulimi (eds) *Eleftherios Venizelos: Koinonia-Oikonomia-Politiki stin Epochi tou [Eleftherios Venizelos: Society-Economy-Politics in his Era]* (Athens: Gnosi).

Petropoulou, J. (1991). 'Intellectual Life in Cappadocia in the 19th Century, an Outline', in L. Evert, N. Minaidi and M. Phakidi, *Cappadocia: Travelling across the Christian East* (Athens: Adam).

Phalbos, F. K. (1957). 'O Teleftaios Typos Astikou Spitiou tis Smyrnis' [The Last Type of Urban House of Smyrna] *Mikrasiastika Chronika* (Athens), 180 (7).

Philippidis, S. (1997). 'Kykliki Diarthrosi Topon sta Diigimata "O Amerikanos" tou Papadiamanti kai "To Lios" tou I. Venezi' [The Cyclical Structure of Places in the Stories "The American" by Papadiamantis and "Lios" by I. Venezis] in *Topoi* [*Places*] (Athens): 61–96.

Politis, K. (1930). *Lemonodasos* [*The Lemon Forest*] (Athens).

—— (1963). *Stou Hatzifrangou* [*At Hatzifrangou*] (Athens: Karavias).

—— (1988). *Stou Hatzifrangou. Ta Sarantachrona Mias Chamenis Politeias* [*At Hadzifrangou. A Forty-Year Commemoration of a Lost Town*] (Athens: Ermis). Turkish translation (1992): *Yitik Kentin Kırk Yılı. İzmir'in Haci Frangu Semtiden* (Istanbul: Belge Uluslararası Yayıncılık).

Politis, L. (1973). *A History of Modern Greek Literature* (Oxford: Oxford University Press).

Popovic, A. (1986). *L'Islam Balkanique: Les Musulmans du Sud-Européen dans la Période Poste-Ottoman* (Berlin, Wiesbaden).

Prevelakis, P. (1938). *To Chroniko Mias Politeias* [*The Chronicle of a Town*] (Athens). English translation (1976): *The Tale of a Town* (London: Doric Publications).

Psalidopoulos, M. (1989). *I Krisi tou 1929 kai oi Ellines Oikonomologoi. Symvoli stin Istoria tis Oikonomikis Skepsis stin Ellada tou Mesopolemou* [*The Crisis of 1929 and the Greek Economists. Contribution to the History of Economic Thought in Inter-war Greece*] (Athens: Idryma Erevnas kai Paideias tis Emporikis Trapezas tis Ellados).

Psilakis, M. (1995). *Kritiki Paradosiaki Kouzina* [*Traditional Cretan Cuisine*] (Herakleion: Karmanof).

Psomiades, H. (1968). *The Eastern Question: The Last Phase: A Study in Greek–Turkish Diplomacy* (Thessaloniki: Institute of Balkan Studies).

Ramsey, W. M. (1916). *The Intermixture of Races in Asia Minor: Some of its Causes and Effects* (London: Oxford University Press).

Reps, J. W. (1965). *The Making of Urban America* (New Jersey: Princeton University Press).

Renan, E. (1990) [1882]. 'What is a Nation?', in H. Bhabha (ed.) *Nation and Narration* (New York: Routledge).

Rodocanachis, A. (1934). *Les Finances de la Grèce et l'Etablissement des Refugiés* (Paris).

Rossi, A. (1982). *The Architecture of the City* (Cambridge, Mass.: MIT Press).

Rovertakis, G. (1973). *Enas Rebetis: Yiorgos Rovertakis* [*A Rebetis: George Rovertakis*] (edited by T. Schorelis and M. Oikonomidis) (Athens).

Rozakis, C. (1997). 'Eisagogi' [Introduction] in K. Tsitselikis and D. Christopoulos (eds) *To Meionotiko Phainomeno stin Ellada* [*The Minority Phenomenon in Greece*] (Athens).

Şahin, M. S. (1980). *Fener Patrikhanesi ve Türkiye* [*The Phanar Patriarchate and Turkey*] (Istanbul).

Said, E. (1991) [1978]. *Orientalism* (Harmondsworth: Penguin).

Salamone, S. D. (1987). *In the Shadow of the Holy Mountain* (New York: Columbia University Press).

Salzmann, A. (1999). 'Citizens in Search of a State: The Limits of Political Participation in the Late Ottoman Empire', in M. Hanagan and C. Tilly (eds) *Extending Citizenship, Reconfiguring States* (Boulder: Rowman and Littlefield).

Sarandis, C. (1993). 'The Ideology and Character of the Metaxas Regime', in *The Metaxas Dictatorship: Aspects of Greece 1936–40* (Athens: ELIAMEP, Vryonis Centre).

Schechtman, J. B. (1962). *Postwar Population Transfers in Europe, 1945–1955* (Philadelphia: University of Philadelphia Press).

Schorelis, T. (1977). *Rebetiki Anthologia [Anthology of Rebetika]* vol.1 (Athens: Plethron).

Scudder, T. (1979). *Expected Impacts of Compulsory Relocation on Najovas with Special Emphasis on Relocation from the Former Joint Use Area Required by Public Law 93–531* (Binghamton, NY: Institute for Development Anthropology).

—— and Colson, E. (1982). 'From Welfare to Development: A Conceptual Framework for the Analysis of Dislocated People', in A. Hansen and A. Oliver-Smith (eds) *Involuntary Migration and Resettlement: The Problems and Responses of Dislocated People* (Boulder: Westview Press): 267–287.

Seferiades, S. (1928). 'L'Echange des Populations', *Recueil des Cours*, tome 24 (Paris: Académie de Droit International).

Sella-Mazi, E. (1999). *La Minorité Musulmane Turcophone de Grèce: Approche Sociolinguistique d'une Communauté Bilingue* (Corfu).

Seyppel, T. (1989). 'Pomaks in Northeastern Greece: An Endangered Balkan Population', *Journal of the Institute of Muslim Minority Affairs*, 10 (1) (London).

Sgouridis, P. (2000). *Thraki – Provlimatismoi sto Katophli tou 21ou Aiona* (Athens).

Shaw, S. J. (1998). 'Resettlement of Refugees in Anatolia, 1918–1923', *Turkish Studies Association Bulletin*, 22 (1) (Spring 1998): 58–90.

Sifnaiou, E. (1996). *Lesbos: Oikonomiki kai Koinoniki Istoria (1840–1912) [Lesbos: a Socio-Economic History (1840–1912)]* (Athens: Trochalia).

Şimşir, B. (1989). 2nd ed. *Sakarya'dan İzmir'e 1921–22 [From the Sakarya to Izmir 1921–22]* (Ankara: Bilgi).

Skalieris, G. K. (1990). *Laoi kai Phyles tis Mikras Asias [Populations and Races of Asia Minor]* (Athens: Risos).

Sofuoğlu, A. (1996). *Fener Rum Patrikhanesi ve Siyasi Faaliyetleri [The Phanar Rum Patriarchate and its Political Activities]* (Istanbul: Üsküdar).

Solomonides, V. (1984). The Greek Administration of the Vilayet of Aidin, 1919–1922 (Unpublished Ph.D., University of London).

Soltaridis, S. (1997). *I Istoria ton Moufteion tis Dytikis Thrakis [The History of the Muftis in Western Thrace]* (Athens).

Sotiriou, D. (1959). *Oi Nekroi Perimenoun [The Dead Await]* (Athens: Kedros).

—— [1962]. 22nd ed. *Matomena Chomata [Bloodstained Earth]* (Athens: Kedros).

—— (1991). *Farewell Anatolia* [English translation of *Matomena Chomata*] (Athens: Kedros).

—— (1978). *Mesa apo tis Phloyes [Out of the Flames]* (Athens: Kedros).

Söylemezoğlu, G. K. (1946). 'Hatıraları' [Memories] *Canlı Tarihler*, 5 (Istanbul: Türkiye Yayınevi).

Spandonis, N. (1893). *I Athina Mas [Our Athens]* (Piraeus).

Spatharis, A. (1964–1965). 'The Ecumenical Patriarchate. A Many Century Old Institution', *International Relations*, (Athens) 7–8: 67–86 (in English).

Stamatopoulos, K. (1985). 'H Kathimerini Zoi stin Sinaso tis Kappadokias' [Everyday Life in Sinasos, Cappadocia] in S. Petsopoulos (ed.) *I Sinasos tis Kappadokias [Sinasos in Cappadocia]* (Athens: Agra): 39–91.

Stavrakis, N. (1890). *'Statistiki tou Plythismou tis Kritis' [Statistics of the Population of Crete]* (Athens: Karavia).

Stavros, S. (1995). 'The Legal Status of Minorities in Greece Today: The Adequacy of their Protection in the Light of Current Human Rights Perceptions', *Journal of Modern Greek Studies*, (13).

Stavrou, T. (1967). *O en Konstantinopolei Ellinikos Philologikos Syllogos [The Greek Literary Society of Constantinople]* (Athens).

Stevenson, D. (1991). *The First World War and International Politics* (Oxford: Clarendon Press).

Sussnitzki, A. J. (1966). 'Ethnic Division of Labour', in C. Issawi (ed.) *The Economic History of the Middle East 1800–1914: A Book of Readings* (Chicago: University of Chicago Press).

Svolopoulos, C. (1977). *Greek Foreign Policy after the Treaty of Lausanne: The Crucial Turning Point, July-December 1928.* (Thessaloniki).

Sychrona Themata. (1994). *Evraioi stin Ellada [Jews in Greece]* (special issue), 17 (52–3) (Athens).

Syrigos, A. (1995). 'Proti Epistimoniki Katagraphi tis Pomakikis' [A First Scholarly Record of the Pomak Language] *Oikonomikos Tachydromos* [Economic Journal] 30 November (Athens).

—— (1999–2000). 'Dytiki Thraki, i Atheati Opsi: Mia Diplomatiki kai Nomiki Periplanisi sti Synthiki tis Lozanis gia tis Meionotites' [Western Thrace, the Unseen View: a Diplomatic and Legal Peregrination through the Lausanne Treaty regarding Minorities] *Nea Koinoniologia*, 29: 43–84.

Takkenberg, L. (1998). *The Status of Palestinian Refugees in International Law* (Oxford: Clarendon Press).

Tambouris, P.(n.d.) a. Compact Disc 'Reminiscence of Smyrna' *The Greek Archives* 4 (ed. P. Tambouris) (Athens: FM Records).

—— (n.d.) b. Compact Disc 'Unknown Recordings of Rebetika Songs' *The Greek Archives* 12 (ed. P. Tambouris) (Athens: FM Records).

Tapper, N. and Tapper, R. (1987). 'The Birth of the Prophet: Ritual and Gender in Turkish Islam', *Man (N.S.)* (22): 69–92.

Terzibaşoğlu, Y. (2001). 'Landlords, Refugees and Nomads: Struggles for Land around Late Nineteenth Century Ayvalık', *New Perspectives on Turkey* (24) (Spring): 51–82.

Tenekides, C. G. (1924) 'Le Statut des Minorités et l'Echange Obligatoire des Populations Gréco-Turques', *Revue Générale de Droit International Public*, tome XXXI : 72–88.

Tenekides, G. (1980) 'Prologos'[Prologue] in *I Eksodos : Martyries apo tis Dytikes Peripheries tis Mikras Asias [Exodus: Testimonies from the Western Asia Minor Regions]* vol. 1. (Athens: Centre for Asia Minor Studies).

—— (1986). *Imbros kai Tenedos [Imbros and Tenedos]* (Thessaloniki).

Tessi, E. (1981). *Anatolika t' Archipelagous [East of the Archipelago]* (Athens).

Texier, C. and Pullan, R. (1864). *Byzantine Architecture.* (London: Day and Son).

Theodorakis, M. (1984). *Star System* (Athens: Kaktos).

Thompson, K. (1963). *Farm Fragmentation in Greece: The Problem and its Setting*, Monograph Series 5 (Athens: Centre for Economic Research).

Thorburn, J. (1996). 'Root Cause Approaches to Forced Migration: Part of a Comprehensive Strategy? A European Perspective', *Journal of Refugee Studies*, 9 (2) (June).

Thornberry, P. (1991). *International Law and the Rights of Minorities* (Oxford: Clarendon Press).

Thrakiotis, A. (1993). 'Anichti Pligi tis Mousoulmanikis Meionotitas sti Thraki' [The Open Wound of the Muslim Minority in Thrace] *Anti*, 7 (2).

Toprak, Z. (1998). 'The Demographic Consequences of the Lausanne Convention for Turkey', (Unpublished Conference Paper, *The Compulsory Exchange of Populations between Greece and Turkey*, Refugee Studies Centre, University of Oxford).

Toynbee, A. J. (1922). *The Western Question in Greece and Turkey: A Study in the Contact of Civilizations* (Boston: Houghton Mifflin Company).

Tsimouris, G. (1997). 'Anatolian Embodiments in a Hellenic Context: The Case of Reisderiani Mikrasiates Refugees' (Unpublished Ph.D., University of Sussex).

Tsitsanis, V. (1979). *I Zoi mou, to Ergo mou* [*My Life, my Work*] K. Hatzidoulis (ed.) (Athens: Nefeli).

Tsitselikis, K. and Christopoulos, D. (eds) (1997). *To Meionotiko Phainomeno stin Ellada* [*The Minority Phenomenon in Greece*] (Athens).

Tsourkas, D. (1981–1982). 'Les Jurisdictions Musulmanes en Grèce', *Hellenic Review of International Relations*, 2 (2) (Thessaloniki).

Tuan, Yi-Fu. (1974). *Topophilia: A Study of Environmental Perception, Attitudes and Values* (New Jersey: Prentice-Hall).

Turan, Ö. (1999). 'Pomaks, Their Past and Present', *Journal of Muslim Minority Affairs*, 19 (1) (London).

Uran, H. (1959). *Hatıralarım* [*My Memoirs*] (Ankara: H. Uran).

Valaoras, V. (1942). *To Demographikon Provlima tis Ellados kai i Epidrasis ton Prosphygon* [*The Demographic Question in Greece and the Impact of the Refugees*] (Athens).

Venezis, I. (1928). *O Manolis Lekas ki Alla Diigimata* [*Manolis Lekas and Other Stories*] (Athens).

—— (1931). *To Noumero 31328* [*Number 31328*] (Athens and Mytilene).

—— (1939). *Galini* [*Tranquillity*] (Athens).

—— (1944). *Akiph* [*Akif*] (Athens: Glaros).

—— (1969) [1943] *Aioliki Gi* [*Aeolian Earth*] (Athens: Estia).

—— (1974). *Mikrasia Chaire* [*Farewell Asia Minor*] (Athens: Estia).

Veremis, T. (1982). *Oikonomia kai Diktatoria* [*Economy and Dictatorship*] (Athens: MIET).

—— (1997). *The Military in Greek Politics: From Independence to Democracy* (London: Hurst).

Vitti, M. (1978). *Istoria tis Neoellinikis Logotechnias* [*History of Modern Greek Literature*] (Athens: Odysseas).

Volkan, V. and Itzikowitz, N. (1994). *Turks and Greeks: Neighbours in Conflict* (London: Eothen Press).

Voutira, E. (1991). 'Pontic Greeks Today: Migrants or Refugees?' *Journal of Refugee Studies*, 4 (4): 400–420.

—— (1996). 'Vestiges of Empire: Migrants, Refugees and Returnees in post-Soviet Russia', *Oxford International Review*, 8 (3) (Summer).

—— (1997a). 'Viaies Metakiniseis, Metanastefseis kai Epanapatrismos. Dilimmata Taftotitas ton Ellinon tis Kentrikis Asias' [Forced Migrations, Migrations and Repatriation: Dilemmas of Identity among Greeks in Central Asia] in *I Diaspora ton Ellinon sti Rossia apo tin Ptosi tis Polis Mechri Simera* [*The Greek Diaspora in Russia from the Fall of Constantinople until Today*] (Athens: Metsovio Polytechneion): 171–207.

—— (1997b). 'Population Transfers and Resettlement Policies in Europe: The Case of Asia Minor Refugees in Macedonia from a National and International Perspective', in P. Mackridge and E. Yannakakis (eds) *Ourselves and Others: The Development of a Greek Macedonian Cultural Identity since 1912* (Oxford: Berg): 111–131.

Vroutsis, C.D. (1999–2000). 'Oi Dikastikes Armodiotites tou Moufti einai Asymvivastes pros tin Elliniki Ennomi Taksi' [The Judicial Competences of the Mufti are Incompatible with the Greek Legal Order] *Nea Koinoniologia*,13 (29).

Vryonis, S. (1971). *The Decline of Medieval Hellenism in Asia Minor and the Process of Islamization from the Eleventh through the Fifteenth Century* (Berkeley, London: University of California Press).

Whitman, L. (1990). *Destroying Ethnic Identity – The Turks of Greece* (New York: Helsinki Watch) (October).

—— (1992a). *Denying Human Rights and Ethnic Identity – The Greeks of Turkey* (New York: Helsinki Watch) (March).

—— (1992b). *Greece: Improvements for the Turkish Minority. Problems Remain* (New York: Helsinki Watch).

Williams, C. (2003). 'The Cretan Muslims and the Music of Crete' in D. Tziovas (ed) *Greece and the Balkans: Identities, Perceptions and Cultural Encounters since the Enlightenment* (London: Ashgate).

Yalçın, K. (1998). *Emanet Çeyiz – Mübadele İnsanları [Entrusted Trousseau – The People of the Exchange]* (Istanbul: Belge Yayınları).

Yerolympos, A. (1994). 'Ekthesi gia tis Synthikes Ygieinis stin Synoikia Vardariou, Thessaloniki 1897' [A Report on the Sanitary Conditions in the Vardar District, Thessaloniki 1897] *Paratiritis*: 25–26.

—— (1995). *I Anoikodomisi tis Thessalonikis meta tin Pyrkaia tou 1917 [The Replanning of Thessaloniki after the Fire of 1917]* (Thessaloniki: University Studio Press).

—— (1996). *Urban Transformations in the Balkans, 1820–1920: Aspects of Balkan Town Planning and the Remaking of Thessaloniki* (Thessaloniki: University Studio Press).

Yiannakopoulos, G. A. (1992). *Prosphygiki Ellada [Refugee Greece]* (Athens: Centre for Asia Minor Studies).

Yildirim, O. (2002). 'Diplomats and Refugees: Mapping the Turco-Greek Exchange of Populations, 1922–1934' (Unpublished Ph.D., Princeton University).

Yorulmaz, A. (1997). *Savaşın Çocukları [Children of the War]* (Istanbul: Bilge).

Zachos, E. (1980). *I Piatsa [The Marketplace]* (Athens: Kaktos).

Zampidis, I. (1954). *I Kappadokiki Neapoli (Nev-Sehir) kai ta Perichora aftis [The Cappadocian Neapoli (Nev-Sehir) and its Surroundings]* (Athens).

de Zayas, A. (1975). 'International Law and Mass Population Transfers', *Harvard International Law Journal*, 16.

—— (1988). 'A Historical Survey of Twentieth Century Expulsions' in A. Bramwell (ed.) *Refugees in the Age of Total War* (London: Unwin Hyman).

Zenginis. E. (1988). *O Bektasismos sti Dytiki Thraki : Symvoli stin Istoria tis Diadoseos tou Mousoulmanismou ston Elladiko Choro [Bektashism in Western Thrace: A Contribution to the History the Propagation of Islam on Greek Territory]* (Thessaloniki).

—— (1994). *Oi Mousoulmanoi Athinganoi tis Thrakis [Gypsy Muslims of Thrace]* (Thessaloniki).

Zetter, R. (1991). 'Labelling Refugees: Forming and Transforming a Bureaucratic Identity', *Journal of Refugee Studies*, 4 (1): 39–62.

—— (1995). *Shelter Provision and Settlement Policies for Refugees: A State of the Art Review. Studies on Emergencies and Disaster Relief Report No. 2* (Uppsala: Norvic Africa Institute, University of Uppsala and SIDA).

—— (1999) 'Reconceptualising the Myth of Return: Continuity and Transition among the Greek Cypriot Refugees of 1974', *Journal of Refugee Studies*, 12 (1): 1–22.

Zizioulas, J. D. (1985). 'I Symvoli tis Kappadokias sti Christianiki Skepsi'[The Contribution of Cappadocia to Christian Thought] in S. Petsopoulos (ed.) *I Sinasos tis Kappadokias [Sinasos in Cappadocia]* (Athens: Agra): 23–37.

Zolberg, A. R., Suhkre, A. and Aguayo, S. (1989). *Escape from Violence* (New York, Oxford: Oxford University Press).

Zürcher, E. (1998). *Turkey, A Modern History* (London: I.B.Tauris).

Appendix

N° 807.

GRÈCE ET TURQUIE

Convention concernant l'échange des populations grecques et turques et Protocole, signés à Lausanne, le 30 janvier 1923.

GREECE AND TURKEY

Convention concerning the Exchange of Greek and Turkish Populations and Protocol, signed at Lausanne, January 30, 1923.

[1] TRADUCTION. — TRANSLATION.

No. 807. — CONVENTION [2] CONCERNING THE EXCHANGE OF GREEK AND TURKISH POPULATIONS, AND PROTOCOL, SIGNED AT LAUSANNE, JANUARY 30, 1923.

French official text communicated by the Greek Chargé d'Affaires at Berne. The registration of this Convention took place January 27, 1925.

The GOVERNMENT OF THE GRAND NATIONAL ASSEMBLY OF TURKEY and the GREEK GOVERNMENT have agreed upon the following provisions :

Article 1.

As from the 1st May, 1923, there shall take place a compulsory exchange of Turkish nationals of the Greek Orthodox religion established in Turkish territory, and of Greek nationals of the Moslem religion established in Greek territory.

These persons shall not return to live in Turkey or Greece respectively without the authorisation of the Turkish Government or of the Greek Government respectively.

Article 2.

The following persons shall not be included in the exchange provided for in Article 1 :

(a) The Greek inhabitants of Constantinople.
(b) The Moslem inhabitants of Western Thrace.

All Greeks who were already established before the October 30, 1918, within the areas under the Prefecture of the City of Constantinople, as defined by the law of 1912, shall be considered as Greek inhabitants of Constantinople.

All Moslems established in the region to the east of the frontier line laid down in 1913 by the Treaty [3] of Bucharest shall be considered as Moslem inhabitants of Western Thrace.

Article 3.

Those Greeks and Moslems who have already, and since the October 18, 1912, left the territories the Greek and Turkish inhabitants of which are to be respectively exchanged, shall be considered as included in the exchange provided for in Article 1.

---

[1] Communiquée par le Ministère des Affaires étrangères de Sa Majesté Britannique.   [1] Communicated by His Britannic Majesty's Foreign Office.

[2] Ratified by Turkey, August 23, 1923, by Greece, August 25, 1923.

[3] British and Foreign State Papers, vol. 107, page 658.

The expression " emigrant " in the present Convention includes all physical and juridical persons who have been obliged to emigrate or have emigrated since the October 18, 1912.

Article 4.

All able-bodied men belonging to the Greek population whose families have already left Turkish territory, and who are now detained in Turkey, shall constitute the first instalment of Greeks sent to Greece in accordance with the present Convention.

Article 5.

Subject to the provisions of Articles 9 and 10 of the present Convention, the rights of property and monetary assets of Greeks in Turkey or Moslems in Greece shall not be prejudiced in consequence of the exchange to be carried out under the present Convention.

Article 6.

No obstacle may be placed for any reason whatever in the way of the departure of a person belonging to the populations which are to be exchanged. In the event of an emigrant having received a definite sentence of imprisonment, or a sentence which is not yet definitive, or of his being the object of criminal proceedings, he shall be handed over by the authorities ot the prosecuting country to the authorities of the country whither he is going, in order that he may serve his sentence or be brought to trial.

Article 7.

The emigrants will lose the nationality of the country which they are leaving, and will acquire the nationality of the country of their destination, upon their arrival in the territory of the latter country.

Such emigrants as have already left one or other of the two countries and have not yet acquired their new nationality shall acquire that nationality on the date of the signature of the present Convention.

Article 8.

Emigrants shall be free to take away with them or to arrange for the transport of their movable property of every kind, without being liable on this account to the payment of any export or import duty or any other tax.

Similarly, the members of each community (including the personnel of mosques, tekkes, medresses, churches, convents, schools, hospitals, societies, associations and juridical persons, or other foundations of any nature whatever) which is to leave the territory of one of the Contracting States under the present Convention, shall have the right to take away freely or to arrange for the transport of the movable property belonging to their communities.

The fullest facilities for transport shall be provided by the authorities of the two countries, upon the recommendation of the Mixed Commission provided for in Article 11.

Emigrants who may not be able to take away all or part of their movable property can leave it behind. In that event, the local authorities shall be required to draw up, the emigrant in question being given an opportunity to be heard, an inventory and valuation of the property left by him. *Procès-verbaux* containing the inventory and the valuation of the movable property left by the emigrant shall be drawn up in four copies, one of which shall be kept by the local authorities, the second transmitted to the Mixed Commission provided for in Article 11 to serve as the basis for the liquidation provided for by Article 9, the third shall be handed to the Government of the country to which the emigrant is going, and the fourth to the emigrant himself.

Article 9.

Immovable property, whether rural or urban, belonging to emigrants, or to the communities mentioned in Article 8, and the movable property left by these emigrants or communities, shall be liquidated in accordance with the following provisions by the Mixed Commission provided for in Article 11.

Property situated in the districts to which the compulsory exchange applies and belonging to religious or benevolent institutions of the communities established in a district to which the exchange does not apply, shall likewise be liquidated under the same conditions.

Article 10.

The movable and immovable property belonging to persons who have already left the territory of the High Contracting Parties and are considered, in accordance with Article 3 of the present Convention, as being included in the exchange of populations, shall be liquidated in accordance with Article 9. This liquidation shall take place independently of all measures of any kind whatever which, under the laws passed and the regulations of any kind made in Greece and in Turkey since the October 18, 1912, or in any other way, have resulted in any restriction on rights of ownership over the property in question, such as confiscation, forced sale, etc. In the event of the property mentioned in this article or in Article 9 having been submitted to a measure of this kind, its value shall be fixed by the Commission provided for in Article 11, as if the measures in question had not been applied.

As regards expropriated property, the Mixed Commission shall undertake a fresh valuation of such property, if it has been expropriated since the October 18, 1912, having previously belonged to persons liable to the exchange of populations in the two countries, and is situated in territories to which the exchange applies. The Commission shall fix for the benefit of the owners such compensation as will repair the injury which the Commission has ascertained. The total amount of this compensation shall be carried to the credit of these owners and to the debit of the Government on whose territory the expropriated property is situated.

In the event of any persons mentioned in Articles 8 and 9 not having received the income from property, the enjoyment of which they have lost in one way or another, the restoration of the amount of this income shall be guaranteed to them on the basis of the average yield of the property before the war, and in accordance with the methods to be laid down by the Mixed Commission.

The Mixed Commission provided for in Article 11, when proceeding to the liquidation of Wakouf property in Greece and of the rights and interests connected therewith, and to the liquidation of similar foundations belonging to Greeks in Turkey, shall follow the principles laid down in previous Treaties with a view to fully safeguarding the rights and interests of these foundations and of the individuals interested in them.

The Mixed Commission provided for in Article 11 shall be entrusted with the duty of executing these provisions.

Article 11.

Within one month from the coming into force of the present Convention a Mixed Commission shall be set up in Turkey or in Greece consisting of four members representing each of the High Contracting Parties, and of three members chosen by the Council of the League of Nations from among nationals of Powers which did not take part in the war of 1914-1918. The Presidency of the Commission shall be exercised in turn by each of these three neutral members.

The Mixed Commission shall have the right to set up, in such places as it may appear to them necessary, Sub-Commissions working under its order. Each such Sub-Commission shall consist of a Turkish member, a Greek member and a neutral President to be designated by the Mixed Commission. The Mixed Commission shall decide the powers to be delegated to the Sub-Commission.

Article 12.

The duties of the Mixed Commission shall be to supervise and facilitate the emigration provided for in the present Convention, and to carry out the liquidation of the movable and immovable property for which provision is made in Articles 9 and 10.

The Commission shall settle the methods to be followed as regards the emigration and liquidation mentioned above.

In a general way the Mixed Commission shall have full power to take the measures necessitated by the execution of the present Convention and to decide all questions to which this Convention may give rise.

The decisions of the Mixed Commission shall be taken by a majority.

All disputes relating to property, rights and interests which are to be liquidated shall be settled definitely by the Commission.

Article 13.

The Mixed Commission shall have full power to cause the valuation to be made of the movable and immovable property which is to be liquidated under the present Convention, the interested parties being given a hearing or being duly summoned so that they may be heard.

The basis for the valuation of the property to be liquidated shall be the value of the property in gold currency.

Article 14.

The Commission shall transmit to the owner concerned a declaration stating the sum due to him in respect of the property of which he has been dispossessed, and such property shall remain at the disposal of the Government on whose territory it is situated.

The total sums due on the basis of these declarations shall constitute a Government debt from the country where the liquidation takes place to the Government of the country to which the emigrant belongs. The emigrant shall in principle be entitled to receive in the country to which he emigrates, as representing the sums due to him, property of a value equal to and of the same nature as that which he has left behind.

Once every six months an account shall be drawn up of the sums due by the respective Governments on the basis of the declarations as above.

When the liquidation is completed, if the sums of money due to both sides correspond, the accounts relating thereto shall be balanced. If a sum remains due from one of the Governments to the other Government after a balance has been struck, the debit balance shall be paid in cash. If the debtor Government requests a postponement in making this payment, the Commission may grant such postponement, provided that the sum due be paid in three annuities at most. The Commission shall fix the interest to be paid during the period of postponement.

If the sum to be paid is fairly large and requires longer postponement, the debtor Government shall pay in cash a sum to be fixed by the Mixed Commission, up to a maximum of 20 per cent of the total due, and shall issue in respect of the balance loan certificates bearing such interest as the Mixed Commission may fix, to be paid off within 20 years at most. The debtor Government shall assign to the service of these loans pledges approved by the Commission, which shall be administered and of which the revenues shall be encashed by the International Commission in Greece and by the Council of the Public Debt at Constantinople. In the absence of agreement in regard to these pledges, they shall be selected by the Council of the League of Nations.

Article 15.

With a view to facilitating emigration, funds shall be advanced to the Mixed Commission by the States concerned, under conditions laid down by the said Commission.

No. 807

Article 16.

The Turkish and Greek Governments shall come to an agreement with the Mixed Commission provided for in Article 11 in regard to all questions concerning the notification to be made to persons who are to leave the territory of Turkey and Greece under the present Convention, and concerning the ports to which these persons are to go for the purpose of being transported to the country of their destination.

The High Contracting Parties undertake mutually that no pressure direct or indirect shall be exercised on the populations which are to be exchanged with a view to making them leave their homes or abandon their property before the date fixed for their departure. They likewise undertake to impose on the emigrants who have left or who are to leave the country no special taxes or dues. No obstacle shall be placed in the way of the inhabitants of the districts excepted from the exchange under Article 2 exercising freely their right to remain in or return to those districts and to enjoy to the full their liberties and rights of property in Turkey and in Greece. This provision shall not be invoked as a motive for preventing the free alienation of property belonging to inhabitants of the said regions which are excepted from the exchange, or the voluntary departure of those among these inhabitants who wish to leave Turkey or Greece.

Article 17.

The expenses entailed by the maintenance and working of the Mixed Commission and of the organisations dependent on it shall be borne by the Governments concerned in proportions to be fixed by the Commission.

Article 18.

The High Contracting Parties undertake to introduce in their respective laws such modifications as may be necessary with a view to ensuring the execution of the present Convention.

Article 19.

The present Convention shall have the same force and effect as between the High Contracting Parties as if it formed part of the Treaty of Peace[1] to be concluded with Turkey. It shall come into force immediately after the ratification of the said Treaty by the two High Contracting Parties.

In faith whereof, the undersigned Plenipotentiaries, whose respective full powers have been found in good and due form, have signed the present Convention.

Done at Lausanne the January 30, 1923, in three copies, one of which shall be transmitted to the Greek Government, one to the Government of the Grand National Assembly of Turkey, and the third shall be deposited in the archives of the Government of the French Republic, which shall deliver certified copies to the other Powers signatory of the Treaty of Peace with Turkey.

(L. S.)   E. K. VENISELOS.
(L. S.)   D. CACLAMANOS.
(L. S.)   ISMET.
(L. S.)   DR. RIZA NOUR.
(L. S.)   HASSAN.

[1] Vol. XXVIII, page 11, of this Series.

PROTOCOL.

The undersigned Turkish Plenipotentiaries, duly authorised to that effect, declare that, without waiting for the coming into force of the Convention with Greece of even date, relating to the exchange of the Greek and Turkish populations, and by way of exception to Article 1 of that Convention, the Turkish Government, on the signature of the Treaty of Peace, will release the able-bodied men referred to in Article 4 of the said Convention, and will provide for their departure.

Done at Lausanne, the January 30, 1923.

ISMET.
Dr. RIZA NOUR.
HASSAN.

No. 807

Index